C0-BUZ-017

TOMORROW

in

THE MAKING

TOMORROW

in

THE MAKING

EDITED BY

JOHN N. ANDREWS, Ph. D.
New York University

AND

CARL A. MARSDEN, Ph. D.
New York University

E
806
A654

Indexed in:
ESSAY INDEX

New York **WHITTLESEY HOUSE** *London*
M c G R A W - H I L L   B O O K   C O M P A N Y ,   I N C .

185095

Copyright, 1939, *by the* McGraw-Hill Book Company, Inc.

All rights reserved. This book, or parts thereof, may not be
reproduced in any form without permission of the publishers.

PUBLISHED BY WHITTLESEY HOUSE

A division of the McGraw-Hill Book Company, Inc.

Printed in the United States of America by The Maple Press Co., York, Pa.

CONTRIBUTORS
TO THIS VOLUME

HARRY ELMER BARNES
Historian and Sociologist

NED H. DEARBORN
New York University

SIDNEY HOOK
New York University

CLYDE MILLER
Teachers College, Columbia University

HERMAN H. HORNE
New York University

RALPH W. SOCKMAN
Minister, Christ Church, New York City

GEORGE E. SOKOLSKY
Author and Lecturer

LAWRENCE DENNIS
Author and Lecturer

NORMAN THOMAS
Socialist Leader and Author

EARL BROWDER
Secretary of Communist Party in America

WALTER RAUTENSTRAUCH
Columbia University

JACOB BAKER
Chairman of the President's Committee of Inquiry on Cooperative Enterprise in Europe

RUFUS D. SMITH
New York University

SAMUEL SEABURY
Lawyer, Counsel to Joint Legislative Committee 1931

LEWIS E. LAWES
Warden, Sing Sing Prison

ALFRED G. BUEHLER
University of Vermont

ABRAHAM EPSTEIN
Executive Secretary of American Association for Social Security

HERMAN FELDMAN
Professor of Industrial Relations, Amos Tuck School of Administration and Finance, Dartmouth College

ARTHUR P. CHEW
U. S. Department of Agriculture

WALTER E. SPAHR
New York University

RINEHART J. SWENSON
New York University

ROY V. PEEL
New York University

HENRY C. WOLFE
Author and Foreign Correspondent

PETER MOLYNEAUX
Editor, The Texas Weekly, Dallas, Texas

GERALD P. NYE
U. S. Senator from North Dakota

CLARK EICHELBERGER
Director, The League of Nations Association, Inc., New York City

To those builders of today and tomorrow who lived yesterday and bequeathed to us certain inalienable rights, this volume is reverently dedicated.

PREFACE

THIS volume has as its motive the enlightenment of Mr. Everyman, upon whom rests the major responsibility of creating a better tomorrow through his efforts today.

During the early days of our republic, President Madison stated that "popular government without popular information is but the prologue to a farce or a tragedy or perhaps both. Knowledge will forever govern ignorance; and a people who mean to be their own governors must arm themselves with the power which knowledge gives." In the light of current world developments that statement is especially significant today.

We are living in an era of rapidly changing governments, crises in old economic systems, and the emergence of new social and political patterns. It is a period characterized by great insecurity; by a quest for security; by industrial strife, far-reaching legislative programs, revolutions, and undeclared wars. All these are manifestations of general unrest and dissatisfaction among the masses, confusion among their leaders, and the presence of important economic, social, and political problems needing solution.

Cynics among us look upon the chaos in contemporary life as a damning sign of man's essential stupidity rather than as a challenge to his intelligence. The critics ignore a very vital consideration: the present generation is being called upon to make more radical and rapid readjustments than any other group of contemporaries in the history of mankind.

We in the United States are committed at least doctrinally to the proposition that the democratic way of life is the best for us. But there are those who in all sincerity and honesty question the basic philosophy underlying "popular" government, on the premise that the average man lacks the capacity for self-government. Others, more optimistic but no less naïve, contend that our present shortcomings can be attributed to the presence of some one feature of existing society which once removed would immediately result in a utopia. To these and to all their blood brothers, the individual who believes in the ideals of American democracy replies that our ills cannot be cured by revelations from on high or from abroad or by panaceas whose sole recommendation is their simplicity, but only by the consistent and unremitting use of intelligence in *all* the focal problems of our day.

We are not all equally capable of intricate or abstract thought. But we can make a beginning. True, we do not know many relevant facts. But we can learn. Therefore, if we are to participate intelligently in the strengthening of democracy, it is imperative that new points of view, new knowledge, and analyses be presented in a way that can be easily grasped by all. This does not mean that we need less research, experimentation, and scholarly treatises; it means that the paramount need is effective popularization of those findings. To popularize is not to vulgarize but to present essentials in a relevant and interesting way. This volume is planned expressly to satisfy partially the basic need of the hour: the creation of an intelligent body of public opinion without which neither programs nor leaders can successfully cope with problems within the framework of democracy.

The disagreements among the experts at the moment should not be disconcerting. For the possibility of progress is dependent not so much upon agreements as upon conflicts and disagreements. Intelligent agreement or disagreement in turn is dependent upon an accurate knowledge of the major alternatives of policy and direction which face us today. This accurate knowledge can best be secured from the protagonists of these alternative and conflicting social policies. Let us try to understand them before we praise or denounce. Understanding may be more deadly to a doctrine than persecution. Just as some malignant organisms flourish best in the dark, so do illusions, phobias, and obsessions. They cannot stand being brought into the light. This is probably true of some of our own prejudices which masquerade as first principles. How many of us really comprehend wherein the ideologies of other political and social philosophies differ from our own and from one another? And, what is more pertinent, who among us can truthfully say that he comprehends fully the implications of democracy and translates his understanding into something more objective than mere lip service?

In the symposium here presented, the editors have invited outstanding authorities to discuss problems and points of view of which they are experts or protagonists. The contributors were selected for two reasons: their familiarity with the problems and positions they expound, and their ability to speak their minds effectively. Each contributor speaks only for himself. The editors have conceived it to be their opportunity and responsibility not merely to make possible a collection of casual individual papers written by several specialists but so to organize the materials presented as to depict some of the significant movements now under way in the United States and in other countries.

Some of these movements may be anathema to the readers— and to the editors. But the editors would have been remiss in their duties as editors, educators, and lovers of democracy if they had excluded them from this volume. The existence of such a volume is not only an illustration of what democracy in the life of mind means; its very possibility is a plausible argument in behalf of the democratic way of life. Let those who are protagonists for totalitarianisms—no matter what their color—explain why such projects in co-operative difference are impossible in the cultures for which they speak; but let no one who holds to the American ideal of intellectual, but not uncritical, tolerance wonder that so many views are expounded within the covers of this book.

This volume is by no stretch of the imagination a complete survey of the field it treats. Its purpose is not to tell the reader what to think or to restrict his vision. A selected bibliography is provided for the interested student as a guide to further exploration.

PREFACE

It now becomes the pleasant duty of the editors to acknowledge that the compilation of this volume has been in reality a co-operative enterprise. The authors are indebted to the contributors of the various chapters who, despite the many demands upon their time and energy, accepted our invitations to participate. Mary Lee Andrews and Helen Allinger Marsden admirably executed the chores frequently delegated to their wives by authors and editors. And last but not least, we are indebted to Ethel Mason Eaton, whose editorial assistance conserved our time and energy.

JOHN N. ANDREWS,
CARL A. MARSDEN.

NEW YORK, N. Y.,
November, 1938.

CONTENTS

Part One
FRAME OF REFERENCE

Part Two
PATTERNS OF CHANGE

CONTENTS

CONTENTS

Part Four
OUR RELATIONS ABROAD

Part One

FRAME OF REFERENCE

Chapter I

THE CURRENT CRISIS: ITS CAUSES

Harry Elmer Barnes

★ ★ ★ ★

O NE of the most difficult of the historian's tasks is to obtain perspective on his own age. It is often much easier to understand the past. It is hard to grasp our relation either to the immediate past or the near future, and it is even more of a problem to view our own generation against the whole panorama of human history.

Yet, unless we are able to do this, historical study is little more than a satisfaction of curiosity. Standing by itself, the past has only a musty antiquarian significance. The main practical service that history can render mankind is the aid it may give us in understanding how the past created the present. Once we comprehend this, we may begin to see what light the past and the present throw on the probable course of future events.

When we apply this thought, we see that the chief lesson which a study of the past will be likely to offer us is the overwhelming evidence that we are living in one of the great transitional periods of human history. It is always dangerous to draw direct analogies with the past, for historical epochs never reproduce themselves exactly. Attempts, for instance, to find explicit lessons for our generation in the later Roman Empire may prove misleading. It is futile to compare in any detail a preindustrial society operating under an economy of scarcity, with an industrial civilization which has attained a potential economy of abundance.

3

HISTORICAL TRANSITION

Yet certain broad historical analogies are useful and illuminating. Most significant is the suggestion that we are living in the early days of the fourth great transitional period in history. The three previous eras of sweeping social and cultural transformation, roughly comparable to ours, were: (1) the passage from prehistoric culture to so-called *historic civilization*, somewhere between 6000 B.C. and 3500 B.C.; (2) the gradual disintegration of classical culture in the later centuries of the Western Empire, around A.D. 300–600; and (3) the supplanting of medieval civilization by early modern culture and institutions between 1500 and 1800.

The third transition probably bears the closest resemblance to our age. In the three centuries following 1500, the typical medieval institutions, such as a decentralized feudal government, an agricultural economy operated according to the manorial technique, the guild control of urban industry, the great unified international ecclesiastical state, the scholastic system of education, and similar institutions, were weakened or supplanted.

In their places were born the forebears of many modern practices. The centralized state came into being along with tenant farming and the domestic or "putting-out" system of industrial production. The economy became increasingly more commercial and industrial, with the consequence that avenues of national and world trade were opened. The capitalistic ideals and methods resulted in a quest for private profits by any means not flagrantly illegal. At the same time the schism in the Catholic world state produced Protestantism, and the scholastic ideals of education declined with the ascendancy of humanism.

Had a scholar suggested in the year 1500 that the civilization of his age was on the eve of a thorough transformation, he would have been ignored or ridiculed. But just this thing happened. By 1800 medieval civilization ceased to exist,

4

except in the more backward parts of Europe. So, likewise, we in the second third of the twentieth century find it hard to believe that we may be in about the same condition in which the western world found itself around 1500. Yet plenty of evidence will be presented to support the opinion that we have already instituted more far-reaching changes than any previous century has ever witnessed—perhaps the most fundamental transition in man's experience on this planet.

The typically modern institutions have reached about the same stage of decay which feudalism, the manor, the guilds, and scholasticism exhibited around the year 1500. There is little probability that the institutions and culture of the year 2000 will closely resemble the civilization of our day. There is a considerable prospect that the contrast will be far greater than that between the civilization of the early Tudor period and culture in the days of Napoleon.

While, in a general way, our age resembles the three great previous eras of social and cultural transition, there are several important contrasts between former transitional epochs and our own. In the first place, it is inevitable that the changes which lie ahead of us, for better or for worse, must be carried through far more rapidly than in the past. The simple pastoral and agricultural civilizations of earlier ages could keep going in one way or another for a long time under adverse conditions. Except for war, invasion, and devastation, a complete breakdown was unlikely. There might be less dried beef, flour, and meal for the larder and less fodder for the cattle. A more than usual number of babies, calves, and sheep might die of malnutrition. The standard of living might be lowered in the few towns that existed. Yet somehow, mankind managed to get along. Scores of causes for the decline of Roman society have been suggested by historians, but despite all these causes, it took several centuries to wreck Roman civilization. Even when conditions were improving in the past, it took a long time to create a new order. The decay of medieval institutions

5

actually began in the late thirteenth century, but the early modern age was hardly complete before 1800.

OUR COMPLEX CIVILIZATION

We moderns will have no such extended period for readjustment. Our own urban industrial world civilization presents an altogether different spectacle. Our culture is so complex, so delicately articulated, so thoroughly based upon an elaborate division of labor that the whole system must work efficiently if it is to work at all. It may be compared to an automobile which, if defective in a single vital part—the carburetor, distributor, or battery—and perfect in all other parts, will not run satisfactorily.

An illustration of this fact was furnished by the "bank holiday" in the opening days of Mr. Roosevelt's first administration. Our industrial system was still operating, transportation lines ran as before, food supplies were not curtailed, electric current was generated in normal volume, and so on. There was merely a temporary suspension of the ordinary credit system. Yet the country was in a veritable panic. Had not a new and colorful administration been installed to give renewed hope and confidence, there is no telling how serious a breakdown of the whole structure of capitalistic society might have ensued. One can easily imagine what would happen if basic industries, transportation, or food production were entirely disrupted.

We now have an economic system which, if it runs well, can do more for man than any earlier one, but it exacts a price for this advantage. It demands relatively efficient control and co-ordination to operate at all. A dynamo can do much more work than a treadmill, but it needs greater attention and is more likely to get out of order if carelessly handled.

Our present economic system is in a serious crisis. In the United States, potentially the most prosperous country in the world, the economy almost collapsed between 1929 and 1933 and has been restored to a semblance of normality only by a

6

kind of "first-aid" treatment in the form of lavish expenditures of public funds to bolster private industry and finance. Candid observers, even if kindly disposed toward Mr. Roosevelt and the New Deal, can hardly maintain that any fundamental changes have been wrought in the system which broke down in 1929 because of basic imperfections. And if it is allowed to collapse again, there is some doubt that such moderate policies will be effective, even temporarily, in restoring normal operations.

Therefore, it is evident that we face the prospect either of fundamental changes which will make the system permanently efficient and trustworthy, or of evasive palliatives which will eventually bring acute crisis and collapse. In either case, it means a striking change in present practices, and a change which may not be delayed beyond a decade or two.

It would take a superprophet to tell us today whether we shall take the road to constructive reform or to temporary disintegration. But it requires only passable literacy and ordinary "horse sense" to discern that we shall take one or the other, and that very soon.

The prospective rapidity of the transition in which we find ourselves is the first of the contrasts between ours and any earlier epoch of transition. Another great contrast lies in the sharpness and magnitude of the alternatives which face us—a fact implied in the preceding discussion. In earlier transitional periods, it was a matter of gradual improvement or gradual decline. Mankind has never before been faced with a rather direct and immediate choice between utopia and catastrophe, but such is precisely the alternative which is offered to Western civilization in our day.

THE CHOICE BEFORE US

If we overhaul our economic system, put our unparalleled mechanical equipment at the service of mankind, and wipe out the menace of war, we can, within a decade or two, step into a condition which will make any of the utopias from Plato to Fourier seem drab, trivial, and uninviting. We could quickly realize Edward Bellamy's dream expressed in *Looking Backward.* This does not even imply that we must wait for future mechanical marvels. The technology and natural resources are already at hand. In the United States we could provide a far higher standard of living than has ever been known and could make it available to the masses with less than thirty hours of work each week. This is probably true of all other industrialized nations. There could be plenty, security, and an abundance of leisure which would enable us to attain the "super-pig" vistas of culture envisaged by Plato in his *Republic.*

This is one side of the picture. If we do not rise to our responsibilities and make the most of our unprecedented mechanical equipment, then the whole economic machine is bound to break down within a few years. It has already so far broken down in several countries as to necessitate a well-nigh complete cessation of civilized traditions and practices in order to save it from complete collapse. In the largest country in the world, capitalism, as we know it, has already disappeared.

If we continue on the road of evasion—and decline—we must face the prospect of collapse through internal weaknesses. The best we could then hope for would be insecurity, lower standards of living, greater unemployment, unrelieved want, misery, and sheer starvation. To this must be added the ever-increasing danger of devastating warfare and a return to barbarism, for warfare today means wholesale destruction of physical equipment and civilized amenities.

We have created a machine age uniquely prepared to serve us or to wreck us. The outcome will depend upon the type of social control which we impose upon our empire of machines.

Thus, to summarize, we are living in a great transitional age. This transition is bound to be carried through with relative rapidity, and we shall either move into a state of culture far ahead of anything hitherto realized by man, or revert to condi-

8

tions unmatched for mass misery since the early Middle Ages and the era of the Thirty Years' War at the close of the medieval period. As James Harvey Robinson has put it, "Our civilization is likely to perish in as stupid a fashion as the hen in the fable who starved to death roosting face out on the rim of a bushel basket filled with grain." Startling as such a statement may seem, it is one of the few general declarations that can be made today with reasonable assurance of accuracy.

CONTRASTS AND CONFLICTS IN TWENTIETH CENTURY CULTURE

The most characteristic aspect of our twentieth-century civilization, and the one which makes our age inevitably transitional in character, is the amazing contrast between the material and the nonmaterial factors in our culture. Never before was there such a gulf between technology and social institutions. We have a thoroughly up-to-date material culture, diverse, and potentially efficient beyond that of any earlier age. On the other hand, the institutions and the social thinking through which we seek to control and exploit this material culture are an antiquated mosaic, compounded of accretions from the stone age to the close of the eighteenth century.

OUR MEDIEVAL INSTITUTIONS

Very little in our institutional life and social thinking dates from a period more recent than the year 1800. The national state was a legalized institution of wide prevalence in 1648. The theories of representative government and democracy were worked out in the seventeenth and eighteenth centuries. The legal theories which dominate us today rest fundamentally upon Roman law, the medieval English common law, and the natural-law doctrines of the seventeenth century. Capitalistic ideals and practices were well established in theory long before 1800. Our basic economic theories appeared in Adam Smith's *Wealth of Nations*, published in the same year as our Declaration of Independence. Indeed, Smith was a much more erudite and enlightened expositor of such theories than many of the business leaders, financiers, and lawyers who hark back to him today. Our educational curriculum and much of its subject matter come from ancient, medieval, or early modern times. The prevailing religious system dates from the beginning of the Christian era and embodies many elements far older than that. Our moral code has developed over a protracted period, stretching from Moses to Augustine, the Puritans, Immanuel Kant, and Anthony Comstock. Nine-tenths of our philosophical speculation is a rehashing and rationalization of mental antiquities, originally suggested by thinkers between the ages of Socrates and Hegel. It is, therefore, no wild generalization to say that the dominant institutions and social thought of our day derive from the eighteenth century or earlier.

Such a situation has never existed before. By and large, material and nonmaterial factors in previous civilizations exhibited reasonable congruity and harmony. The only earlier examples of conspicuous discrepancy were manifested by the Attic Greeks and, to a lesser extent, the Romans. But in each of these earlier instances the situation was exactly the reverse of that which prevails in our age. Among the Greeks and Romans social institutions and social thinking were far in advance of their material culture. Technology and economic life never caught up with classical thought, and this was the outstanding reason for the decline of classical civilization.

THREE INDUSTRIAL REVOLUTIONS

We may now look a little more closely into this gulf between our material equipment and our institutions and social thinking.

The first industrial revolution after 1750 created our modern methods of textile manufacturing, the new iron and steel industry, the steam engine, and the beginnings of steam transportation on land and sea. This first industrial revolution had hardly been established in many countries before a second came on its heels, introducing the application of chemistry in the steel, rubber, oil, and other industries, together with synthetic products of many kinds, new methods of transportation and communication, large-scale industrial establishments, and the like. Today, we are in the midst of the third industrial revolution, characterized by varied applications of electrical power—the age of electrification, automatic machinery, electrical control over manufacturing processes, air transport, radios, and so on.

OUR MATERIAL ACHIEVEMENTS

Few of us can understand the principles on which these machines operate. Our own material achievements defy our comprehension. We have giant turbines, four of which can generate more energy than the whole working population of the United States. We possess automatic machinery of the most amazing efficiency. One plant can, for example, turn out 650,000 light bulbs each day, or 10,000 times as many per man as was possible by the older methods. This automatic machinery can be controlled by a photoelectric cell, or the electric eye, which is absolutely dependable and unfailing and all but eliminates the human factor in mechanical production. We have giant autobusses, clean, quiet, and speedy Diesel-motored trains, safe and swift airplanes. We have skyscrapers that make the tower of Babel seem almost like a depression in the ground, accessible through elevators which are mechanical marvels. Our bathrooms would fill a Roman emperor with envy. Our system of communication is incredibly extensive and efficient. Our radios would appear a veritable miracle to persons who died even so recently as the period of the World War. Our modern printing presses would utterly stagger Gutenberg. We might thus go on indefinitely through all the provinces of our great "empire of machines."

Let us now turn to the other side of the picture and consider our archaic institutional life and social thought, through which we vainly attempt to control and exploit our new mechanical age.

OUR ARCHAIC INSTITUTIONS

In spite of the revolutionary changes that science and technology have wrought in our material culture, our opinions and institutions have altered but slightly in a century. Any person who was a member of the Constitutional Convention in 1787 would be completely astounded and absolutely at sea when faced by modern material culture, but he could discuss economics, politics, education, and religion with any one of us in terms mutually intelligible.

In contrasting our material culture and institutional life, it is useful at the outset to emphasize the fact that the intellectual outlook of the masses remains much as it was in primitive times. Anthropologists have described the primitive mind as characterized chiefly by an all-pervading supernaturalism and credulity, a corresponding lack of precise and logical thinking, and ignorance of scientific methods and accomplishments. If we apply these standards, it becomes apparent that the great majority of moderns are still overwhelmingly primitive in their ways of thinking. Moreover, much of the specific content of earlier superstitions has been carried over to the modern era. There is a remarkable hangover of the primitive belief in luck and chance, and of other prescientific mental attitudes.

We may now consider more specifically the archaic nature of the prevailing opinions and institutions in contemporary society. Our political opinions and institutions represent a mosaic compounded of: (1) the veneration of the state derived from the oriental emperor worship; (2) Roman legalism and the conception of secular omnipotence; (3) the classical obsession with the merits of monarchy, aristocracy, and democracy; (4) archaic views of representative government that developed between the sixteenth and the eighteenth centuries; (5) seventeenth- and eighteenth-century doctrines of natural

rights; and (6) the eighteenth-century view of the perfecta-
bility of man, linked up with the nineteenth-century
enthusiasm for democracy. While there is much vital political
theory expounded by modern thinkers, this has found but
slight adoption in political practice, and there has been sin-
gularly little effort to adapt our political institutions to the
needs of an urban, industrial age. We in America continue
to revere a Constitution and a political system that were
created in a simple agricultural society, in spite of the fact
that material culture in America has been altered more in the
last century than did Western civilization in the previous
millennium.

Law, likewise, is founded upon ancient theories and practices. It is based primarily upon oriental practices, formulations of Roman jurists, precedents of English common law,
and the natural-law doctrines of the seventeenth and eighteenth centuries. Little progress has been made in the way
of introducing the historical and sociological point of view into
juristic practice. We attempt to regulate a twentieth-century
civilization by applying to it legal concepts and methods which
have changed but little since the year 1700. The rules of legal
evidence are hopelessly out of date and confused.

The attitude taken by the courts toward crime and criminal
responsibility is a composite of archaic legalism, religious
superstition, and false metaphysical conceptions. With the
exception of certain advanced work in juvenile courts, there is
hardly the slightest acceptance of the modern socio-
psychological conception of human conduct and its relation
to the causation of crime. Even when insanity is pleaded, the
conventional legal conception of the free moral agent is still
retained; the test of insanity is strictly legal and not medical.

Our attitudes toward property are equally full of primitive
vestiges. The unique sanctity surrounding property is in part
an outgrowth of primitive mysticism and superstition. Our
contemporary view of property rights is a compound of
ancient legalism and sixteenth- and seventeenth-century

Protestant opinions of God's approval of thrift and profit. To these have been added the seventeenth- and eighteenth-century notion that the chief purpose of the state and of legal institutions is to protect private property. Nothing more modern than this is needed to explain the decisions of the conservative majority of the Supreme Court of the United States on matters pertaining to private property in the twentieth century. Indeed, there is little or nothing in present American conceptions of property rights that cannot be discovered explicitly or implicitly in the writings of John Locke.

In the matter of sex morality we are likewise at least medieval, if not prehistoric. We have been especially reluctant to bring the control of sex and the family into harmony with scientific and esthetic considerations. Our sex mores and family institutions embody: (1) a primitive reaction to the mystery of sex and of women in particular; (2) Hebraic conceptions of patriarchal male domination; (3) patristic and medieval views derived from the church fathers and from the medieval world regarding the baseness of sex and sex temptation, especially as offered by women; (4) the formal medieval esteem for virginity in women; (5) the sacramental view of marriage, which leads us to regard marriage as a theological rather than as a social issue; and (6) the property interests of the early bourgeoisie.

EDUCATION, JOURNALISM, AND RELIGION

As to our system of modern education, this, too, has changed but little in comparison with the recent vast alteration in our ways of living. Certain basic strains in our educational doctrine are derived from the oriental and medieval notion that the chief purpose of education is to make clear to man the will of the gods or of God. From the Greeks and the Romans we derived the high esteem for training in rhetoric and argumentation, which was considered by them to be essential to a successful career in politics. Humanism contributed the view that the classical languages embody the flower of secular learning

14

and represent the most exquisite form of literary expression. In some educational centers—recently at the University of Chicago—there has been proposed a frank abandonment of modernism and a revival of classicism and overt medievalism. The democratic tradition is responsible for the dogma that all are entitled to participate equally in a complete system of education. The solemnity and the punitive psychology, which still dominate the greater part of our educational ideals and procedure, were derived from the Christian philosophy of life and the Puritan urge for an exacting discipline of the will. As Professor Horace Kallen has observed, education is today more of a distraction from life than a preparation for it. Few of the real problems involved in living an intelligent and successful life in urban and industrial society are touched upon vitally in our educational system from the kindergarten to the graduate school. Nor has there been much effort to harmonize our pedagogical methods with the modern psychological principle that a student's interest in the subject matter should be an important element in determining educational procedure.

Journalism has not yet been notably successful in educating the public on contemporary issues and providing general intellectual direction concerning the problems of modern life. It still remains chiefly a method of providing wholesale mechanical dissemination of something very much like neighborhood gossip, now that the neighborhood, as such, has largely disappeared and face-to-face gossiping has become more difficult. The same subjects which made juicy gossip in prenewspaper days are still "hot news" for the contemporary press. Personalities are much more highly esteemed than principles. No scientific discovery of modern times, no engineering achievements, no social-reform program will receive the publicity bestowed upon a notorious murder trial or kidnaping. The Lindbergh kidnaping case crowded the war in China off the front pages. The Dionne quintuplets outweigh the fall of a government. Few newspapers that have made a serious effort to devote themselves primarily to informing the

15

public on vital topics of economic, political, and sociological import have been able to survive.

It is scarcely necessary to point out the many archaic elements in religion. The fundamentalists today, among whom are numbered the majority of religious communicants, live under the domination of the same intellectual patterns which prevailed in primitive times. William Jennings Bryan openly declared at the Dayton trial in 1925 that no statement whatever would appear to him preposterous or unsupportable, provided it be found in Holy Writ. Even the great majority of liberal theologians today are in rebellion only against seventeenth- and eighteenth-century religious and philosophical views. It is probably no exaggeration to say that only a minority of modernist theologians are really adjusted to contemporary knowledge and ways of thinking. Most of them are merely attempting to restate archaic views in contemporaneous phraseology.

Of all the phases of human culture which we have been considering, religion is perhaps slower than any other in readjusting itself to new ways of living and thinking. This fact was demonstrated by Dr. and Mrs. Robert Lynd's important book *Middletown*, an admirable case study of the relative change of opinions and attitudes in American culture since 1890. Even more, orthodox religion is a leading influence in producing cultural lag in other fields of human activity. It is a primary intellectual factor in discouraging mankind from making a candid and secular approach to the essential task of reconstructing human knowledge and social conduct.

Not only does this vast gulf exist between material culture, on the one hand, and social thinking and institutions on the other, but we are constantly widening the abyss. We provide almost every imaginable incentive to extend our material equipment. Scientific prizes, patent royalties, industrial profits, social prestige, and every conceivable reward are offered to those who will provide us with better machines and more convenient gadgets.

16

OBSTACLES TO PROGRESS

At the same time, we set every possible obstacle in the way of those who seek to improve our antiquated institutional machinery. There are no prizes for the social inventor; on the contrary his plans are not given even tolerant consideration. Indeed, in most modern countries, an individual who shows any real ingenuity in social planning is ridiculed or threatened with a jail sentence. Instead of showering the social inventor with honors, the very best we do is to make him a social outcast and deride him as a crank. In this way, the gulf between our material equipment and our institutional life is still more alarmingly broadened.

We are restrained from improving this serious situation because of sharply contrasting psychological attitudes with respect to material and mental antiquities. We demand the most up-to-date models of automobiles, radios, bathtubs, and electric-light fixtures. The average man would be utterly embarrassed if he drove through a public thoroughfare in a 1925 automobile, even though the vehicle were in perfect condition. Yet the same man may cherish ideas and institutions which date from the stagecoach era. Many a plutocrat who demands the latest supermotorcar venerates unreservedly our Constitution, model 1787. So long as this state of mind exists there is little hope of closing the gap between material culture and institutions. Indeed, we feel that there are plenty of good reasons why we should not do so. Nevertheless, until we recoil from outmoded ideas or institutions as decisively as we do from an old-fashioned vehicle or gadget, there is no hope of closing the gap, which is only another way of saying that there is no hope of preserving civilization, since we cannot go on for long with one foot in an airplane and the other in an oxcart.

Another phase of this paradox lies in our reaction toward expert guidance. When a man desires to have a bathroom faucet repaired, a spark plug replaced, or a tooth pulled, he deems it necessary to have recourse to an expert. Yet in the

17

much more difficult problems of social, economic, and political life, he is completely satisfied with the opinions of the layman. He wants a "brain trust" to design his automobile, but not one to plan his government.

What has just been said is no mere idle gossip or amusing reading. It lies at the heart of our social crisis. No matter what aspect of our social problems we consider, it is always a secondary and incidental manifestation of the chief defect of our civilization—the gulf between machines and institutions. For example, if our economic thinking and institutions were on the same level of efficiency and modernity as our mechanical equipment, we could be living in a veritable utopia where man would be relieved of exhausting physical labor. If we could manage under capitalism the problems involved in the consumption of goods as well as we can th problems involved in their production, there would be no crisis. We produce goods with the very latest machinery, but we utilize them on the basis of ideas and institutions which originated a century or a millennium ago.

THE CHALLENGE AHEAD

However lightheartedly some may view this striking discrepancy between our machines and our institutions, it has already exacted a frightful penalty in the form of severe depressions and other economic disasters. It has almost destroyed democracy. It has made our legal system inadequate and produced widespread contempt for law in general. We have an annual crime bill equal to a fifth of our total national income, and crime itself is so well organized and protected that the more serious criminals are never even molested by the public authorities. It has bred religious indifference, moral chaos, and educational futility. It may easily exact the supreme penalty of the extinction of civilization. The upshot, if we go on as we have so far in the twentieth century, is the impending collapse of western civilization from internal

18

weaknesses, with the grave probability that the process will be hastened by a devastating world war.

If society awakens in time and closes the gulf by bringing our institutions up to date, we may literally "inherit the earth." If we proceed as we have since the turn of the century, there is not even a gambling chance of preserving civilization much longer. Our unique mechanical civilization has created, perhaps unwittingly, grave responsibilities. Unless we shoulder them, we shall soon enter another dark age—perhaps darker than that which followed the Roman Empire.

Chapter II

SOCIAL PROGRESS THROUGH EDUCATION

NED H. DEARBORN

★ ★ ★ ★

SOCIAL progress from the viewpoint of material culture did not just happen, for progress is not inevitable. It resulted only from the union of worthy aims and effective planned efforts. That human beings first directed their aims and planned efforts toward the satisfaction of fundamental material needs is not surprising; history is replete with the tragedies caused by scarcity. Now, however, with victory in sight—in the sense that production is potentially capable of satisfying the full material needs of mankind—the lines waver. A new and perhaps a more difficult problem in our economic life has arisen—that of distribution. We are attempting to meet this problem as we have tried to meet many others —with outworn ideas. As the writer of the preceding chapter has stated it, we are trying "to utilize the products of our power age in accordance with outmoded ideas and institutions." The only avenue to a successful solution of our present dilemma is education.

The aims, broadly stated, of a progressive society—truth, beauty, and justice—are almost universally accepted even though philosophers have struggled through the ages with their definitions. Beyond those broad concepts there comes a divergence of opinion due to differing points of view. Liberty, equality, and fraternity, for instance, are proclaimed by the defenders of the democratic faith and denounced by adherents

20

of the aristocratic belief. Thus honest conflicts arise, and to complicate the situation, methods or means are confused with aims or ends. Democracy, for example, is primarily *a method* of group life, although it may also have aims. To those who believe that the *means to a very large extent determine the ends*, method becomes of great importance. There follows, then, the necessity of considering both worthy aims and effective planned effort as underlying and interdependent bases of social progress.

Acceptance of social progress implies some faith in humanity. Human beings are constantly struggling to control environment. They struggle to conquer insect pests, vegetable life, poisonous and vicious animals, disease, climate, air, water, and land. And to an encouraging extent they are succeeding. On the whole, human beings seem to combat and, in some instances, to overcome, the opposing forces of environment through rational intelligence that is superior to that of any other form of life. All of which seems to justify allegiance to rational human effort in the control of environment. Knowledge and skills intelligently used seem to have a better than even chance over any form of sheer physical force in advancing social progress.

It is necessary for human beings to agree upon values if society is to progress. These values will change as conditions of life change. What was good for the Puritan settler may not be altogether advantageous for the New England farmer today. Modern man has electric light and power, the telephone, the telegraph, and the radio with its infinite possibilities. He has automobiles, streamlined railway trains, speed boats, and airplanes. He often works in huge factories and lives in large population centers. Gone are the days in this country of the relative independence of the pioneer American of one or two centuries ago. Evolution continues, but man now must recognize new values if progress is to be realized. The values of humanity determined by the conditions of the times result in recognized aims and in rational planning to

21

185095

achieve those aims. The greatest good for the greatest number poses social problems that cannot be ignored: society is a group of two or more people, and as the number increases the social problems multiply and become more difficult of solution. The story of Adam and Eve in contrast with the story of twentieth-century America with her one hundred and thirty millions of people proves the point.

Current conditions emphasize the necessity of our learning to live together more effectively. Our progress in material culture has both caused and resulted in an increasing interdependence of each individual upon the other and upon the whole. Individual welfare is dependent upon the general welfare and, as a consequence, sensible selfishness would in reality be selflessness. But individuals conditioned by past procedures find it difficult to adjust their thoughts and behavior to changed conditions. Our task, then, is not one of education alone, but in most instances one of re-education—which is frequently a more difficult matter.

Knowledge and skills result from education. Knowledge in a broad sense means an understanding of the conditions of the present as well as of the past. It is not a mere accumulation of unrelated facts, but a mastery of facts in all their relationships. Skills obviously relate to action and become the instruments of knowledge. It is on the foundations of knowledge that human beings build their values and select the skills seemingly best suited to a realization of the values. Hence, knowledge and skills are part and parcel of aims and methods, and without this harmonious wholeness social progress is a metaphysical concept. Thus education becomes the direct instrument of human progress.

Education can mean many things. Psychologically, any experience is educative, *i.e.*, it causes the nervous system of a human being to react in one way or another. More narrowly, the experiences of reading, seeing, and hearing have possible educational results. Books, magazines, newspapers, the forum, the pulpit, travel, the cinema, the phonograph, and the radio

22

are instruments of learning. Education, however, in a technical sense, is systematic directed learning. Out of this more limited idea of education, schools emerged as a social agency, a product of evolution, and a possible agency for social progress.

Education and social progress are logically related to each other. Without the results of education social progress is impossible. Knowledge and skills are the forerunners of aims and methods and justify education. It would, therefore, seem that progress must rely entirely on education. Society has recognized the relationship between education and social progress and established a program of formal education. That action places a neat package of responsibility on the doorsteps of our schools. An examination of what the schools have done with the package is not encouraging, but it is necessary. A consideration of what the schools can do may not be a pleasant task either, owing to the gap between what is and what can be, but it may also be necessary. Both the examination of present educational practice and the consideration of needed procedures are presented here in terms of contemporary American education and in terms of a practical and contemporary concept of social progress in American life.

CRITIQUE OF FORMAL EDUCATION

Teaching as a profession has its handicaps in modern industrial America, but those handicaps do not justify the conditions within our schools that threaten the present status of organized education. Ignorance, indifference, personal ambition, incompetence, timidity, chauvinism, chicanery, and complacency may be explained, but never justified. That they exist in all large occupational groups should be no comfort to educators, for no group in the present stage of human advancement is so much in need of social understanding, fundamental scholarship, zeal, selflessness, competence, courage, broad social statesmanship, integrity, and alertness.

23

The infirmities that have been mentioned and others, similar to them in kind, are personal and must be treated as such. But the teaching profession also has been attacked by a group infirmity that is devastating to the ideal of the school as a social agency of supreme importance. It is institutionalism. Indeed, it is hyperinstitutionalism. It has attacked all social agencies from the beginning of civilization and with disastrous consequences. The symptoms are unmistakable. The social agency invariably acts as if it were no longer answerable for its purposes, plans, and programs to the people that it was established to serve. Its conduct indicates a supernatural sanction or a self-sufficiency that is arrogant and intolerable. In any case, the effects of institutionalism are obvious: decline in influence, diminution in social usefulness, and, when not apprehended in time to be halted and cured, elimination. This is exactly what is happening in our schools and colleges, especially in those supported by funds derived from taxation. In this country, recognition of the public school and colleges as social agencies imperative to a democracy has become so nearly universal that to question their usefulness or integrity at any point is to subject oneself to calumnious epithets like *traitor* or *heretic*. With isolated exceptions, the public schools and colleges of our day have been the recipients of relatively generous and substantial financial support. As a consequence, the present generation of schoolmen has come to expect support and protection as natural rights. It is education that is a natural right, but, like liberty, it can be enjoyed only at the price of eternal vigilance.

Since 1900 there has been little opposition to public education as a social agency, *i.e.*, little opposition of the kind known to Horace Mann. The growth of schools and colleges in America is evidence on this point. In 1890 there were 202,000 students enrolled in our public high schools; today there are about 6½ million. To a large extent this development has taken place despite the isolation of schoolmen. Paradoxically, isolationism has canceled out effective opposition. Had the schools taken their place in society as powerful agencies for social progress, opposition would have been notable, and we should have needed a great many Horace Manns. The lack of effective opposition has resulted in unwavering faith on the part of schoolmen in society's acceptance of public schools and colleges; the assumption by schoolmen that society no longer questions the primacy of schools as now organized and conducted; and a group apathy that has rendered our profession well-nigh inarticulate.

One of the few isolated attacks on public education occurred during the early years of the present decade. The fundamental cause was economic, of course, and the immediate occasion was a panicky fear that frequently found expression in groups, such as taxpayers' associations. In this discussion the kinds of attacks are most pertinent. Demands for the reduction of school costs, through the elimination of the "fads and frills" of education, were due to the fact that the general tax-paying public did not understand the value of music, art, health education, health services, recreation, playgrounds, vocational guidance, the activities of visiting teachers, modern vocational instruction, and a host of other things not common in schools a generation ago. The public did not understand their value because we professional educators had not taken the pains to discuss with laymen our understanding of the need for these activities and services, to say nothing of validating our practices in terms of social values. It is as simple as that.

If fatal consequences are to be avoided, institutionalism must be eradicated from our educational system. Tinkering with present practices will not suffice. The problems of learning must be approached from an entirely new point of view.

In fairness to our schools and colleges it must be recognized that formal education is the "kept-child" of the *status quo*. Some few schools—all too few—have attempted to take their places as agencies for social progress and have found themselves beset by a horde of heresy hunters. Professional casualties which resulted serve as grim reminders of probable consequences to those educators who sense the need for change and would do something about it. In a situation wherein society assumes the paradoxical position of establishing schools as instruments of social progress and, at the same time, in reality prohibits them from doing just that, it is far safer for teachers to concentrate upon the tools for learning rather than upon education itself. Unfortunately, even that instruction which pertains to the "tool" subjects is not too well done. Frequently, our methods are so deadening that, after the individual has mastered the mechanics of learning, the appetite for education, far from having been whetted, has been completely destroyed.

ADULT EDUCATION

Should the schools face tomorrow the conditions of life as they actually exist, the chances of social progress would be improved and its tempo hastened. However, the need of the hour is even more deeply rooted than that. Changes today occur with such startling rapidity that thought and behavior patterns adequate for the needs of yesterday become obsolete overnight. It is therefore incumbent upon each one of us to attune our thinking and actions to the constantly changing conditions. The need, therefore, for each of us is one of unending education, for in the final analysis it is the adult population which has the power and the instruments to stimulate social progress. That is the paramount obligation of citizenship in a democracy. The schools have a great contribution to make, but it must be said that theirs is not the sole responsibility for the current lag between our material and institutional cultures. The adult citizen must share the load.

The developments in adult education in this country during the last decade seem to point the way to a vitalized type of learning for all age groups. It is not surprising that adult education should play the role of pathfinder. In fact, the history of education in European countries clearly shows that adult education grows out of dissatisfaction with the inadequacies of the established order in school offerings. The pattern of adult education varies from country to country, of course, just as elementary, secondary, and collegiate education varies. In our own country, adult education seems to have accepted as its aim what may be called the preparation for complete human living. This concept, if applied to all levels of educational activity, and if intelligently interpreted, would dispel the evils of institutionalism now threatening the leadership of our American schools and colleges.

EDUCATION FOR THE COMPLETE LIFE

Complete human living must be the recognized end of all education. Enlightenment in these terms is not new, but it is almost completely foreign to present practice. Johann Comenius, Friedrich Froebel, Johann H. Pestalozzi, Bertrand Russell, L. P. Jacks, and others have stated the case in one way or another. Its major aspects may be said to include: *general:* (1) developing a satisfying, growing, definite, and articulate philosophy; (2) creating and applying the art and science of human relations; (3) adjusting individual, personal rights to the conditions of an advancing social order; (4) facilitating human adjustment to rapidly accelerating transitions in the conditions of group life; *specific:* (5) maintaining and operating good government; (6) perfecting the conditions of labor; (7) establishing industry in its appropriate place in the social structure; (8) facilitating desirable policies and practices of trade and commerce; (9) providing adequate housing for all; (10) producing, distributing, and using food to the best advantage; (11) obtaining healthful and adequate clothing for every one; (12) adding to the knowledge, skill, and habits of health; (13) increasing and improving the resources of recreation including the arts; (14) using and conserving natural resources in terms of the common good;

27

and (15) accounting for the discovery and development of human resources.

Such a plan must utilize all fields of learning for the realization of one or more of what we may continue to call the major aspects of complete human living. These fields of learning will continue to exist and to expand, but they will not be ends in themselves. Social perspective will become one important goal. Sociology, history, economics, the mother tongue, and psychology will assume added significance, not less, in the new setup. The approach, however, is different, because life itself, rather than the classroom with its textbook, becomes the laboratory. Arts, letters, and science will become increasingly important in our social structure, not less so. Science, to cite one of the three, now contributes directly to the welfare of mankind, everywhere, except in schools. Occasionally a teacher of science with a repressed desire to catch a glimpse of the new day offers a course entitled, let us say, The Contributions of Chemistry in Industry. That is really a red-letter effort in present practice. It is good as far as it goes, but it isn't good enough, and, what is worse, it goes in the wrong direction. It is still making life serve the purposes of subject matter instead of making subject matter serve the purposes of life. It is still facing the western horizon.

Emphatically opposed to present practice is the methodology implied in this general analysis of complete human living. It suggests an approach to "the good life" through the understanding, the insight, and the foresight that come by constant use of analytical, reflective, and judicial thinking. The implication of dynamic action also should be noted. There is nothing static even in the ultimate objective. This is the way of life. To make the way of enlightenment, of education, if you please, conform to the way of life leaves nothing to dispute. Because of our settled habits in schools and colleges, it leaves much to discuss and to do. It means an about-face and a new approach to the problems of modern life.

28

If the fitting of the individual, and through him, of society, for complete human living is an acceptable goal in education, there are three steps to take. First, some agreement should be reached as to what are the major aspects of this educational goal. Those that have been suggested (page 20) are merely illustrative of the new approach. But assuming for the moment that they are acceptable, the second step would be the analysis of what is involved in each one. Each indicated phase of the problem—as, for instance, the study of the art and science of human relations, together with one of its integral parts, the perfecting of the conditions of labor—becomes on closer analysis an ever-growing, fan-shaped outline of related experiences that have found expression in action and knowledge. The third step is the integration and use of these experiences in the full realization of the major aspects of complete human living.

The novel characteristics of this proposal will raise many questions that cannot be answered in one brief chapter. Reflection leads to the conclusion that education for complete human living, accepted generally by educators as a worthy goal, will operate in the interests of the entire population. Democracy requires just that kind of an educational program. Acceptance of this new goal for American education will enhance the advantages of scholarship and will establish disciplines in learning calculated to bring about functional results. These are matters that can scarcely be considered disputable. The organization and administration of education must be changed as radically as the program of studies and the general approach to learning. This problem, however, is almost a separate matter in itself, and consideration of it must be deferred to another time and place. In passing it is worthy of note that organization and administration affect Federal, state, and local programs.

The challenge is unmistakable. Whether or not the unification of educational resources and effort will result in a program similar to the one herein proposed is subject to debate.

Just how far education can become enlightenment for complete human living under present working conditions in our schools and colleges is a matter of grave concern. That there will be change, no one can deny. That change is necessary in the general direction suggested in this discussion seems too obvious to be argued. All the college professors and school teachers in the country cannot stem the tide of progress, not even if they were to try. Neither can all the professional educators combined carry the entire load. If our democracy is to survive, each citizen must subject himself to the discipline of continuous education. In the light of the present tendency toward overproduction in lip service to democracy, that discipline might well begin with the re-examination of what democracy really is as a method of group life.

Chapter III

DEMOCRACY AS A WAY OF LIFE

SIDNEY HOOK

★ ★ ★ ★

THE greatest tribute to democracy as an ideal of social life is unwittingly paid to it in the *apologias* of the dictators of the modern world, Hitler, Stalin, and Mussolini. For all of them insist, in the shrillest tones, that the regimes they control are actually, despite appearances, democracies "in a higher sense." For example, Mussolini in a public address delivered at Berlin in September (and reprinted in *International Conciliation* for December, 1937), proclaimed that "the greatest and soundest democracies which exist in the world today are Italy and Germany"; while Stalin, after the worst blood purge in history, praises the constitution that bears his name—a constitution that openly provides in Section 126 for the control of all socio-political institutions by the minority Communist party—as the most democratic in all history. And here in America, owing to the needs of the foreign policy of the various dictatorships, their partisans now wrap up their program of blood and steel in the American flag and make a great verbal play about being defenders of American democracy.[1]

That the greatest enemies of democracy should feel compelled to render demagogic lip allegiance to it is an eloquent sign of the inherent plausibility of democratic ideals to the modern mind and of their universal appeal. But that its enemies, apparently with some success, should have the audacity to flaunt the principles they have so outrageously betrayed in practice is just as eloquent a sign that these

31

principles are ambiguous. Agreement where there is no clarity merely cloaks differences; it does not settle them. The analysis of the concept of democracy is not merely a theoretical problem for the academician. The ordinary man who says he believes in democracy must clearly understand what he means by it. Otherwise, the genuine issues that divide men will be lost in the welter of emotive words which demagogues skillfully evoke to conceal their true intentions. There is such a thing as the ethics of words. And of all the words in our political vocabulary, none is in greater need of precise analysis and scrupulous use than *democracy*.

SOME METHODOLOGICAL CONSIDERATIONS

Anyone can use a word as a sign for any idea *provided he makes adequately clear what he means by it*. For example, if a man says, "By democracy I mean a government in which the name of the ruler begins with a D," we can smile at his peculiar nominal definition and pass on. We have no right to dispute the legitimacy of his use if he always accompanies it with a parenthetical explanation of what he understands by the term. However, if he introduces the term into a political discussion without stating explicitly the special meaning it has for him, we have every scientific and moral right to object. For, where words of a certain kind are already in use, to employ them as signs of new meanings without posting, so to speak, a clear public notice, is to be guilty of a form of counterfeit. New verbal signs can always be found for new meanings

Democracy is a term which has customarily been associated with certain *historical* practices and with certain writings in the history of culture. Instead of beginning with arbitrary nominal definitions, it would be preferable to describe and critically evaluate the growth of democracy in Western Europe from its origins in the Greek city (slave) states to the present. But this could only be essayed in a systematic treatise.

The third alternative—one which we shall here follow—is to begin with a definition which formally is acceptable to most people who distinguish democracy from other forms of political organization and which is in consonance with at least traditional American usage. We shall then indicate what it implies as far as the structure of other present-day social institutions is concerned, to what techniques of settling differences it commits us, and what fundamental ethical values are presupposed. In this way we shall combine the advantages of an analytical and "contemporary-historical" treatment.

THE MEANING OF DEMOCRACY

A democratic society is one in which the government rests upon the freely given consent of the governed. Some ambiguity attaches to every term in this preliminary definition. The least ambiguous is the term *governed*. By the *governed* is meant those adult participating members of the community, with their dependents, whose way of life is affected by what the government does or leaves undone. By the *government* is primarily intended the law and policy-making agencies, legislative, executive, and judicial, whose activities control the life of the community. In the first instance, then, government is a *political* concept, but in certain circumstances it may refer to social and economic organizations whose policies affect the lives of a large number of individuals. In saying that the government rests upon the *consent* of the governed, it is meant that at certain fixed periods the policies of the government are submitted to the governed for approval or disapproval. By *freely given* consent of the governed is meant that no coercion, direct or indirect, is brought to bear upon the governed to elicit their approval or disapproval. A government that "rests upon" the freely given consent of the governed is one which *in fact* abides by the expression of this approval or disapproval.

33

CONSEQUENCES OF THE DEFINITION

A direct consequence of this definition may be that there is no complete democracy anywhere in the world. This no more prevents our employing the term intelligently and making comparative evaluations than the fact that no one is "perfectly healthy" prevents us from making the concept "health" basic to medical theory and practice. There is no absolutely fat man, but we can easily tell whether one man is fatter than another. So long as our definition enables us to order existing communities in a series of greater or less democracy, our definition is adequate.

If a democratic government rests upon the freely given consent of the governed, then it cannot be present where institutional arrangements—whether political or nonpolitical—obviously obstruct the registration or the implementation of the common consent. We do not have to settle any metaphysical questions about the nature of freedom in order to be able to tell when consent is not free. A plebiscite or election which is held at the point of a bayonet or in which one can only vote "Yes," or in which no opposition candidates are permitted, obviously does not express freely given consent. These are only the crudest violations of the democratic ideal, but they are sufficient to make the pretence that the present-day regimes in Italy, Russia, and Germany are democratic sound almost obscene.

There are less obvious, but no less effective, ways of coercively influencing the expression of consent. A threat, for example, to deprive the governed of their jobs or means of livelihood, by a group which has the power to do so, would undermine a democracy even if its name were retained. In fact, every overt form of economic pressure, since it is experienced directly by the individual and since so many other phases of his life are dependent upon economic security, is an overt challenge to democracy. Where the political forms of democracy function within a society in which economic controls are not subject to political control, there is always a standing threat to democracy. For in such a society, the possibility exists that economic pressure may strongly influence the expression of consent. Where it cannot influence the expression of consent, it may subvert or prevent its execution. This is particularly true in modern societies in which social instruments of production, necessary for the livelihood of many, are privately owned by the few. A political democracy cannot function properly where differences in economic power are so great that one group can determine the weal or woe of another by nonpolitical means. Genuine political democracy, therefore, entails the right of the governed, through their representatives, to control economic policy. In this sense, it might be said that where there is no economic democracy— a phrase which will be explained later—there can be no genuine and widespread political democracy. The exact degree of economic control necessary to political democracy will vary with changing conditions. It is clear that today modern economic organization plays such a dominant role in social life that political democracy cannot be implemented if it is unable to control economic policy.

A further consequence of *freely given consent* is the absence of a *monopoly of education* where education includes all agencies of cultural transmission, especially the press. As important as the majority principle is for a democracy, the expression of consent by the majority is not free if it is deprived of access to sources of information, if it can read *only* the official interpretation, if it can hear *only* one voice in classroom, pulpit, and radio, if, in short, all critical opposition is branded as treason to be extirpated by heresy trials, re-education in concentration camps, and execution squads. The individual has no more freedom of action when his mind is deliberately tied by ignorance than when his hands are tied with rope. The very dependence of modern man upon the printed word, greater than ever before in history, makes the public right to *critical dissent* all the more necessary if *common consent* is to be

35

free. Not many years ago this would have been a common-place. Today apologists have so muddied the waters of truth that its reaffirmation must be stressed. Look at the following item from *Pravda*, a paper used not only for domestic consumption but for export to Western countries to prove that the Soviet Union is "the freest and most democratic country in the world":

> Only patriots of our fatherland and people loyal to communism can work on any of our newspapers in any position, from copy-reader to editor. Only party and non-party Bolsheviki are worthy of working in and guiding the press of the freest and most democratic country in the world—the Soviet Union. (Reprinted in *The New York Times*, July 26, 1937.)

Similar statements can be culled from the press of other totalitarian countries.

POSITIVE REQUIREMENTS OF A DEMOCRACY

So far we have been considering conditions in the absence of which democracy cannot exist. But the effective functioning of a democracy demands the presence of a number of other conditions. Among these, the active participation of the governed in the processes of government is primary. By active participation is meant not the attempt to do the scientific work of officials but free discussion and consultation on public policies, and voluntary co-operation in the execution of man-dates reached through the democratic process. Where the governed feel that they have no stake in the government, indifference results. And political indifference may be called the dryrot of democracy. "The food of feeling," as Mill well says, "is action. . . . Let a person have nothing to do for his country, and he will not care for it." The country or com-munity, however, is never a homogeneous whole. There may be common interests, but the conceptions of the common interest are never common. Nor in this world can all interests ever in fact be common. If they were, government would be a mere administrative detail. The variety of interests that is

36

always to be found necessitates that no interest be excluded from voicing its demands, even though these demands may, in the process of democratic deliberation, be compromised or rejected. The only historical alternative to the participation of the masses in the processes of government is the ancient, artful, and uncertain technique of "bread and circuses." That the modern bread is smeared with oleomargarine and the circuses are cinematic makes no essential difference. Such a technique conceals differences and trouble centers, whereas the methods of participation and consultation uncover them, articulate new social needs, and suggest instrumentalities of handling them. The wisest policy cannot succeed in face of popular indifference or hostility. Even those who believe that the professional wise men or experts must govern exclude, at their own peril, those whom they would govern from their counsels.

Another requirement for the effective functioning of democracy is the presence of mechanisms which permit prompt action, through delegated authority, in crucial situations. What constitutes a crucial situation and what specific administrative mechanisms are best adapted to meet it cannot be settled in advance. But it is clear that there is nothing incompatible with democracy in freely delegating specific functions to authority *provided that at a certain fixed time an accounting is made to the governed who alone have the prerogative of renewing or abrogating the grant of authority.* That such grants of authority may be abused goes without saying. It may even be acknowledged that there is no absolute guarantee against the risks of abuse and usurpation. But unless these risks are sometimes taken, democratic government may be destroyed by evils whose urgency will not wait until the close of prolonged debate. Common sense recognizes this in case of flood and plague. Flood and plague have their social analogues. But whatever the crisis may be, the recognition that it is a crisis must come from the governed or their delegated representatives; grants of power must be renewed demo-

37

cratically; and the governed cannot, without destroying their democracy, proclaim that the crisis is *permanent*.

The fact that the preservation of democracy sometimes demands the delegation of far-reaching authority and the fact that the possession of such authority may corrupt those who wield it reinforce another positive requirement of democracy. To understand this requirement we must take note of the psychological effects of holding power and the historical evidence which indicates that many democratic organizations, sooner or later, become instruments of a minority group which identifies its interests with the interests of the organization as a whole and which keeps power by fraud, myth, and force. Taken literally, Lord Acton's maxim, "power always corrupts and absolute power corrupts absolutely" is an exaggeration. But there is sufficient truth in it to give us pause when we are about to invest individuals or groups with great power, even temporarily. Similarly, Robert Michels' "iron law of oligarchy," according to which democrats may be victorious but democracy never, goes beyond the data he has assembled. But no one can read his powerful case studies and the data presented by other writers like Pareto, Machajaski, and Nomad without realizing how plausible Michels' induction is. And when we add to this the degeneration, under our very eyes, of the Russian Revolution which began avowedly as a workers' democracy, developed into the dictatorship of the Communist party *over* the proletariat, and finally took form as the bloody rule of a camarilla that has piled up more corpses in a few years than the Roman emperors in as many centuries of Christian persecution, the lesson is driven home with sickening force. This lesson is that a positive requirement of a functioning democracy is an intelligent distrust of its leadership, a skepticism, stubborn but not blind, of all demands for the enlargement of power, and an emphasis upon critical method in every phase of education and social life. This skepticism like other forms of vigilance may often seem irritating to leaders who are con-

38

vinced of their good intentions. The skepticism, however, is not of their intentions but of the objective consequences of their power. Where skepticism is replaced by uncritical enthusiasm and the many-faceted deifications which our complex society makes possible, a fertile emotional soil for dictatorship has been prepared. The most convincing aspect of Plato's analysis of the cycle of political decay in the eighth book of the *Republic* is the transition from a hero-worshiping democracy to an absolute tyranny.

Another positive requirement of democracy we have already referred to as *economic democracy*. By economic democracy is meant the power of the community, organized as producers and consumers, to determine the basic question of the objectives of economic development. Such economic democracy presupposes some form of social planning, but whether the economy is to be organized in a single unit or several ·and whether it is to be highly centralized or not are experimental questions. There are two generic criteria to decide such questions. One is the extent to which a specific form of economic organization makes possible an abundance of goods and services for the greatest number, without which formal political democracy is necessarily limited in its functions, if not actually endangered. The other is the extent to which a specific form of economic organization preserves and strengthens the conditions of the democratic process already mentioned.

There are certain kinds of economic planning which are so conceived that they may give security—the security of a jail in which in exchange for freedom the inmates are given food, clothing, and shelter of sorts. Closer examination will show that any type of planned society which does not provide for the freest criticism, for diversity, for creative individuality, for catholicity of taste cannot ever guarantee security. Security in such a society is conditional upon accepting arbitrary bureaucratic decree as the law of life. This is conspicuously true wherever the instruments of production are socialized by a nondemocratic state. When Stalin tells us that "the dictatorship of the proletariat is *substantially* the dictatorship of the [Communist] Party," he is telling us that the Russian worker can purchase a problematic security only insofar as he accepts this party dictatorship. The upshot, then, of our analysis is that just as political democracy is incomplete without some form of economic democracy, so there can be no genuine economic democracy without political democracy. Some may call this socialism. But it is certainly not the "socialism" of Hitler or Stalin. Nor of Roosevelt.

THE ARGUMENT AGAINST DEMOCRACY

Our discussion would be incomplete if we did not consider the chief objections which have been urged against democracy by some of the outstanding thinkers of the past and present. Most of these objections are variants of two fundamental arguments—practical and theoretical.

The practical argument, from the time of Plato down, stresses the imperfections in the actual functioning of democracy. It draws up a detailed indictment of the blundering inefficiencies of democracies, the influence of demagogy and prejudice in the formulation of their policy, and the operation of certain political mechanisms which actually place the power of selection of the rulers of the community in the hands of a minority. And from this largely accurate description of the way in which democracies do in fact function, it is concluded that democracy must be scrapped for another alternative. Now the description may be granted, and yet the conclusion not be justified, for unless we know the precise nature of the alternative and how *it* works out in practice, we may legitimately reply that the cure for the evils of democracy is better democracy. This is not a catch phrase, for by better democracy is meant the realization of the conditions and requirements already outlined or, at the very least, the struggle for them.

And what is the alternative to democracy with all its imperfections? Upon analysis, all alternatives turn out to involve some form of benevolent despotism—whether it be a

40

personal, class, or party despotism. The fatal objection to a benevolent despotism—aside from the fact that people with different interests have different ideas of what constitutes benevolence—is that no one knows how long the despotism will remain benevolent, not even the despot himself. We may appeal from Philip drunk, to Philip sober, but who is to keep Philip sober?

Every benevolent act of a despot recorded in history can be matched with scores of malevolent acts. For every guilty man a dictator spares, there are thousands of innocent men whom he dooms. The *ideal* benevolent despotism is a figment of the imagination; even as an ideal, it is no more promising than *ideal* democracy. Moreover, it is logically impermissible to compare the ideal form of benevolent despotism with the actual practice of democracy. If we intelligently compare the practices of both, whether in antiquity or in the modern world, the lovers of democracy need not fear the outcome.

The second type of argument against democracy is theoretical and is really presupposed by the first. It holds that the ultimate end of government is human welfare and that the discovery of the nature of human welfare is a difficult pursuit in which the best qualified are those who have the best knowledge and the highest intelligence. Since the problems of government are largely administrative, demanding knowledge and intelligence, and since an effective democracy presupposes the possession of both by the majority of the population, and since even the lover of democracy must admit that this rarely is the case—democracy must be rejected. Plato put the nub of the argument in a metaphor: Who would propose that, setting out on a perilous journey, we should elect the pilot of the ship? And yet the pilot of the ship of state has a task infinitely more difficult, and the course of the vessel is beset by many more perils. What rhyme or reason exists, therefore, for electing him? Or as Santayana, a direct lineal descendant of Plato in political philosophy, puts it: "It is knowledge and knowledge only that may rule by divine right."

41

Space permits only a brief indication of the Achilles' heel of the argument. There may be experts in knowledge of fact, but there are no experts in wisdom of policy. Ultimate welfare presupposes that there is an ultimate good. But a conclave of philosophers gathered together to determine the nature of the ultimate good would resemble nothing so much as the Tower of Babel. Wisdom of policy depends upon knowledge of one's interests. It is true that some men are not clear as to what their own interests are, but it is arrant presumption for others to pretend to them that they know what their interests really are, or what they should be. A parent dealing with children may sometimes be justified in asserting that he knows better than they what their real interests are; but any ruler who justifies his abrogation of democratic control by proclaiming that he knows what the real interests of the governed are better than they do themselves is therewith telling them that they are no more responsible than children. Besides oppressing them, he is insulting them, for he envisages their childhood as perpetual. It is not accidental that we call dictatorial government paternal. In paternal government, however, there is more evidence of authority than affection. The paternal ruler often mistakes his political children for guinea pigs upon whom he can try peculiar experiments. Their peculiarity lies in this: no matter how the experiments turn out, they are fatal to the generation of guinea pigs which serves as the test.

To be sure, there is no wisdom in electing a pilot or a cobbler. But, in the last analysis, as even Plato was compelled to recognize, it is the user and not the maker who is the best judge of work well done. He who wears the shoe knows best where it pinches. On this homely truth every theoretical attack on democracy founders.

DEMOCRACY AS A WAY OF LIFE

Democracy is more than a pattern of institutional behavior. It is an affirmation of certain attitudes and values which are more important than any particular set of institutions, for they must serve as the sensitive directing controls of institutional change. Every mechanism of democratic government has a critical point at which it may run wild. It may be formally perfect but actually murderous. For example, the principle of majority rule is a necessary condition of a functioning democracy. But so far there is nothing in what has been said which would prevent a majority from oppressing a minority. Numbers, even less than knowledge, give divine right, or immunity from folly. A just government may rest upon the consent of the majority, but it is not therewith good government. The tragic history of the oppression of minorities indicates that. It is a history to whose lessons no one can be indifferent; for every member of the community is part of a minority at some points or on some issue.

It is helpful, but not sufficient, to insist that democratic communities must provide for autonomous self-government by voluntarily organized minorities on all questions which concern the minority rather than the community at large. It is not sufficient because minorities are often in opposition on communal issues and because the very willingness to extend autonomy on other "local" issues is contingent upon acceptance of the values of democracy as a way of life.

There are three related values which are central to democracy as a way of life. The first is found in many variant formulations, but common to them all is the belief that every individual should be regarded as possessing intrinsic worth or dignity. The social corollary of this recognition is that *equal opportunities* of development should be provided for the realization of individual talents and capacities. To believe in the equality of opportunities does not mean to believe in the equality of talents. But it does carry with it a recognition that, under conditions of modern technology, marked inequalities in the distribution of wealth or in standards of living are prejudicial to equal opportunities of development. It is absurd to expect that the same technical opportunities

43

of development should be accorded to the artist and the engineer, the machinist and the administrator. It is not absurd to expect that their living conditions be approximately the same. The ideal of equality is not to be mechanically applied, but it must function as a regulative principle of distribution. Otherwise, endemic conflicts, latent in all human associations, take such acute forms that they imperil the very existence of democracy.

The belief in the equal right of all members of the community to develop their personalities must be complemented by a belief in the value of difference, variety, and uniqueness. In a democracy, differences of interest and achievement must not be merely suffered but encouraged. The healthy zest and opposition arising from the conflict and interchange of ideas, tastes, and personality in a free society is a much more fruitful source of new and significant experiences than the peace of dull, dead uniformity. To be sure, there are limits to difference as there are to specialization. However different people are, they live in a common world, they must communicate in a common language, and accept the common constraints which safeguard the species from extinction. In nondemocratic societies the admission that men are always bound in some way by the necessities of living together is a premise for constructing vast techniques of repression to choke off differences in almost every way. In democratic societies, the admission must serve as a condition for enlarging the scope of variation, free play, growth, and experiment.

It is obvious that no matter what the values are to which a democracy is committed, situations will arise in which these values conflict or in which they are challenged by other values. No decision made in one situation necessarily stands for all others. The ultimate commitment of a democracy, then, must be a faith in some *method by which these conflicts are resolved.* Since the method must be the test of all values, it would not be inaccurate to call it the basic value in the democratic way of life. This method is the method of intelligence, the method of critical scientific inquiry. In a democracy it must be directed

44

to all issues, to all conflicts, if democracy is not to succumb to the dangers which threaten it from within and without. It is not mere chance that the greatest philosopher of experimental empiricism—John Dewey—is also the greatest philosopher of democracy.

To say that the method of intelligence is essential to the democratic process seems like worrying a commonplace. But not when it is realized how revolutionary the impact would be of giving the method of intelligence institutional force in education, law, and politics. Policies would be treated as hypotheses, not as dogmas: customary practices as generalizations, not as God-given truths. A generation trained in schools in which emphasis was placed upon method, method, and still more method, could hardly be swayed by current high-pressured propaganda. The very liberties granted by free institutions in a democracy provide opportunities for special interests to forge powerful instruments to undermine it. There is no protection against this save the critically armed mind. Minorities know that the majority may be tyrannical. The tyranny of the mass flows from its insensitiveness to the consequences of means and methods, not only for the minority but for itself. An insistence upon evidence, relevance, and deliberation is not incompatible with action but only with blind action. The method of intelligence cuts under the fanaticisms which make a fetish of ends, by stressing the conditions and consequences of their use. It both uncovers and enforces responsibilities in social life. It, and it alone, can distinguish between social conflicts which are negotiable and those which are irreconcilable, and the degree of each. Where conflicts are negotiable, it approaches social problems as difficulties to be solved by experiment and analysis, not as battles to be fought out in the heat of blood lust. It is reliable without claiming to be infallible, and its self-critical character permits it to learn from the history of human error.

What other alternative method can be embraced by a society which permits and encourages plural values and plural associations? The more intelligence is liberated in a democratic community, the greater its control of nature and the sources of wealth; the greater its control of nature, the greater the possibility of diversifying interests, values, and associations; the greater diversification, the more necessary the function of intelligence to mediate, integrate, and harmonize.

NOTES

[1] The leader of the American Nazi Bund maintains in a recent letter to *The New York Times* that many of his members have rallied to the program of his organization because of their loyalty to the democratic institutions of the United States; Stalin's chief American lieutenants have been performing even more humorous contortions in an effort to convince us that their party is the heir to Jeffersonian democracy. Both blithely assume that American citizens either cannot read or have no memories. One need only turn to the literature written in a franker mood, like Hitler's *Mein Kampf* or William Z. Foster's *Towards Soviet America*, to refute them.

Chapter IV

TODAY'S PROPAGANDA AND TOMORROW'S REALITY

Clyde R. Miller

★ ★ ★ ★

REVELATIONS made since the World War have enlightened us as to the powerful influences that may be deliberately set in motion to form public opinion. We are coming to see that what we will believe and do tomorrow depends in great measure upon what we are being told to believe and do today. In a word, we are becoming "propaganda conscious" without considering very accurately what we mean by that phrase. However, an increasingly important body of literature treating the subject from psychological, political, and ethical standpoints has become available, and it is now possible to test and clarify our impressions of what constitutes propaganda and of how its uses may be judged.

THE NATURE OF PROPAGANDA

Speaking broadly, all form of communication involves propaganda because it involves suggestion of mind acting upon mind. Opinions and actions which are not deliberate or purposeful nevertheless do influence other people. Such actions and opinions fall within the category of customary ways of thinking and behaving, customary ways of dressing, eating, worshiping, amusing ourselves, marrying, bringing up children. Because these ways are *customs*, they are generally considered to be *right*. The ordinary citizen would no more think of departing from them than he would think of appearing

47

on Broadway in a suit of yellow silk pajamas. These customs are in the mores to which most people conform because it is the easiest way, the way of habit rather than of thought, and thought, particularly when it has to do with changing some long-established custom, gives most people a wrench. So the majority prefer to leave things and people as they are, and by so doing become unconscious propagandists for preserving the *status quo*. If, on the other hand, we are for change, we become more or less conscious propagandists for changing the *status quo*. Even if we express no opinion because we are not interested or because we are afraid, our unconscious conformity or deliberate neutrality still has the net effect of propaganda, inasmuch as it helps to preserve the things as they are.

As generally understood, however, propaganda is action or the expression of opinion by individuals or groups deliberately designed to influence opinions or actions of other individuals with reference to predetermined ends. The Boston Tea Party was a propaganda action. It was planned to help crystallize sentiment against the British government. The burning of the German Reichstag is thought by many to have been a propaganda action deliberately planned by the Nazis to discredit the communists. Whether the Nazis planned and executed the burning of the Reichstag or not, one thing is certain: they took immediate advantage of the fire by blaming it on the communists and immediately placing communists under arrest. The reaction in Germany was immediate. To have an idea of it, imagine that the Capitol in Washington was destroyed and that the president and other responsible officials, the newspapers and radio commentators immediately placed the blame on the communists. It is easy to believe that popular feeling against the communists would run high. Substantially the same techniques are employed by the Russian communists against real or alleged dissenters as evidenced in the conflict between the Stalinists and the Trotskyists.

While much propaganda takes the form of specific acts, most of what is generally considered to be propaganda consists of words, printed and spoken. By our definition, propaganda is action or the expression of opinion *deliberately* designed to influence opinions and actions of others. It is this deliberate propaganda which claims our attention if we are to understand the forces which make for social change, forces which will make tomorrow different from today.

"GOOD" AND "BAD" PROPAGANDA

We cannot go far in our consideration of the subject without intimating, as we have already, that propaganda is associated with *conflict*, with the pro and con of opinion. We do not have opinions in a vacuum. We have opinions about things and people. We take sides. We line up "for" or "against." When changes are proposed, people are for them or against them. A century ago a committee of citizens in Lancaster, Ohio, asked for the use of the schoolroom to discuss a new invention, the steam locomotive. The school board deliberated and rendered its decision. "If God in His infinite wisdom," declared the board, "had intended men to be hurtled through space at the outrageous speed of fifteen miles an hour, He would have said so in His Holy Scripture. Petition denied." Similar prejudice greeted the first "horseless carriage." Older people still recall the ridicule with which short skirts and bobbed hair were hailed, and the outcry against girls' smoking cigarettes. It required propaganda direct and indirect, propaganda of word and action, propaganda deliberate and continuous to bring in the age of rapid transit and to create a generation of women smokers.

Propaganda is usually considered to be "good" or "bad" according to the end it serves and the means it utilizes. What is good propaganda? What is bad propaganda? Good for whom? Bad for whom? One cannot answer these questions without first setting up some standards. Suppose we start with the simple statement that life ought to be worth living. Immediately we run into questions which take us into spheres of religion, ethics, race, economics, politics. Life ought to be

49

worth living for whom? Jews? Nordics? Chinese? Negroes? By the Christian concept life ought to be worth living for all people of all races. "Come unto me all ye who labour and are heavy laden . . . " Jesus added no footnote stating that the invitation applied only to pure Jews or pure Nordics.

To live mentally and spiritually, people must live physiologically; they must have air, food, water, clothes, and shelter. Here we are brought face to face with the clash of economic systems.

Propaganda is thus inseparable from conflict. It is always associated with it, as cause or as effect, or as cause and effect. Regarding it in this light, we can see propaganda, in the form either of action or the expression of opinion, as the dynamic element, not only in today's conflicts, but in the recorded conflicts of history. Copernicus, Galileo, Descartes, Thomas Edison, and Henry Ford were all propagandists in their day. They expressed definite propagandas in the sense that they gave voice to suggestions or opinions which ran counter to the accepted beliefs of their times, and were met by the counterpropaganda of orthodoxy.

AREAS OF CONTROVERSY

One of the great fields of conflict in the past was the constantly shifting borderland between science and theology. Here, where the questions at issue were still highly controversial, even the proponents of natural science were propagandists fighting for truths not yet generally accepted. In Copernicus' time people believed the earth was flat, that it remained stationary while the sun moved. The Scriptures said so; to believe otherwise was heretical. Copernicus knew it was heretical. He knew that heretics (*i.e.*, persons with opinions not commonly accepted) faced drastic treatment, ostracism, and possibly torture and death. He waited until he was on his deathbed before publishing his theory of the universe. The printer who published the book did not wish to be punished as a heretic either. So as a precaution, he wrote a foreword which

50

stated in effect that Copernicus' theory really was just an amusing whimsey, not to be taken seriously. But it was taken seriously, as Galileo found to his grief when he announced that by his crude telescope he had confirmed the Copernican theory. Galileo was forced to recant. The new teachings were condemned by virtually all the theologians, Catholic and Protestant alike, and centuries passed before the battle was won by natural science against the propaganda of the theologians and the superstitious masses. In the same way the propaganda of today may become the accepted truths or the rejected fallacies of tomorrow.

At the present time the great areas of controversy are not theological; they are political and economic and social. Hence we should expect to find the most heated propaganda centering about these subjects, and this, as every one knows, is actually the case.

PROPAGANDA AND DEMOCRACY

In a book which devotes a chapter to the examination of democracy, it is not necessary to analyze or define it here but merely to indicate the relationship which it bears to the problems of propaganda. Only statements of a general character need be made at this point for a consideration of some of the questions specific to the use of propaganda in the United States will be given later in this chapter.

Most Americans think they believe in democracy, but they would do well to check their belief against the political, economic, social, and religious freedoms offered under actual conditions of life in the United States. For it is apparent that democracy, insofar as it is a reality, must consist of *specific* freedoms applied to *specific* situations, one of these freedoms being the right of everyone to be a propagandist. With all of these freedoms are associated responsibilities and restrictions. Freedom of speech does not include freedom of libelous, obscene vituperation. Freedom of assembly does not include the freedom to assemble on the right of way of a trunk-line

51

railroad and block passage of trains. Freedom to drive an automobile does not mean freedom to drive it on the wrong side of the street or to travel through city traffic at sixty miles an hour. Complete, unrestricted freedom would be tantamount to anarchy, in the popular sense of that term. As human activities and associations become more intricate and complex, we see the need for more restrictions and controls. Paradoxically, such controls are required to maintain and extend specific freedoms.

In the democratic state, ideally, authority flows from the top down and obedience from the bottom up; also, authority flows from the bottom up and obedience from the top down. No democratic state, of course, is wholly democratic; its people must constantly wage battle against the authoritarian trait which is common to all humanity.

CONFUSION OF TONGUES

In the democratic type of human organization, whether it be government, business group, labor union, school, or church, there are many conflicting wills, accompanied by their conflicting propagandas. To the superficial, the resulting Babel of voices, warnings, charges, propagandas, and counterpropagandas is a dismaying confusion of tongues, a sign of dissolution and decay. Out of such confusion of opinions come actions which bring variations and change; and change, as we already have observed, is not welcome to people attuned to the easy way of long-accustomed habits of thinking and acting.

Something of the dismay caused by this confusion of tongues may have been in the mind of a speaker at the 1937 Institute of Human Relations at Williams College. According to a *Springfield Republican* editorial, the speaker "referred somewhat despairingly to Americans as 'a most propaganda-ridden people' with the implied suggestion that something should be done about it."

To those who see in the free but admittedly confusing conflict of propagandas the sign of a vital democracy and to those who envisage democracy as the only mode of living based on the axiom that life should be worth living to all people, what *The Springfield Republican* went on to say about the speaker's thesis will summarize extraordinarily well the function and challenge of propaganda in a democracy:

Propaganda and liberty are inseparable. Freedom of speech and of the press, to the extent that Americans enjoy them, necessarily afford full scope for propaganda from everybody, everywhere, any time.

Free propaganda is nothing but free publicity for the views, interpretations, arguments, pleadings, truths and untruths, half-lies and lies of all creation. Propaganda is good as well as bad. "We are surrounded by clouds of propaganda," complained the speaker at Williamstown; and so we are. It is up to each of us to precipitate from those clouds the true and the false, the near-true and the near-false, identifying and giving to each classification its correct label. If this task is far beyond the facilities or ability of most of us, the fact has to be accepted as the price we pay for liberty . . .

The American press is as honest as any press in the world; certainly it remains the freest in the world. . . . Yet the freest press in the world abuses its privileges shamefully. The deliberate misrepresentation and distortion of truth all the time going on for the promotion of some interest, political, financial, social or patriotic, is staggering.

The philosophy of liberalism rationalizes this endless abuse of freedom by assuming that truth meets falsehood eventually in fair contest, and overthrows it. It is safe, in the long run, to leave truth and falsehood to fight it out in a free and open field, although "in the long run," as someone has observed, we shall all be dead . . .

As they see free speech and free press, there is more or less lying in all directions at the best. And so they conclude that the lying had better be done in a single direction instead of many. But this carries propaganda to the other extreme where there is no battle allowed between truth and falsehood and it is 1000 to 1 that falsehood will prevail. Give Thy children oh Lord! "clouds of propaganda" as the lesser evil.

With reference to the same speaker and the same subject, *The New York Times* observed:

What is truly vicious is not propaganda but a monopoly of it. When we are asked to suppress any "propaganda," let us be sure that we are not merely being asked to shut down on one side of a controversy and leave the field free to the other.

A population long subjected to germs of a certain type begins to develop some immunity to them. It might occur to some of those who are in such dreadful fear of propaganda that the more Americans are bombarded by it the more easily they will recognize it in its various forms and the more practiced they are likely to become in dealing with it. If Americans could be thoroughly protected from "propaganda" (which is usually our invidious name for the other fellow's ideas), is it certain that the protection would work only good and no harm? Might it not be useful to apply in this case the logic that Milton applied in his noble plea against censorship:

"I cannot praise a fugitive and cloistered virtue, unexercised and unbreathed, that never sallies out and sees her adversary, but slinks out of the race where that immortal garland is to be run for, not without dust and heat."

PROPAGANDA AND THE AUTHORITARIAN STATES

It is a *monopoly of propaganda* which we see when a powerful group takes over the government of a nation, applies all controls to restrict freedom of action and opinion, and uses those controls to prevent dissemination of any adverse criticism of its own means and ends. Such propaganda is typical of the authoritarian state.

In such an authoritarian organization there is one will; hence, one opinion, one voice, one propaganda. All avenues to the minds of the people—press, radio, cinema, theater, school, church—must be made to reflect that one will. When a government is authoritarian no other opinion, no other propaganda than its own, is tolerated. The people are told exactly what to think, what to do. Methods of coercion, extending even to imprisonment and death, are used to enforce the monopoly of propaganda. In short, in the authoritarian state, authority flows from the top down and obedience from the bottom up. The state, in essence, *is* the dictator or dictatorial group. The authoritarian state utilizes its power not to effect controls to afford the maximum amount of freedom to the majority of its citizens but rather to effect controls which will give a monopoly of freedom to the dictator or dictatorial group.

In such a type of human organization, the conditioning of the peoples' minds is a matter of first importance. In Nazi Germany, as in communist Russia and fascist Italy, pains are taken to train children to respond to beliefs and acts to which the dictator wants response and to reject others. The school system is as thoroughly regimented as labor, agriculture, and industry. Children are gathered into youth organizations, so that even in leisure hours their thoughts will be conditioned to respond to the dictatorship.

Parents are arrested when their children report them as expressing opinions not favorable to the regime. The home supplements the school in conditioning the people of an authoritarian state to accept the propaganda of the state.

Even among countries ruled by dictators some difference in method, however, is to be observed, as well as differences in level of appeal made by the propaganda of a single dictator at different times or on different subjects. Hitler and Mussolini have both paid lip service to democracy by asserting that the virtues of a democracy were all to be found in their own forms of government, and Stalin in order to find allies among the Western Powers has committed communists everywhere to a verbal defense of democracy. At other times the mask has fallen, and Hitler is quoted as having said: "Democracy is a creation of the Jews, it is the foul and filthy avenue to Bolshevism," and Mussolini: "Democracy is a rotting corpse"; and Stalin: "The theory of 'pure democracy' . . . was formulated to camouflage imperialism . . . The dictatorship of the proletariat is the rule of the proletariat over the bourgeoisie, a rule unrestricted by law, based upon force. . . . " When Hitler speaks of "strength through joy," he has hit upon a psychological truth capable of broad application to education and to life, and one which is in marked contrast to his usual vituperative and brutal method of propaganda. But in actual practice it is simply a technique of consolidating the power of a minority political party. Similarly, in Italy and

55

Russia some slogans and devices have been evolved which are capable of being employed to further social purposes and to increase material welfare, but since they function within a totalitarian framework of thought and action, their primary use is to weld the population into an uncritical, undifferentiated mass of enthusiastic believers in the supreme virtue of the ruling party.

In the main, however great the differences, the authoritarian states, in their use of propaganda, lean heavily upon compulsory education and police power to enforce the party-imposed standards from which no appeal is permitted.

THE PROBLEM OF PROPAGANDA IN AMERICAN DEMOCRACY

The good life with the maximum of freedom for all the people is the ideal if not the actuality in a democracy like our own. But here, too, controls may be set up by powerful private individuals to restrict, in the interest of their own private freedoms, the rights of other individuals. Such controls may be seen in the United States in "company towns" where nearly every aspect of life—housing, education, press, cinema, religion, purchase of groceries, clothing, and medical service— is regulated by the major industry which controls the town. Sometimes powerful gangsters or racketeers may restrict the freedom of employers or of a labor union, and any of these forms of control may make use of mediums of propaganda of which education, the press, the movies, and the pulpit are the most outstanding examples. Sometimes freedom to disseminate opinion and propaganda is restricted by a political leader in a local community under his control.

During the course of a Federal Trade Commission investigation into the financial structure and practices of the utilities, covering the years 1927 to 1930, an immense amount of evidence was uncovered bearing on the organized propaganda carried on by the electric and gas companies. The evidence reappeared in a book entitled *The Public Pays—A Study of Power Propaganda*, by Ernest Gruening, from which a few examples are chosen. The director of public information of the Electric Light Association, and spokesman for the American Electric Railway Association and the American Gas Association, speaking before representatives of these bodies in 1922, reported as follows:

> There are twenty-three states with bureaus functioning in such a way that newspapers in six states are using an average of 8500 column inches of material every month of which approximately one-fourth or about two thirds is editorial comments favorable to public utilities. That means something more than 500 pages of reading matter every month . . . with a total circulation running between two and a half and three millions of readers.

On the theory that "the college can say things that we cannot say and be believed," the utilities organized courses as part of college curriculums, contributed guaranteed subscriptions to such courses, arranged summer research work of a "practical" character for professors of economics, and provided that lectures should be given at various universities by utility officials. Something like a "horror list" of textbooks marked "bad" by the utilities bear names of men like William Z. Ripley, William Burrell Munro, John Albert Woodburn, and Thomas Francis Moran. Charles A. Beard's *American Government and Politics* was designated as one of the worst. To eliminate school textbooks containing expressions favorable to public ownership of utilities, an assistant director of the Illinois Committee on Public Utility Information stated that two courses of action were open to the utilities:

> One was getting at the thing locally right away and stopping it in the local schools, and the other was reaching the authors and publishers and taking such steps as would prevent publication in the future of textbooks containing misinformation. The latter is a very slow process, but has to be gone through with. The other . . . gets action in the form of the immediate removal of the books from the schools of a city.

In the face of propaganda of which these examples are only notable for their crudity, but are not otherwise exceptional or rare, it would be folly to deny the right of a democracy to use the tools of propaganda in its own defense, provided only that facts are not distorted or the sources of information closed to the public. As to the right of political parties to propagandize there is, of course, no dispute save as that right is exercised by parties advocating socialism or public ownership of productive property. As for the government itself, most citizens probably would agree that it must not be debarred from the right of propaganda within the democratic frame of freedom and accountability.

ANALYSIS OF PROPAGANDA

Democracy, then, means free play for all manner of ideas, opinions, propaganda. As we in America become increasingly propaganda conscious we shall, as intelligent individuals, undertake to analyze the propaganda offered us. Such propaganda analysis, possible only under democratic conditions of government, involves examination of three angles of the subject.

The first we may dismiss quickly as falling under the head of the unconsciously exerted forces of propaganda comprised in the more or less static conditions of climate and particular cultures. As we have already indicated, the way we look upon life is determined by our ways of earning a living, our home environments, amusements, religion, and traditions generally. From these flow opinions. A sudden change in these life conditions involves conflict, and the more violent the change the more explicit and potent the conflict becomes, and the more inevitable the appearance of conscious and deliberate propaganda. The depression which began in 1929 was one such violent shift from accustomed patterns of thought and living. The Nazi dictatorship, the aggressive action of fascist governments in Ethiopia, Spain, China, Austria, and Czechoslovakia, the Bolshevik revolution in Russia were other formidable examples. These are the sensational realities out of which flow clearly defined propagandas. With reference to them we "take sides"; we become excited, bitter. We utter violent opinions.

58

The second angle for analysis is the channels through which these opinions come to us—the business and labor groups, the schools, churches, cinema, radio, and press. All these have factors of distortion which vary with the backgrounds of the individuals and groups in control. Any objective study of propaganda entails evaluation of these channels. A healthy skepticism should keep us alert to the dangers inherent in accepting information issuing from prejudiced sources, and at least some elementary sense of historic perspective should guide us in discriminating between the raw stuff of selfish and intolerant bigotry and the disinterested and matured processes of scholarly minds. Even the reading of our daily paper should be to some extent an exercise in our powers of discrimination, and for this there are certain simple rules which may be followed. One is to observe how far a headline is used to guide or to mislead the reader; another criterion is the relative importance of news appearing on the front page and that which is inconspicuously placed on inner pages; another is the use of "color words" designed to make a favorable or unfavorable impression in what purports to be a news article and not an editorial. Mr. Paul Hutchinson, who makes these suggestions to newspaper readers in his little pamphlet "How to Read a Newspaper" summarizes his conclusions as follows:

> In general, it is a safe rule to be on guard against propaganda under circumstances such as these: When the sources of news are not clearly identified. When the news contains only an *ex parte* statement, that is, when only one side in a disputable matter is presented. When news originates in places where censorship operates. When news is printed in papers with a reputation for violent partisanship . . . When what is printed as news is seen on close examination really to be argument—or in other words, editorial.

The third angle, which brings us back to our starting point, is the nature of our individual or collective minds. Our minds are so conditioned by the character of our environment that we are susceptible or not susceptible to propaganda; accessible to some forms of propaganda and disposed to reject other forms. The enlightened individual will be at pains to take stock of himself and of his environment and set controls over his own mental processes and adjustments.

From the foregoing it is apparent that minds are "conditioned" in democracies as well as under dictatorships, but in democracies, as we have observed, many individuals and groups compete in the process. There is no monopoly of power, hence no monopoly of propaganda, but rather constant competition. Thus, there is a tendency to cancel out some of the consequences of the various authoritarian conditionings which go on within a democracy. Authoritarianism makes for strong orthodoxy and violent propaganda against all heresies.

Such violent propaganda, given a people deliberately conditioned to accept the orthodoxy, can be highly effective, as we Americans learned during the World War when our own government was authoritarian. Democracy makes for examination of propagandas; it does not make for strong orthodoxy. Hence the violence of authoritarian propaganda is not effective in a democracy, when education and experience have taught its citizens sagacity. In the 1936 campaign, unmeasured vituperation against the New Deal helped Roosevelt win in forty-six of forty-eight states. Leftist groups, as well as rightist reactionaries, make the same mistake. Whether a cause be regarded as "good" or "bad," extremism in advocating it often has a boomerang effect when channels for counterpropaganda remain open.

Conditioned to accept their own views as the only true orthodoxy, violent propagandists of today are as zealous in attacks on heretics as were the theologians in the Middle Ages. They make devils out of individuals and groups who hold other orthodoxies. Psychologically there is no difference between a reactionary businessman who voices intense hatred for the New Deal, a communist who derides the businessman, as an actual or potential fascist, and a religious fundamentalist who sees every wind of modern doctrine in science or economics as a force blowing us toward perdition.

It might be said in conclusion that for the people of the United States who have accepted democracy as a condition of life, all propaganda that strengthens and develops the democratic ideal is "good" propaganda and any that debases or weakens democracy is "bad." But substitute the word "authoritarian" for "democratic ideal," and "tyranny" for "democracy" and the generalization takes on quite another hue. Democracy exposes the propaganda of its enemies to the pitiless light of analysis and publicity; authoritarianism meets the propaganda of its critics with rope, ax, or bullet. In this lies their unbridgeable difference.

Under democracy *all* propaganda is to be challenged and analyzed; all that is honestly conceived is to be tolerated to the extent of being heard in the faith that it is inherent in the true democrat to seek the truth for himself, and that it is the habit of educated minds, when seeking information, to follow the scientific method and reduce the incidence of error.

Chapter V

ACADEMIC FREEDOM

Herman Harrell Horne

★ ★ ★ ★

THE discussion of academic freedom taken alone, abstracted from its general social setting, would be only *academic*. In fact, the subject cannot be properly understood except in relation to other important matters which are closely integrated with it. So, in this chapter, we shall undertake to make clear not only the nature of academic freedom, its importance, and its limitations, but also its connection with freedom in general and with freedom in specific situations other than those which are present in institutions of learning. Our discussion will close with some practical applications for social and educational leaders today.

THE CONCEPT OF FREEDOM

What does *freedom* signify? The term has different meanings in different connections. A physical body is said to move freely when there is no obstruction in its path. A man is said to be free when he is not the slave of another man; or, again, when he carries out his own purposes instead of those foisted upon him contrary to his own choice; or, again, when he has the power to choose between two alternative courses of conduct. A nation is said to be free when its laws are made by its own members in assembly or by its representatives duly elected by its voting citizens. Societies and communities may be spoken of as free in the same sense as nations. (We shall have to return later on to the question of a free society, when dealing with free schools.)

62

By contrast, a physical body does not move freely when its path is obstructed in some way. A slave is not free. A person living to fulfill another person's purpose, which is not voluntarily accepted by himself, is not free. A person whose responses are all predetermined by antecedent causes, without choice between alternatives, is not free. A nation, a society, or a community which lives by laws forced upon it, not made or chosen by itself, is not free.

A man may exercise his free choice in breaking a law of nature or a statute of society, but he finds himself in consequence suffering some form of penalty, and to this degree his freedom of action, his freedom from restraint, is abridged. A law of nature may be violated in ignorance, but the penalty is none the less inevitable. Strychnine may be taken by mistake for quinine, but it still acts as strychnine. This shows that the proper exercise of freedom requires knowledge and intelligence.

In the light of these views, we may define freedom as *the intelligent self-expression of individuals and societies.* Freedom belongs both to individuals and to societies, and both are free when they express themselves intelligently.

There are conditions conducive to, or inhibitive of, true freedom as intelligent self-expression. These conditions may be natural, political, or social. Arctic dwellers lack physical conditions for full freedom. Subjects of a despotic government lack political conditions for full freedom. Victims of race prejudice, religious intolerance, or economic exploitation lack social conditions for full freedom. Among the things that inhibit freedom are ignorance, error, ugliness, and evil. Full freedom is possible only under conditions favorable to knowledge, beauty, justice, and unrestrained pursuit of truth. Artificial restrictions of all kinds hamper that intelligent self-expression which is true freedom. The self-expression of an individual or of a nation is both subjective, originating in the self, and objective, expressing the self. It is thus both inner and outer: the inner life is not repressed through hindrances to outer

63

expression, and the outer expression is not artificial and hollow through lack of inner motivation.

All men really want freedom. The slave, the prisoner, the person in bonds of any kind, whether intellectual, social, or political—all these persons want freedom. As John Stuart Mill said: "After the prime necessities of food and raiment, freedom is the first and strongest want of human nature." This may not always appear to be the case, for, when outer freedom is lacking, even the inner desire for it cannot be manifested except through underground channels.

It is right and proper that man should be free. The course of human history, according to the philosopher Hegel, reflects the development of man's increasing freedom. It is man's nature to be free. It is his destiny to be free. The denial of freedom to man is reversion. One of the profoundest and most ethical of philosophers, Immanuel Kant, said men should always be treated as ends in themselves, never as only means to ends. It is a mistaken interpretation of Darwin's law of the survival of the fittest in the plant and animal world to hold, as Nietzsche did, that in the human world most men should be only tools in the hands of the few.

If the universe of which man is a part were only a mechanism, devoid of life, purpose, and freedom, there might be some philosophical justification for denying that man has, or can have, any freedom. But science in our day is denying that the cosmos is a machine; it is more like a living organism with an inherent purpose. Man in his increasing freedom may be only becoming what it was and is intended that he should become.

It is not easy to be free. It is not even easy to know what freedom is. Freedom is not a gift, it is an achievement, and the race of man is slowly and painfully learning what it is to be free. But the goal is clear: the intelligent self-expression of individuals in an intelligent self-expressive society.

ACADEMIC FREEDOM AS ONLY ONE PHASE OF FREEDOM

The term *academic freedom* refers to the freedom of teachers in educational institutions. Related phases of freedom are

64

these: political freedom, religious freedom, racial freedom, freedom to exercise the right of petition, freedom of assembly, freedom of speech, freedom of the press, freedom of the person against unwarranted arrest and search, and freedom of movement within one's country. Academic freedom is set in a very large and important framework; essential as it is, it is inwrought with even larger matters.

Political freedom, the practice of self-government, is the prime basis of all freedoms. Under dictatorships, freedom languishes. In self-governing nations, freedom can flourish, but even so, "eternal vigilance is the price of liberty." The term *dictatorship* is unwelcome to the dictator. He prefers the more complimentary and more democratic term of *leader* or *secretary*. These terms disguise the absolute power he wields. In Italy, the people are taught to believe *Il Duce, i.e.,* Mussolini, is always right. In Germany, the most educated country now under a dictatorship, thought is regimented, behavior is manipulated, dietary habits are controlled, and educational institutions have become tools of propaganda and centers of indoctrination. Count Hermann Keyserling has said:

National Socialism represents an exceedingly narrow and exclusive outlook, the essence of which is hostility to the intellect.

The absence of freedom in the Union of Soviet Socialist Republics, still commonly called Russia, is thus portrayed by a disillusioned communist, Eugene Lyons, in his work, *Assignment in Utopia:*

Above all, I had the sense of leaving behind me a *nation trapped.* Trapped physically, with bloodhounds and machine guns guarding the frontiers, with a passport system to prevent them from moving freely inside the country. Trapped intellectually, with every thought prescribed and mental curiosity punished as heresy. Trapped spiritually, through the need of practicing hypocrisy as the first law of survival. There was no longer even the solace of martyrdom for the defiant; a technique had been evolved for breaking their spirit and dragging them into the limelight for slobbering confessions of guilt.

In an authoritarian state, the state speaks with final authority on all matters, even those of the church. In a totalitarian state, all the social, political, and economic agencies of

65

the state, in fact its whole life, are organized to defend and to propagate one set of ideas—the ideology of that state. In these states, minority race groups and minority religious groups lack freedom and recognition. To dissent is treason. There are concentration camps and prisons for political offenders. The unity is supposed to be homogeneous. In a self-governing society, minority racial and religious groups have equal right to life, liberty, and the pursuit of happiness. Not that these rights are always freely enjoyed, though they are guaranteed by the fundamental laws of the land and redress may be had in the courts. The unity is heterogeneous and all the more real because it is voluntary.

The totalitarian states imprison the minds of their subjects. They read what is allowed; critical foreign newspapers are banned, and they hear from home sources only the government's side of every issue. The advent of the radio is necessarily changing this situation. The wall of silence erected between the totalitarian state and the outside world is penetrated by foreign short-wave broadcasts. It is easy to prohibit listening to such, but not easy to enforce the prohibition. The radio is a great liberator of intelligence. Concerning freedom of the press and related freedoms, *The New York Times* published a significant map on January 3, 1938. An editorial in the same paper two days later described the map as "vivid and terrifying," and ended by observing:

> What has happened in Germany, Italy, Russia and elsewhere is enough to show that no private "monopoly" of the news, even if such a thing should be conceived to be possible, could be as complete, as unscrupulous or as ruthless as that of a Government determined to keep itself in power.

Not that America has the perfect exercise of all the freedoms so denied in the dictatorship countries. Far from it. We have our Civil Liberties Union and need it as a private organization operating under the Constitution to assist in protecting citizens against the infringement of their rights. We too have race prejudice, religious prejudice, and minor political despots. There are those among us, too, who would stop the mouths

66

of those who utter opinions that they do not like. There are many even in democratic countries who do not share the views of Voltaire expressed in a communication to Helvetius: "I do not believe a word of what you say, but I will defend to the death your right to say it."

In the United States there are about 2,100 daily newspapers, 13,000 newspapers in all, and 19,000 periodicals of all kinds. Here is an immense agency for informing public opinion. These publications manifest all shades of political and religious views. Various newspapers, in some cases as many as twenty-five, are linked under a central management, voicing a common editorial sentiment. But propaganda is harmless when it can be exposed and met with counterpropaganda. It is very true that even so good a principle as freedom of the press can be abused, as when it is appealed to in the interest of publishers against employees or to keep secret their sources of information when such are demanded by a competent public body.

The real test of a man's love of freedom of speech is his readiness to defend that right when exercised by an opponent. America repeatedly sees such violations of freedom as are indicated in the following headlines on the front page of *The New York Times,* January 7, 1938:

15,000 CHEER HAGUE FOR BAN ON CIO; "REDS" ARE DEFIED

———

Civic, Religious, Labor and All Veteran Groups Represented at Big Mass Meeting

———

PARADES PRECEDE RALLY

———

Governor-Elect and Others Praise City Heads—Mayor Reiterates His Stand

In all the cases cited we have an abridgment of that freedom which is the intelligent self-expression of an individual in an intelligent self-expressive society. Such abridgments exist, more or less, in all societies. The same is true of academic freedom, which is set like a diamond in the midst of these other jewels of freedom.

WHAT GIVES PERTINENCE TO THE TOPIC OF ACADEMIC FREEDOM

The discussion of academic freedom would be without point if there were no need for such discussion in the educational scene throughout the world today. Among the facts that give pertinence to the discussion of this topic are these: the destructive influence upon academic freedom of the dictatorships abroad and certain hostile elements in the situation at home. In President Butler's recent annual report to the trustees of Columbia University, referring to the institutions of higher learning in the countries under some form of despotism, he writes:

> The universities in these countries are in a state of coma. Some of these institutions were, not long ago, the world's leaders in almost every field of philosophy, of letters, of science and of the arts, but now their mouths are closed save to echo empty and futile formulas which for the ruthless despot have taken the place of the multiplication table and the Ten Commandments.

Dr. William E. Dodd, former ambassador to Germany, on his recent return from that country, made a public statement in the course of which he observed, in reference to the Rome-Berlin-Tokio axis:

> Over that vast area freedom of religion has ceased to exist and universities no longer govern themselves. In a single country sixteen hundred professors and teachers in high schools have been dismissed, the Rockefeller Foundation having given more than $500,000 to help the helpless. . . . In a vast region where religious freedom is denied, where intellectual initiative and discovery are not allowed, and where race hatreds are cultivated daily, what can a representative of the United States do?

Poland, which owes its existence as a free country to the democracies of the world, lying as it does between two absolutisms, is following the example of Germany in persecuting the Jews. In schools and universities, the Jewish students are

68

segregated, being required to occupy the so-called *Ghetto benches*. This situation is inimical to freedom, culture, and progress. The Polish Ministry of Education has received requests and protests from several groups of Americans, some of which are non-Jewish. Among those making such appeals are the American section of the International League for Academic Freedom, representing 994 teachers, associated with 110 universities in our country; the American Committee on Religious Rights and Minorities; and the American Writers' Committee to Aid the Jews of Poland.

Many Americans are sensitive to abridgments of academic freedom abroad because they are fearful that something similar may happen here. At the beginning of the year 1938, a number of prominent educators were asked to forecast lines of progress for 1938. The answers were published in *The New York Times*, Sunday, January 2. Among those answering was James L. McConaughy, president of Wesleyan University, who is also president of the Association of American Colleges. He wrote:

First, the problem of freedom for teachers and academic freedom in general bids fair to become more acute than at present. There are many indications of increasing interference with reasonable freedom of teaching; in many institutions teachers will, I fear, lose their positions because of an honest, forthright attitude on controversial subjects. College professors in many States are much less secure in tenure than they were. Furthermore, college professors are divided on the question of affiliation with a union, probably the C. I. O., to protect their rights. The American Association of University Professors and the Association of American Colleges face grave difficulties in 1938 along these lines. Many teachers and some administrators are likely to be sacrificed in the effort to preserve academic freedom.

In our own land of freedom, twenty-three states and the District of Columbia require loyalty oaths of teachers, through fear that some will teach subversive political doctrines. Teachers in the District of Columbia were not permitted to instruct the children concerning the tenets of communism. State institutions suffer under more pressure from political groups, whether conservative or radical, than denominational colleges receive from religious groups. The new orthodoxies are

69

political and economic rather than religious. Teachers' contracts are in some cases not renewed or the teachers themselves are actually dismissed because of opinions held or because of religious or racial affiliations. In view of the increasing competition for positions, teachers learn to conceal those views, honestly held, which menace their living and the living of those dependent on them. The most celebrated recent case of alleged breach of academic freedom is that of Prof. Jerome Davis of Yale University. (For one side of this case, see the pamphlet *The Jerome Davis Case*, published by the American Federation of Teachers, 506 South Wabash Avenue, Chicago.)

Patriotic pressure groups insist on certain texts being used or certain types of teachers being employed. The "100 per cent" brand of Americanism is adulterated but nevertheless is spoon fed to many of our people. Legislatures have sometimes undertaken to determine by law what science the schools shall teach. Children who, because of the religious scruples of their parents, did not salute the flag have been expelled from school, and their teachers dismissed. In New York State, religious scruples are not allowed to stand in the way of saluting the flag; in Pennsylvania they are. The propaganda of the private power companies has entered the classroom in the guise of the voice of economic wisdom. Patriotism, which is really devotion to the Constitution of our country and to the processes of orderly social change guaranteed by it, has been misread by conservatives and reactionaries as support of the existing economic order of competition, wages, and profits. Criticism of this order as allowed under the Constitution, or any appreciation of a competing order, or even joining a political party, legally existing, which is committed to social change, or joining a teachers' union, has been made grounds for bringing charges of *disloyalty*.

Looking backward for a moment, we find there are those who hold that the American Civil War might have been prevented had it not been for the suppression of freedom of teaching. The slavery issue could not be discussed in schools and colleges, either in the North or in the South. There are facts enough, both abroad and at home, to give great pertinence to the problem of academic freedom today.

WHAT ARE FREE SCHOOLS?

Academic freedom is not possible in a school or institution that does not itself enjoy freedom. It may not be found even in a school that does enjoy some other kinds of freedom.

A free school may have some or all of these things: free tuition, a free library, free texts, free lunches, free dental and medical service. Under systems of national education supported by general taxation, these things have gradually come about, usually one at a time. They are found in largest measure in democracies in which the education of the citizenry is necessary for wise participation in the processes of self-government. Such free schools are the intelligent and protective self-expression of a democratic community.

But not all schools called free are so in every respect. There are many hangover restrictions on the so-called *free schools*, such as hampering traditions, outworn subject matter, antiquated methods of instruction, ancient forms of repressive discipline, a nonflexible organization, an autocratic administration.

A free school is the expression of a free society. A free society is what most men really desire, though actually they do not have it today. It is itself a product of intelligent self-direction, self-determination, and self-expression on the part of the members of a society. It has usually originated in revolution, has often suffered from a reaction, and has finally gained stability by intelligence and social justice.

There are three forces that control societies, which in turn control schools. These three forces are habitual action, which is conservative and non-progressive; direct action, which is radical and revolutionary; and intelligent action, which is flexible, adaptable, and progressive. Old societies are likely to be conservative, new societies are likely to be radical, while

71

intelligent societies of all ages are progressive. True intelligence is both ethical and social. As a free school exists in a free society, so should academic freedom obtain in a free school.

WHAT IS ACADEMIC FREEDOM?

What then is this precious and rare thing in the modern educational world known as *academic freedom?* It is the privilege enjoyed by teachers and educational institutions of thinking their own thoughts, speaking their own minds, and acting on their own beliefs. Here is indeed a weapon of great power! It is important that it be used, and that it be used aright. But before we speak of its importance and limitation, we need to understand it better.

The great obligation resting upon the teacher is to teach the truth. He is free when he is bound only by the truth. This is a paradox indeed: freedom in bondage, when the bonds are those of truth. The academic freedom of the teacher means: (1) that he is unfettered in his investigation of the truth; (2) that he is unrestrained in his teaching of the truth; and (3) that he is at liberty to publish and proclaim the truth he knows. As a citizen he has freedom of speech and as an employee of an educational institution he has freedom to teach. No ultimate harm can come from the knowledge of the truth. It is the knowledge of the truth, involving performance, that sets men free.

Yes, one may say, but the teacher may be mistaken and take error for truth. He may mislead his students and the people. He may harm the institution which employs him. True enough, just as a small torch may give a poor light and set a great fire. But the remedy is not to put out the poor torch and live in darkness. The remedy is to light a better torch. All of which means that the possible evil results of academic freedom are not to be avoided by restraining academic freedom but by using it better and more fully. To convict a man of being mistaken in his view is a service to him and society; to forbid him to express his view is a disservice to the truth itself, for

72

truth is served best by free investigation. Unless our deeds are evil we need not fear man's knowledge of the truth. We do not need so much to defend the truth as to unveil it. The truth is its own best apologetic. The truth does not need to be protected at our hands by abridging freedom of speech and freedom to teach.

THE IMPORTANCE OF ACADEMIC FREEDOM

Academic freedom has a sixfold importance: for the educational institution, for the teacher, for the pupil, for the advancement of knowledge, for the formation of ideals, and for social progress. To each of these we will devote careful attention, though the discussion must necessarily be brief.

1. *Academic Freedom Is Important for the Institution of Learning Itself.* To deny academic freedom and so forbid the expression of certain views is *ipso facto* to assume responsibility for those views that are expressed. In this way, the institution carries a collective responsibility which is heavy for it and repressive of individuality. Under such circumstances neither the institution nor the individual teacher is freely and intelligently self-expressive. But an institution that does not restrict freedom of teaching is not responsible for what one of its teachers does say, any more than the government of the United States is responsible for what one of its private citizens says. Allowing freedom of speech is thus a happy convenience for both institutions of learning and civil governments.

2. *Academic Freedom Is Important for the Teacher.* The liberty to disagree is important to the teacher, that he may be a voice and not an echo, that he may be himself and not the weak imitation of another, that he may avoid intellectual mimicry and maintain his self-respect, that he may have the sense of personal dignity and individual responsibility. If teachers as a class were deprived of academic freedom, they would labor under restrictions not present in the case of other learned professions, such as law, medicine, and engineering. Such discrimination would be both invidious and stultifying.

73

It would serve to repel the most independent and capable minds, whereas, in fact, the teaching profession should be made more attractive than it is to the more able minds of any generation. A teacher should be the mouthpiece of truth, not a parrot. Beware of classroom psittacosis!

3. *Academic Freedom for Teachers Helps to Develop the Right Sort of Pupil.* A teacher whose instruction is regimented necessarily produces regimented pupils. To have independent pupils it is necessary to have free teaching. Critical, high-minded, serious youth cannot develop in an intellectually stifling atmosphere. Society needs youth who do not accept without thinking and do not accept at all an idea which cannot stand scrutiny. When youth is permitted the critical attitude toward the existing social order and is even encouraged to improve upon it, comparing with open mind the values of different regimens, there is hope for removal of the major ills of society. Fortunate are the students who can say:

> For vigorous teachers seized my youth,
>   And purged its faith, and trimmed its fire
> Showed me the high white star of Truth,
>   There bade me gaze, and there aspire.

4. *The Most Rapid Advancement of Knowledge Requires Academic Freedom.* A free interchange of economic, political, sociological, and other opinions will necessarily be stimulating and challenging. Errors under constant scrutiny and investigation cannot survive. Orthodoxy or opinion held to be right and enforced by authority is a blight on science. Questions are settled before they can fairly be raised. Conclusions are already contained in the acceptable premises. A fascist physics or a communist chemistry are as absurd as would be a Methodist multiplication table or a Baptist botany. A dogma cannot settle the question of race superiority or the most desirable kind of economic order. Just as social progress in a democracy depends on freedom of speech, so does scientific progress the world around depend on freedom of inquiry.

74

5. *Without Academic and Institutional Freedom, Individuals Can neither Form New Ideals for New Situations nor Voluntarily Realize Old Ideals.* A worthy ideal is an idea for the improvement of man chosen as a plan of action. Freedom gone, one accepts the standards prescribed by others. There is no stimulus to independent thinking, and life becomes, as with the lower creatures, adjustment to an environment one does not control as a basis for physical survival. The few at the top who retain their freedom impose their ideas on the many by all the arts of propaganda.

But education is not propaganda. Education is the liberation of intelligence; propaganda is its seduction. Education involves free investigation in the pursuit of the knowledge of the truth; propaganda decides in advance what the truth is or shall be and inculcates that view alone by instructional methods and emotional appeals. Education distinguishes between fact and opinion; propaganda calls opinions facts and indoctrinates accordingly. Education is concerned to make the face of truth appear; propaganda is concerned to make a given ideology appear the truth.

6. *Academic Freedom Is One of the Conditions of Social Progress.* It aids that general circulation of thought without which a society languishes. Especially in a democracy is freedom of teaching a beneficial grace, even as in a dictatorship it is a menace. Through variation in opinion and clash of views in a self-governing community, progress comes about. Without constant social reconstruction, democracy lapses into complacency and lethargy, and for effective and guided social change intelligent citizenship is a prerequisite. Without freedom to teach and to learn, there is no enlightened citizenship. The critical estimate of the present state of political and economic affairs in a democracy, and action in accordance therewith, is the safety valve against violent revolution.

It was John Stuart Mill who regarded liberty as "the inalienable prerogative of man." Liberty may be denied for a season, but the sentiment of liberty will not be alienated from man. When he lacks it, he will nevertheless call what he has by its good name so as to make it tolerable. Thus we find in the totalitarian states that the precious thing called *academic freedom* is still claimed as present, even after the dictator has liquidated all parties but his own, has purged his own party of all those who are suspected of holding different opinions, and has turned over the education of youth to members of the only surviving party.

For these six and other reasons, we see that the importance of academic freedom is great and manifold. But it is time to speak of the limits of this privilege.

THE LIMITS OF ACADEMIC FREEDOM

No one who has followed us thus far will doubt our belief in academic freedom. At the same time, like all other things, except the absolute itself, it has its limits. One may even claim that the absolute has self-imposed limits.

Now the limits to the exercise of freedom of teaching are precisely those of any other ethical right, *viz.*, a due regard for the rights of others; "a decent respect for the opinions of mankind," as the American founding fathers said; a proper esteem for the laws of the land; a proper sense of obligation to the employing institution; and that precious thing, good taste. But no one of these limits, properly understood, takes away or even unduly abridges freedom of teaching.

It is not good taste to use American freedom of speech to advocate systems denying freedom of speech without at least a word of appreciation for the privilege of so doing. It violates the rights of others if we abuse our freedom in uttering libel, slander, or indecency. We violate the laws of the state if we engage in subversive and seditious action, but there is no violation in a calm and serious consideration of the best form of human government for Americans, whatever that form may be. We should remind ourselves that radical political parties may have legal status in our country. It does not show "a decent respect for the opinions of mankind" to see no good

76

whatever in a foreign system which millions of the human family espouse.

It does not show the proper sense of obligation to the employing institution, say a college under particular religious auspices, to challenge the principle upon which it is founded; it were better to resign first, and then speak. Contractual obligations must be scrupulously observed; such should be warily assumed, but, being assumed, their violation gains us nothing. It is the spirit as well as the letter that must be kept. In accepting employment we obligated ourselves in certain ways; no plea of academic freedom can waive those obligations.

No enjoyment of academic freedom gives us the right to force our personal political or economic opinions on our pupils who are under compulsory attendance laws; or to make converts to any political party or religious sect; or to violate the civil liberties of students or parents; or to defeat the purpose for which the school system is established and supported by taxation, *i.e.*, to improve the citizenship in a democracy; or to advocate the overthrow of organized government by force or violence; or to use our classroom as a forum for specific propaganda rather than study and instruction; or to use an unsound and unscholarly method, giving offhand, ill-formed, and half-baked opinions as final.

For any teacher to express unpopular views successfully, without damaging his cause, requires skill, much applied psychology, and many valuable community contacts. We are to lead in thinking without giving general offense. Yet we are not to be mealymouthed or to be the friends of everything at the price of espousing nothing. The teachers of America have a great opportunity to assist in forming public opinion, which itself controls our form of government. And this brings us to the question of means of using academic freedom.

SOME PRACTICAL APPLICATIONS

Our aim is to induce pupils to think for themselves. There is no pupil too young to think, but there are many problems too difficult for him to think about intelligently. Grade the problems to suit the ability of the pupil. Our aim is not to transmit orthodoxy of opinion, nor yet to detect heterodoxy, but to train in thinking. Our aim is not, primarily, even to seek recruits for democracy, but to practice the democratic process of inquiry, open-mindedness, respect for facts, and the testing of hypotheses by experimentation and observation, with recognition of the right of minorities to their opinions. There should be freedom for the dissenter to express his view. What cannot be tolerated is advocacy of the violation of law and order, which is not the democratic procedure.

Controversial issues are to be allowed in the classroom. They stimulate and challenge thought. Some of the most important questions in life are not yet finally settled. The habit of intelligent controversy is to be cultivated. Dangerous issues are not to be avoided or shelved, nor yet lugged in. The aim in intelligent controversy is the discovery of truth, not winning a debate. The teacher should not lend the weight of his opinion to one side or the other but should see that all sides receive a fair exposition. If his opinion is wanted by the class, then he should disclose it, but not dogmatically. The question itself may be left undecided, with the relative strength of the two sides indicated by vote. The function of the minority is to show that the truth as envisaged by the majority is not the whole truth. In fact, the minority may more closely approximate the truth than the majority. Genuine differences of opinion are not only to be tolerated, they are to be welcomed.

Teachers do not need to be agitators. Their views should be as objective and impartial as possible. They do not need to be propagandists for any cause. Their pupils should not have lock-step minds. But convictions on the live issues of the day teachers should have, which upon suitable occasion they are willing to state and defend, and for which they cast their ballots. Teachers are not likely to be too active in behalf of unpopular causes. Their jobs, their living, and the living of those dependent on them, all serve to make teachers cautious. As a social class we are rather followers than leaders.

Agencies, organizations, newspapers that act as pressure groups, restrictive of freedom, are to be opposed and withstood by teachers. The schools should be free to teach the truth as they see it. Aristotle said, "Plato is dear to me, but dearer still is truth." Teachers are more than hired men and women, more than servants employed to do as they are told and to teach what they are told to teach. There is an inalienable and unpurchasable intellectual obligation to know and to teach the truth.

Teachers' loyalty oaths are reprehensible because of the design behind them. This design is not only to keep subversive persons out of the classroom, but also to hamper the discussion in the classroom of such alien forms of government as communism and fascism. But these doctrines and practices have to be understood in order to be properly evaluated. A really subversive and disloyal teacher will not be deterred or detected by an oath. A loyal teacher will not be benefited by taking an oath. Those teachers who have been compelled to swear allegiance to the Constitution of the country of which they are citizens may all the more stand upon their constitutional right of freedom of speech.

Teachers and their superintendents should stand together in defence of their freedom. Teachers should support their superintendents in a fight for their freedom, for the superintendents' freedom is the teachers' freedom. And the superintendent should stand for the freedom of the teacher, lest the minds of the children of the community be improperly indoctrinated. Both superintendents and teachers are to be free to inquire for themselves. Otherwise education becomes a travesty. The late Newton D. Baker once observed, "What the nations of the world need is educated men. The great trouble with most men is that they become uneducated just as soon as they stop inquiring and investigating problems for themselves."

It is a very striking thing that the Nobel prize winners appear to come mainly from the free countries of the world. One hundred and ninety-four of these awards have been made since 1901. This number is too small for safe generalization, but the simple fact, whatever its significance, is that five little countries which allow great personal liberty have had from two to twelve times as many Nobel prize winners in proportion to population as the other countries of the world. These five are: Denmark, Sweden, Switzerland, Norway, and Holland. Then follow in order: Scotland, England, Germany, France, Belgium, Ireland, the United States, Argentina, Austria, Canada, Italy, Spain, and Russia.

Since science requires freedom for its greatest and most rapid growth, it is not surprising that scientists in the free countries of the world are uniting against political oppression. Professor Edwin Grant Conklin, Princeton biologist, retiring president of the American Association for the Advancement of Science, recently said, "Intellectual freedom has been essential for the advance of science, and the time has come when science should stand for freedom, especially in those countries where force, war, and unutterable ferocity are used to compel acceptance of political, social, or economic creeds."

Something new in behalf of academic freedom is taking place in our own country: The National Education Association is protecting the freedom of teachers. It both assails academic restrictions and deplores the discharge of teachers for expressing their views, holding that "Teachers should be accorded the full right of all citizens to express publicly their views and ally themselves with organizations of their own choosing." Nothing like that has ever taken place before in our history. Never before have our educational leaders been so aware of the need for social change, for freedom of teaching in order to preserve the democratic process, and for the protection of teachers against loss of their living because of opinions held.

In the days when Germany was cosmopolitan, the philosopher Fichte gave a series of lectures at the University of Jena called *The Vocation of the Scholar* (1794). One of his lectures was "Academic Freedom," in the course of which he said:

The Scholar can be guided only by his own determination, can have no other judge but himself, and no motive external to himself. . . . In the Divine Idea he carries in himself the form of the future age which one day must clothe itself with reality; and he must show an example and lay down a law to coming generations, for which he will seek in vain either in present or in past times.

Chapter VI

GOALS IN A CHANGING WORLD

RALPH W. SOCKMAN

★ ★ ★ ★

A FEW years ago one of our popular authors wrote a book under the title *Life Begins at Forty*. Since that time others have made playful and serious copies of the expression in their attempts to tell us when we really begin to live. May we offer a rough parallel and say that life begins with its ends?

In life planning, both individual and social, the first point to be fixed is the goal. A youth may be uncertain for a long time as to his choice of vocation, but he ought early to become clear as to the kind of man he wants to be, for a person cannot play the game of life intelligently until he knows at least where his own goal posts are. For this reason, it is foolish to say, as so many do, "It doesn't matter what a man believes, so long as he does what is right." A man's creed determines what he thinks is right and, consequently, his conduct.

Louis Pasteur has become a household hero, not only because of his contribution to science but also because of his courageous spirit in the face of stupidity, pride, and professional jealousy. When at last he was elected to the French Academy, he revealed in his inaugural address one secret of the strength which sustained him on his hard road to victory. He said, "Blessed is he who carries within himself a God—an ideal, and who obeys it: ideal of art, ideal of science, ideal of the gospel virtues, therein lie the springs of great thoughts and great actions." The end which we seek is the primary formative factor in life. The goals on which we fix our eyes give direction and dynamics to our lives.

The illumination of life's ends is a service expected of religion. It must be confessed frankly, however, that religion has often served to confuse rather than to clarify. What different and destructive things have been done by persons who thought they were doing God's will. Mahomet thought he was doing the will of God when he took plural wives and sanctioned polygamy. Certain devout sects in India think they are doing the divine will when they preserve insects and rodents which spread disease and devour crops. The Spanish inquisitors centuries ago thought they were doing God's will when they put heretics on the rack, and today Christians are divided in their support of the two warring factions in Spain, each section of supporters believing its side is making for the Kingdom of God. During the World War a German kaiser sent his soldiers to their slaughter with the pious, and probably sincere, slogan, "Gott mit uns," while the English and French chaplains were summoning their troops to die in a "holy" cause. When the churchman, therefore, says in catechetical fashion that the chief end of man is to do the will of God, he must beware lest he confuse the "divine will" with his own wilfulness.

And when we turn from religious to secular guides, we should examine the goals which they set up. Aldous Huxley in his recent book *Ends and Means* assumes that there is general agreement as to what are the ends of life. He says, "From Isaiah to Karl Marx the prophets have spoken with one voice. In the Golden Age to which they look forward there will be liberty, peace, justice and brotherly love." But, although it is true that these are the ideals which men say they are agreed in seeking, do all men have the same things in mind when they use these four great words? Most certainly they do not.

LIBERTY AND FREEDOM

Take liberty, for instance. The cry for freedom may be the plea of a poor victim to be delivered from the clutch of cruel circumstance, or it may be the petulant plaint of a pampered child for more indulgences. It may be the longing of the underprivileged to get a place in the sun, or it may be merely the desire of the overprivileged to do as they please. When men say they want freedom of speech and of press, some may mean the right to spread the truth for the benefit of society; others may have in mind the license to send pornographic pictures and poisonous reading matter through the mail. "O Liberty! what crimes are committed in thy name!" Hence, when we shout the rallying cry of liberty, we ought to consider what we mean by the term.

Is it freedom of thought that we want? That is a boon which we prize very highly in America. The idea of it was sown in our mental soil by colonial settlers who had almost all suffered under oppressive governments in the Old World. The Puritans of New England, the Quakers of Pennsylvania, the Roman Catholics of Maryland, the Huguenots of the Carolinas—all came as minority groups which had felt the repressive heel of intolerant majorities in the Old World. They were therefore determined that in this new land men should be free to think and speak and worship according to the dictates of conscience. We pride ourselves that we have preserved these tenets of freedom. Yet with all our boasted liberty of speech and thought, just how free are our minds? When we examine our processes of thought, we are surprised to find how many of our ideas are led around by prejudice and fear and wishful thinking. Many of our minds are only about as free as the stray dog of the street which takes up with any passerby, even a tramp. We are the easy victims of the charlatan in business, the demagogue in politics, the fanatic in religion. And a majority is sometimes only a mob.

Freedom of action, as well as freedom of thought, needs to be examined. The old individualistic liberty of the pioneer is no longer feasible or even safe in the crowded high-powered mechanized world of today. We are not free to drive our motors on Fifth Avenue as were our fathers to drive their horses in the

84

horse-and-buggy era. Dean Wicks of Princeton puts the contrast cogently when he reminds us that our grandfathers went to school in little one-story country schoolhouses, whose windows and doors were all on the ground floor. If a fire broke out in a building of that type all that was necessary was to cry, "Fire! Everybody for himself!" But now our pupils go to school in large buildings, several stories high with probably several hundred or several thousand persons in them. Were a fire to break out in one of these modern structures and the cry to go up, "Fire! Everyone for himself!" what would happen? Panic, chaos, probably disaster. No, we are not free as our fathers were. When each one tries to do what he pleases, no one can long do as he pleases, and, what is more, no one is long pleased with what he does. Liberty must be sought within the limits of group action and self-restraint.

In a Christian civilization, the basic rule for living together is that we must restrain ourselves before trying to restrict others. That is what we are not doing today. We pass innumerable laws and pile immeasurable armaments to hold others back, but few of us are willing gracefully to hold ourselves in. Unless we learn to hold our persons and our property with reverent regard for the rights of others, we can have no social freedom.

PEACE AS A GOAL

Or consider the goal of peace. All men profess to desire peace, although some are still brutally frank enough to assert their belief in war as a means of developing morale. Signor Mussolini, for example, is quoted as saying, "War alone brings up to its highest tension all human energy and puts the stamp of nobility upon the peoples who have the courage to meet it." Such belated militarists, however, are growing rarer. But with all our multiplying pleas for peace, what do we mean by the term? Is it the drowsy contentment of those who have plenty and do not wish the *status quo* disturbed; or is it the stability which is founded on justice? Can we say we are at peace when we have an armed truce filled with economic strife? Is peace simply an absence of open military warfare, or is it a state of co-operative activity for the general welfare?

If peace is to be attained, it must be conceived as a positive program and not as a mere negative of war. We do not drift into peace by denouncing war any more than we shall land in the Kingdom of Heaven merely by shying off from hell. We must take over into the peace movement those concepts which have hitherto been the monopoly of the warmakers. Patriotism, for example, has been so much colored by its war connections that we think of patriotic celebrations and patriotic societies almost entirely in relation to past military achievements or in preparation for future ones. A basic question now is, Can we arouse the noble sentiment of love for one's country by peaceful means as well as by warlike gestures? Can we make patriotism as colorful and contagious in peace as in war? We believe so, but it can only be accomplished by a steady persistent program of education, involving our teaching of history, economics, and ethics.

Preparedness is another concept which needs to be incorporated into the peace program. So ingrained is the idea of force as the means of preparedness that the terms automatically link themselves together in the public mind. Yet those who advocate big navies and backbreaking militarization do so with a resigned fatalism, knowing that the race for armaments runs inevitably toward war. The way to check this is not to disavow preparedness, but to change the conception of what constitutes a nation's best security. Also, we need to re-define our national defense. For the defense of what are we building our navies? As Dorothy Thompson pointed out recently in her column, "The richest nations tomorrow will not be the ones with the farthest scattered empires to defend. They will be those countries with the greatest scientists, the most brains, the most skillful populations, and the most efficient social organization. The new worlds to conquer are not horizontal, they are vertical. They are in men's minds."

86

Yes, men desire peace, but we should seek to clarify what it is we want as well as the way to it. If we could end international strife, there would still remain those insecurities which destroy our peace of mind. Without a sense of security there is no peace worthy the name; but even security is an ideal of various interpretations. To some it means shelter *from* struggle; to others it means strength *in* struggle. To some it means a future guaranteed against want or disaster; others ask for their security only a foundation sufficiently firm to enable them to build their own futures. Marcus Aurelius is credited with the statement that weak men seek retreats, strong men carry their retreats with them. That stoic principle is also Christian. A Christian civilization, if true to the temper of Him from whom it takes its name, does not soften its citizens with exemption from struggle and guarantees of future plenty, but strengthens them with fortitude in struggle and foundations of law and justice on which they can build their own tomorrows.

JUSTICE IN THE WORLD

Let us turn then to justice, the third of these goals which Huxley says all men are agreed in seeking. Oliver Goldsmith once defined justice as "that virtue which impels us to give to every person what is his due." But how diverse are the ideas of what is justly due to persons! The mother and the judge have very different opinions of what would be just to the wayward boy standing before the bar of the court. The shiftless tramp and the thrifty seeker of work have different things in mind when they say, "The world owes me a living."

Many persons say very glibly that all our social problems could be solved if men would only practice the simple golden rule—and as ye would that men should do to you, do ye also to them likewise. But the trouble is that most persons have not imagination enough to see intelligently what they would want done to them if they were in the other person's place. The result is that they do to him what they think is good for him,

87

and that usually irritates him. The golden rule practiced without imagination is usually sheer irritation.

Justice, therefore, is an ideal to be approached by the imagination rather than by definitions. That approach should start in the home. The writer can recall a home wherein a mother's missionary interest served to free the child's mind from any antiforeigner complex, a home in which the attitude toward a Negro employee made for an understanding of the relationship between races. It was a household, too, which enjoyed neighborly exchanges with certain Jewish families, and as a result the children grew up with none of those anti-Semitic prejudices which are so pernicious in contemporary society. The home is the first training ground of the imagination in attitudes of justice.

The church also can contribute to the concept and cultivation of justice. The week-by-week worship of God, if at all sincere, serves to widen the horizon and sensitize the sympathies. Minds are illumined by the flaming denunciations of injustice uttered by the great Hebrew prophets and by the radiant compassion of Him who so put himself in the place of the underprivileged that He could say "Inasmuch as ye have done it unto one of the least of these, my brethren, ye have done it unto me."

And, of course, this imagination so essential to justice must penetrate the courtroom and the legislative assembly. The classic figure of justice as a blindfolded woman with a scales in her hands is hardly adequate. The just treatment of citizens, whether lawbreakers or lawkeepers, requires more than the mere weighing of facts in hand. The blindfold should be removed and the eyes of justice equipped with bifocals, so that the dispensers of justice can get the close-up view of the individual and the long-range vision of the system in which he is caught.

BROTHERHOOD

The fourth goal included in all utopias is, according to Huxley, brotherly love. Here is an expression so expansive and

88

empty that it resembles those high-sounding and hollow-toned phrases which political parties often put into their platforms. The realistic mood of the present no longer takes seriously the mouthing of the words *brotherly love*.

During the war of two decades ago, Gilbert Murray walked around the quadrangles of Oxford, so he told us, with a heart made heavy by the thought that splendid young men were dying for him in France. Today, as we write, babies are being bombed in Barcelona, frightened Jews are taking their own lives in Vienna, and only God knows what tragedies are occurring in China. How heavy does that make our hearts here in America? Have we grown so callous to horrors in the last twenty years that we cease to shudder at them? It is possible that the mighty agencies of the radio, the press, and the cinema are making us so familiar with the sufferings of others that we have grown callous toward them. It is possible that the means of travel and communication which are making the world into a neighborhood are leaving us less neighborly. In fact, that seems to be the case. We are getting closer together physically and often, because of that fact, farther apart socially and fraternally. The sinister situation is that mere physical proximity often serves to accentuate our sense of difference.

But what does this ideal of brotherly love demand of us? We must be realistic in defining it. Much talk about loving neighbors and enemies falls on deaf ears because it sounds too sentimentally impossible. To think that we can feel the same love toward a stranger as toward a twin brother seems as far beyond human nature as the mathematics of Professor Einstein's relativity theory are beyond the use of the paperhanger measuring the walls of our living room. But while the natural intense affections of the family can not be stretched to include strangers, we can have toward them an active, aggressive good will. Both the law of Leviticus and the law of Christ command, "Thou shalt love thy neighbor as thyself." Our own self-respect is thus the yardstick by which we are to measure our regard for another. We are to consider his rights

89

as carefully as our own. We are not to force our opinions on him any more than we allow him to thrust his views on us. We shall not try to use him any further than we wish him to use us.

Yet brotherly love is to be defined by its positives rather than its negatives. It is more than tolerance which lives and lets live. It is active co-operation which lives and helps live. It is this activity of good will which generates its increase. Pagan love is kindled by the lovableness or attractiveness of its object; brotherly love is aroused by the activity of the subject. As Lincoln turned Edwin M. Stanton from enmity to loyalty by putting him in his cabinet, so men can beget love even for enemies by acts of co-operation and advances in friendship. Since it is thus self-generating, brotherly love is a possible ideal even in a world as brutal and belligerent as ours.

It was not a sentimentalist but a great strategist, Marshal Foch by name, who said, "We must always seek to create events, not merely to suffer them." It is on this principle that we can break the vicious circles of social habit in which succeeding generations repeat the errors of their predecessors and thus are shunted away from the goals of liberty, peace, justice, and brotherly love. We no longer need to surrender to the spell of the old fatalistic doctrine that "You can't change human nature." With our modern means of communication and concerted programmization, we can create events and deliver our tomorrows from the dictatorship of our yesterdays.

In this progress, however, the means which we use are no less important than the ends which we seek. Let us be done with the musty theory that the end justifies the means. It was said recently of a certain well-meaning, but ineffective, person who forfeited a strategic opportunity that "he had a penchant for doing the right thing in the wrong way." One of the most devilish ways by which good men have been defeated is by setting them to fight evil with the wrong weapons. Yet despite the evidence of history, men still succumb to the theory of fighting wars to end war and of getting liberty through dictators.

90

One dark and rainy night the late Dr. John Henry Jowett was leaving the home of his Scottish host for the railroad station. His host pointed out to him the station light as the guiding beacon, but he also gave him a lantern to help him pick his way along the muddy, slippery path. In our dark and stormy time we need the station lights to show us the ends we seek. But we need equally as much the lantern of intelligence to help us pick the ways toward those ends.

Part Two

PATTERNS OF CHANGE

Chapter VII

CAPITALISM WILL SURVIVE!

GEORGE E. SOKOLSKY

★ ★ ★ ★

FROM the American Revolution to Sarajevo marks a period in human history. Feudalism in all its manifestations disappears from the most progressive countries and begins to disappear even in backward countries. The slogan of that century might be summed up in the two words, *Liberty— Freedom*.

The land, which used to be held by kings, dukes, bishops, and other feudal owners, is broken up among free farmers, and those who are unable to possess soil in the land of their ancestors migrate to the new worlds on the North and South American continents, Africa, Australia, and New Zealand. The free farmer becomes so much a character of the age that even in backward countries like Russia and China the struggle over the ownership of the land marks the principal political and economic movements.

The free farmer is a capitalist. He owns property. He becomes the truest capitalist because he lives in the least limited freedom. He not only owns his own property, but he freely merchandizes the product of his soil. He possesses wealth in the forms of cash, land, cattle, and machinery. He constantly increases the amount of machinery that he employs until he is often freed from the backbreaking toil characteristic of agriculture. He enslaves steel machinery, the tractor, the binder, etc., to do his work. He employs labor. His standard of living rises as he comes into increasing possession of machinery. His children go to school and to college. Agricultural colleges

95

dot every agricultural area, and science improves both his methods of work and his products. He partakes of the political life of his community and country.

Serfdom disappeared in Europe, and finally in Russia at the same time that Negro agricultural slaves in the United States were given political and economic freedom. It is thus possible to set the limit to human slavery in the Western world in the sixth decade of the nineteenth century. In Asia and Africa, slavery has not yet disappeared.

The disappearance of economic and political slavery is a definite product of the struggle between feudalism and capitalism and the victory of capitalism in the nineteenth century. That victory is marked, ideologically, by the growth of freedom for the individual, the growth of democracy in government, the growth of uncontrolled competition in economics.

TRANSITION PERIOD IN INDUSTRY

Simultaneously, in industry, government control of the means of production and distribution was constantly being lessened. The guilds, which controlled wages, hours of work, quotas of production, and qualities of commodities, lost their usefulness, and where they continued, they existed only as social and charitable institutions. The apprenticeship system and the system of indentured workers also ceased to function and their place was taken by the free worker in the industrial field, the man who could shift from industry to industry, who could develop such skills as he chose, who could combine with other workers in self-defense and mutual association, and who could become a capitalist out of his accumulation of wages.

Both the employer and the worker became capitalists in the sense that both owned or could own property and tools. Both were free to do as they chose with their accumulations of surplus wealth. Both were free to work or not to work, to select their occupations, and to move from place to place. Ideologically, they were supported by the concept of equality of opportunity.

It was the operations of this economic and social system, uncontrolled by government, unhampered by ruler and politician, which freed millions of human minds for the cultivation of the industrial process. Out of it came the use of steam and electricity; the development of thousands of fabrics, not only out of the usual fibers, but out of trees and weeds and the stalks of the farm; the growth of the fundamental steel industry and the infinitely variegated utilization of steel products. As a result of this free play of the human mind, the automobile and airplane and submarine appeared. Out of it grew a thousand food products and household gadgets which freed the woman from unending toil and made it possible for her to be elevated from a slave position in the kitchen to the freedom of social and political equality.

For thousands of years prior to the century of which we speak, man made little progress in his equipment for producing either agricultural or fabricated materials. He made little progress in the materials themselves. During periods of peace, his variety increased because he was not altogether dependent upon his own locality, but government and guild controls prevented him from altering ancient methods or producing altogether new commodities. Often governments, to finance themselves, granted monopolies which not only limited production, but prevented new ideas from fructifying.

Capitalism, as soon as it appeared, fought these government controls and limitations, and, if Adam Smith, the first great philosopher of capitalism, stressed freedom of operations too much, it was because under feudalism, the limits upon freedom were too great. Capitalism can only operate in freedom, which involves an irreducible minimum of regulation and no control whatsoever.

WHAT IS CAPITALISM?

Capitalism is the principle of the production and distribution of goods and services by individuals with their own capital and as a result of their own ingenuity. The objective is to make a profit which the investor retains and to which he has a legal right. The same rule applies to wages, which may be spent or saved. If saved, wages may be invested in enterprise to earn a profit.

This profit the individual may keep, spend, reinvest, or lose. That is within the province of his own decision and conscience. Usually such capital is reinvested in the same enterprise or in new or additional enterprises.

The formation of American capital, the development of American enterprise, the American standard of living, and the growth of the American nation is due entirely to this process of investing capital, earning a profit, and reinvesting that profit, which thus becomes new capital.

This procedure involves risks, but the risks are wholly individual. Just as the profits flow to the individual investor, so do the losses fall upon him. But there are never losses to the entire community under this system, for wealth, once created, is never destroyed, except by wars and revolution.

The essence of the capitalist operation is that wealth is never lost, except by war or revolution, but is transferred from one individual to another, from one group to another. Thus, although some may suffer from their own errors in judgment, from their own inability, or from shifts in the processes of production and distribution, or from geographical causes, the total accumulation of wealth continues and is constantly in use for the whole of society. Occasionally—but only as a recognition that any system may become diseased and needs a purgative—the accumulation becomes so uneven as to require some type of redistribution. In a free system, this can best be accomplished by tax arrangements and by increased investments in agencies of production which increase the value of the commodity but lower its price. The best example of that is the American automobile.

The center of all economic activity is the marketplace. Under all other systems, the government dominates the market place. Under capitalism, the government plays a

98

meager role in the marketplace. Certain police powers continue to be exercised. But on the whole the market is free, in the sense that those who are engaged in it enjoy a very large measure—larger than under any other system—of the privilege of independent and individual action based on individual judgment. They may profit or lose as their judgment dictates—and the government usually does not and always should not guarantee profits or provide safeguards against losses. To do so is to lessen the element of risk which is the incentive force that makes for increased ingenuity and productivity.

In this freedom, capitalism developed three processes: mass production, mass distribution, availability or stimulated marketing.

Mass production is a system of manufacturing by machinery in which a rhythmic flow of a vast variety of commodities, labor, and services are synchronized in tempo, so that at a given point and at a given moment a finished commodity of high quality and comparative cheapness is produced. It is premised primarily upon repetitive demand for identical or similar articles and depends for its economies largely on the element of repetition of its productive processes.

Mass distribution is the movement of vast quantities of goods, agricultural, raw, and manufactured, from the point of production to widespread markets with swiftness and a reduction of loss through breakage and rot. This further reduces the price. Mass distribution of agricultural products of every type has enriched the farmer, while at the same time it has made available for all human beings commodities which once were the relish of only the ruling classes.

Availability is an end result of mass production and mass distribution. Its theory is that every product and service shall be present when and where it is desired. To create that desire, demands are stimulated by advertising and by financial arrangements which make it possible for the purchaser to possess the commodity in advance of the actual accumulation of purchasing power. This process for the speedier rise in the standard of living exists only under capitalism and is its crowning glory. It has brought the riches of kings to every household. Carpets, fine furniture, furs, automobiles, radios, electrical devices, every type of food product—anything becomes available to an increasingly larger number of human beings.

AMERICAN LABOR UNDER CAPITALISM

Labor, under traditional capitalism, is a commodity. Its price is subject to the law of supply and demand. Its value is determined by the quantity and quality of work which an individual worker can turn out in a given unit of time.

Under mass production, human labor as a commodity may lose in value because it may be required to contribute less skill and no tools. When skill is employed, it receives high compensation because it is more effectively applied and thus is worth more. Strictly, the common laborer contributes to production only his time and a minimum of skill and knowledge.

But in American capitalism, the laborer has taken on another role. He is also a large consumer of goods and services. Both as to quality and quantity, the American laborer, under capitalism, consumes on a par with the middle classes of Europe and the rich of Asia. Mass production and mass distribution and the stimulation of demands make consumption on such a scale available to the laborer and the farmer. Therefore, both must have the means to make these purchases.

Wages, therefore, are not paid on the basis of labor as a commodity but on a complex of bases, the principal factor being that an exchange shall be continuously maintained between the laborer in industry on the one hand and the farmer and other groups of the population on the other hand.

This principle has resulted in the American wage scale, which is the highest on earth for the work that is done. Under American capitalism, it is correct that this wage level was not extracted from the employer by force, but was a voluntary raising of the wage level, in nearly all the principal industries of the country in response to a general raising of the level of purchasing power in the market. It is American capitalism's fundamental contribution to economic progress.

It is important to note at this point that if all the proceeds of industry were expended on wages, it would have been impossible to develop either American industry or the American form of government or the American standard of living. Some of the proceeds must be retained for taxes and as a reserve for the development and protection of industry and for reinvestment in new enterprises.

LIVING STANDARDS UNDER CAPITALISM

It is this which has produced, under American capitalism, the highest standard of living known to man.

Standards of living are best measured by the yardstick of the use of consumption goods. And by that measurement, it is, beyond peradventure, true that the highest standards exist in the countries which are capitalistic. The United States, Great Britain, France, the Scandinavian countries, Holland, Switzerland—these are the leading capitalist countries. In them the standards of living for each occupational group are higher than for similar groups in countries under other economic systems.

Poverty continues to exist in capitalist countries. But whereas it is possible in countries which are not capitalistic to point to an entire nation in poverty, under capitalism, poverty may be defined as an out-of-step rise in the standard of living. Marginal groups of this type in American capitalism would generally not be regarded as living in poverty in the noncapitalistic countries.

Poverty, however, is intolerable under capitalism because the poor individual is an inadequate consumer. The task of capitalism is constantly to find means for increasing the productive capacity of those who are poor, so that their earnings may be increased and, therefore, their purchasing power increased. This is accomplished by the development of new commodities and services which provide increasing work at adequate wages. There is an inevitable lag and an attendant maladjustment in this process which keep part of the population below the current subsistence level. Except during periods of economic crises, their number is small and is constantly being reduced.

THREATS TO CAPITALISM

Just as capitalism had to struggle against feudalism and overcome it, so today capitalism is defending itself against rejuvenated forms of feudalism. This struggle, in widely differing manifestations, has been eternal with the human race.

The immediate cause for the present struggle was the Great War. As the War prolonged itself and grew in intensity, government was forced, in pursuit of military victory, to increase its controls over the means of production and distribution. The freedom of man was first curbed and then destroyed in many countries. Money lost its value and in some places its currency. Plants and equipment were expanded to meet war needs, *viz.*, destructive needs, but far beyond reasonable productivity in peace time. Inflation followed the so-called peace. Revolutions effected changes in government. Not only were tariff barriers raised, but other economic barriers were erected which clogged the arteries of commerce and broke down trade among nations. Large masses of the population were demoralized as a result of the War and men were accustomed to dependence upon government for an easy but unambitious and unprogressive existence.

In some fourteen countries in Europe, capitalism and, therefore, freedom for the individual either disappeared altogether or is being so modified that it is losing its primary characteristics. In Russia, a form of socialism was imposed upon the country by a politically effective group. The government took possession of the means of production and distribution

102

and of the total wealth of the country; and, seeking to develop as high a standard of living for the masses as exists in capitalist countries, but without utilizing the incentive processes of capitalism, they have, after twenty years of experimentation, shown some interesting but, on the whole, inconclusive results. To accomplish the little that they have, it has been necessary for the Communist party in Russia to resort to murder, suppression of human liberty, and, finally, to the despotism of a single individual. Their tremendous losses in human values do not compensate for their small gains in the standard of living of their people.

The anticapitalist system which is making startling progress throughout the world is fascism. Starting in Italy, it has spread through Europe and is taking on all the paraphernalia of a religion in Germany. Even the United States is not altogether free of fascistic influences; many of the most pressed reforms of the New Deal, particularly in agriculture and industry, definitely and unmistakably reflect fascistic tendencies.

Fascism is a reactionary movement which reverts to medieval governmental controls for its processes. It is government control of the means of production and distribution; private ownership of wealth is tolerated by government but the control of the flow of capital lies with the government. Democratic forms which abound in capitalism and which are the declared objective of socialism, are destroyed as wasteful. In their place appears the principle of leadership, *viz.*, that one man endowed with unusual gifts having possessed himself of political and economic power, employs it at his discretion.

Fascism is an ugly social system because its foundation is force. All forms of human freedom, of the liberty of man, of the rights of man, are obliterated. The spiritual gains of man under capitalism since the American Revolution are ground under the heel of despotism. And this tyranny is made, by fear and propaganda, to have the sanction of the people.

Capitalism and fascism cannot thrive in the same atmosphere. For capitalism requires freedom for the individual man

103

if it is to function, while fascism abhors freedom in any form. The struggle between fascism and capitalism is then to the death, and all suggested compromises between them are doomed to failure. The error, for instance, in such a process as the NRA was that it represented a compromise between capitalistic idealogy and fascistic practice. The ensuing confusion was inevitable. Similarly, the Roosevelt depression of 1938 was a result of the confusions arising from a desire to reform capitalism into fascism while retaining democracy. This is an impossible objective because its elements are irreconcilable.

WILL CAPITALISM SURVIVE?

The future of capitalism, as of democracy, for the world is in the United States. Should fascism develop in the United States as a product of the New Deal, then a new economic and political system will become fixed in Europe to last until the next war or a series of revolutions frees men from despotism. War is inevitable under fascism because the dictators, *i.e.*, the leaders of fascistic states, have to offer their literate masses stimulants in nationalist grandeur to offset the loss of incentives to personal improvement. Already, the principal fascist countries have engaged in expansion—Italy into Ethiopia; Germany into Austria; Japan into China. And this is by no means the end. Even the United States and Great Britain have been forced into the costly diversions of armament races to meet what is everywhere regarded as the inevitable forthcoming war.

On the other hand, if the United States and Great Britain can weather the current demoralization, they will remain the beacons for a new freedom. For their people will continue to enjoy both the highest standard of living and the greatest amount of human freedom. Wherever men will know of conditions in those countries, they will be increasingly dissatisfied with tyranny. They will ask, "Why must we be slaves to a despotism if we do not live as well as free men?"

No devices of propaganda, no suppressions of news and knowledge, can be devised which will be so efficient that they will blind men to the truth of the superiority of a free to a controlled system of life.

The principal battleground between capitalism and fascism then will be in the United States. Many battles have already been fought and the results are not clear. As in Europe, many who have regarded themselves as liberals and progressives are really supporting the approaches to fascism. The rallying cry here, as in Europe, is the improvement of the lot of the underprivileged, but here as in Europe, the process is one of leveling the whole of society down to the condition of the lower middle class with the government gaining power with every move in the process. The mark of fascism is the growth of power by government.

Nevertheless, in the United States fascism is not making as rapid progress as in Europe. Its political tactics depend upon the speedy gain of power—before the people resent it. Here speed has failed. The democratic selection of public officials continues and the revolt against the corruption of the electorate grows stronger. The two most fundamental acts of legislation designed to bring about a concentration of power in government, the Supreme Court Packing Bill and the Reorganization Bill, both failed. The tax bill for 1938 modified a prior fascistic measure.

It is, therefore, possible to suggest that the American people are resisting the fascistic trend here, as that trend was not resisted in Italy and Germany. It is possible to be optimistic that this resistance will increase in fervor and power until fascism is crushed in the United States, where communism seems at the moment to have no chance at all.

Chapter VIII

IS FASCISM THE WAY OUT?

LAWRENCE DENNIS

★ ★ ★ ★

FASCISM, unlike communism, does not promise utopia. We must go on living, working, fighting, and striving in the never-ending struggle for existence. As fast as we get out of one set of difficulties we shall get into another. The zest of life is in struggle rather than in achievement. Fascism, however, does hold out the promise of order, discipline, co-operation, kinship, and comradeship in the collective adventure of the struggle for existence. The main problem is how to get most spiritual and material satisfaction out of the adventure rather than to reach any particular sort of heaven on earth.

PROMISES VS. ACCOMPLISHMENTS OF COMMUNISM

The communist utopia is supposed to be without poverty, inequalities, class war, or international war. The Russian experiment does not support these claims. As for ending poverty, it is unlikely that any new social system, ushered in after a long period of disorder and the depletion of capital, culminating in a grand collapse, would be able in any near future to surpass the living standards enjoyed under a flourishing frontier capitalism. Neither fascism nor communism should be expected to excel liberal capitalism in its prime. They have had to take it over in its collapse; wherefore most of the comparisons unfavorable to communism and fascism are highly irrelevant. Both fascism and communism could afford a higher standard of living were it not for sacrifices demanded in the interests of national defense and economic self-sufficiency. Yet, without a strong national defense and a diversified economic production, a nation might expect to meet crushing defeat in war. In reducing poverty or raising living standards, communism must be expected to do worse than fascism, because communism starts out by destroying the managing personnel and all the capitalistic motivations.

As for the communist promise to end inequalities of reward and the class war within countries, nothing can be found in the Russian record to support it. In order to induce production on a large scale, communism—exactly like fascism and every large American corporate bureaucracy—offers great inequalities of rewards. These, in conjunction with the inescapable features of any hierarchy, necessarily mean that, under communism, instead of a classless society, there will be classes and class interests in perpetual conflict with one another. Communism, of course, will try to mitigate inequalities—but so do fascism and the New Deal, largely through progressive taxation and regulation. Communism will also try to prevent class warfare, but this it can only do by waving the flag and invoking nationalism and patriotism—again exactly like fascism and the New Deal. Today it is not communism, but the mystic bonds of racial and national unity, that is, love of country and of kind, which must hold together Russian communists. These are the very ties which communists used to deride before they had a show of their own to run. For these reasons Russia is going fascist about as fast as the United States, though with a head start on us in the matter of political organization.

The promise of the Communist party to end international war is amply refuted by the size of the Russian army, Russian policy in Spain, and by the fundamentals of international relations. It has always taken an outside enemy to unify a people and produce a nation. In religious associations, the devil serves this necessary function.

These contrasts between promise and performance are not peculiarities of the Soviet situation. If the entire world were communist, it would still be a world of nations, with the same conflicts of interests, traditions, and tongues now dominant. The communist nations would still be divisible into the "haves" and the "have nots." There would remain the same old inequalities in the distribution of raw materials; the same strategic inequalities; the same cultural, racial, and technological inequalities; the same inequalities both in greed and in bargaining power.

Communism, it will be said, is a cult of world peace and brotherhood. But nothing furnishes a surer motivation and a better rationalization for war—especially a "holy" war—and for doctrinal schisms than a universal religion like Christianity or communism. As Hegel said, wars are caused by conflicts between right and right, rather than by conflicts between right and wrong. Wars of this kind are made by peace lovers like Woodrow Wilson and Franklin D. Roosevelt, who love peace so much that they must fight for it.

A communist world of nations, like a fascist or a liberal-democratic world of nations, would need periodic selfish wars to maintain national unity as well as to effect necessary changes in the *status quo*. Without national unity, patriotism, and the technique of national sovereignty, the state would soon disintegrate into a plethora of warring factions, or gangs, such as kept all Europe in continuous petty warfare before the rise of strong nations, supported by national, instead of private, armies. The rise of nationalism resulted in fewer and bigger wars, with long intervening periods of peace and order during which civilization has flourished. The motives and techniques of the soil, the market, or the monastery will never, by themselves, hold together a people in the bonds of a strong national unity such as is necessary for prolonged periods of peace and cultural advance.

DEGREES OF COLLECTIVISM

Mr. Walter Lippmann, in *The Good Society*, is perfectly correct in saying that fascism, communism, and the New

108

Deal rely on the martial spirit and would not work without the unifying force of a crusading militancy. What he fails to add, however, is that all nations, including those he contrasts with what he calls the collectivisms, were born in war and have been developed by the same martial spirit and experiences which he makes peculiar to the fascist countries. All nations are collectivisms, although their respective degrees of collectivism vary with the moment and the exigencies of the moment. In war time, it runs to extremes; in periods of prosperity and ease, when no external danger menaces, collectivism declines along with the moral stamina of the people. The rugged individualism, however, of a brief frontier era, combined with a period of industrial revolution, is not to be regarded as traditional or as the vital principle in any of the great liberal states, all of which have been not only as militant but as collectivistic as any of the present-day fascist states. The chief difference at this point between the two groups is that the latter are now facing equals in their struggle for power, while the former, during the greater part of the eighteenth and nineteenth centuries, were facing inferior adversaries, usually semicivilized, or unwarlike peoples and undisciplined savages. The collectivism, for instance, of our own Indian wars was less totalitarian than that of European nations today, mainly because the conquest of the American Indians and their lands was comparatively easy.

The significance of the all-embracing type of collectivism, now commonly called totalitarian, lies in the fact that the day of easy, democratic wars on primitive peoples is about over. That brief day, be it remarked in passing, was considerably shorter than any one of several dynastic eras of China, Persia, Babylon, Egypt, Peru, or Mexico. Privileged conservatives, mostly in America, who owe their privileges to a particularly radical system called liberal democracy, or economic *laissez faire*, are completely at sea when they talk pontifically about getting back to fundamentals and first principles. That is just what Hitler, Mussolini, and Stalin are doing. But they are getting back to the fundamental ways of authority and discipline—the traditional norm of the ages —ways for antedating the radical and experimental document called the American Constitution.

Some optimists still believe that compromises and bad checks can stave off the day of totalitarian discipline and planning. Other optimists, like the parliamentary socialists, believe that, between fascist discipline for capitalists and the communist firing squad, there is an intermediate formula. But a parliamentary socialism will not work any more than a system of voluntary enlistment and loans will work in a modern war. Today there are too many, too powerful, and too ruthless minority interests both in the camp of capital and in the camp of labor to make possible any sort of voluntary, half-and-half socialism.

FASCIST TREND IN AMERICA

Against this background it is now in order to trace some of the causes that are influencing the trend toward fascism in liberal democracies like the United States. Inasmuch as the purpose of a political label is to dramatize a cause and attract supporters, rather than to furnish an accurate description of the thing labeled, it seems likely that an American fascism will not be called by that now unpopular name. In France, the term *conservative* is as unpopular as the terms *fascist* or *communist* are in this country, whereas the terms *radical* and *socialist* are as good vote getters as the terms *Republican* and *Democratic* are in Maine and Mississippi, respectively. So, quite naturally, the most conservative faction of the so-called *Socialists* of France, the faction whose members are neither socialists nor radicals, calls itself *Radical-socialist*. That is perfectly logical. So it would be for an American fascist party to call itself antifascist, anticommunist, democratic, and constitutional. An American fascism may come as a result of a war against European fascism.

Some of the principal causes of fascism, such as the growth of big business, the rise of tariff and immigration barriers, the spread of economic nationalism, the anarchy of minority groups, and the absence of sufficient incentives for normal business recovery, are to be found operative here exactly as they were operative in the European countries which have gone fascist. The fact that fascism first manifested itself in certain less favored European countries has about the same significance as the fact that the financially weaker countries preceded us in going off the gold standard in the order of their weakness. In fact, the trend away from liberalism and toward fascism is very like the trend away from the gold standard and toward a managed currency. It embraces the entire world, not excepting ourselves.

European businessmen and capitalists, who so eagerly assented to fascist dictatorships, were threatened with a worse fate than that of being ruined by government competition, government prosecution, and government persecution—the fate now confronting American big business. They were threatened with liquidation before a communist firing squad. In America, most investors and businessmen, instead of demanding survival under workable regulation and adequate business stimulation, are asking for more freedom and less governmental interference. Curiously enough, they cannot grasp the obvious fact that the unprosperous can destroy the prosperous with the liberal ballot quite as effectively as with the communist bullet, though possibly with less speed and logic.

The main issue in the matter of government relationship to business is not liberty but self-preservation and security. The modern political machine cannot work if minorities be allowed to exercise their present constitutional rights to influence government by group pressures—as the minority interests are doing in America and France. In England, a powerful, and power-conscious, ruling class, is developing

111

a kid-gloved fascism and maintaining a fair degree of order while paying lip service to the outward forms of parliamentary democracy. Unlike Americans, the upperclass Englishman never forgets that his privileges depend more on a system than on his own ability to out-do and out-trade the other fellow.

Wherever it is found, democratic liberalism assumes that the compromises of the parliamentary process add up to a sum total which is both the will of the people and their greatest good. Actually, the compromises do not so add up. They determine only who gets what, when, and how. The total result may be willed by few, and found to be unsatisfactory by the majority. The essence of the parliamentary process of give and take is the continuous passing out of overdrafts. Conflicting interests are all demanding the impossible. Workers and farmers demand more for producing less. Business demands larger profits than the traffic will bear. Cotton growers want larger foreign markets at the expense of markets for northern industries, and vice versa. The only way in which all these minorities can reach a democratic or parliamentary agreement is by exchanging bad checks. It is because many of the minority groups receiving these bad checks find it subsequently impossible to pass them, that they smash the system. The dying phase of this system must be currency inflation and devaluation, now incipient in the American scene.

If it be asked why the method worked so well for nearly a hundred years, the answer of course is that, during the frontier and industrial revolution era, the overdrafts were, for the most part, made good by reason of the exploitation of virgin lands, international division of labor, the doubling of the population every thirty years, thus insuring continuously rising land values and diminishing public-debt burdens, and the continuous gains from science and invention. Liberalism was like a community of prodigal sons who kept their credit good while continuously accumulating debts which were periodically being paid off out of a new legacy. One day, alas, the last rich relative dies and leaves the final legacy, with the result that no more debts can be paid off out of windfalls. And so we enter our ninth consecutive year of deficiteering.

The wheels of liberal democracy are supposed to turn by reason of the assertion and the exercise of private rights, and of the protection and enforcement afforded those rights by the state. In such a system, the state works most for those who have most rights which are legally enforceable—another way of saying for those who have most property. The Protestant Reformation and the French Revolution, with their respective ideologies, overstressed certain rights and underemphasized certain duties. They overstressed the rights of conscience, property, and equality before the courts. But equality, under the French Revolution, meant obliteration of distinctions of birth and rank, not equality of bargaining power. The rising class of economically powerful, and legally underprivileged tradesmen of that era wanted for themselves equality with the classes above them; they did not want or allow equality with themselves for the working classes beneath them. In all their talk about the rights of man, they never mentioned the right to a job. These traditional ideologies are being liquidated the world over by the collectivist revolutions of fascism and communism. Fascism emerges as a new system of rights and duties in which the emphasis is on duties. The liberal state, of course, enforces duties—the obligation of contract, for instance, or to avoid trespass—but not the duty to provide work and food for the unemployed, or to quote a fair price in driving a bargain. In liberalism, a fair price is a free market price, without regard for the inequalities in bargaining power between a billion dollar corporation and a common laborer. It is of the essence of liberalism that most duties of the individual are enforced only in response to a justiciable assertion of private right—the right to a job and to a fair bargain not being so enforceable. In other words, the core of the system is the competitive assertion and exercise of private rights *under the rule of law* written and interpreted to favor those richest in

113

property rights. The jig is up for such a system once the competitive process gets out of the courts and the market place into the halls of legislature, as has happened recently in America and France. Now the best side is the one which can exert most pressure and get most advantages by trading votes and favors with other selfish minorities. In this game the unprosperous, organized and led by demagogues of the same ruthlessness as our captains of industry and finance, should prove more than a match for the less numerous ranks of the prosperous. For one minority, like the manufacturers or small businessmen, to lecture the CIO or the farm raiders of the Treasury is a case of the pot calling the kettle black. Sermons on "my rights and your duties" are no longer in order.

Of course, it can easily be shown that the results of the new class war on the floor of Congress must be chaos, and that any grant from the prosperous might momentarily be better for the unprosperous than chaos. But it cannot be expected that the unprosperous, given more technical and unmoral education, will not eventually "gang up" in a perfectly legal democratic way, and march in organized minorities on Congress, on the public Treasury, and into the purses of the privileged. No wonder we hear so much about a lack of business confidence.

It has already been implied that present-day methods of minorities make the economic machine as unworkable as the political machine. There are causes for this into which we may look a little closer.

The economic machine will not work (which means that *all* of us will not eat) if investors, bankers, and businessmen are left free to cause depressions, however innocently, by reason of the sum of their individual decisions. It matters not what explanations may be advanced in defense of decisions to hoard rather than to invest, to contract rather than to expand bank credit, to curtail, rather than to increase, industrial production, to sell, or to postpone buying rather than to buy. Only the consequences matter. If the net result is increased unemployment and hunger, violent remedies will be tried. The victims of insecurity are no longer demanding the right to exercise constitutional liberties which do not fill their bellies, but rather to have imposed upon all, including themselves, duties and obligations so that their bellies may be filled. They are asking security and public order, not expositions of sound economics. It is easy to say that in so doing they are demanding that they become slaves. Perhaps they are. But what of that? We have always been slaves of our appetites, our families, our religions, our principles, and even of our country, in time of war. There are, and always have been, a number of demands to which, as a practical matter, we may not say no.

SUSPENDED COLLAPSE IN AMERICA

Since 1933 we have been supposed to be enjoying recovery, yet during all of this period nearly twenty per cent of the total population have been subsisting more or less outside of the national economy and on the Federal pay roll. This has not been recovery but suspended collapse. Mr. Roosevelt has suspended collapse only by *deficiteering*. Only in this way can collapse be suspended in either America or France today. But *deficiteering* must eventually end in collapse, and as that collapse approaches, the alternatives of fascism or communism become clearer.

The balancing of the budget in a depression is impossible for a system which cannot impose social discipline. Starvation, in the absence of relief or recovery, is a swift process. It cannot be allowed to go on while we grope toward a sound, constitutional equilibrium, assuming that we could ever attain it, which is improbable. Our present system allows government but one means of swiftly accomplishing unemployment relief and business stimulation, *viz.*, the printing press. The only trump card that can be played against the depression is inflation.

115

Mr. Donald Richberg, the brains of the late NRA, has pointed out the chaotic state of government regulation of business in the United States. Its uncertainty, inefficiency, and waste are proverbial. Government does not know what it may constitutionally permit, command, and forbid: businessmen do not know what they may and may not lawfully do. Although Mr. Richberg tries to take a more cheerful view of the matter, it is apparent that under economic liberalism, under our Constitution, under the decisions of the Supreme Court in the AAA and NRA cases, under the doctrines of Solicitor General Jackson—in short, under traditional rules—it is impossible either to regulate business or to conserve our natural resources. Our lawyer-ridden system obstructs efficient social control and public administration; it displays congenital impotency to meet crisis in a day when crisis is perpetual.

If every pants presser, as well as every billion dollar corporation, enjoys an imprescriptible right to challenge government regulation at almost every step by means of interminable litigation, on the ground that regulation constitutes confiscation without just compensation or that it does not constitute due process of law, workable regulation in our complex society becomes impossible. However beautifully it may be idealized and however convincingly it may be rationalized in the abstract, regulation by litigation will not work in the concrete. Against its successful operation stand the perversities of human behavior and the eternal conflict between self-interest and public interest. Either business frustrates social control through the use of good legal tactics, or social control paralyzes business, as happened in 1937 under the New Deal, when inflation was turned down.

The most fundamental error in the philosophy of regulation by law enforcement is its failure to recognize that business today requires stimulation as well as regulation. Take labor regulation, for example: regulation, *i.e.*, the fixing of reasonable wages and hours, is obviously humane and desirable.

116

But what if one of the results is a drastic increase in unemployment? Should the welfare of the employed be sacrificed for the sake of maintaining or increasing employment? Or must the state, by means of artificial stimulation, force a sufficiency of employment under the humane wages and hours it may prescribe?

Take financial regulation, for another example: the effort of the SEC to purge the security markets of speculation and manipulation may seem highly commendable. But what if the sequel is such a curtailment of investment as to cripple new capital formation? This is precisely the result of the New Deal efforts at reform in Wall Street. The problem then, becomes that of economic stimulation. The mortal sin of capitalism is not exploitation of workers or investors; it is insufficient activity. The New Dealers have attempted to make capitalists good, when the real problem is to make them work. It appears that the more capitalism is purified and reformed, the less active it becomes. If capitalism will not work at full capacity under reform, then the unemployed must be fed by a *deficiteering* state. Thus, the New Deal has merely substituted deficiteering for brokers' loans. Not unnaturally, in view of current economic theories, the New Dealers have felt that their chief problems were to hasten by pump priming a process of recovery considered to be inevitable and to work in, at the same time, as much reform as possible. It came as a terrific jolt both to the New Deal and to Wall Street to discover in 1937 that as soon as Washington reduced the hypodermics, the only thing that recovered was the late depression. A recovery normal to capitalism could not have taken place without a resort to practices forbidden by our present Securities Act and stock-market regulation.

ECONOMIC STIMULATION BY THE STATE

Economic stimulation is not pump priming, as it is so often and so erroneously called. The problem is not priming the pump but providing power to run the pump. Economic stimulation by the state, which is a new imperative for public order, has, of course, as many aspects of coercion as of stimulation. Investment in capital goods may be stimulated or forced by the fear of drastic inflation as well as induced by the expectation of profits—as under normal prewar capitalistic conditions. Investment may also be forced by government fiat to the institutional investors. This is the fascist method, and it is much sounder than that of inducing a flight from money to goods by spreading fear of drastic inflation and the ensuing devaluation of currency. In the case of France, the instrument of fear has worked badly for French prosperity, for it has driven French capital into foreign currencies. In the United States, there has been no attempted flight of American capital, but there occurred in 1937 a definite sitdown strike by American capital. Notwithstanding the inflationary danger implicit in the New Deal policies, American investors most illogically indulged in a big flight from securities and commodities to money during 1937. Washington, of course, can turn this flight to money into a flight from money by cheapening money through inflationary creations of bank deposits to finance relief deficits caused by such flight to money. In France, a fascist government must establish exchange control and stop the flight of French capital, while in both France and America a fascist government must either force capital and labor to co-operate and produce in a patriotic, rational manner, or else restore prewar incentives to capitalist expansion—but just how the latter can be done no one can show.

It is a cardinal principle of liberalism that the capitalist or banker shall be free to use or not use his resources as he may see fit. Fascism denies such freedom to private capital, holding that capital has no more right than labor to strike against the public welfare. The liberal maintains that, if savings are not promptly and fully invested, if banks contract credit and business enterprise lags, it is because the profit incentive is lacking; that the profit incentive can only be restored by letting nature take its course. The fascist admits that the lag is due to loss of business confidence, but denies that business confidence can be restored by *laissez faire*. He points out that nowhere since the war have the rules of orthodox economics been followed—least of all during the depression. The problem, in the fascist view, is not that of stimulating business recovery by an impossible restoration of prewar conditions, but that of stimulating business recovery within the conditions of today. This problem can be solved only by state compulsion of both capital and labor to accept reasonable and fair wages, hours, production norms, prices, and profits. Whether emphasis is put on the coercive or the stimulative aspects of government matters little. What does matter is that government intervention proves efficient and moderately successful.

The liberal proceeds on the assumption that it is the interest of both labor and capital to secure the maximum output, and that the only solution is to be found along the lines of voluntary co-operation, better education, and more democratic representation. The fascist contends that if the problem could be solved along these lines it would never have arisen, and, moreover, that education without a totalitarian morality makes the situation worse by intensifying class conflicts.

THE FASCIST PROGRAM

The fascist solution of social disorder and class conflict has three parts: first, making public interest under a unified plan paramount to private interest; second, making the plan explicit; third, making the plan effective.

The breakdown of capitalism and the rise of fascism have been strongly influenced by two important postwar developments of a financial nature. These are the increasing institutionalization of savings and investment, and the increasing preference for liquidity in investments. Institutional investors are insurance companies, savings banks, the trustees of trust funds, and the finance companies, many of which are mis-called *investment trusts*. In an ideal liberal-capitalist system, composed of small enterprises, small capital contributions,

119

and great diversification of investment by the wealthy, losses would tend automatically to be taken and fully written off by investors more or less as fast as they occurred. Institutional investors, however, proceed on the theory that such investors must limit themselves to certain types of investment, bonds, mortgages, and hand-picked common stocks, and should hold only liquid investments, that is to say, investments which can be readily sold in an organized market for such securities.

The result of this policy has been to concentrate financial control in New York City. Through the institutional investors, the savings of the entire country are drained off into a large pool to which only large companies, capable of offering blocks of at least several hundred thousand dollars, have access. Small business enterprises cannot tap for long-term uses this reservoir of institutionalized savings, while promoters of excessive and unwise investments by large corporations have unlimited access to these funds.

Another evil resulting from institutionalization of the nation's savings is rigidity of investment values or of the price structure in capital goods. Under a system of large-scale institutionalization of savings and investment and of extreme liquefaction of capital, the progressive readjustment of capital values to earning potentialities is impossible. Readjustment is postponed as long as possible, and then an avalanche of liquidation occurs which carries all before it and forces state intervention with the aid of inflation.

These evils are part of what Justice Brandeis has called *the curse of bigness*. But, contrary to the view of those of his school of thought, there is no escape possible by a return to littleness. Restorations have seldom succeeded. Having created super-corporate organisms to handle our funds and to produce our goods and services, we may not now destroy them without wrecking our present social order. We must now create a superstate competent to make these frankensteins function in an orderly fashion. The fascist corporate state is the logical outgrowth of the liberal capitalist mammoth corporation.

For the failure of private capital to provide enough jobs and to open the reservoirs of credit to small business enterprises, we have now only the corrective of relief expenditures and government loans to business financed by bank purchases of government bonds. A permanent solution must either put capitalistic enterprise on a working basis or inaugurate a workable state socialism.

SAVING CAPITALISM THROUGH FASCIST DISCIPLINE

Putting capitalism on a working basis today would involve a fascist discipline over both capital and labor. This result might not be accurately described as capitalism. But terminology is unimportant. It would be social order which is supremely important. An adequate social discipline must control not only prices and wages, but money, credit, and the flow of savings into investment. The New Deal is being driven inevitably in this direction. Control should be attempted only to the extent strictly necessary to avoid disorder and log jams in the flow of money and production.

In reducing the major problems of the hour to a few formulations which may seem somewhat oversimplified, it would be a great mistake not to interpose due reservations for two highly fortuitous factors in shaping human destiny: the one is chance; and the other is human irrationality. The element of chance in determining history we may dismiss as unpredictable and useless to discuss. Rational ideals as expressed in laws, customs, attitudes, and institutions, should, rationally, conform to certain dominant interests, rationally defined. But life is so often irrational. Irrationalities, like chance, are also unpredictable.

It would appear, however, that the choice between communism and fascism must be determined by ultimately predominant interests and ideals—ideals being the rationalizations of interests. The national interest is probably the noblest ideal around which working institutions can be formed. It allows the largest number of persons to live in peace and co-operation that it is possible so to unite. It is not possible to make a community of the entire world for any of the practical purposes of government or group co-operation. It is a strange paradox that those who are professedly desirous of saving liberalism should favor international collectivism among the nations while denouncing intranational collectivism within a nation. As a matter of fact, collective security is not in the best liberal tradition. The liberal states have always been extremely individualistic in their international behavior as nations.

COLLECTIVE SECURITY AN UNATTAINABLE IDEAL

Collective security in the international field seems to the fascist to be an unattainable ideal, the pursuit of which can only lead to futile warfare. World peace through the reign of one law and one authority is an ideal unsuccessfully pursued for centuries by the Papacy and the Moslem Caliphate. The pursuit has invariably meant religious or "holy" wars and chaos, escape from which has been found in the rise of strong nations which fight only for national self-interest. International wars for power can be localized and made fairly infrequent, but they cannot be prevented. The entry of the United States into the World War, and the British use of holy war propanganda started the liberal democracies on the road back to the principles of religious and moral wars which are the antithesis of nationalism. These wars lead to social disintegration from which an emergent nationalism is the only salvation. The World War was our one bad war: it gave us only a series of rubber checks and a pestilence of internationalism. Fascism does not regard war as an end always to be pursued, but rather as a possible means to certain ends for given countries under given circumstances. Fascism approves of selfish wars that are profitable, like our war with Mexico, or Britain's opium war with China, but disapproves of wars which have no chance of achieving their alleged objectives or yielding an advantage to the winner, such as a war to make the world safe for democracy. The now rich nations have grown rich because they have waged profitable wars. They cannot now expect other nations to desist from wars which may profit the aggressors. They can only propose to defend what they now have, but not to defend weaker nations against aggression and conquest by other expanding powers.

Fascism holds aloft in a world of spiritual, as well as economic, confusion and decay, the ideal of a national community, the only community under which a high and humane civilization has ever been achieved. Fascism is the present-day version of nationalism, whereas liberalism was the nationalist formula for the frontier era.

Within the nation, the interests of the majority should be dominant. Often they are not. Frequently human irrationality gives consent to such monstrosities as human sacrifice in accordance with the ritual of certain ancient religions, or to depressions as a ritual of modern liberal capitalism. The priests of old, however, conditioned their devotees to blind acceptance of human sacrifices as being essential to the welfare of the whole tribe, whereas the victims of modern capitalism have not been so conditioned. On the contrary, the priests of capitalism have conditioned the people to expect a chicken in every pot and two cars in every garage. They then express surprise that the masses are indisposed to make sacrifices for a balanced budget.

The great problem of fascism, from a humanitarian standpoint, is that of rationalizing or harmonizing the ideals and interests of the majority. The larger and more inclusive the majority, the more humane the result. For a country as heterogeneous as America, both as to racial stock and religious convictions, a racial or religious nationalism would seem somewhat inhumane as well as most impracticable.

The answer of fascism to the question what is the greatest good to the greatest number has already been indicated. Fascism says that it is a unified and totalitarian greatest good; liberalism, that it is the sum of minority interests or greatest

123

goods. Obviously, there is but one way to meet the postwar march of minorities upon the warpath, and that is along the line of the assertion of duties—the duty of every individual and every group to work together for one common good. Fascism means a socialized national community, integrating all persons, functions, values, institutions, and ways deemed worthy of integration. Fascism is democracy as well as nationalism. It is the democracy of the majority of integrated citizens, whereas liberalism is the democracy of a majority of unintegrated individuals and minorities. The liberal type of democracy is now doomed for the excellent reason that, at last, the unprosperous minorities have learned to play the game, whereas, in the days when liberalism worked, only the prosperous minorities really played the game because they alone wrote and enforced the rules.

Liberalism has no solution for unemployment except continuous government deficits or uncontrollable inflation. The frontier no longer makes good the overdrafts. The liberal state cannot impose social discipline. Present-day liberalism is a matter of practicing the assertion of one's own rights and preaching the performance of the other fellow's duties. Fascism can make everyone practice the performance of social duties. Liberalism is supposedly a competitive economy, but actually it is an economy of monopolies which the liberal state can neither regulate nor stimulate. Fascism is an economy in which large monopolies are recognized, regulated, and assured a market. Fascism preserves the nation, democracy, and private property rights which were formerly basic to liberalism, and which liberalism is no longer able to preserve. In a word, fascism means preserving order by social discipline, something the liberal state is incapable of doing.

124

Chapter IX

WHAT DOES SOCIALISM OFFER?

Norman Thomas

★ ★ ★ ★

Two facts stand out in ever clearer light as we consider the decades following the World War. One is the breakdown, first, of laissez-faire capitalism and, then, of private-finance capitalism of the sort familiar in America. The other is the fact that the immediate successor to the old capitalism in Europe has not been true socialism but the totalitarian state which, whatever its avowed aim, fascist or communist, is the enemy of any genuine fellowship of free men.

The first fact needs no protracted argument. It fairly shrieks at us from the pages of the daily newspaper. Writing even before Hitler came to power, the acute and scholarly Austrian economist and foe of socialism, von Mises, punctuates many of his closely reasoned pages with his lament for the betrayal of a sound capitalism by its friends. He finds evidences of "socialism"—as the opponent of laissez-faire capitalism—in every advance of state interference in the economic order, in the apologetic attitude of capitalism's own defenders, and in the concessions they are willing to make. How much deeper must be his grief in 1938!

Now I do not find true socialism in the rampant economic nationalism, the state capitalism of Italy or Germany, or in the pragmatic reformism of Roosevelt's New Deal in America. But it is enormously significant that nowhere in the world, outside of books (Walter Lippmann's *The Good Society* is an example), is there any movement toward an economic order based on "the automatic controls of the market," as opposed to state intervention and some form or degree of collectivism. Those books have a wistful utopianism in their aspirations for a capitalist "liberalism" which never fully existed and never, in the degree to which it did exist, seemed to satisfy men's elementary demands for security and the most modest abundance.

The age of power-driven machinery and the social evolution which has accompanied it has made a high degree of collectivism inevitable. The question before us is the degree of that collectivism and whether it can be controlled under the forms of the co-operative commonwealth as opposed to the totalitarian state.

PALLIATIVES

Before we turn to that great question, it is important to remind Americans that the Roosevelt effort to make the profit system work by reforming it has already failed. Some of its reforms were of themselves good. Especially good were such measures as encouraged the dynamic forces of labor. But it is precisely because those reforms have been good that the failure of the New Deal to give us even the old seven-year cycle of comparative prosperity is the more striking. While these Roosevelt reforms can be criticized in some detail, and while economists after the event can give more or less ingenious reasons for this depression—perhaps we should say *recession*—those reasons are often mutually contradictory and do not alter the fact that capitalism under the New Deal, as under the old, has not used, and apparently cannot use, our resources and machinery so as to provide that security which technological resources lead the poorest of us to expect.

As this is written, the newspapers proclaim: "One Sixth of the Population of New York City on Relief"; "Three Million More Unemployed Since August 1937." And this emergency has recurred in a country where President Roosevelt asserts that "one third of our people are ill-fed, ill-clothed, and ill-housed." In the presence of such need, the machinery and the men who could meet it stand idle!

126

Economists and politicians may be able to ridicule the quack remedies of the social doctors who spring up like mushrooms after the rains of adversity; they may point out the evils of regimentation and the difficulties of a planned economy of abundance, but they cannot save their capitalist system so long as men *and nations,* divided into the houses of the "haves" and "have nots," find no reason for poverty and insecurity except unjust social arrangements and human exploitation. John Blair, an able young economist, postulates in a forthcoming book certain reasonable demands that the masses may make of a going and satisfactory economic order. These demands include security of employment and the avoidance of unemployment; a steadily increased production of wealth and a more generous sharing of it among the workers under the wage and price system. All this, on an examination of the evidence, he does not find. Hence an unrest that will not be quieted.

Hence also the danger of war. For men who cannot find jobs, or markets for the crops they raise, offer weak resistance to the shot in the arm which war provides. They forget for the time being its horrible cost. And the occasions for war abound in a world organized under the twin loyalties of capitalism and nationalism into classes and nations so unequal in respect to economic opportunity and advantage.

Clearly the present system is failing men in those eternal and elementary demands, ever present if not always fully articulate, which, and correctly so, they make of life: bread, peace, freedom, fellowship. But with equal clearness it is evident that out of the breakdown of the old no desirable new order is automatically arising. In the complexity of the machine age a desirable society must be a conscious creation. Mere drift is movement toward chaos, new dark ages, or the tyranny of rival totalitarian states.

Between the avowed purposes of the Soviet Union and the fascist dictatorships are great and important differences. Nevertheless the instrumentality of the totalitarian state which both fascist and communist dictators use tends to narrow

127

the gap between them. It is a state for which the individual exists, a state governed by one party, no, by one bureaucracy within a party. At the head of each is a beloved, half-deified leader, who rules by bread, circuses, and appeals to patriotic ardor. There are no civil liberties, as we understand the term, under any totalitarian state. The state takes from the workers in town and country what may fairly be called the "surplus value" of their labor—that is, value which they create beyond what is socially necessary to sustain them, and apportions it, without democratic processes, for the military, the bureaucracy, and its favorites.

This is true in varying degree in all totalitarian states. In the fascist states, there is still an owning class but it is increasingly regimented by the bureaucracy and increasingly subject to taxation and "voluntary" contributions to the state. In Russia, the control of the state over the economic life is direct. Coercion, brutality, purges are as much facts of government in the U.S.S.R. as in fascist countries. And while government in Russia is more truly *for* the workers than in Germany, it is scarcely more truly *by* the workers under the domination of the Stalinite bureaucracy. Emphatically Lenin's hope that the state would "wither away" with the overthrow of capitalism is not even on the way to fulfillment. In this situation there is little satisfaction of the socialist hope. Socialism never promised merely to make the workers better off than under the czar. It never promised merely to overthrow capitalism and then to establish a society scarcely freer than a herd of more or less well-fed and contented cows—with condign punishment for those who are discontented. True socialism is concerned not only for plenty, but for peace and freedom. In the long run, plenty is always menaced by the dry rot of bureaucracy, and this is true of even such inequitable sharing of scarcity as the totalitarian states afford to the poor.

Today, the critics of socialism in increasing numbers are telling us that there cannot be any planned economy of abundance such as socialism demands except under a totalitarian state. None of those who make this argument or who defend the New Deal can tell us how the capitalism which is failing under New Deal or old, can meet the imperative demands of the workers for security.

THE PROGRAM OF SOCIALISM

In this dilemma, what has socialism to offer?

In the first place it reiterates its fundamental analysis of the capitalist economy: it points to the internal contradictions, to the development of monopoly out of competition, to the inherent wastes, the exploitation of natural resources and, above all, of the workers who never receive the equivalent of what they produce. Socialism insists that in the last analysis profit depends on relative scarcity; hence, such partial planning as is done under capitalism is scarcity planning, the sharing, to some degree, of poverty. Consider, for example, agricultural restrictions such as we have in the United States, where a well-fed population ideally needs more of every foodstuff except wheat! Or think of the tragic farce of telling share croppers without decent clothing, without sheets, without anything, that the trouble is that they have raised too much cotton! This is the capitalist system. In it crisis is inherent.

Under this economy liberty and democracy are always relative and often hypocritical terms. Those who own will rule. Governments, subject to such restraints and qualifications as the workers can enforce, are the agents of that owning class which tends to preserve its power, political and economic, by its control of the means of production.

And this capitalism is to be judged by its fruits: poverty, insecurity, repression, and war, the use for death and destruction of the machinery that might mean life and abundance.

The logical alternative to capitalism is planned production for use; not production for the private profit of owners— increasingly *absentee* owners—of our natural resources and the great means of production and distribution. To end the predatory society, the ancient struggle between a privileged class and those whom it exploits, let the workers with hand and brain become collectively the owners. Then the engineers, in Thorstein Veblen's phrase, can work for society as they now work for absentee owners, and the real social revolution will be accomplished. Let men be rewarded no longer according to *breed and greed*, but according to *need and deed*. In short, make machinery, mechanical power, applied science the servants of us all, across lines of race, nation, and creed.

Such, put briefly and in broad untechnical terms, is the underlying philosophy which socialism has to offer.

It has more than that. It has something of great value to say about the dynamic forces which may produce the new society. In particular it affirms that it is the historic destiny of the workers to achieve their own emancipation. The builders of the new society in which every able-bodied adult will work, and none shall seek work in vain, or be defrauded of the abundance and the leisure that modern technology makes possible, must be the workers themselves, in the fullest and richest sense of that great word. The basic organizations to which we must look for the winning of the new society are labor unions and associations of working farmers, consumers' co-operatives, and a labor or farmer-labor party.

A farmer-labor party is not to be identified with a progressive party or a popular front within, perhaps, the Democratic party. This needs emphasis not only against a certain school of liberals or progressives but against the new line of the communists who, intent primarily on saving Stalin's Russia as the holy land, have temporarily declared a moratorium on Leninism in favor of defensive action against fascism. Now a popular front may have uses in an emergency struggle *against* fascism but it lacks any unity of class interest or any philosophy by which to achieve the socialist society. So much at least is proved by its history in Spain and France.

Socialist logic supported by experience indicates that the workers will form a party in their own interest before they are ready to identify that interest with a full socialist program. Properly they will welcome to it all sympathetic individuals of every class. Socialists will support such a party and work within it. They will not oppose it in election campaigns. But their usefulness depends upon keeping their own identity and organization for educational and agitational work. That work must be done in mass organizations other than political parties, but it must be done openly, democratically, not on a Jesuitic or rule-or-ruin basis.

"All this," I can hear some reader say, "is well enough, but you don't tell us what program socialism offers to avoid, on the one hand, a repetition of its defeat in Germany or, on the other, the ills of the totalitarian state."

It is quite true that in these days, in addition to a philosophy and a party, socialists must be asked for a program. That program must be developed in thought and action more effectively than any socialist party has yet done. Socialists can point proudly to what they have done for the masses within the general confines of capitalism. They can emphasize their record of support of civil liberties and their positive achievements in social well-being in municipal governments here and abroad and in national governments in New Zealand and Scandinavia. But nowhere can we socialists say: "We have established socialism free from totalitarianism."

The tragic failure in Germany arose from many causes: lack of boldness and forthright socialization following the flight of the kaiser; the sharp division in labor's own ranks; the socialist failure to win the peasants; the postwar weariness and fear of the victors. None of these would have been banished by the simple device of a socialist embrace of totalitarianism.

PRINCIPLES STRESSED BY SOCIALISM

Nor has the case been proved that economic planning requires the totalitarian state. Democracy can and must be made to work functionally. Men must be citizens in industry as well as in political units. Specifically, as against totalitarianism, socialism must stress these principles:

1. Not even in the difficult transition period to a workers' society can we tolerate the dictatorship of one party under one omnipotent leader or dictator.

2. Civil liberties, including the right of association, the right to fair trial, and the right "to know, to argue and to utter according to conscience" must be protected. There must be no racial discrimination. Only overt acts and conspiracy against the government should be punished. There must be no weakness in dealing with such acts.

3. In season and out of season men must be taught that the state should be used as an instrument; that while it is a necessary social organization possessed of coercive power it is an instrument to be used for the whole company of individuals. It is not a half-mystical and all-sufficient entity for which (as in fascist countries) the individual exists.

4. The machinery of social control of industry must be elastic; it must recognize the role of the engineer (in Veblen's sense of the term) and yet permit democratic control; it must be decentralized and permit of socialist emulation or competition. It will have to develop careful cost accounting and will make use of money and the price system to permit a high degree of consumers' choice. (This is possible in a country where production is so far advanced that goods do not have to be rationed as to a beleaguered garrison.)

I envisage a society in which the political state will not be "omnicompetent"; where consumers' co-operatives will carry on many activities; where socialized industries will be administered under boards representing both the consuming interest and the workers of various categories in that industry; and where the economic planning board or boards, while, of course, subject to ultimate political control, will be divorced as far as possible from nagging partisan interference. The fact of world interdependence will find its political expression not in a centralized world state but in a federation of co-operative commonwealths, with enough world government to prevent war, allocate raw materials, establish minimum working standards, and a world fiscal system.

So destructive is modern war of all sorts, including warfare between classes, so important is the maximum possible good will in the difficult struggle for the co-operative commonwealth, that a socialist government could well afford some compensation to present owners of key industries, natural resources, and distributive agencies that it takes over, *provided that such compensation is the price of peace.*

Land now farmed under the plantation system or under corporation-owned, or chain-farm, control should be organized into co-operative agricultural collectives, but there should be a forced collectivization of family farms. Title should be based on occupancy and use. Henry George's principle of appropriation of the rental value of land by a tax may be used to deal with landlordism.

None of this logically compels the totalitarian state. Quite the opposite; socialization requires democracy and civil liberty in order to avoid the death of initiative and the dead hand of a fixed bureaucracy.

More than most of us, more even than most socialists, the writer has realized that war and militarism are responsible for totalitarianism. If the nation is the unit in a perpetual war system there is a grim logic to totalitarianism. Practically and psychologically, the totalitarian state is the expression of the nation always ready for war to keep what it has or gain what is desired in a world divided into the houses of the "haves" and the "have nots." Fascism itself is the ugly child of capitalism and nationalism in our modern world.

Not only, then, must socialism seek to end those divisions which breed war and strife, but in the struggle it must make every effort to find and use substitutes for the method of war. War, especially under modern conditions, entails not only brutalization, but a military organization of those who use it which tends to frustrate the noblest aims.

133

In particular, we must abandon the fallacy that war can cure what war has caused; or in other words, the delusion that capitalist nations, still relatively democratic, in a second war for "democracy" against "aggressor nations" will undo the harm they did in the treaties of Versailles and St. Germain. On the contrary, they may conquer certain aggressor nations and once more accentuate the causes of aggression. They will either reduce the world to a chaos of despair, or make new and worse treaties of Versailles. The *dramatis personae* will change but not the tragic drama of brutal frustration. Today, the hope in the Far East is not in the blundering police power of the United States after a costly victory; it is in the awakening of the Chinese masses so vividly described in Edgar Snow's *Red Star over China*. It is in the Japanese workers who are slowly learning to hate militarism.

Capitalist nations will never destroy the fascism or totalitarianism that capitalism and nationalism have bred. That is the task of new loyalties, new organizations, primarily of workers.

The one certainty, then, is the certainty that the only results of America's entry into war would be the brutalization of America, the destruction of what liberty we have, a military totalitarian state of indefinite duration. On no other terms can or will our government wage war.

DUTY OF AMERICAN SOCIALISTS

The outstanding duty of American socialism is to fight American entry into that war, for socialism knows that every year of peace gives time for the education and organization of the forces which must build the new society. We reject as the worst of socialist heresies the communist effort to get America into a war which communists think will help Stalin's Russia. It might help Stalin but not socialism. It is a betrayal of the best that Lenin taught.

Our European brethren are caught in a mesh which we, by the fortune of our geographic and historic position, may escape. Because socialism teaches world co-operation for peace, American socialists are not compelled to urge their nation to join a suicide club to prove good will. The maximum possible isolation from war is consistent with socialism. We are in no danger of invasion. American fascism threatens from within, not from without. Even in Europe it is not the external might of Germany or Italy which can seriously threaten Britain and France and Russia, provided western bourgeois democracy and Stalin's totalitarianism are not themselves destroyed from within.

It will take planning and educating and some economic preparation to stay out of a new world war. It can be done, and the effort to do it is vital to socialist integrity in America. The immediate necessity of our struggle against the totalitarian state is to keep America out of war even if we cannot immediately keep war out of the world.

The slogan of collective security is attractive to idealists. Logically, however, capitalist nations can hardly be expected to unite to impose economic or military sanctions for true democracy. The history of their failure when the omens were more auspicious than today bears out this logic. In the present crisis there will be no effective economic sanctions collectively imposed for democracy. Joint action of America with any European power, if it occurs, will be in the old line of national interest. Whether or not we are allied with Britain, the British Empire will be just as willing to settle with Hitler or Mussolini, or both of them, if she can do it cheaply enough or at some other nation's expense.

Effective economic sanctions, if imposed at all, would be a prelude to war, not an alternative to it. You might be happier thinking you were fighting for collective security, but you would die in vain.

Hence the activity of American socialists against the absurd supernavy, unnecessarily large for reasonable defense, but quite insufficient, no matter how large, to enable us to play Lord God Almighty to protect our "national policies" around the world! Hence our activity for housing, not battleships, and for the democratic right of the people to vote on war. Hence, in general our immediate program which may change in detail but is always based on our purpose to keep America out of war. We utterly reject the prowar popular front which so strangely unites at this late date the followers of Woodrow Wilson and the professed followers of Lenin.

I make no apology for stressing even in a short article, the position of American socialists on war. It is central to our philosophy and program. Though the crisis during which I write may abate or change, the menace of war will remain. The fight for socialism and against totalitarianism is bound up in the fight against American participation in a new world war.

But socialism offers more than a negative program, more than opposition to capitalism and war. It offers a glorious affirmation of the possibility of the conquest of poverty and exploitation. It offers a sure hope, worth the struggle, that men can harness machinery for life, not death, in a fellow-ship of free men. That is its supreme service to mankind.

Chapter X

DOES COMMUNISM POINT
THE WAY?

EARL BROWDER

★ ★ ★ ★

*Hold members
of the family*

URING the past few months the New York newspapers
have very systematically and persistently been attempting to transform the Communist party into an
illegal conspiracy engaged in preparing to overthrow the
American Constitution and American democracy by a violent
coup d'état in order to establish over America's 130 million
people the dictatorship of our 75,000 members in the Communist party. In fact, among the new and younger members
just coming into our party and still under the influence of the
New York newspapers, we have to engage in a purification
process to make sure they leave at the threshold to our party
all conceptions of communism that have been given them by
the New York newspapers; otherwise those newspapers might
have a certain degree of success in penetrating the Communist
party with their spurious ideas. They would like our party to be
a conspiratorial organization advocating force and violence.
Because we reject their plans for us, they try to bring about this
condition by suggestion and innuendo. I have had occasion, in
combating this newspaper campaign, to make a number of
statements repudiating the libelous theories and programs
attributed to the Communist party. Let me here cite from a
recent statement of mine made before a gathering of more than
6,000 of the most active members of our party in New York:

The Communist Party opposes the overthrow of American democracy.
On the contrary, it supports American democracy and urges the widest
possible common front of supporters of democracy in order to maintain it.

137

The Communist Party does not advocate force and violence. It is not a party of anarchists, terrorists, or conspirators. By no stretch of the imagination does it come under the terms of the criminal anarchy statute or any law patterned after that statute.

The Communist Party is an American Party and is not subject to any foreign control. The Communist Party is an American Party from the ground up. Its policy is based entirely upon American needs and it is absolutely not subject to any decisions except its own Conventions and the officials elected thereby.

. . . undemocratic legislation like the McNaboe measure can only lead the country along the road to Hitlerism. The McNaboe bill starts off ostensibly with the Communists but always winds up, as we see in the tragic case of Austria, with the Schuschniggs, the Miklases, the Catholics, Jews and liberals. You and I and our fellow-Americans in the state legislature certainly do not want such developments here.

This categoric declaration of policy I believe meets most of the charges brought against us. It is a statement based upon the solemn actions of the national convention of our party and one which we shall reiterate at our coming convention in May, in terms that even a New York newspaper editor cannot distort. We believe that it will help to clear the ground for a general consideration upon their merits of the program and problems of the Communist party.

First, what is the final aim of the Communist party? What are the basic needs which bring the party together and create over many generations, not only in America, but in every advanced country in the world, the vanguard party of the working class and of all the exploited and oppressed? The objective is the establishment of a new system of organization of society based upon the common ownership of the most important economic institutions, including the means of production and distribution of wealth, by all the people, through the medium of their government; or, in other words, the transference of the ownership of these economic institutions of society from the small group of present monopolists to the entire people acting through their government. This is the state of society which we call socialism. We maintain that this sort of social organization is absolutely necessary if the

138

human race is to continue not only to progress further but even to preserve the rights and liberties threatened by rampant reaction and fascism. The need for this sort of social reorganization arises not from our theories, not from our minds, but from the existing conditions of society itself.

CRITIQUE OF CAPITALISM

The present organization of society that we call capitalism, has reached a point in its development at which it is no longer compatible with human progress; at which it is destroying human rights; at which it is eliminating a large proportion of the population from every organized participation in our common life, except that which is based upon charity or the dole. We believe that the present capitalist system is destroying the productive forces of our country, and, instead of expanding our ability to produce wealth, is choking our capacities for wealth production, and so actually destroying the existing means of production. In a nation like the United States, the most advanced capitalist country in all the world, where capitalism has given its best example of expanding the technical and human productive forces, even here, especially here, capitalism now exhibits most sharply and most emphatically those characteristics that I have just described.

Certain important data that throw light revealingly on this situation are contained in the *Monthly Statistical Bulletin* of the League of Nations for December, 1937. Those figures, giving an index of our present state of production, show the following:

INDEX OF INDUSTRIAL PRODUCTION IN THE UNITED STATES
(1929 = 100)

	March, 1937	November, 1937
Total production....................	92.2	75.6
Consumption goods................	102.6	62.4
Capital goods......................	93.8	82.8

139

In the basic steel industry, the drop was appalling severe—from eighty per cent in the middle of September to less than twenty per cent in the last week of December.

During the early months of 1938 the curve of production went continuously downward.

If we study the teachings of Karl Marx and his collaborator Friedrich Engels, joint fathers of the modern socialist movement in the middle of the past century, we understand why these things are so. Life has demonstrated that the Marxian criticism of capitalist society is in every particular scientific and correct. Marx scientifically disclosed the laws of motion that inevitably control the development of society; he specifically disclosed the causes of the rise and downfall of the present system that we know as capitalism. In a later, declining epoch of capitalism, Lenin concretely analyzed the laws of motion of *monopoly capital* and showed the way to the socialist transformation of a society as achieved in the Soviet Union.

Capitalism is, relatively speaking, a recent comer on the historic stage. Many of us do not realize that, and so we have become accustomed to thinking of the capitalist system as something eternal, something that has existed from the foundation of the world and must necessarily exist for all time. But the most casual examination of history makes clear that capitalism as we know it today is the product of the last hundred and fifty years at the most, and that the present stage of capitalism—by which is meant the domination of monopoly capital, involving concentration of the main productive resources of humanity in giant corporations and trusts, their ownership being in the hands of a small group of people, an infinitesimal proportion of the whole—is characteristic only of the last forty years. Whatever its present defects, the capitalist system when it first appeared had many virtues; it was a distinct historic advance over the previous era of society. But the virtues of capitalism in its youth have all disappeared. It is one of the essential principles whereby history develops, according to the Marxian theories, that each stage of historic

140

development contains within itself certain basic contradictions which, on maturing, inevitably precipitate a crisis, and force society to go forward to a new system of organization. Our analysis of the capitalist system reveals that the present stage of monopoly capital, which we also call the imperialist stage of capitalism, has arrived at the point when the whole capitalist system is about to collapse, that there is no possible way whereby it can be reconstituted, and that the only way out for the human race is to abandon this system and establish a new one.

Space does not allow us to enter into a detailed examination of the workings of the economic laws of capitalist society that make this condition inevitable. But this examination is rendered the less necessary because the results are so clearly before us that every serious thinker on this question has already observed them in one form or another. Seventy-five years ago, through his study of the economic laws of capitalism, Marx was able to predict with marvelous clarity some of the main features of the present stage of the capitalist system. He pointed out that the capitalist system of society would pass from the historic scene at that moment when it changed from a system that feeds humanity, that produces the means of life for humanity, into one that denies the means of life to humanity. The early stage of capitalist development was plainly one of expanding production unprecedented in history; but it is clear to everyone that now our capitalist system is not expanding the production of wealth. The figures just quoted show that since 1929, wealth production, in this most favorably situated country in the whole world, far from advancing, has dropped to forty per cent of its level at the outset of the crisis. This has happened in a country which has unmatched resources for production.

What is there to prevent the production of five times as much wealth as we produce each year in the United States? It is not the lack of raw materials; we have almost every necessary raw material in our own land, in quantities sufficient for any possible demand of ours for at least the next hundred years. We have machinery, developed to the point at which it could produce five times the present output, reckoned at peak. We have labor, the most highly skilled labor in the world, in unlimited quantities; and if there is a shortage of any particular kind of skilled labor, as employers sometimes complain, that is only because society has refused to give food, clothing, and shelter to those who want to train themselves for special types of work. We do not use the means we have at hand. What prevents us?

Examine the situation as you will, you can find nothing that stands in the way of the utilization of America's resources for wealth except the obstacle of private ownership. This country's wealth is produced on terms laid down by a small group of private owners, and the terms which these private owners must lay down, according to the operation of the laws of capitalism, prevent the production of wealth, except where it increases the rate of profit to the owners without any regard to the needs of society. By resisting at the present time the progressive measures which the Roosevelt Administration is bringing forward in response to the people's demands, these monopolist owners are resorting to economic sabotage, to a veritable sitdown strike of capital. Production is not limited by social needs; it is limited only by effective demand in terms of money. So long as this situation exists there is no possible way out of the crisis for the capitalist system. There are, of course, ways in which conditions are alleviated here and there, and such ameliorative measures will be necessary so long as we have the present situation. The Communist party does not fight against them, it fights for them; but we point out that all these measures which will fit only within the limits of the capitalist system cannot in any way change the fundamental crisis of capitalism which already has 10 million people permanently divorced from jobs.

Without in any way introducing the elements of a new social system, but in attacking the problem within the limitations of capitalism itself, what measures are offered to change this situation? The first law that capitalism has laid down is that government must, under no circumstances, organize these masses of unemployed in order to produce the food, clothing, and shelter that they need. In other words, capitalism prohibits a government facing this crisis from taking the obvious and direct method of providing food, clothing, and shelter because such a course would put government in competition with private industry. The consequence is that every measure which is proposed, instead of attacking the very foundation of our difficulty, which is the system of private capital, is directed toward public works. We build great public buildings, we repair our streets, we build national highways, we even use public money to build magnificent golf courses; but we cannot through our government organize for the production of food, clothing, and shelter for the people. So we have today an outstanding paradox: at the moment when our country is suffering the most, when millions are starving, when the general standard of living in the country has gone down forty per cent—at this precise period a visitor from Mars would have the impression of our having entered into a greater period of prosperity. When we were really in a period of prosperity there was almost no development of these public improvements. When life became a problem, a question of existence for millions of people to be solved day by day and hour by hour, we suddenly burst forth with the most extravagant public building. That is a very sharp expression of the fundamental contradiction in capitalism, the contradiction between our way of life and the constantly increasing needs of our population. Our President estimates that one-third of our population is actually below the bare subsistence level. The rest of the population is gradually being forced closer and closer to it. We of the Communist party say that no solution is fundamental which does not boldly break through the limitations set by the capitalist mode of organization. And we say that once you go beyond those limitations set by capitalism

143

you must proceed rapidly to a complete reorganization of society—which is possible only under a new system. This must be the system of the common ownership and operation of our economy by the people through their government; a system which will eliminate private ownership and profit; ensure the distribution of the fruits of production among the population solely according to their contribution to that production; and offer a full program of social legislation. There is no other alternative. Even the most fertile imaginations have never been able to figure out a third way in which society could be organized. We believe that it is necessary to effect this reorganization as rapidly as possible. Our program arises out of the necessities of the people, the people in their great and overwhelming majority.

PROGRESS WITH SOCIALISM

In order that the human race may continue to exist and develop, it will be necessary for it to abandon the present system of chaotic production and go on to socialism. Our theoretical leaders, those who first developed the program of scientific socialism, foresaw that socialism is not only inevitable because it is the only alternative to extinction, but that socialism is very desirable in itself because it would bring about a tremendous expansion of human powers, the release of all the possibilities of human development.

Many people who accepted the necessity for socialism thought that Marx and Engels had overestimated the possibilities of what socialism could do. Our generation, however, has had the opportunity to see with its own eyes a socialist system in operation under the most unfavorable conditions and to contrast it with the capitalist system operating under what should be the most favorable conditions. I refer to the contrast between the development of life in the Soviet Union and of the capitalist nations in the rest of the world, especially our United States. At the end of the last World War, the United States had achieved the position of leader of the world. America had half the productive resources of the world, more than half its accumulated wealth, and the rest of the world was in debt to us to the tune of billions. Russia at that time was a ruined country, completely shattered by the war and the civil conflict that followed. Always a backward country, economically as well as politically, it had been thrust to the very bottom of the scale, suffering enormous famine that swept all areas; its factories, so far as they existed, were ninety-five per cent out of commission. Contrast the two countries twenty years ago—America at the very top, Russia at the bottom. Socialism began in the new Russia right at the very bottom, with the whole world against the Soviet people who were fighting for their life with nothing to fight with but their bare hands. In twenty short years, by the methods of their social organization, the methods of socialism, they transformed that ruined and backward country to the foremost in Europe economically, culturally, and politically; from a crushed and helpless nation into one of the most powerful. During the same period the ruling class of America took such good care of our inheritance that it brought disaster and starvation to our own people and reduced our living standards forty per cent. By their socialist system, the people of the Soviet Union not only solved their pressing needs but multiplied their national production of wealth by four hundred per cent and raised the standard of living of the masses of people by more than seven hundred per cent. One may entertain all the doubts one pleases as to the details involved in revolution and the establishment of a new system with its multitude of problems, but whatever these doubts are, one cannot avoid these obvious facts of wealth production and its distribution among the people. Whatever may be your opinion of the socialist system of government, whatever may be your opinion of the economic theories of Karl Marx, Lenin, and Stalin—this practical result of socialism in the Soviet Union you cannot get away from. The Soviet people are producing wealth, increasing the production of wealth of their society at a rate five times as fast as any rate of increase ever experienced in the United States under capitalism. And they are distributing this production of wealth throughout the entire population, limited only by the necessity of diverting a large part of this wealth production to the military defense of their society.

If we in the United States could do just half as much in the next five years as socialism has done for the Russian people in the last five years, we would greatly increase our average income, which is now about $1,000 per year. Four years from now, if we kept up with the rate of the Soviet Union, we would have $4,000 per year as the average income. If the American people could really be sure that they could accomplish as much for themselves by socialism in this country as the Russian people did in that backward country, how many of us would be so attached to our present capitalist system that we would reject the socialist reorganization of our society? What reason have we for thinking that we in America are less capable than the Russians of accomplishing these things?

Clearly the problem is how we can arrive at this new organization of society.

THE NEED FOR EDUCATION

The great majority of the American people have not yet even thought about socialism as a system of society; in fact, there has been an organized effort on the part of public channels of information to prevent the majority of the people from facing the question of socialism, from even understanding what socialism is. And there has been widespread misinformation about it. We are told that communism or socialism is nothing but a lot of elaborate and nonsensical theories with the most harmful and immoral content; that it advocates the destruction of family; that it encourages the theory of free love; that it prevents anyone from having any kind of private property; that it implies the destruction of civil liberties. So long as the problem of the crisis of the capitalist system and the alternative of a socialist system is approached with intent to protect the capitalist system at all costs; so long as the newspapers of America, the schools, the universities, join in a general conspiracy of misinformation, it is going to be a difficult job even to get immediate economic and social betterment pending effective transition from our present chaotic system to a new system of society. Socialism cannot be produced by imposing the new system upon the people against their will. The Communist party is accused of desiring this. We have sense enough to know that, however much we might desire it, it would be impossible to bring about a socialist state without the support of the mass of the people. Capitalism is the kind of system that can be organized by a small minority of capitalists. Socialism cannot be so organized; it can be established only when the masses themselves decide that it must be done, and take charge of actively doing it. Our task, therefore, is to organize ourselves for the education of the people to that end. However, if we merely become schoolmasters and propagandists, the job is so enormous that capitalism would destroy the human race before we would get through educating the majority. But we have found a way whereby education on a mass scale can be identified with the daily life of the masses in their struggle for a better life under the present system. This is by fighting for constantly improving standards of life under the present system. Precisely through that means we bring people to understand finally the necessity for socialism. That is why, though we have no faith whatever that capitalism can be rejuvenated, we are the best fighters for better conditions under capitalism. That is why at the present time when capitalism is brought to the stage where all the democratic achievements of society under capitalism are threatened with destruction by fascism and war, we are the most consistent defenders of democracy. We know that democracy as it now exists and by itself will not produce socialism; we also know that with fascism threatening the destruction of this democracy, as it does today, to defend democracy is the shortest road to educating the masses in the need for socialism.

We want to unite with all other democrats in a democratic front to preserve democracy without regard to ideas of the future socialist society. We want to unite our efforts with all progressives for even the slightest improvement of the conditions of life for the masses of the people now and today under capitalism. We are convinced that the struggle for a better life, the very experiences of the struggle, and the knowledge of the better life that will have been gained through fighting for it are going to educate the American people to the understanding of the need for socialism. The way to a better life is blocked by monopoly capital. Only by defeating monopoly capital, by getting its hands off our governmental institutions, by getting the people in charge of them, can the better life be achieved. Only by tackling their economic problems through organized effort, above all through governmental effort, and by learning more and more through experience that the carrying out of improvements has gone beyond the limits of the capitalist bounds will the majority of the people become revolutionists; and when the majority of the people want revolution and change, we will organize them to bring about the change. We hope that it will be accomplished with a minimum of difficulty, with a minimum of struggle; but as we educate, we warn the people always that the democratic majority, in all stages of history in which a democratic majority has expressed itself, has always had to overcome the resistance of a reactionary minority. The people must be prepared for struggle; that is the very essence of democratic development.

COMMUNISM AND SOCIALISM

This in brief outline is the theory and the practice of communism. Communism is that movement of the workers for the socialist stage of society which is the next stage after capitalism, and the preliminary stage in the development toward a full communist society. Some people are confused by the existence of a Socialist party and a Communist party, both of which say they want socialism. Many people think there is a fundamental difference between socialism and communism. That is not true. Originally our movement arose with the names *socialist* and *communist* used interchangeably. The first program of modern socialism was called the *Communist Manifesto*. Later on, under the influence of the development in Germany of the Social-Democratic party, the whole international movement changed its name to *socialist*. With the advent of the imperialist epoch which opened up the era of transition to socialism for the world working class, the necessity arose for reconstituting the proletarian party on the principles of revolutionary Marxism. Under the leadership of Lenin, the first sector of this new world party was formed in 1903 in Russia—the Bolshevik party, which was the first to realize the historically necessary split with reformist social-democracy. During and soon after the World War, there was a deep split over the question whether we should press forward immediately to socialism. The dominant leaders of the German Socialist party were afraid, even when they had power. After the war, although they had the power, they handed it back. This policy produced a split on a world scale. Those who wanted to follow the line of the Leninists had to sever themselves from antirevolutionary social-democracy. They therefore constituted in each land the party of revolutionary Marxism and reverted to the old original name of *communism*. Scientifically, of course, there is a difference between socialism and communism in that socialism, as we have said, is the stage of communist society that comes first after capitalism is abolished, and that still bears traces of the capitalist society, such as a strong state organization and a system of wage payment with lingering inequalities and limitations. With the full development of our productive forces under this socialist society, we foresee that we shall enter a higher stage which we call *communism*, when society produces enough to provide for every need without limitation. We shall come then to the era when there is no limitation on distribution, when each contributes according to his abilities

149

and receives from the common product according to his needs. That is the ultimate goal of communism, not achieved in the first establishment of socialism which operates under the law from each according to his abilities and to each according to his service.

THE WAR MENACE

While charting the course to the ultimate goal of humankind, the Communist party is constantly responsive to the urgent day-to-day demands and needs of the people and formulates concrete policies of guidance for their achievement.

Inextricably connected with the issues of economic betterment, of progress, of the defense and extension of the democratic gains is the great issue of peace.

The vital question that occupies the American mind today is, What should we do in this international situation, characterized by the most severe undeclared war? Every other question is subordinate to this in importance.

Let us not be consoled with the thought that, after all, we in America should concern ourselves only with our own future. Upon our decision will rest at least the immediate fate of the civilized world, accepting the term *civilized* in its usual newspaper sense to exclude that *uncivilized* land, the Soviet Union. All the lands of the civilized world are depending upon what we do in America. And if throughout those lands there appear the most lamentable weaknesses, hesitations, divisions, fears, retreats, and surrenders among those whom we expect to be the defenders of democracy and peace, let us not be too hasty to assume a holier-than-thou attitude toward our weaker brothers in Europe until we are prepared to answer the question, What have we done to help them face their difficult task? To be honest, we must admit that, far from having strengthened the world forces of peace and democracy, the practical force of our government has been permitted to encourage and to strengthen the camps of the bandit fascist governments that are destroying democracy.

In the debate that rages about this question throughout America, there is clearly taking place a revaluation of America's role in the world. A short year ago, America was so overwhelmingly isolationist in sentiment that the few voices which were raised for a policy of concerted action to defend peace and democracy were hardly heard, and in most of the deliberative assemblies of our nation the issue almost went by default; today that is no longer characteristic of the thought and sentiment of the American people. A tremendous awakening is taking place. The old dreams of isolation are fast disappearing. Those who have met the world crisis by withdrawing America within its own borders in attempting to shut out the influences of the rest of the world are no longer able to answer the practical questions of the day in any way that will satisfy the simple common sense of the American people. Today the arguments for American isolation are being revealed in their full inconsistency and danger for the future of our country and for the whole world.

The fascist warmakers themselves have boldly thrust their schemes of world domination onto the American continents through their penetration of Latin America, their establishment of an advisory direction over the Cuban military dictatorship at our doorstep, their preparation for an armed uprising to turn the government of President Cardenas over to the fascist agents in Mexico, and their insidious encroachments upon Canadian provinces. Yet even more than these acts of fascist penetration, even more than the arrogant parading of the gold-shirt troops right on American soil itself, what should alarm us as most fundamental, most menacing, is the development here of an American fascism with powerful forces behind it.

We have in America today a profound and far-reaching antidemocratic movement which operates upon a line of policy that fits into the views of Hitler, Mussolini, and the Mikado, and one that links up strongly with the policy of Chamberlain.

151

In Spain, the fascist advance was long prepared by conspiracy and intrigue within the Spanish government. We Americans should be able to understand the Spanish struggle because in so many respects, Spain parallels our own experiences, especially in the period of our own Civil War. Like Spain's, our government also, almost up to the moment of the outbreak of the Civil War, was in the hands of an enemy preparing an insurrection precisely through the government against which it was to rebel. Our army also was dispersed and its supplies delivered over to the enemy by official military heads, who later went over to the rebels, just as Franco did in Spain. Our government also was charged with being an undemocratic government, just as the Spanish government is charged today, and with more justification, because, while the Spanish Republic, established in the spring of 1936, had an absolute majority of the votes, Lincoln was elected by a minority of the popular vote—an indisputable fact in American history. These are parallels which should make us alert to new and sometimes obscure dangers which threaten us today.

Communists have been the most uncompromising and energetic advocates of a policy of international concerted action to halt the fascist warmakers whose arrogance and greed are constantly increasing. We have consistently pointed out that America is in an especially favorable situation to apply such a policy. We are the only great power in the world which can throw its full economic and moral resources, which are tremendous, on the side of peace and democracy without the immediate menace of warlike retaliation by the fascist dictators.

The logic of our isolationists, who emphasize this privileged position of ours, is that precisely because we could help at less cost than any other people, we must not help.

But already the development of world events has demonstrated to the American people that, while we have this relatively privileged position today, if we continue to use it as an excuse for withdrawing from world affairs and abandoning the threatened democracies to their fate, our privileged position will rapidly disappear—disappear not only by aggression from without, but, more important, by disintegration of our democracy from within. We cannot maintain American democracy upon the foundation of abandoning democracy in the rest of the world.

A UNITED FRONT

We of the Communist party are profoundly convinced that the solution of the problems of our country and of the whole world will certainly require the abandonment of the present capitalist system of economy and social organization; that it will be necessary for America to go over to a socialist system in order to solve our problems fundamentally; that it will be necessary to take our economy out of the hands of the small group of monopolists who now own it, exploit it, and prevent its utilization except to the degree that it contributes to their profit; that it will be necessary to place this national economy in the possession of the people of the nation acting through their government, in order to provide the possibilities of anything approaching a prosperous life of well-being for the whole of the people.

Although we are fully convinced of this, we know that the great majority of the American people are not yet convinced, are not yet ready for socialism. While continuing to the fullest extent our educational work for winning the majority of the American people for socialism, we cannot wait for the successful accomplishment of that before preparing to meet the immediate menace of fascism and war. We consider that the advent of fascism in America would create such chaos and destruction as not only to postpone the successful realization of socialism, but to destroy the limited security and democratic rights which the American people have won under our democracy. *We believe, therefore, that in this crisis, in the emergency that exists, it is necessary, first of all, for all of us, sincere democrats,*

153

enemies of fascism, and lovers of peace, to unite our efforts, regardless of differences as to the future society. We must unite to preserve the democratic achievements of the American people, to protect our standard of life, to protect our peace, and, as a necessary accompaniment to that, to unite our efforts with the peace-seeking and democratic-minded peoples of all the world, including the solid peace policy of the people of the Soviet Union. We must unite to halt the fascist aggression before it is too late, to establish guarantees that our efforts to arrive at a more fundamental solution to our problems shall not be destroyed and brought to nothing by the rise of fascist dictatorships throughout the world, including our own country.

That is the policy of communists everywhere—to give their complete devotion and support to the building of the people's front against fascism and war. And in the United States, where the masses of the people are still politically unorganized, this policy finds its expression in our proposal for the united democratic front, the fullest unity and consolidation of all labor and democratic forces without regard to labels, without regard to program, to protect American democracy, to protect the achievements of the people, and to make our great country a force for the preservation of peace and democracy throughout the world.

154

Chapter XI

TECHNOLOGY DEMANDS A PLANNING ECONOMY

Walter Rautenstrauch

★ ★ ★ ★

THE forces which determine the economic and social destiny of any group of people are various and complex. It is beyond the capacity of any human being to understand them completely. When we attempt to determine the effects of any specific group of forces on our economic and social life, such as those associated with the new technology, we are confronted with a most difficult problem because of the necessity of separating these from the effects of many other social and economic forces acting at the same time. While the use of power and machinery has increased at an enormous rate since the beginning of the century, we find that vast changes in business and financial practices have also occurred during the same period of time, and therefore it is extremely difficult to comprehend our present social trends in terms of the new technology alone. The most we can hope to accomplish in any study of this character is to discover one or more significant happenings which may serve as partial indicators of probable future trends.

In what particulars may we feel reasonable certainty that technology has affected our national economy?

THE NEW TECHNOLOGY

The phrase *new technology* symbolizes modern methods of production by means of the extensive use of power-driven machinery, by which natural resources are converted into

155

useful goods with less expenditure of human energy than in former times. The new technology itself is characterized by three important factors, which are (1) high-speed automatic machinery operated by power, (2) improved methods and processes of production resulting in new materials and new products, and (3) improved systems for the organization and management of productive enterprises.

We are generally aware of the importance of power and machinery in modern society because of our daily contacts with automobiles, trains, elevators, electric refrigerators, washing machines, power tractors, and countless devices in daily use in farms, factories, offices, and homes. We also have some notion of what the chemist, physicist, and engineer have done through research and design to develop new materials and new methods of production and, in general, to bring the benefits of science to the service of mankind. But what is not generally realized is that one of the most significant events which has transpired since the beginning of the century is the improvement in types of organization and methods of management of industrial enterprises.

With the advent of power and the accompanying new types of machinery and new processes for production, industry found that these could not be most effectively utilized by the old types of shop organization and methods of shop management. A complete revolution in factory organization and management had, therefore, to be brought about, and as rapidly as this was accomplished, increasing productivity and lower costs were realized. Industry found that the highly mechanized units of production had to be co-ordinated in their operations and that all processes from the purchase of the raw materials to the shipment of the finished products had to be united in a systematic plan of operation. Thus a planning economy is already an accomplished fact in the modern manufacturing plants of private enterprises, and it was due to the use of planned procedures that private enterprises were able to reach their present pinnacle of productivity. Therefore, to state that the modern age is a machine and power age somewhat obscures one of the most important contributions which the new technology has made to modern civilization. Important as the design and perfection of new machinery and processes have been in the fields of power generation and distribution and in manufacture, mining, and agriculture, these new devices and equipments could never by themselves have accomplished the great economic changes of modern times. Without the use of the new types of organization and methods of management which the new equipments demanded, private industry would never have made the great advances that we have noted.

Not only did the use of new processes and equipments of production compel revolutionary changes in the co-ordination and integration of operations within the factory itself, but its influence was felt in the channels of distribution and in the market places of the world. Market analyses of sales trends, estimates of the consumers' purchasing power, and many other investigations of similar character are currently made by private enterprise as a basis for forecasting probable output, raw-materials requirements, cash and capital demands, and other short- and long-term needs. It is this aspect of the new technology which needs continual emphasis if we are to become fully aware of the conditions under which modern science and engineering can be of greatest service to the human race. What the new technology has meant in the reorganization of private enterprises seems to have escaped public attention.

What is to be its effect upon the national plant as a whole? Is it not reasonable that the industrial activity of the entire nation must be reorganized and operated by improved methods of management in order that all the agencies of this process we call civilization may be brought to their most effective use in the service of mankind? It appears, therefore, that the real problem now before us is to make proper use of the equipments which science and engineering have provided

157

us with, and that this can be accomplished only by the perfection of a new type of national organization which will bring the nation as a whole to a high state of sustained production and consumption. In a word, we need to do the same constructive work for the national organization as was found necessary for private enterprise if we hope to realize fully the benefits of modern technology.

The claim cannot be made on behalf of private industry that it has forseen and understood all of the implications of the problem of reorganization either within its own limits or in its relation to society as a whole. Nor have the changes which we have noted in its organization and management been brought about without considerable opposition and resistance from those who did not understand them. It is not surprising, therefore, that any proposals to apply these same principles to the business of the nation as a whole should be stubbornly opposed by those who do not recognize their benefits. When once the principles of a national planning economy are thoroughly grasped by the majority of mankind, the benefits will not be long delayed. *It would appear, then, that one of the conditions which must be fulfilled, if we are to enjoy the benefits of modern means of production, is to organize ourselves as a nation in accordance with the principles by which the new technology works.* When we are so organized we shall find that the benefits extend beyond the range of material assets and have a direct bearing upon the balanced development of individuals and of society at large.

THE SHORTCOMINGS OF MODERN ECONOMY

Private industry, as we have seen, found it could not operate modern industrial equipment along old patterns of organization. The business of the nation as a whole has broken down because we have failed to remove the shackles of old organization patterns which do not permit modern methods of production to serve the needs of mankind.

158

In what ways do the present practices of our national economy prevent us from obtaining the benefits which science and technology are ready to bestow? And what factors did private enterprise fail to include in its plans which caused the national plant as a whole to break down?

It would require a rather long outline to state clearly the many particulars in which the present organization of the nation's business blocks the power of the machine to provide us with the plenty of which it is capable. We will give consideration to only two of these particulars: (1) our national organization as now constituted does not permit the continuous employment of those who are able to work, nor their employment at those services in which they can make their greatest social contribution; and (2) it fails to distribute the national income in workable proportions, by which is to be understood that the national income is not distributed to the citizens of the nation in such proportions that a balance of purchasing power with productive capacity is continuously maintained. These deficiencies of operation which are due to our national organization are closely related to each other. They have occurred because the planning economy of private enterprise failed to provide for the creation of the purchasing power which would assure the consumption of the goods it could produce. This failure was due largely to the fact that the use of machinery, and particularly the financial arrangements made by the owners of the new means of production, altered, as we shall see, the relative shares of the workers and the owners in the goods produced.

Before the extensive use of machinery, the costs of production were largely wage costs. This meant that the wage earners had a predominate claim on the goods produced and that the production and consumption of goods were in closer balance than now. The new technology and the ownership of the machinery and other properties of business enterprise by "investors" have changed the relation of the workers to the

159

goods produced. In 1919, for example, for every dollar paid in wages in the manufacturing industries in the United States, fourteen cents was paid to individuals in interest and dividends, *i.e.*, to those who owned the means of production, but in 1930 whenever the wage earner was paid one dollar there were thirty-two cents paid to individuals in interest and dividends. This means that in 1919 when the wage earners (not including salaried employees) in manufacture received one hundred loaves of bread, the owners of stocks and bonds received fourteen loaves of bread, but in 1930 when the wage earners received one hundred loaves of bread the owners received thirty-two loaves. If the owners could consume all the bread they received, consumption and production would be in balance. Of course, neither wage earners nor owners actually received bread; they received money with which they could buy bread. The wage earners did use their money to buy bread but the owners could not consume all the bread their money could buy. The owners invested most of the money they received, which means that they made arrangements, through the banking system, with builders of machinery and factories to give these builders claims to bread in return for more machinery and more factories. By this process the capital-goods builders were able to obtain food with which to sustain life. But in 1930 it was not profitable for the owners to make such arrangements with the capital-goods builders, and it was then that the great era of unemployment set in.

At this point private enterprises did not get together and plan for the distribution of purchasing power nor for the continuous employment of labor. It was believed that these matters would take care of themselves by certain assumed natural economic laws such, for example, as the laws of supply and demand. Many of those who refer to the relation between supply and demand do not realize that demand is determined by purchasing power and that because we did not plan for purchasing power it failed to equal the supply of goods we could produce. The relation between supply and demand is

160

man-made in the sense that the demand for goods is dependent on how we distribute the claims to goods.

Modern technology demands not only planning for production but also planning for consumption for the national plant as a whole. What are the elements of a nationally planned economy? The first thing to be considered is, of course, what the object of the planning is to be. We do not want to make the mistake which was made by private enterprise when it planned for high-speed production only and did not take proper account of mass purchasing power. In other words, we must include all people in the plan and not only the few who receive profits.

A desirable performance of our national economy should accomplish the following results:

1. The most efficient use of the non-renewable material resources such as coal, iron, and gas.

2. The most efficient use of, replacement of, and additions to the renewable national resources, such as the land and its derivatives, wheat, timber, hogs, and cotton. These objectives raise the problems of maintaining and developing the physical assets of the national plant. Much of our so-called prosperity of former days was but the faulty accounting of wasting assets as profits.

3. The growth of the social capital as expressed in the physical, intellectual, and spiritual well-being of every man, woman, and child. This raises the problem of providing those conditions which will assure all persons an opportunity to take part in and contribute to the processes of civilization and culture, and through such participation to derive nourishment for their physical and spiritual development.

The present processes of civilization have not been operating specifically toward these ends. Our objectives have not been rational because our social philosophy has been faulty. Social conditions do not just happen; they are due to social practices, and social practices arise from the rules man makes for playing the game of civilization. This game is played by

161

rival teams called private enterprises seeking profit and fortune by hiring for wages the mass of human labor.

It should be emphasized that many so-called economic laws which are generally believed to be "natural" laws are no more than the recorded results of man-made processes. They are no more natural economic laws than the baseball rule "three strikes and out" is a natural law. The entire economic framework in which our business processes are set is wholly man-made, and there is nothing sacred about it. We have evolved an economic process for operating the nation's business which is based on a false sense of values, and the stockholders of the national plant are wondering if they have not been deceived by faulty accounting methods because of which the real changes in the values of the national assets are not disclosed. It seems, therefore, that the real objective of any economic planning must be such use of our physical and social capital that their values are at least not impaired but shall preferably be increased for the use of future generations.

METHODS IN A PLANNED ECONOMY

The next problem in national planning is that of organizing our conduct, *i.e.*, setting up methods by which the purposes of the national economy may be attained. Here we begin to have difficulty with words. A plan of action to most people means controlled conduct or regimentation and the consequent restriction of freedom. An effective program of action should be a way of life, an evolving pattern of behaviors from which greater satisfactions are being gradually realized. This is a difficult idea for most people to grasp because there are so many experiences in human affairs in which the mass of people have been exploited by being forced to follow a plan of action which a few powerful leaders have devised for their own benefit. A properly constituted organization, on the contrary, consists of a constantly changing group of activities from which spring improved methods for meeting new situations. Such

162

an organization gives life to all its parts. When we deal with an organized activity we are not concerned with a blue print or a structure or an inert aggregate of things, but rather with a living process, an activity, a group life, or organism which when functioning properly gives nourishment to all of its parts, and the parts in time contribute to the life of the organism as a whole. Because by it men will live, and live more abundantly, such an organization will bear the seeds of its own renewal.

The life process is well illustrated by the biological organism and its development from the simple forms to the complex organisms of which man is the present ultimate in development. We shall also see that the life process is the prototype of the great engineering developments, such as the railroads and the power systems.

The living organism has equipments for eating, digesting, moving, and other responses to its environment and its changes. Its equipments for seeing, hearing, smelling, feeling, and tasting enable it to sense its environment and, together with its organized nerve centers, to adjust its behavior.

The growth of the organism from the simple one-celled types, such as the amoeba, to the complex types of animal life, including man, seems to be characterized by two coincident developments: (1) the addition from time to time, in response to environment, of specific equipments which permit the organism to adapt itself to a wider range of environment or the more complete utilization of a specific environment; (2) and the development, refinement, and extension of a nervous system which serve to give the organism a more complete sense of its surroundings and a greater capacity of adaptation to them. Thus biological growth does not reside wholly in the additions of functional equipments but rather in the proper balance of these with other factors. The disappearance of certain forms of animal life which existed in the distant past may be explained in terms of the inadequacies of their own organs, their relationships to other elements, or both.

163

The technological process, such as a power system, is provided with functional equipments such as electric generators, steam turbines, boilers, pumps, heaters, and coolers by which potential energy is converted into the dynamic energy of the electric current. While the more complete utilization of fuels has been accomplished by the addition to the system of new and improved equipments, these of themselves would never have made the modern power systems possible. As we trace the growth of the power plants from their earlier simple forms to the complex interlocking continental networks of today, we find that, as the engineer developed larger and more efficient machinery and added more kinds of apparatus to the system, he was compelled to develop, perfect, and install the necessary co-ordinating and integrating systems which would make it possible for the functional equipments to act in unison and in response to load demands.

An industrial enterprise, such as a company manufacturing furniture or automobiles or food products, operates in an environment, the principal divisions of which are raw-materials supply, the consumer market, and the state. It is provided with functional equipments for converting raw materials into products useful to society. But its existence and prosperity do not depend on these alone. It must have adequate integrating equipment for sensing its environment, its raw-materials supply, the domestic and foreign markets, and the demands of the national, state, and local governments. Its capacity to sense this environment correctly determines in large measure the adequacy of its policies.

The social organism, such as a municipality, a state, or a nation, exhibits the same elements of organization structure. The modern state sustains itself in its environment by functional equipments, embodied in mass-production factories, cavernous mines, steam-trawler fishing fleets, power-cultivated fields, transcontinental railways, bus routes, airways, steamship lanes, vast banking systems, and national and international merchandising agencies. Not only has society grown

164

by adding to its productive and power equipment, but it has also endeavored to develop, extend, and refine its systems of integration. It endeavors to sense environment and its changes by means of educational systems and news agencies, by meetings, conventions, and other processes for the formulation of opinions and for disseminating information. Further integration is attempted through public-utilities commissions, federal trade commissions, statutory laws, trade practices, and social agencies and customs.

Thus, these four widely different types of organization seem in each instance to be made up of the same structural elements, and their healthy growth is characterized in all cases by extensions and refinements of their nervous systems for purposes of integration, coincident with the expansions and additions of functional equipments.

CHARACTERISTICS OF GROWTH

It is also interesting to observe that the growths of these organisms in magnitude follow, in time, the same general pattern. A tree, for example, grows in height; the automobile industry has grown in number of cars produced; the growth of coal production, in time, follows the same general trend. The growth of population in the United States has also followed the same trend. One would therefore suspect that each of these forms of organization had control mechanisms for balancing size with environment which operate in a surprisingly uniform fashion. Since such controls appear to reside in mechanisms for integration, one is led to the suggestion that the elements of organization of each type of organism reviewed have the same operating characteristics.

Just as the growth processes in each case seem to conform to uniform laws, so also do we find that each is subject to the same processes of disintegration. When a complex organism breaks down into simple elements it is said to be in a process of disintegration. The biological organism, for example, returns to the earth from which it was formed by processes of

165

disintegration. When the life-sustaining properties which build, maintain, and unite the cells into a complex organized entity disappear, then disintegration into the elements replaces the integrating forces of the life processes.

It is apparent also that disintegration takes place when the units of the organism begin to feed on the organism as a whole without, at the same time, making their contribution to the life of the whole. In the biological processes of healthy growth, the organism as a whole provides the environment from which each cell and each group of specialized cells receive assistance from and contribute to the whole. This balanced flow of energy into the cells, and from them out to the body as a whole, is the life principle of interdependent relationships, of rights and responsibilities by which the life processes are sustained.

The healthy functioning of the technological processes is dependent on the same principles of energy intake and outflow. The fire under the boiler, for example, imparts energy to the shell of the vessel. If an imperfectly functioning shell stores up this energy beyond a certain amount before it is passed on to the water, the temperature of the shell will rise to the point of burning and the whole vessel will be destroyed. Every engineer knows the serious effects of excess energy storage in any part of a power system, a machine tool, an electric generator, or a motor; therefore, in the design of such equipments the inflow and outflow of energy is a problem of primary consideration.

The industrial engineer is always concerned with the storage and flow of economic values in industrial enterprises. An excess storage of values in fixed assets which do not contribute proportionately to the productive process, or an excess of outflow in dividends which depletes working capital, or the high cost of an overhead service which does not contribute adequately to the effective working of the organization may be a focal point of disintegration which, if not curbed, may destroy the whole organization. When it is proposed to buy a

166

new machine or add a new department, the engineer asks the question, Will it pay? The question, put in other words, is, Will the new cell or group of cells contribute to the growth of the whole, or will it (or they) absorb more energy from the environment than is returned to it by the additional cellular activity? Will the new unit be a parasite feeding upon and sapping the economic strength of the business, or will it do its part in strengthening and rebuilding the environment to higher levels of economic strength?

The social organism also is subject to the same type of disintegrating process. If any considerable number of units derive energy from society as a whole in the form of excess profits, unemployment doles, interest charges, bonuses, excessive salaries, or graft, then there are parts which feed on the whole but do not make a proportionate contribution to the life of the organism. When the lumber industry depletes the forests, the oil industry drains the oil pools, political groups graft on the citizens, or powerful economic groups exploit labor, then we find the processes of disintegration tearing down the complex structure of society, and this results in a tendency to form aggregates of dissociated individuals and groups. In the normal processes of social growth the environment reacts on the individual to impart energy (physical, mental, and spiritual) to him; the individual in turn rebuilds and refines his environment so that by the action and reaction between the individual and his environment increasingly higher forms of society are attained. When, however, the individual feeds on his environment but fails to contribute to its regeneration, then the unregenerated environment restricts its nourishment of the individual, and decreasingly lower forms of society result. All of these examples of similarity of behavior of widely different forms of organisms seem to confirm the opinion that all have similar structures and principles of operation. We accordingly have reason to believe that the state tends to grow into a more complete realization and embodiment of these principles of organization. If

167

human society ever hopes to fulfill its highest possibilities, it must direct its conduct toward understanding and stimulating these principles of growth.

THE PROBLEMS OF A PLANNING ECONOMY

The importance of these observations to the problem of a planned economy lies in the fact that if a planned economy is to be successful it must conform in its design and structure to those principles which experience indicates are inherent in successful organized procedures. Accordingly, the plan must be based on the following:

1. An understanding of the operating characteristics of the functional equipments by which society converts the materials of its environment to its needs and all of the purposes these equipments serve.

2. An appreciation of the fact that the life-giving principle of an organization lies in the excellence of its equipments for integration, *i.e.*, its nervous system. Society provides itself with its material requirements by its functional equipments for agriculture, forestry, mining, manufacture, and transportation, warehousing, and retailing. It facilitates these transactions through its many agencies of money and credit. Its churches, schools, museums, libraries, theaters, and parks serve its spiritual, intellectual and recreational needs.

If the functional equipments of society are to be maintained in a healthy state so that they can best serve society's needs, they must be integrated and their operations co-ordinated. No sound economic system can be devised on any other principle. No system of government through which planning for economic performance is to be accomplished can be operated successfully in disregard of the foregoing principles of organization structure.

The technical skills with which these many functional equipments have been designed are rightly counted as partial evidence, in themselves, of the growth of civilization. But these industries and institutions serve other than technical functions. They establish the conditions under which people associate with one another, *i.e.*, they determine ways of life out of which the culture of the race develops; and they also serve as agencies for distributing the national income, *i.e.*, the claim to the goods and services produced. Obviously, then, any plan for better economic performance in the technical sense must also take account of these social and economic functions. It is generally agreed, for instance, that we must reorganize the distribution of the national income, by taxation or other methods, in better and more workable proportions; and it is becoming increasingly plain that, because of the cultural consideration just stated, we must also reorganize it as to the ways in which it originates. The functional units of the business process are in a healthy state, individually and collectively, only when they operate in harmony with (1) technical, (2) economic, and (3) social principles of interdependent relationships.

It is the integration of these functional divisions of social activity, such as manufacture, agriculture, mining, that determines the state of health and vitality of the whole social organism. If our study of the operation of organisms—biological, technical, and industrial—reveals anything, it is that the very life of the organism, its capacity to grow and adapt itself to changing environment, its capacity for serving the needs of all its parts, and its ability to resist disintegrating processes, depends on the vital processes of its nervous system. The nervous system of our society is represented by the process of education, by all the means employed for learning the truth, and all the methods used for arriving at decisions and for formulating the laws and rules by which we live. If we accept the economic and social objectives and the principles of organization structure suggested, how may they be embodied in an operative social system? At this point, we face a most difficult obstacle. It is the same obstacle that has retarded the advance of civilization and culture for thousands of years. Less so in recent times, but yet a real obstacle. The inability of the mass of mankind to think objectively, the binding fetters of fixed and familiar patterns of action, the inertia in adapting to new and changed environments, these are the obstacles to social progress as much as they were the obstacles to scientific progress that hindered the work of Harvey, Galileo, and other scientists of former times. Against these men was raised the cry that they were undermining the teachings of the church and defying the laws of God. Today, the same cry is raised in the sacred name of the Constitution, of liberty, and of freedom.

Any planning for economic performance must take this fact into account, recognize it as an obstacle, and deal with it intelligently. We must take people as we find them. Any procedure is impractical which ignores this fundamental condition. The problem now raised divides itself into two main parts: first, the setting up of a social and economic system, a planning economy, which our objective analysis informs us will mean most in social and economic results; and, second, the devising of a practical means of redirecting our present social behavior at minimum social cost.

A PROPOSED PLAN OF NATIONAL ORGANIZATION

Space limitations will only permit us to suggest what the ultimate form of our national economy may be, if we are successful in overcoming the inertia to social change and in organizing our conduct intelligently. The tremendous significance of the adventure is—and this is important to realise—that the form of the organization and the types of activities induced by it are the determining factors in economic and social progress. This is true because intelligence springs from activities and has no meaning apart from action.

Experience indicates that if technology is to serve mankind to the fullest possible extent, its processes should be embodied in a form of national organization approaching the following:

1. All group activities such as agriculture, manufacture, mining, transportation, and banking, as well as public health, public works, social science, political science, and the natural

sciences, to mention only a few, would be represented in a national congress.

2. The representatives of such groups would be elected as trustees of the national interests by the people who work in these groups.

3. These trustees would form the Congress of the United States of America; they would elect one of their number as chairman for a period of one year.

4. Regional trustees would be elected in each state in the Union and serve the region in the same manner as the national trustees serve the nation.

5. Local trustees should be elected to serve the local community.

6. Institutional trustees should be elected for each incorporated body and administer its properties as the trustees of a university now function in a similar capacity.

Mankind has developed and operated a type of organization which seems to embody the vital principles of an organized procedure; an organization which has borne the torch of civilization through the dark periods of history and given to man the most enduring and cherished values in life. That organization is the university. Our colleges and universities, churches, libraries, museums, parks, and educational and research foundations, learned and professional societies, and associations of many kinds have enriched the life of humanity not only in bringing forth the best in character and personality of the individual but also in their contribution to the physical well-being of mankind.

It appears, therefore, that we already possess a familiar pattern of organization to which our entire processes of civilization may be adapted and in which will be found a wholesome and vitalizing relationship between functional equipments and systems of integration. How will our national organization appear when made to conform to the university type of organization? The trustees would be charged with:

1. Holding the socially productive plants and natural resources of the nation in trust for the citizens in precisely the same way in which the property of the university is held by its trustees.

2. Directing the use of the physical plant and resources according to sound principles of national economy.

3. Providing opportunity to all citizens capable of service to be employed in creating wealth and under conditions which will release their creative faculties and stimulate their intellectual and spiritual well-being.

Each productive unit would handle its own funds, accumulate reserves for the expansion of plant, depreciation, and obsolescence, and maintain the unit on a sound economic self-sustaining basis.

All production would be delivered to designated places, administered by the trustees of warehousing and retailing and paid for at cost including all reserves. The consumer's price would be the average standard of costs from all production units plus service and other costs necessary to maintain the service of distribution.

All social service institutions and their employees would be maintained by a tax on production determined by popular vote. Any group of citizens would be free to organize and operate any kind of religious or social activity they care to support on their own account.

The trustees of banking and credit would administer the credit requirements for new plants, plant expansions, and other purposes on the basis of sound economic principles. A competent board of technical and economic experts would determine the probabilities of credit risk. Loans would be amortized over prescribed and predetermined periods of time with only such charges as are necessary to pay for the cost of the service and insure the average risk.

National examiners functioning as those who now serve our national banks would be employed not only for banks but for all industries and other enterprises. Boards of properly qualified competent persons would furnish the national, regional, and local trustees with statistics and analyses from which adequate policies of operation might be formulated.

Private property for individual use would be acquired, possessed, and transferred as each individual might prefer. Socially used property could not be held in restrictive possession nor could any individual or groups of persons establish claims on future production through the instrumentalities of interest and dividend rights to goods socially produced.

This is the general form of national organization structure, according to the university pattern, which seems to embody life processes of organized endeavors toward which our national economy is tending. When it will be adopted no one can tell. The best we can hope for is that its normal growth will be stimulated by intelligent co-operation instead of being retarded by the stupidity of man.

There appears to be no way of evaluating the probability of social change either in magnitude or time. Both as to rapidity and extent, social change probably depends on the sum total of social pressures and the paths along which the resultant forces flow. The chances are most favorable to efficient transition to high social levels if the emotional drive of the people is intelligently directed. Accordingly, there is immediate need for the most vigorous campaign of education and widespread discussion on the causes of our social and economic ills and of the principles upon which their remedies may be founded. We must repair our processes of integration which have fallen to such low estate that we cannot sense our environment nor formulate adequate policies of meeting its challenge. It is impossible to operate our civilization on a plane above the capacity of the people to function in it. No matter how excellent a plan for economic performance may be devised, it cannot be made to work unless there is a sufficient number of people having skill and a sense of trusteeship to operate the plan. Therefore, the first step in the technique of transition is education. If the educational program is effective, it will

173

probably result in a desire to formulate more adequate rules for operating the processes of civilization. This may take the form of a constitutional convention called for the purpose of bringing social and economic practices in closer accord with the operating characteristics recently developed in our industrial civilization, and in harmony with the ways of life to which our better natures aspire. Devising plans for economic performance within the framework of rules and regulations which prohibit co-ordination is a waste of time. Not until the structure of our social organization is reshaped to embody the life-sustaining processes can adequate planning for economic performance be accomplished.

Chapter XII

THE CO-OPERATIVE WAY

JACOB BAKER

★ ★ ★ ★

THERE is a current and growing understanding that political democracy without economic democracy is a mockery. There is developing a feeling, also, that the right to vote without the right to live, and to exercise a measure of control over the economic processes that yield security is an idle thing. Not only one-third of a nation, but nearly the whole nation finds itself contributing in apparent helplessness to the concentration of wealth and control in the hands of a few. The people have handed over or let slip from them the management of so many and such important functions that they are in an economic and social condition little better than slavery. This is a condition as stunting to the development of personality as slavery itself.

Farm tenancy, which sometimes results in the standard of living of the Southern share cropper, is increasing in the United States. Figures for 1935 show that nearly half of our farmers have lost their lands and have become tenants. Taken in connection with unemployment generally the fact is sinister. Among the Danes, on the other hand, where co-operatives became active at a critical moment in Danish economic history, tenancy is on the decrease. In 1850 Denmark had forty-two per cent farm tenancy. Figures for 1935 show it to be all but eliminated.

Co-operation is claimed by its proponents to be the method by which the people can recover their lost control and the economic system can be reshaped to serve its true end—the profit of the community, not merely of the few. They further claim that it is the only method which will preserve among us such commonly accepted values as civil liberties and the rights of the person, protected by the institution of private property, the democratic process, and the technical advantages and social values of group effort. It is not an exclusive movement, scorning all others; on the contrary, without directly involving itself in such efforts, it commends tax revision, organization of labor, proper inspection of foods, the maintenance of standards of quality and quantity, and the encouragement, indeed, of all socially progressive measures.

The co-operative way can be begun immediately and in one's own neighborhood. It is not dependent upon capturing control of the political machine or the mobilization of vast numbers under one leadership. Unlike the primarily political formulas being advanced for the relief of world distress, it has a history of nearly one hundred years and a performance record in several countries in which its principles have been tested and against which its claims can be evaluated.

In Sweden, where the co-operative distributive function has been reinforced in a notable way by efficient manufacture and management, the strangle hold of the trusts or cartels has been broken on such essential commodities as flour, rubber (galoshes, tires, etc.), and electric light bulbs. In a very real sense, the people themselves set the price for these necessities and influence the price of others by their implied, and proved, power to compete with the great industrialists. This has been done without sacrifices on the part of labor by creating a new and workable technique of *production for use* with no profits sequestered by management or capital.

In Great Britain, where the influence of government upon the economic life of the people is much less than in the Scandinavian countries, the effect of the co-operatives, powerful though they are in point of numbers, has been ameliorative rather than curative. But even here, between the years 1929 and 1934, 600 million dollars was returned as profit dividends to members. Wallace J. Campbell, in a

Factual Survey of the Consumers' Coöperative Movement, is able to say that the co-operatives increased their membership by 50,000 during the years of the depression. Moreover, "While private profit business was adding to the breadlines, the co-operative movement in Great Britain continued to increase both the number of employees and their real wages."

In Novia Scotia, the resurrection of an entire community is happening before our eyes. *Co-operation together with the education of adults for life* has brought it about.

In our own country, where the co-operative movement is taking on new vigor, there are a thousand indications of its power to improve the conditions of life for its members. The crying need is for more education, and a greater awareness on the part of the general public. There is one point of complete unanimity of interest in every society: we are a brotherhood of consumers. There are some who do not work, but everyone consumes. It is at this point of unanimity that the co-operative is potent. John Dewey has said, "The basis of interest is the annihilation of distance"—of distance between minds and between classes.

Although co-operative enterprise has developed more widely in Europe than in America, its growth in America each year, in proportion to the business done by it in the previous year, is more rapid than is the expansion of either governmental enterprise or private business. The actual co-operative sector, which is still a very small one in America, bulks very large in Europe. In Finland and Denmark, co-operatives of one kind or another occupy a sector of economic activity that is probably a little larger than that occupied by either private business or by the government. In a number of other European countries, co-operative activities are overtaking the other forms of economic organization.

VITAL PRINCIPLES OF CO-OPERATION

Co-operation in the broader sense is simply the voluntary joining together of people in mutually helpful efforts—as

177

among neighbors on informal occasions or in emergencies. Indeed, the movement originated in the banding together of a small group of nearly penniless English workers to meet a desperate economic emergency in their own lives. What we now call the co-operative movement is organization on a wider basis by means of which consumers supply themselves *at cost* with the goods and services they need. The following is a workable definition:

A co-operative enterprise is one which belongs to the people who use its services, the control of which rests equally with all the members, and the gains of which are distributed to the members in proportion to the use they make of its services.

The English workers in the village of Rochdale, who in 1844, "co-operated" to save themselves from starvation after a futile strike in the Lancashire woolen mills, called themselves the "Equitable Society of Rochdale Pioneers." They invested a small capital of $140, painfully saved when wages were about forty-five cents a week, in a stock of groceries on which they proposed to save for themselves the profit usually made by the retailer. Instead of ignominiously failing, as by all precedent they should have done, they made a spectacular success of the venture and became the model for the great development of consumers' co-operatives in Great Britain and on the Continent. The reasons for their success appear to lie in the principles which they applied. These have been formulated and restated in the literature of the movement as follows:

1. Open membership, irrespective of race, nationality, politics or religion.
2. Democratic control—one member, one vote.
3. Limited returns on capital; and return of gains to members through patronage refunds.

Consumer co-operators are also generally agreed upon the following as essential to successful co-operative action:

4. Regular provision of funds for promotional and educational work.
5. Cash trading.
6. Trading at market prices.

178

Still another principle has received almost universal acceptance and is included in the bylaws of many co-operative societies:

7. Regular provision for the building up of substantial reserves.

Essential business transactions usually take place at the point of exchange; hence co-operative enterprises first engage in buying and selling, and that remains, perhaps, their most important function. Other activities which they undertake are primarily for the purpose of making their buying and selling more effective—as when consumers' co-operatives promote the manufacture of goods in overpriced fields, or farmers' marketing societies undertake the grading and standardizing of farm products. Even banking, credit unions, insurance, and other social services performed by co-operatives may be viewed as transactions in buying and selling.

EUROPEAN CO-OPERATIVES

In Europe, the co-operative movement has taken a variety of forms, influenced, of course, by natural and commercial conditions. In an agricultural country like Denmark, it was the farmers who first developed a co-operative method which took shape in farmers' marketing and purchasing societies and rural credit unions. Some idea of the importance of these farmers' co-operatives, which are active in most of the non-fascist countries of Europe, may be gleaned from the fact that in Denmark the co-operatives handle over a third of the meat and cattle export, forty-six per cent of the butter export, and ninety per cent of milk produced by dairies. These are figures quoted by the co-operatives for 1934. Although rural by first intention, the Danish co-operatives have gradually pushed out into other fields, such as manufacture, housing, and banking. The obligation to enter the manufacturing field is often forced upon co-operatives by methods of boycott and discrimination employed against the co-operative wholesale societies by private business.

179

A wide variety of co-operative enterprises has been organized throughout Europe. Farmers' purchasing societies have been augmented by farmers' marketing societies. Groups of industrial workers infrequently own the enterprise in which they labor. Consumer distributive societies operate many stores to supply their members with part or all of their household goods. There are likewise numerous special service groups wherein members are supplied with medical treatment, hospitalization, and burial. Dry cleaning and laundering are also among the services provided co-operatively. Co-operative housing societies are successfully operated in England, Denmark, and Sweden. Electricity is frequently distributed by consumers' co-operatives, and it is interesting to note that in Sweden where this plan is followed, three-fourths of the farms have electricity. In the United States less than one-eighth are similarly equipped. Co-operative credit, insurance, and banking societies indicate additional fields of activity.

CO-OPERATIVE, GOVERNMENTAL, AND PRIVATE ENTERPRISE

It is apparent that a co-operative is a business enterprise that must command the attention of economists and of all those who are interested in social movements. As a business enterprise, it differs from both governmental and private undertakings in its actual constitution, and this results in certain differences of business policy and development.

If one thinks of organized economic enterprise as a triangular structure, the three points of the triangle are private, governmental, and co-operative organization: Government enterprise rests upon sovereignty; private enterprise on contract; and co-operative enterprise upon continuing agreement.

Co-operative enterprise is something like government enterprise in that its membership is open to all, in the same way that municipal enterprise is supported by all residents. In both cases, the benefits are proportional to the use made of the proffered service.

It is like private enterprise in that it must keep the adherence of its members by day-to-day service—the term upon which the continuing agreement remains in force. There are other points of resemblance: its capital is secured by voluntary investment, and its development is dependent on individual initiative.

In actual practice, co-operatives sometimes partake of the nature of either government or private enterprise. In Denmark and Switzerland, for instance, agricultural co-operatives are entrusted with certain governmental responsibilities concerned with the enforcement of decrees in connection with government subsidies and governmental control of production. In other places we find both consumer and agricultural societies profiting by the trade of nonmembers; and to the degree that they do so they assume the aspects of private enterprise.

Bearing in mind the figure of the triangle, the experience of Europe and conditions in the United States indicate that within thirty or forty years the field of organized business may be roughly divided between the three forms of enterprise, not equally, but with each having a substantial fraction. There can be no fixed rule as to which shall be the greatest. All that we know is that private business can do some things well, that government can do others very well, and that co-operation also performs some functions admirably. Private enterprise appears to be particularly adapted to those segments of the economic structure where the element of risk is largest and the speculative returns are proportional; governmental enterprise is requisite in those cases where security of continued function is the prime consideration.

As to co-operatives, it would appear that services which can be directly rendered to the participants are the ones that can be most easily undertaken; and that only by way of extension to make these most effective can co-operative enterprise proceed to secondary operations, such as manufacture. Such segments of organized enterprise as farming or heavy industry seem, at least at the present time, to be unsuitable for co-operative effort—just as other segments, such as water supply, are not suited for private industry.

CO-OPERATIVES IN THE UNITED STATES

Historically, co-operative enterprise in the United States has not shown the consistent growth that has been conspicuous in European countries. Only a year after the movement originated with the Rochdale Pioneers, a consumers' co-operative made a good start in Boston, acquiring about five thousand members and spreading over several states, but it soon declined and was unable to survive the Civil War. Bad management, depressions, booms, and a population constantly tending to seek new frontiers, all contributed to weaken various efforts promoted by the Grangers, the Sovereigns of Industry, and the Knights of Labor. A few scattered groups survived among those racially predisposed to co-operation, and especially in cases where the organization kept faithfully to Rochdale principles. In New York City, there is an outstanding example in the Workmens' Mutual Fire Insurance Coöperative, which was organized in the early seventies by a small group of German carpenters and has today 68,000 members and policies to the amount of 85 million dollars. Other examples of survival are found among the Scandinavian settlements of the Middle West.

Just before the World War, the American Federation of Labor strongly endorsed the co-operative movement, but again, bad management and the dislocations due to war itself took toll of all but a few of the hardiest and best organized of what have been called the *union co-ops*. Nevertheless, the sympathetic attitude of labor and its active participation are to be viewed as primary aids upon which American co-operatives may rely. The president of the American Federation of Labor recently sent the following message to the last congress of the Cooperative League of the United States of America:

The American Federation of Labor is ready to work with any constructive movement for consumers' cooperation. We realize what cooperation can mean to wage earners, and are anxious to see a strong and lasting movement built up in this country.

President Roosevelt's Commission on Cooperative Enterprize in Europe has this to say on the subject of co-operatives and their relations to their employees:

Cooperative spokesmen claim that their workers are better paid and better treated than those of private competitors. That seems to be true in all of the countries visited. In most of these countries, cooperative enterprises started as a labor movement. Cooperatives and labor unions are friendly and work together. Unions use cooperative labor standards to bring pressure on private employers. In many cases, cooperative enterprises operate on a closed shop basis, regardless of the attitude of their competitors. . . .

Higher wages are particularly characteristic of employment in stores and offices. In manufacturing and transport, rates, in many cases, already are set up by the unions, and cooperatives offer their membership substantial advantages.

Another strong ally of co-operation is the farmer. It is to be noted that in the revival of co-operative organization that has been going on in this country since the nineteen twenties, the farmer has been the actuating force. Because farmers were primarily interested in selling their produce, the farmers' marketing co-operatives were the first to develop extensively. It is perhaps a fair statement to say that these co-operatives have been successful in the United States in proportion to their opportunity to control the market for the commodity. There are crops in the United States where production is so large, and the area of cultivation so vast, that a total or even substantial control of the market is almost impossible. For these commodities we may expect some extension of co-operative activity in the way of storage and processing, but only to the degree that these services can be performed more economically for the farmer than they are now performed by private milling and packing interests. There are, however, many lesser agricultural commodities that we may expect to

183

see marketed co-operatively, as California oranges and raisins, or Washington and Oregon apples, are now marketed. In general, the development of co-operative marketing will, perhaps, be twofold: (1) organization of associations covering crops not now organized, in cases where substantial market control is possible; (2) organization or extension of service co-operatives in processing or handling such commodities as wheat and pork, when the costs of private handling appear excessive.

Recently the most rapid development of consumers' co-operation has been in rural areas. It is the farmers' view that consumer co-operatives will assist them in stabilizing the outlets for their marketing co-operatives. Already there has been a great expansion of present farm marketing co-operatives into general purchasing co-operatives, and of farm purchasing societies into consumers' and general-purpose co-operatives. Both farm and labor groups may be expected to give increasing support to this movement—especially to the organization of consumers' co-operatives in the cities. The Ohio Farm Bureau and other farm-bureau organizations have recently begun to give direct assistance to consumers' co-operatives in cities within their territories. These local consumers' co-operatives have developed with the expansion of groups formed originally to purchase one or two farm requirements, such as seed, fertilizer, or feed. The volume of sales, as well as the membership, of this class of co-operative has shown the most rapid increase of any type in this country. Many small stores have been set up which handle a variety of goods, and undoubtedly the service will expand until it furnishes a complete range of consumers' commodities.

The strength and soundness of the movement are well exemplified by the amazing increase in the co-operative distribution of gas and oil—commodities that are particularly suitable for this kind of distribution. The price margin is such that reserves accumulate much more rapidly than in other lines, such, for instance, as groceries. From the Middle West to the Pacific, two thousand farmer-owned co-operative bulk gasoline plants and filling stations are in operation, together with several oil compounding plants in Indiana, Kansas, and Minnesota. It has been estimated by co-operative agencies that 48 million dollars' worth of petroleum products were handled by co-operatives in 1935. Two great wholesale co-operatives are reported to have supplied local co-operatives of the Pacific Northwest with 20 million gallons of gasoline a year. A Kansas wholesale co-operative has begun shipping oil to co-operatives in European countries. A local oil co-operative organized by the farmers of Albert Lea, Minnesota, began operation in 1925 with a capital of $500. In ten years it reported assets of $125,000, and patronage dividends to consumer members of $250,000. The saving to members is estimated at an average of ten per cent. Such outstanding development in one commodity may be expected to influence the growth of co-operatives generally. Indeed the tendency of farmers' organizations to move toward full consumer service will lead, in all probability, to the development of joint enterprises between farmers' organizations and urban consumers' co-operatives for the processing and effective distribution of farm products now processed largely, and distributed wholly, by private enterprise. Very few such joint enterprises exist in the United States, and there are not many in Europe, but there is opportunity in this country for developments that will reduce the spread between producer and consumer.

We may also expect, in urban and industrial communities, a continued growth of existing consumers' organizations and the creation of new ones. Local co-operative stores will undoubtedly become larger, memberships will increase until branch stores are required, and, in general, the normal process of consumers' co-operative expansion will go forward.

It takes the usual consumers' co-operative society about twenty years to develop sufficient reserves so that it can operate without debt and with interest-free funds. In the

185

United States, the established consumers' co-operatives—found in industrial centers and suburbs of great cities—are now reaching that point of maturity. They have proved their business ability and are ready for expansion. Many societies which were founded by particular language groups are now outgrowing the characteristics that marked them as European, and are recruiting new members from among their neighboring communities. New groups or branch services are constantly being established, and funds are becoming available for new ranges of service, some of which, like the funeral service and the laundry service of the European co-operatives, will require regional organization.

The distribution of milk by co-operative effort is certain to go forward and will show a very great increase in the next ten years. A joint enterprise of producers' and consumers' co-operatives in Geneva, Switzerland, has developed one of the most successful methods of milk distribution in Europe. Other cities have followed the Geneva plan. In this country, some steps have already been taken; one or two societies already perform this function very successfully, and encouragement by two governors, Aiken of Vermont and Lehman of New York, will undoubtedly strengthen the movement. In his recent message to the New York Legislature, Governor Lehman said:

> Establishment of consumer cooperatives for direct distribution of milk from producer to consumer should be definitely encouraged. These undertakings could be made yardsticks for the measurement of fair and just distribution costs. . . . Properly operated consumer cooperatives can supply milk at better retail prices and yet not impair a fair return to the producer.

The type of consumers' co-operative—usually rural—which is called the General Purpose Cooperative, offers to its members every kind of business service that they require. It markets their varied farm products, purchases their farm requisites, and operates a store for home requirements. Although it has proved effective in communities of widely varying economic character, it is particularly suited to areas where the land is poor or overpopulated. The economic results in parts of Europe where a wide range of co-operative service has been made available by such general purpose enterprises, show that wherever the resources of a community are meager, the general purpose co-operative will be of great value in helping to bring the income of the residents up to the minimum requirements for reasonable living. The Federal government might advantageously promote such organizations in areas like the southern mountains, or wherever there are "stranded populations."

One of the most effective services rendered by the co-operatives of Northern Europe, Switzerland, and elsewhere is the distribution of electricity in rural areas. In our own country the Rural Electrification Administration has found its most considerable response among rural co-operatives of electricity users. Other utility services, such as telephone lines, water supply, waterways, bridges, and dock facilities, all of which have developed co-operatively in Europe, seem more completely given over to private and municipal operation in this country. We have many rural co-operative telephone lines, however, and other facilities may develop. In any event, we may be sure that in the next ten years there will be a great increase of rural electrification co-operatives, aided by the government.

The great development in Europe of co-operative housing is almost always closely linked, as to financing and building, with governmental or municipal aid, or both. Because co-operation is a continuing enterprise, repeated from day to day, it seems better adapted to the operation of housing projects than to their financing and building—big jobs that are done once and for all. The need for new construction, however, is enormous, and co-operatives may be able to enter the field. Whatever developments we may have in this country in co-operative housing will probably be linked, as in Europe, with governmental or municipal aid, although such an enterprise as the Amalgamated Housing Corporation, promoted by the Amalgamated Clothing Workers' Union, compares so favorably with governmental and private projects as to suggest that other purely co-operative housing ventures may be set up.

We are familiar in the United States with mutual insurance companies, many of our largest companies being of this type. A mutual company does not have the quality of full co-operative participation, its policy holders may vote by proxy at the annual meetings, and the management may go on from year to year with little check or change. Smaller and more nearly pure co-operative companies usually have a great deal more of membership co-operation, but small companies —whether mutual or fully co-operative—although they operate at very much lower margin of cost than the large national mutual companies or joint stock companies, cannot take every class or risk. They, therefore, frequently reinsure some of their risks. In this field of reinsurance of co-operative companies, as well as in the organization of new ones, there has been considerable development. Several of the state farm bureau federations—notably that of Ohio—are operating co-operative insurance enterprises. Beginning with automobile insurance, these farmers' co-operatives have extended their service to cover fire and life insurance. The Cooperative Life Insurance Company of America, organized as such in 1935, reports an increase of coverage every week from $50,000 to $100,000, and policies in force of more than $2,000,000. There are several other large co-operative ventures in the field of insurance, covering automobile, fire, and life insurance.

The growth of credit unions during the past five years has been one of the notable advances made by co-operatives in the United States. The Credit Union National Association, with headquarters at Madison, Wisconsin, reports that over two hundred of these unions are being organized each month, with a million and a half members included in co-operative associations formed by workers in industrial plants, labor unions, teachers' groups, government employees' associations,

188

and other organizations. Wherever small-salaried workers, professional or otherwise, need emergency funds, these credit associations may offer the escape from the exorbitant interest charges of the loan sharks. The unions enable their members to buy an automobile or to pay their doctor bills; they are a way of managing debts so as to get back on a cash basis. Furthermore, they make their members favorably acquainted with the co-operative idea and method and are a possible source of credit for other co-operative ventures.

The development of medical and health services on a co-operative basis is an extension of benefits which will commend itself increasingly to Americans. It may develop quite independently of any theories of state control, rather on purely co-operative lines involving the reduction of costs and the covering of risks by group organization. The various health and hospitalization insurance plans are modes of accomplishing a co-operative health service. Another way, notably illustrated in Elk City, Oklahoma, is the co-operative ownership and operation of a hospital.

The extent of co-operative ownership and enterprise in the United States has been only briefly outlined. There are, unfortunately, no comparable figures for the whole of co-operative enterprise in this country. No government department collects over-all figures on all co-operatives, although the Farm Credit Administration has a complete record of all marketing organizations and of many other farmers' co-operatives. The Bureau of Labor Statistics of the Department of Labor has some figures on consumers' co-operatives, but because of the recent rapid growth of these organizations, the statistics change almost as fast as they can be accumulated. It is to be hoped that the Federal government will soon have available comprehensive figures for the whole of co-operative enterprise throughout the country.

Summed up, the incomplete or estimated figures for the United States show 6,500 local consumers' co-operatives, with members representing 2 million families, and a business turnover of about half a billion dollars in 1936. There are thirty-six regional wholesale societies which serve the local societies. Seventeen wholesale societies affiliated with the Cooperative League had a net turnover, in 1935, of $72,102,000. Eight of the regional wholesale societies have formed a superwholesale, the National Cooperatives, Inc., the sales of which, in 1935, exceeded $25,400,000.

Although it has been recognised in this study that co-operative enterprise only originates and grows when the actual member consumers feel the need of the service which the co-operative can provide, there are contributing factors which sometimes stimulate growth.

A sense of regional identity and loyalty is one of those factors, expressed in a common concern for keeping the income of a region at home where it originates. There is often antagonism to outside banks and insurance companies that loan money or make investments in a given region, and then withdraw part of the regional income in profits and interest. An economist in a Western university has estimated that thirty per cent of the total profits of all industrial enterprise in his own state is drawn outside. Other states present the case even more forcefully.

SOME SOCIAL AND ECONOMIC IMPLICATIONS

The only method of organization of industrial enterprise which assures that the gains shall go to the users is the co-operative method. It is also true that anything which contributes to regional self-sufficiency, to the decentralization of wealth and of economic organization, strengthens the total national economy. A successful co-operative, deeply rooted in its local community, probably offers greater satisfaction to the participants than would a private enterprise of the same size in the same place, and although local or regional loyalty and the desire to keep profits at home may not be powerful enough to induce co-operative organization, their help may be depended on to keep it going.

Our teachers of economics and sociology may very well give widespread approval to the co-operative idea, for not only will its effect upon the national economic stability be plain to them, but they will be the first to see how basically it reinforces the structure of democracy. It is not without reason that dictators abroad have wrecked the co-operatives as soon as it became possible to do without their aid.

It is unquestionably true that co-operatives assist in restoring to the people the economic controls that have passed out of their hands. When this fact is more generally recognized by the American public, it will stimulate the growth here of the co-operative method.

In Sweden, the co-operative movement, by entering the fields of processing and manufacture, has forced one trust after another to lower prices to a fair level. Not only have co-operators benefited, but every consumer in Sweden of such essential commodities as margarine, flour, or rubber has reaped the benefits. The people can buy more goods with their present incomes, and, as a result, they have been able to increase production and put men back to work. Whereas our own experiments in antitrust legislation are as profuse as they are futile, the Swedes have no antitrust laws, and with the exception of the international monopolies in munitions, they have no private monopoly problems. Although this is not wholly due to the influence of the co-operatives—government monopolies, well administered, and other factors have done their share—the approach to the problem by the co-operatives has been direct and logical. The people believe in the effectiveness of their own competition rather than in legislation. The greatest victory of the Scandinavian co-operatives has been won by the federated wholesale societies of Sweden, Denmark, Finland, and Norway, known to us as the Scandinavian Wholesale Society. This organization, after careful analysis of all the problems involved, undertook to compete in the manufacture of electric light bulbs with the General Electric Company and its European affiliates. They were able to

191

secure the services of one of the cartel's most able European managers, and, after building a modern factory and withstanding both the conciliatory approaches and the threats of the cartel, they brought the Swedish price of light bulbs down from thirty-seven cents to twenty-two cents. The manufacturing company was organized as the North European Luma Cooperative Society, and as such it produces about one-third of the bulbs used in Sweden and exports to a number of other countries. In view of the effect of its operations upon the price of all lamps sold in Sweden, this co-operative enterprise may claim to have saved its Swedish consumer 5 million kroner, or $1,200,000 annually.

Aside from its economic results, co-operative enterprise has a number of social effects and implications. Education, especially the education of the adult, is one of the strongest allies of co-operation, and there is a mutual interplay of benefits between the two. In many cases, the effect of a strong co-operative movement in a community may be comparable to the influence of night schools and university extension courses, especially, of course, as to the economic thinking of the members. In the development of fellowship among its members, its influence is similar to that of religious institutions. In the judgment of many competent observers in Europe—both co-operators and others—it is these social elements that give to co-operative enterprise its greatest significance and its continuing appeal. In view of this, the importance to co-operatives of reserves for educational purposes becomes increasingly evident.

Proponents of a functional religion, alert to the influences of environment upon character, are manifesting an interest in co-operatives. The success of the outstanding Christian leader of Japan, Kagawa, in building up co-operative enterprise as part of his Christian missions, has awakened many in this country to the importance of the movement. The leaders of the Federal Council of Churches have contributed to this awakening by sponsoring Kagawa's recent tour through the

United States. Then, too, an achievement comparable to Kagawa's in America has taken place on the Canadian side of our border. The economic plight of the miners and fishermen in the village of Antigonish, Nova Scotia, was so acute that a commission appointed by the Canadian government saw no other course than removing them bodily to some more favorable section. Fortunately, the educational program of St. Francis Xavier University, at Antigonish, was broad enough to include a sense of responsibility for the underprivileged folk of this community and wise enough to hit upon measures that were to prove successful in helping them. Various enterprises, such as instruction in agriculture and a People's School, upon the pattern of the Danish Folk Schools, had been under way for many years, and, after a thorough survey of the possibilities of adult education and its application to community problems, an extension department of the university was founded in 1931. The first object of this group of specially selected teachers, with Dr. M. M. Coady as their leader, was to awaken the people to the advantages of planned effort along co-operative and educational lines. The study club was the entering wedge, after which simple co-operative groups were instituted by the people themselves, under guidance from the priests and teachers. Co-operative buying and selling are studied by the club members and applied realistically to the actual conditions of the group. Credit unions are not only supplying them with capital on reasonable terms but are educating them in the elements of finance. Among the fishermen, the study of a co-operative industry, such as lobster canneries and fish processing, is undertaken, while farmers consider the operation of flour and saw mills, creameries, tanneries, and other projects connected with rural developments. In 1935, such study clubs numbered close to a thousand, with a membership of over seven thousand. Credit societies were transacting $175,000 worth of business; twelve co-operative lobster factories; and five fish-processing plants were under operation by the fishermen themselves. Co-operative stores, marketing agencies, buying circles, and handicraft guilds were each contributing to the increasing well-being of these people. Dr. Lester, of the Carnegie Corporation, refers to the movement as representing "some of the most original and effective extramural work which has come to the attention of the Corporation." A member of the provincial department of agriculture, familiar with the villages in the days of their distress, has said that "an entire region, once in despair of soul because of its economic despair, has been given a new standard of living and a new spirit of courage and hope." In the mining sections, the people had turned in desperation to communism as a way out, but when they discovered what the fishermen were doing to solve their problems through co-operation, they, too, have become co-operators by conviction. Communism is rapidly disappearing from the provinces. Co-operators believe in the gradual extension of what is sound in our system and the elimination from it of the unsound. They know from experience that, as such growth and elimination take place, many problems of a political or social nature have a tendency to solve themselves because the economic conditions causing them have gradually disappeared. They believe that co-operation is a democratic process that restores society by functioning now: it has no need to wait for the destruction of our present social forms.

THE GOVERNMENT AND CO-OPERATIVES

Co-operative leaders state that co-operatives require nothing directly from government, and any approach to a subsidy is abhorrent to the co-operative method. Nevertheless, friendly interest on the part of the government is helpful to any institution, and it is possible that such interest may take the definite form of encouraging expansion by offering credit facilities. The local banking structure does not ordinarily provide credit which would enable a co-operative enterprise to be assured of parity with its competitors, unhampered by discriminatory credit arrangements.

194

The Farm Credit Administration has the chief responsibility for contracts of the Federal government with farmers' marketing societies and credit unions. Because of limitations of the law, the Farm Credit Administration cannot make loans to co-operative organizations for handling consumers' goods, and no other agency of the government is charged with the responsibility of concerning itself with co-operative organization. As farmers' co-operative trading societies move into the field of consumers' goods, they require the same credit facilities for that activity that they have in purchasing farm requisities. This aid the Farm Credit Association is now unable to give.

Federal credit is available in the United States to private trade and to farm-purchasing co-operatives, as indicated by these figures given by the American Retail Federation on outstanding loans, June 30, 1936:

> To private trade: Reconstruction Finance Corporation
> loans to wholesalers and retailers.............. $5,909,917
> To farm-purchasing co-operatives: Farm Credit Administration loans for the purchase of petroleum
> products and other goods and supplies.......... $3,379,127

None was indicated to consumers' co-operatives.

As co-operatives gain strength, they will have funds of their own to draw on for all capital needs. In the meantime, the Federal government and the state governments have the responsibility for seeing that parity of credit is established for co-operative enterprise. We may expect action in this respect.

In most European countries, the government has done two things for co-operatives: (1) It has subsidized a good deal of educational work. (2) Through governmental or government-aided credit agencies, it has made credit available to the co-operative societies on the same terms on which it has been available to commercial enterprises. The credit associations of Denmark, which have helped to promote co-operative undertakings, operate under government franchise. In no case does the co-operative have access to easy credit. Since it moves as rapidly as possible toward a cash basis of operation, all that it requires is that it shall be enabled to borrow on equal terms with its competitors.

Co-operative enterprise does not ask for and should not have special legal privileges, nor should it be subject to any legal discrimination. Its distinctive methods of organization and ways of doing business should be recognized, as they were in the Robinson-Patman Act, which specified that patronage refund to members of co-operatives should not be held contrary to anything in the act.

In a number of federal departments there are now widely scattered and disjointed efforts directed to the study or encouragement of consumers' co-operatives. The efforts are varied in intention, and while none of them is injurious, or contradictory to any of the others, they do not all fit together smoothly, and there are wide gaps that are not covered at all. Government activity touching co-operative enterprise should be co-ordinated and given a solid consistency as a logical part of the government's whole range of activity in behalf of the consumer. It should be integrated with government services which are concerned with the standards of commodities, the maintenance of purity in food and drugs, the spread of legal standards of weights and measures, with its accompanying state and municipal inspections. These are all indirectly stimulating and helpful to the growth of the co-operative method; local co-operative leaders use the rather potent argument that under co-operative ownership there is no temptation for a store manager or employee to short-weight or shortchange a customer. However that may be, the consuming public in America has become greatly interested in getting specific advise as to the quality and content of consumers' goods. The various agencies of the Federal government that have any means of distributing information to consumers are under continuous pressure for more help than they can give: similar pressure is felt by other agencies of the Federal government that have no means of making their facts available to the public. The same thing is true of states and municipalities. One of the private testing agencies has begun to do work for some of the co-operatives, testing goods that the co-operatives propose to sell, advising them as to quality, and making available to them tests of competitive products. This kind of service, whether governmental or private, not only helps the co-operative to maintain its standard of quality but enables it to make a sales point of that quality and, by fostering consumer consciousness, may readily give stimulation and leadership to co-operative effort in this country.

Federal and state departments giving technical information and general advice on problems of business and social organization are asked for advice and information concerning co-operative enterprise. An interesting phase of this service is the increasing volume of correspondence from small businessmen who are considering the problem of transforming their small business enterprises into co-operatives. Such a tendency will mean that many poor enterprises will be turned over to co-operation, but, along with the hazard that this will bring to co-operative enterprise as a class, it will result in considerable expansion of the co-operative method. Wise guidance on the part of government agencies can do much to reduce the fatalities in this field.

Education in co-operative organization is a matter which has interested local school boards and state universities only recently. In a number of towns throughout the country, local school boards have authorized the use of school funds for courses in co-operation in connection with elementary and high schools and adult evening classes. Such courses are included in the teaching of economic and industrial history or as part of workers' educational courses. The state of Wisconsin has by law required the inclusion of courses in co-operative organization in tax-supported schools. It should no longer be possible for an educated man to say that he has gone through high school, college, and graduate work in economics, and has never heard co-operatives mentioned.

PROGRESS THROUGH CO-OPERATION

There is every reason to believe that co-operative enterprise will expand to considerable proportions in the United States in the next generation. This expansion, as we have seen, has already begun. The volume of consumer co-operative enterprise has multiplied fivefold in the last five years. Although marketing co-operatives have not shown the same recent proportionate increase in volume, they too are expanding, and at the moment are, perhaps, consolidating ground already gained.

It is to the advantage of both the agricultural producer and the urban and rural consumer to reduce the spread between producers' receipts and consumers' payments, so that the producer may get more and the consumer pay less. The only way that either producers or consumers can positively control this is by the organization of their own co-operative enterprise. At the point where they meet, there may well be difference of opinion as to price; but the major purpose of co-operative organization on both sides is to make that price a just price. This impulse to the just price is a vigorous one in America, and the will of the people to organize in order to attain it is strong. It is only by co-operative organization that a direct control can be established.

The facts here briefly given as to co-operative enterprise in part of Europe and the United States have their significance for the whole of this country. The course of co-operative development in different European countries has shown much variation; and presumably it will vary in this country to a similar degree. Co-operative enterprise is flexible. Co-operators have been able to adjust it so as to do both complicated and simple things. In any country or district in Europe in which people are habituated to co-operation, they think of it as a method of meeting all group economic needs that may appear. For this reason, any forecaster would be unwise to say that it is from certain starting points that co-operation must grow in this

198

country. Some of the points already listed here may turn out to be important, while others may mean little ten years from now. Other starting points not yet apparent will certainly be discovered and some may come to overshadow those that we now think most essential.

As one looks at the countries where co-operation has made the greatest advance, one sees unemployment and tenancy decreasing, with a corresponding increase in the ownership of farms and homes. One finds a happier and more contented people, with high cultural standards, and with no conspicuously high extremes of poverty and wealth. We find with a curious consistency that they are more fully in control of the economic and political conditions of their lives. There is little trend toward communism and none toward dictatorship. While making all due allowance for homogeneity, racial habits of thrift, governmental attitudes, and imponderables generally, it would seem that the largest single contributing cause at the back of these appearances is co-operative organization. In its various European manifestations, co-operation has generally brought the benefits of stabilization of the national economy, of an influential check upon monopoly, and of a broadening purchasing power. These benefits indicate the possibilities inherent in the co-operative method of economic organization for America.

Part Three

OUR RELATIONS AT HOME

Chapter XIII

· A GOVERNMENT OF MEN

Rufus D. Smith

★ ★ ★ ★

IT MAY not be wise to say with the poet

> For forms of government let fools contest,
> That which is best administered is best. . . .

but it is certainly true that the happiness and liberty of a people depend upon much more than the form of government. As the processes of government become more complex, as its structure becomes more detailed in organization and more inclusive in scope, as its tasks grow in size, and as its services enter more and more into the daily life of the people, the administration of a government takes on greater and greater importance. The government of Great Britain, from a purely formal point of view, can be described in terms of the pageantry of kings and lords, privy councillors and ministers, and commons, but from a practical, and possibly a much more important approach, *viz.*, its relationship to the man on the street, the description might better begin with an account of His Majesty's permanent administrative service with its small band of carefully selected university men who carry on the affairs of England so quietly and effectively. Government in the United States, to give another example, has been taught almost universally in terms of constitutional forms and theories, but actually it may be more important to the citizen to discuss it in terms of fiscal practices, expanding governmental services, the interrelationships of the party machine, and the like.

203

GOVERNMENT COSTS

When government in America—local, state, and national—collects taxes and spends them to the extent of twenty to twenty-five per cent of the nation's income, then the administration of these activities looms up as the largest and most important single item in the family budget, greater perhaps than the cost of food, clothes, or rent. There is great pother, for example, in the halls of Congress over the reduction of the nation's private electric light bill, whereas infinitely more money might be saved by turning public opinion on the government's bill for services rendered. One might well start the reduction of public expenditures in two relatively minor items in the Federal budget: the travel bill for employees, which runs into several hundred millions of dollars and the franking of party propaganda which comes out of the post office till. If the American people are really interested in reducing the high cost of living, then the easiest, quickest, surest, and most profitable avenue of saving will be found in a reduction of government waste, corruption, and inefficiency, and in the attainment of a balanced budget. The millions sunk in the Passamaquoddy Dam, to take a glaring example of waste, will have the same disastrous effect in the long run on the economic welfare of the nation as losses incurred through improper private utility investment manipulation. Socially both are equally bad. If Wall Street needs a Security Exchange Commission to oversee its stock and bond transactions, then the American people need, quite as urgently, the same truthful accounting from the government concerning its activities. An impartial investigation of the TVA is just as important to the public as the one made into the operations of the American Telegraph and Telephone Company. Political manipulation of the people's pocketbook for party purposes is just as reprehensible as the issuance of a dishonest prospectus by an investment bond house. It is well to remember furthermore that an industrial recession can be brought about by the practice of unsound economics in Washington as well as by unwise speculation in Wall Street. President Roosevelt has stated the issue so clearly, "Too often in recent history liberal governments have been wrecked on the rocks of loose fiscal policy. We must avoid this danger."

Now that twenty to twenty-five per cent of the nation's income goes into billions of dollars of government servicing, the searchlight of public opinion must be turned on public administration. It makes little difference under what form of government one lives if the administration of vital services breaks down through faulty methods. When a navy goes into action, it is of little importance whether it be fascist, communist, democratic, republican, or New Deal. It must be a navy with its ships soundly constructed, expertly maneuvered, ably officered, and efficiently manned. What is true of the navy is equally true of every other administrative service of the government. These services must be directed by experts in administration, who are left free to carry on their technical tasks without political interference.

WANTED: A FOURTH ARM OF GOVERNMENT

The Massachusetts Bill of Rights contains a famous phrase, "to the end that this may be a government of laws and not of men." Has this ever been true in the history of government? No matter how a government is organized, can it be anything more than one of men? One which grows out of their conscience, their intelligence, their expertness, and their application? In America, political theory has paid vastly more attention to the laws than to the men who exercise the law. This country has more law per acre of territory than any other civilized nation. Local law is administered by countless overlapping agencies; state law finds its way onto the statute books in an endless stream; national law outruns the mind of man. These laws are administered by three or four million men and women, one-tenth of the gainfully employed in the United States, who operate in no less than 175,418 legally organized units of government. Yet the day-by-day application of the law to the lives of the people seems to grow ever more confused and ineffectual with the result that this nation is one of the most poorly administered in the world.

Certainly with these countless laws, these thousands of governmental units, these millions of employees, the United States should be supreme in at least the first and most fundamental task of government, the administration of criminal justice; yet it ranks rather low with a high rate of crime and a general contempt of law. Some years ago, former President Taft, who was also the Chief Justice of the United States Supreme Court, called the administration of criminal justice a disgrace to American civilization. It is neither prompt nor efficient; trials are of inordinate length and, when the verdict has been given, months or years may elapse before the sentence can be carried into effect. The maladministration of criminal justice is one of the greatest evils from which the people of the United States suffer. But it is only typical of the low state of public administration in general.

Where may be found the cause of this defective condition of American administration? It is imbedded in the lack of understanding and lack of appreciation of sound principles of public administration on the part of the people of this country. An American is less certain than he might be of his life, liberty, and pursuit of happiness, not because of too few laws, but because he has yet to learn the elementary lessons of sound, efficient, expert, and nonpolitical administration of public affairs. In this complex world, government is good or bad according to the spirit and efficiency of its administration of law. "The letter killeth, but the spirit giveth life." The life of the law, in other words, is to be found in the methods used to apply it through countless channels to the daily living of millions of people. Law must be administered by men; the test of government is in its application of law.

There are those who claim that the state is something apart from the men who run it, that the state is super, mythical, supreme. In actual practice, however, the state can never become more than the men who control and administer it. One reads much these days of the virtues of government planning as if it were some abstraction of the mind. Yet translated into action, government planning may become nothing more than a New Deal operated by mortal and finite men working completely at economic cross-purposes, although united politically. Supergovernment calls for supermen who are rare individuals, who arrive on the historic scene but once or twice in a century. Supporting the superman, if there is one, will be found millions of average individuals working for the government on salaries derived from taxation. The administrators of this mythical superinstitution, the state, are men and women no different from the rest of mankind. They make speeches, they study letters, read papers, eat and over-eat, and they become petulant, careless, irritable, and tired. Those who govern are like the rest of mankind, some sane, some insane, with the dividing line frequently indistinct. Nevertheless, we must live under law administered by men and we are concerned primarily with the quality and quantity of their public service.

The reasons for the relative failure of administration in the United States will be found in the backgrounds of American history and psychology. Space permits only a passing reference to a few underlying causes. Early in colonial history, the legislature became the supremely important power in the functioning of government. Liberty, to our early democrats, was safe only in the halls of the legislature, which soon became the symbol of American democracy, the bulwark of colonial liberty, and the guardian of the well-being of the people. America thus became most expert in the usages and organization of the legislature. This cult of the legislature made an ideal springboard from which to jump to the supremacy of courts, judges, and constitutions. Thus the judiciary soon became of equal importance in the scheme of American political philosophy, and, with the legislature, became the

207

dominant notes in the early political theory of the United States. The executive, because he represented the king and thus became the symbol of opposition to the people's representatives, came out of the colonial period subordinate in American estimation as a function of government and came into balance only through the formal constitutional application of the threefold separation of power among legislature, executive, and judiciary. But nowhere did the fourth function of government, *viz.*, administration, make its appearance in any early statement of political theory. Administration via the political party was overlooked completely in the writing of constitutions.

Political science in the United States has only recently begun to build up a body of administrative tradition. Many European countries, in contrast, carried over the superb experience and traditions of the leading administrative agency of all times, the Roman state. England began early in the last century to build a permanent administrative service of surpassing excellence, placing its faith in the leadership of university men, trained for public careers, permanent in tenure and free from party domination. In America, however, custom and democracy ran counter to expertness and permanency. At the outset, the theory of American government did not provide for the political party. Soon after the adoption of the Constitution, however, the party machine came to the fore, and in Jackson's regime swallowed completely, for patronage purposes, the administrative services of government. Never since has it relinquished its control. The administration of government in a territory of which only 100,000 square miles were inhabited did not loom large in importance to some two million whites, of whom five-sixths lived in rural tracts or small towns. Yet these early agrarian philosophies have been carried over as a part of American tradition to our present complex and highly urbanized economic and social conditions.

During the colonial period, the idea of short terms and rotation in office became the typical American legislative practice. Early Americans banked on the ability of untrained

208

and inexperienced men to handle the affairs of state. To them the machinery of democracy was so simple that any man could easily understand and participate in the running of it; they had an abiding faith in the ability of an American with little or no training to fill satisfactorily any government job, an idea still deep in the psychology of the people. We prided ourselves on a shirt-sleeve diplomatic corps. A professional police force did not appear until about the middle of the century, while government engineers were self-trained surveyors. The forefathers of this country, in brief, put their faith in a multiplicity of jobs, in short terms of office, in many elected officials, in numerous elections, and in rotation in office, ideas which when combined made an excellent seedbed of principles in which party patronage could grow luxuriantly. These ideas, incidentally, were opposed to efficient methods of administration. Later they were embodied in American textbooks, and finally became part and parcel of American political folklore.

The very form of American government lent itself to the subordination of sound principles of administration. Power was divided between the states and the Federal government, and functions were separated within the Federal government among the executive, legislative, and judicial branches. These distinctions were carried down to local government, where they are out of place. In spite of our theories, no government can function without unity; yet where was it to be found in the American system of government? No one foresaw the logical answer; the authors of the Constitution could not have anticipated the part that political parties were to play. But in a few years political parties became the dominating and cementing forces which brought unity where formerly only separation and division had existed. Lying close at hand to the party boss were jobs. Since there were no generally accepted traditions of public administration in the United States, the political party soon seized government jobs for patronage purposes and leaped into the saddle of control. Since Jackson's time, the major task of the American people has been to break party power expressed in spoils. It has been a long difficult road, and the end is not yet in sight. The success or failure of American government now rests upon its ability to develop the fourth arm of the government, administration, to an equal place with those provided for in the Constitution—the legislative, the executive, and the judicial.

THE STRUGGLE FOR THE MERIT SYSTEM

The prevailing philosophy of public service was summed up by President Jackson in his first annual message to Congress which was delivered in December, 1829:

> The duties of all public officers are, or at least admit of being made, so plain and simple that men of intelligence may readily qualify themselves for their performance; and I cannot but believe that more is lost by the long continuance of men in office than is generally to be gained by their experience. . . . In a country where offices are created solely for the benefit of the people no man has any more intrinsic right to official station than another. Offices were not established to give support to particular men at the public expense. No individual wrong is, therefore, done by removal, since neither appointment to nor continuance in office is a matter of right. The incumbent became an officer with a view to public benefits, and when these require his removal they are not to be sacrificed to private interests. It is the people, and they alone, who have a right to complain when a bad officer is substituted for a good one. He who is removed has the same means of obtaining a living that are enjoyed by the millions who never hold office. The proposed limitation would destroy the idea of property now so generally connected with official station, and although individual distress may be sometimes produced, it would, by promoting that rotation which constitutes a leading principle in the republican creed, give healthful action to the system.

Senator Marcy gave the name to the system when he said of his followers, "They see nothing wrong in the maxim, to the victors belong the spoils of the enemy." Ever since, it has been called the *spoils system*. It was the political philosophy of Lincoln's day, but before he died he made his famous remark, "Those men," pointing to a crowd of officeholders, "are more dangerous to the life of the Republic than the rebels."

210

Until after the Civil War, these principles dominated the administration of public service. By 1872, however, following the scandals of the Civil War period, both major parties were forced to reform. The Democrats put forward a plank which said:

The civil service of the government has become a mere instrument of partisan tyranny and personal ambition, and an object of selfish greed. It is a scandal and reproach upon free institutions, and breeds a demoralization dangerous to the perpetuity of republican government. We therefore regard a thorough reform of the civil service as one of the most pressing necessities of the hours; that honesty, capacity, and fidelity constitute the only valid claim to public employment; that the offices of the government cease to be a matter of arbitrary favoritism and patronage, and that public station become again a post of honor.

The Republicans countered with a similar plank:

Any system of the civil service under which the subordinate positions of the government are considered rewards for mere party zeal is fatally demoralizing, and we, therefore, favor a reform of the system by laws which shall abolish the evils of patronage and make honesty, efficiency, and fidelity the essential qualifications for public position, without practically creating a life tenure of office.

It took the assassination of President Garfield by a disappointed office seeker to initiate the modern civil service movement. While the President lay dying, the National Civil Service Reform League was organized to bring about reform. Faced with an irresistible demand, Congress later yielded to pressure and passed the Pendleton Act of 1883, which still remains the basis upon which the American Federal civil service rests. President after president, under the wide discretionary powers of the bill, has expanded the system to a larger and larger percentage of Federal employees. President Arthur transferred 15,573 jobs from a basis of partisan appointment to that of the civil service; Cleveland, in his first term, 11,757; Harrison, 10,535; Cleveland, in his second term, 49,179; McKinley, 19,161; Theodore Roosevelt, 128,753; Taft, 47,657; Wilson, 165,515; Harding, 1,500; Coolidge, 20,365; Hoover, 35,398; F. D. Roosevelt, first two years, 10,865.

211

The movement during the last fifty years is a vivid picture of struggle, disappointment, and gradual progress against great odds. Theodore Roosevelt, particularly in his second term, attacked with great zeal the problem of the extension of the civil service, winning for it steadily greater public support. The classified civil service has, since the introduction of the Act of 1883, grown steadily in numbers, and the trend, in spite of some losses of territory once gained, has been moving slowly toward greater dependence upon the merit system. The World War period and the present economic emergency have led to the employment of many new officers outside the classified lists. Although the present incumbent in the White House on numerous occasions has given lip service to the merit system, actually, the spoils system has operated at a high rate under the aegis of the chairman of the Democratic National Committee. Although the President may say, as he did at the Yale Commencement in 1934: "I can't tell today the party affiliations of most of the responsible people in government, and it is a mighty good thing I can't," it is perfectly clear that Mr. Farley is fully acquainted with the facts. His philosophy as to appointments is well known and is summed up in these quotations which are taken from an article by him entitled "Passing Out the Patronage" which appeared in the August, 1933, issue of *The American Magazine:*

Patronage is a reward to those who have worked for party victory. It is also an assistance in building party machinery for the next election. It is also—and this the public usually forgets—the test by which a party shows its fitness to govern.

I think it is only fair that those men who worked to put Mr. Roosevelt into the presidency should be given jobs in the federal service and be given an opportunity to help him carry out his program. I think it is not only fair, but reasonable and intelligent as a policy.

A man may be a fine executive, but unless he's willing to work hard all day and sit up all night to help along the President's plans, we don't want him.

In other words, Loyalty is an aspect of merit.

In contrast to the acts of President Roosevelt's administration is the report submitted to Congress early in 1937 by his committee on administrative management which urges an extension of the merit system "upward, outward, and downward" and to include all positions in the executive branch other than policy-forming ones. Specifically the committee made five recommendations for the extension of the merit system:

(1) The merit system should be extended to positions in new and emergency agencies whose activities are to continue, and the President should be authorized to place such positions, including those in governmental corporations, in the classified civil service. (2) The merit system should be extended to permanent high posts and all other civilian positions in the regular departments and establishments. Exceptions should be made only in the case of such of the highest positions as the President may find to be principally policy-determining in character. (3) The merit system should be extended to the lowest positions in the regular establishments including those filled by skilled workmen and laborers. (4) The incumbent of any position which is placed within the classified civil service should receive civil-service status only after passing a special noncompetitive examination, following certification by the head of his agency that he has served with merit. (5) All civilian positions in regular departments and establishments now filled by presidential appointment should be filled by the heads of such departments or establishments, without fixed term, except under-secretaries and officers who report directly to the President or whose appointment by the President is required by the Constitution.

SPOILS SYSTEM VS. PUBLIC ADMINISTRATION

The fight is between the spoils system for party purposes, on the one side, and service administration for the American people on the other. Every apologist for spoils has advanced, in favor of its retention, the argument that without patronage the party cannot exist, and that the biparty system must disintegrate. European countries have shown, however, that a particularly vigorous party life can be maintained after reform in civil service. England is a particularly happy example. No upheavals occur in the permanent service of that country when there is a change of cabinet, yet England has an aggressively effective party system linked with a thoroughly efficient nonpartisan administration. Less than a hundred

213

offices in a civil service numbering many thousands are affected by a change in government, and these are purely political in nature and stamped as such. Elihu Root was of the opinion that "The spoils system is not essential to effective party organization but on the contrary. . . . it tends to keep out of the organization the men whose services would be most effective."

The evils inherent in spoils far exceed any potential benefits. Among the disadvantages are the complete demoralization of the government service, the gigantic turnover in personnel with a dislocation of long-time policy, slovenly and incompetent service to the public, graft and corruption, the pressure of job seekers on the executive, and enormous cost and waste. A nation pays a terrible price when it adopts the spoils system. William Bennett Munro, a man of mature judgment and a noted scholar, is authority for the statement that "The American city does not get more than sixty cents on the dollar for its pay-roll expenditures."

The gradual assumption by administration of its rightful role will remove the greatest weakness in American government. Sound principles of administration require, first of all, that politics be confined to its proper sphere—that of policy making. In other words, the determination, crystallization, and declaration of the will of the people. Policy making must be handled through elected officials, but no government requires too many agents of this type since only major executive positions are involved, such as president, governor, or mayor, members of the legislature, and the chiefs of local offices. The dividing line between elected political control and permanent administration should be set high up in the scale, although it is well to remember that the question of policy is closely intertwined with administration at points of transfer, necessitating at all times a proper balancing of functions. Nevertheless some line must be set where the political officer must keep hands off the administrator, since the misuse of an army of job holders by politicians is the major problem in

214

American government. It should be remembered that it is impossible for a government of spoils to do a job well and that the more a government has to do, the more vital it is that such a system be rooted out; otherwise, administration will break down completely under the gigantic burden of present-day tasks. To allow all-important services to be used to consolidate a party in power will be disastrous, and the American people must prevent such an outcome at all costs.

The danger is great. It should be remembered that in most of the agencies established since the beginning of the depression appointments have been authorized without regard to the Civil Service Act of 1883. Out of these new nonmerit jobs, totaling by the end of 1935 over two hundred thousand, an enormous patronage control has been established for the perpetuation of political power. The bulk of these appointments fell into the hands of the Democratic National Committee. So great was the patronage that this committee at one time rivaled the United States Civil Service Commission in its employment possibilities.

THE SERVICE STATE

War and depression have brought to the fore the new concept of the service state. Government now deals directly and intimately, and to a degree never before known, with the personal affairs of its citizens. The mere business of operating our national government is now the most extensive, complicated, and difficult administrative task in the world. The co-ordination of the hundreds of official agencies, each with the other, presents a problem not matched by any other nation. Millions on relief, loans extended to thousands of local subdivisions and private enterprises, low-cost home building on ninety per cent mortgages, individual bank deposits of some fifty million people guaranteed, supervision of millions of farm operations, and the training of some three to four hundred thousand young men in CCC camps make necessary a new concept of public administration in the United States.

215

It is folly to think of carrying a government of these gigantic services without putting at its disposal the finest administrative skill the country produces. These newer services require men and women equipped with the rigid discipline, the broad training, and the wide perspective gained through college and university training, supplemented by those who come up through the ranks, by virtue of native ability. American government must build an administrative personnel intelligent enough to meet the challenge of modern times. To do so, however, will require many adjustments in the American attitude toward government. Political control of administration must go. The upper levels of our permanent service must be strengthened with career men and women, while those entering the lower ranks must be afforded an opportunity for advancement on merit over a period of years. Finally the public service must be dignified and made more attractive so as to inspire continuous growth.

RECENT TRENDS

The casual observer may see little progress toward the attainment of these desirable objectives. He reads in the newspaper of the removal of a commission chairman. He hears the story, from a friend of the right political faith, of how jobs are being handed out to the faithful. He is not aware of the countless ways in which the principles of sound administration are being introduced by efficient civil service commissions. He is not acquainted with the newer types of civil service examinations which are being introduced here and there in order to attract the best of America's university and college graduates. He may read of a gift to establish a school of public administration at Harvard, but he has not been told of the rapid introduction of public service training among the outstanding institutions of the land. The student of administration, however, knows that many threads of examinations, of service, of training, and of tradition are being woven into a new pattern of American public service.

216

Progress has been made and is being made. The civil service—local, state, and national—is being extended and strengthened. Within the forty-eight states, the trend runs steadily in the direction of merit. Budget systems are being established, state governments reorganized, city manager plans introduced in more and more cities, and new personnel methods introduced in countless government offices. In time these efforts will consolidate in a tradition of American administrative policy. It may be well to outline a few of these later and more interesting developments in this newer phase of American politics.

The present movement toward a career service may be said to have begun with the suggestion of President Hoover's Research Committee on Recent Social Trends, January 1, 1933, that the Social Science Research Council pursue further the problem of public personnel. The Council appointed in December, 1933, a Commission of Inquiry on Public Service Personnel. This commission reported its findings and recommendations in January, 1935. It declared:

> The establishment of *career service* is, in the judgment of this Commission, the required next step in the history of American government. In the federal government, the state governments, and in the local governments, what we now need is the transformation of the public service to a career basis. This is the method by which our various governments may draw into their services their share of the capacity and character of the man power of the nation.
>
> Recruitment to each one of the career services should be articulated with the American educational system and with the age levels of young men and women who have reached the state of education and development fitting them for the lower grades of the various services.

The conclusions of the commission have met with an unusual response from our citizenry and from the civil service commissions of the Federal, state, and local governments. We are unmistakably at the beginning of an epoch in the development of our civil service even more significant than the period of reform which began in the eighteen eighties.

UNIVERSITY SUPPORT

More than a score of our universities and colleges have either inaugurated divisions of public service training or have greatly extended such facilities as they possessed for this purpose. Still others have announced research programs in the field of public administration looking toward training activities. Harvard University, University of California, University of Southern California, University of Michigan, University of Wisconsin, Wayne University of Detroit, American University, and New York University have each, among others, entered this field. Their programs have been accompanied by modifications in public recruitment policies which greatly increase the opportunities of college and university graduates for entrance into the public service. Even greater opportunities will flow from adoption of the recruitment standards outlined in President Roosevelt's Committee on Administrative Management of January, 1937. State and local civil service commissions, particularly those of New York, New Jersey, Wisconsin, and California, are no less inclined toward the standards of a career service.

NEW TYPES OF EXAMINATION

In the Federal service, there is not merely a continuance of and new emphasis on the traditional profession and technical examinations which have long been conducted at a high level of training, but there has been also an even more important trend toward recruitment on a university and college training basis in the general public administration examinations. Two outstanding examples can be cited. In 1935, the Federal commission established a general register entitled the Junior Civil Service Examiner List. This list was selected by an examination geared into the social science instruction of the colleges and universities of the country. It was used not merely by the civil service commission but by almost every operating department of the Federal government as well, and today the operating departments have advanced young men and women taken from this general register to important posts of responsibility. This was the first outstanding example of recruitment in the United States by an adaptation of the technique by which the British select general administrative ability. The appointments from the list number close to a thousand.

The second outstanding example is the recent examination given for social science analyst. This general register extends from junior to very high positions in the Federal government and is divided into approximately fifty sublists. It will be used by the operating departments of the Federal government as a general pool of outstanding potential administrative ability. It marks a second step in the recruitment of administrative ability on the college and university level and confirms the trend which the Federal government has announced in this field. Certain of the new operating units, such as the TVA, have even more advanced policies in this direction.

The state civil service commissions reflect the same general policy of recruiting at the college and university level for important and increasingly numerous administrative positions. In New York State, one can cite as examples the recruitment policies for placement and unemployment insurance in the Department of Labor and recruitment for the social service staff in the Department of Welfare. Connecticut and New Jersey, to cite the two neighboring state commissions, have the same marked policies.

In New York City, the policy of the public personnel agency has kept pace with Federal and state trends and, in some respects, has been in advance of them. Since 1934, the local commission has been engaged in a reclassification of the whole city service. The guiding policy behind this reclassification has been to reorganize the city service in such a way as to increase the opportunities for recruitment at the college and university level. Recent examinations reflect the determination of the local commission to recruit on this basis. The most important illustration is the recent creation of an administrative service in the city, a new departure for American local government and one which reflects official endorsement of the general policy of recruiting administrative capacities on a career basis geared into college and university training.

BUILDING FOR TOMORROW

No good thing can come about in a democracy without the whole-hearted support of the people. It takes time to supplant old ideas with new when people in the mass must be converted. The old philosophy of spoils will disappear slowly. Sooner or later, however, it must be supplanted by a new tradition of permanent nonpartisan administration and reinforced by a tradition which no politician will attempt to destroy. Certain of the English expressions have great significance. "It isn't done that way." "It isn't cricket." "It is unthinkable." Applied to government these expressions embody many constitutional maxims. They imply that certain ways of doing things aren't acceptable in good government. They just aren't done. Permanent administrative officers, for example, in England are not thrown out for political purposes—it isn't cricket. Civil officers are dignified servants of the king selected to perform a certain function necessary to any well-governed nation, just as the revered judges are chosen. These officers are permanent administrators. They do not mix in partisan politics—that would be unthinkable. They make no political speeches for a party; that would be bad form since they are on the king's business of administration. They must not be interfered with by the elected officers of the king—to do so would be unconstitutional. In America, however, traditions have run counter to these ideas. We shall have to build anew. The English tradition that politics and legislature must keep hands off the administrative domain is only slowly developing here. To bring about the complete acceptance of such an idea, the public must be educated to the real purposes and worth of the administrative branches of the government and to the realization that evolution of the modern service state demands impartial administration. Textbooks and teachers must drive home the paramount importance of the fourth arm of government.

The expansion of the fields of public service, the necessities of careful budgeting, the complexities of public finance, the interrelations of city planning and real estate, the growth of housing management, a nation looking to government insurance for its economic security, and the growth of technical knowledge are making a necessity for a new tradition of public administration in the United States. Technology cannot be handled by political hacks and lame ducks. Banking, law, medicine, civil and sanitary engineering, and a host of other vocations and professions offer careers in public, as well as in private, business. If public business is to survive, it must demand the same expertness as private enterprise, offer similar rewards, dignify administration with advancement, and provide permanency and retirement.

It will take vision on the part of public officials, as well as strong support on the part of the people, to evolve such a system. Civil service must become an aristocracy of ability not only in the scientific and professional fields but in administrative positions as well. To bring this about is the major task of American politics.

MUST DEVELOP AMERICAN WAYS

In doing so we may observe British, German, and French experiments, receive ideas from other countries, and, in some cases, adopt them, but the American problem is distinct and must be developed in American ways and approached in American terms. For example, there is no equivalent in the United States of an Oxford, Cambridge, or Edinburgh education. America has little enough of the classics left in its colleges and universities; therefore, a classical education can never become the basic preparation in this country for entering the permanent service. Germany offers much that is admirable

—its permanent civil service is expert, thoroughly trained, a picked class, but the relationship of university to the state in Germany is inconsistent with American theories of education. France culls out step by step from its educational system those students who do not measure up to its intellectual standards, finding at the end of the weeding-out process an aristocracy of brains capable of entering L'École Politechnique, where graduation leads to administration in the technical branches of the French civil service. America must and is working out its own problem in accordance with its own pattern. At times we may become discouraged and impatient with spoils backsliding and the continuous outcropping of outworn ideas. Yet the setback is temporary, for, when a broad view is taken over a long period of time, the progress being made is both astounding and stimulating. People in the United States are learning that they live under a government of men who must be trained to administer impartially and without political bias the law of the land. In a hundred different ways the dikes of sound tradition are being raised around a permanent service of administration in American government.

Chapter XIV

REFORM BEGINS AT HOME:
THE AMERICAN CITY

SAMUEL SEABURY

★ ★ ★ ★

THE American city, like most institutions, derives from a multitude of sources. It has both point of difference from, and resemblance to, its ancient predecessors.

The ancient cities did much to protect the health, safety, and convenience of their citizens. Rome, for example, in its great water system, its public baths, its police regulations of traffic, the removal of waste, the repair of its streets, its regulations limiting the height of buildings and their frontage upon the streets, discharged many functions which seem to correspond to those discharged by the modern city. Notwithstanding all this, the municipal problems created by our modern industrialism are fundamentally different from those with which ancient and medieval cities were required to deal.

Any modern city differs from the cities of the ancient and medieval world, not merely in the fact that it represents a greater concentration of people in a relatively smaller area, but in that it is state controlled and not autonomous; further, in that its population is composed of legally freemen, and even more fundamentally, in the fact that the modern city is the most highly concentrated expression of the industrialism of the age in which we live.

The American city originated from the chartered boroughs or municipal corporations, which, during the seventeenth and eighteenth centuries, were established in the English colonies. These charters were granted by the provincial governors on

223

the same basis as royal charters had been granted to the English boroughs. Like their English predecessors, they included judicial, legislative, and administrative powers which were limited and were subject to English law and the law of the Assembly of the province.

The inventions of the eighteenth century, which were but the forerunners of the great inventions which were to come with the introduction of steam and electricity, changed the methods of the production of wealth. While under the preceding order the workman labored in his home or his shop with the assistance of his apprentices and journeymen, all the problems which come from the concentration of great numbers in the modern factory were absent. With the concentration of great populations engaged in industrial processes, there developed political and economic consequences of vital import.

THE MODERN CITY HAS DISTINCTIVE PROBLEMS

Immigration and the growth of transportation facilities contributed to the rapid increase of the population and industry of American cities. With this increase went the extension of manhood suffrage, the popular election of the mayor and local officials, and the establishment of the bicameral legislative council. Concurrently with these innovations, the spoils system had taken root and became a distinctive attribute of municipal as well as of our state and national governments. Under it, municipal service ceased to be the primary object of municipal government, and for municipal service was substituted the definite objective of operating the municipal government so as to get the largest profits to strengthen the local political organization and enrich its leaders.

Remedies have been sought in a variety of ways. A host of new laws have been enacted, designed to eliminate sweatshops, regulate the hours of labor, and prescribe the conditions under which certain kinds of labor shall be performed. Problems as to the effect of the operation of factories and the effect of certain industries on the lives, the health, and the property

224

of those living and working in or near them were met by laws relating to nuisances and offensive or dangerous businesses. The danger of converting our streets into deep and unwholesome canyons has been met by zoning and building regulation and other laws.

The economic pressure in the cities, from which poverty, destitution, and social evils of various kinds result, presents a separate group of municipal difficulties which must be dealt with. The administration of charities has long been recognized as a proper function of a city. The manner in which these duties are discharged is reflected in our municipal hospitals, clinics, orphan asylums, and our unemployment relief bureaus.

The problem of policing a city, both in the prevention and detection of crime, presents peculiar difficulties which have been augmented by the advent of the automobile.

The supplying of the food which the city consumes calls into existence a multitude of municipal activities. The city is dependent for its food supply on outside agencies. In order to protect the health of the members of the community, it becomes necessary for the city to place regulations upon the importation of food, with a view of preventing unwholesome and adulterated foods from finding their way into the city.

Safeguards against the potential danger of plague, epidemics, and contagious diseases must be provided. The danger incident to fire hazards and the utilization of effective equipment to deal with them present great difficulties in their solution—difficulties greater in nature, as well as in degree, as the population grows and the height of buildings increases.

Industry is dependent upon transportation. A large city supports itself by its intercity industry and by participating in the commerce of the world. It becomes essential, therefore, for the city, sometimes in co-operation with another state or city, to lay down roads, highways, and streets in order to facilitate travel. Tunnels under rivers, and bridges over them are, of course, a part of the necessary highways which must be

225

established. Some of these require not only the highest degree of engineering skill but also sound methods of financing, without which they could not be created or economically administered.

The modern city is required to give attention not only to the physical and economic needs of the community; there is a vast realm which has to do with the establishment of schools, colleges, and universities, as well as providing the means which enable its people to satisfy their desire for recreation and cultural improvement. The establishment of museums of art and of natural history, opera houses, and, in many cases, municipal theaters, is essential. Playgrounds for the children of the city and gymnasiums and recreational facilities for its adult population are but the recognition of the necessity for satisfying natural and essential needs.

The city is a growing body. It expands not only geographically but also in the nature and extent of its activities. The lines along which its growth must develop cannot be left merely to chance, but, if the best results are to be achieved, must follow a carefully developed plan, made sometimes in co-operation with neighboring cities whose populations are affected by similar social and economic influences. In this way, proper planning activities may not be limited merely to the city boundaries, but become regional in character.

I am not attempting to describe all the functions of the modern city, but merely to refer to some of the most important, to indicate what tremendous tasks are involved in the conduct of the city of today. Nowhere else, I venture to think, can so many gigantic problems which affect so directly the lives, health, and happiness of so many people be found as those that are involved in the conduct of the modern city. In attempting to visualize the intricacy and difficulty of meeting these problems, bear in mind that the American city is the abode of more than a third of the people of the United States, and that the agelong tendency of people to drift from the rural districts to the city still continues. One-half of the people

226

of the country live within fifty miles of a city of a hundred thousand or more, and over eighty per cent reside within one hour's motor journey of a city of twenty-five thousand or more. The American city of today is bounded not only by the territorial limits of its "greater cities," but its far-flung influence covers the vast populations which inhabit its metropolitan area. The same social and economic forces frequently operate over an area which is subject to the legal and political jurisdiction of different cities or states. The result is that millions who are one people, respecting social and economic considerations, are subject to the laws and regulations of different civil divisions. In other words, the economic and social groups do not coincide with the civil boundaries which have been prescribed, thus revealing the difference between the "real city" and the "political city." These metropolitan districts contain populations so great as to be comparable only with the populations of states and nations.

CITIES VARY IN GOVERNMENTAL STRUCTURE

The proper performance of functions as multifarious, as diversified, as important, and as difficult as those involved in the administration of our great cities requires, of course, a large, carefully organized staff, operating under competent and honest executives and trained administrators. The veritable army employed in the enforcement of laws and regulations presents a variety of economic, administrative, and political problems of the first magnitude in municipal administration.

Our several cities vary in the types of governmental structures which have been created to accomplish the performance of these functions, particularly with regard to the exercise of executive and administrative powers. Some cities have the commission form of government, in which the executive power and much, if not all, of the administrative power are lodged in an elected group, each one of whom has co-ordinate powers.

227

In other cities, the people elect a mayor, who is the chief executive and appoints the heads of the various administrative departments. In still others, the people elect a council which, in turn, selects a city manager to act as chief executive and administrator. Some cities have a legislative branch, or even two legislative bodies, elected by the people. In some cities, the members of these bodies consist of representatives elected from districts, counties, or boroughs; in others, their election is city-wide. The method of election varies. In some places the officials are elected by plurality vote; in others, by preferential voting; and in some cases, as for instance in the election of a council of multiple members, by proportional representation. Where a plurality of the votes cast is sufficient to elect a candidate, it can, and frequently does, happen that the person elected is, in fact, the choice of only a minority of the voters. Where a candidate is elected by preferential voting, the voters indicate not only their first choice, but their second and subsequent preferences among the candidates, and if no candidate receives a majority of first-choice votes, the second and subsequent choices of the voters are given effect until some candidate has a majority. In elections to a multiple-member body by proportional representation, each voter, though entitled to have his ballot counted for one candidate only, indicates on his ballot the order of his preferences among all the candidates. Candidates receiving the necessary quota of first choices are elected. By a process of transferring to subsequent choices the votes cast for persons who do not receive sufficient first-choice votes to reach the quota, the ballots ultimately concentrate upon candidates who represent the choices of sufficient voters to constitute the quota. In this way every group is assured of representation in the body, according to its relative voting strength.

In every properly governed city the administrative functions are segregated according to the type of function to be performed, and those charged with responsibility for the proper performance of each are answerable to the mayor or the city manager or the council, according to the nature of the governmental structure.

The types of city government to which I have referred represent the entity which we know as a city as it is described by charter and statute. This entity might be called the *city of the statute book*. It has its executive head or heads, its legislative branch or branches, and its administrative departments or bureaus, all of which co-operate, theoretically, to supply the people of the city with a government which secures the greatest good for the greatest number.

OFFICEHOLDERS SOMETIMES BETRAY THEIR TRUST

In his *City of God*, St. Augustine compared the Earthly City, "the queen of the world and the slave of her own ambition," with the Heavenly City, only to find the greatest differences between them. Without wishing to compare the American *city of the statute book* with the Heavenly City, it is nevertheless true that the differences which exist between the *city of the statute book* and the *city of reality* are as great as were the differences in the two cities which St. Augustine compared. *The differences result largely from political and illegal discrimination in the enforcement of the law by those who secure control of government and operate it, not for the benefit of the governed, but for their own enrichment.*

The structure of most of our modern city governments is intricate and complicated in the extreme. In it is an elaborate system of boards, bureaus, and commissions whose function it is to issue permits of one kind or another—permits for buildings, permits for the sale of food, permits for conducting various kinds of businesses, permits for the operation of transportation lines, and permits for many other things. These agencies are created ostensibly to protect the public against the issuing of such permits to persons not fit or qualified to receive them, by requiring the submission of proof of due compliance with the salutary conditions prescribed by law.

Yet, as a matter of fact, each and all of these functions have frequently, in the modern American city, been utilized as a

229

means of personal profit to those who control the administration. Police departments in our great cities have been prostituted to the function of protecting, rather than detecting, crime. Dealers in narcotics pay the police to be let alone. Other illegal enterprises are subject to a fixed charge which is met with the regularity of an honestly imposed rent. Racketeers of various kinds assist political leaders in controlling primaries and elections, and these leaders, in return for this and other considerations, provide the racketeers with protection against police interference. Those who conduct the fire departments of our cities are sometimes as much interested in the collection of illicit commissions from the suppliers of fire-fighting apparatus as they are in extinguising fires. Political favoritism and other considerations produce official blindness to infractions of laws enacted to reduce fire hazards or even to prevent loss of life from fires. Money eases the way of the transgressor even after conviction and during confinement in penal institutions, and if the price is high enough, representations can be made, through the control of parole boards, which apparently justify a governor in granting a pardon. The suppliers of the food and clothing which the wards of our charitable institutions and insane asylums use, pay their toll to those in charge of administering the charities of the city. In some cases, profits are derived by the delivery of unwholesome foods to city institutions, although the city pays the current price of good food. Even in the distribution of emergency relief, the local political organization in New York City has collected its toll. The right to participate in such relief funds was supposed to be determined by cards issued to those in need by the Public Welfare Department, but, in fact, they were distributed to the district leaders of Tammany Hall and by them apportioned among their faithful followers while an election campaign was in progress.

In schools, the relatives and favorites of political leaders may obtain the choice teaching and supervising positions. In the matter of improvements, whether they have to do with the granting of franchises, the cleaning of streets, the building of bridges and sewers, or the maintenance of public parks, the same system of plunder operates. The contracts under which much of the work is let are given nominally to the lowest bidder, but they reach the hands only of those who pay for the contracts they obtain. Transcripts of sworn testimony might be quoted, showing the money extorted in the administration of zoning regulations, the granting of franchises, or in the matter of sewer contracts, for the making of which contracts a borough president went to jail.

The activities of these licensing and contract-awarding agencies, instead of being bulwarks against injustice and danger to the people, may create more privileges which are for sale to the highest bidder. Under such conditions, the man who is entitled to relief for the asking, frequently can get what is justly his only by paying for it, while the man who is not entitled to assistance can, nevertheless, get it if he is willing to pay the price. Practically every license, from a permit to run a pushcart to a permit to run a transportation system, in many cities must be bought. The price goes, not to the city, but to the corrupt group who control and manipulate these agencies for their own enrichment. At the same time, the racketeer, protected by politics and, indeed, often in partnership with it, takes his toll at every stage in the life of the city. Cars of material which reach the city by rail, cargoes that enter its port, pay in some form for the privilege of unloading. Fruits, groceries, vegetables—indeed everything we eat and drink; sand, brick, stone, cement—everything that goes into the buildings over our heads must pay its toll to the politician-protected racketeer. These costs are added to the expense of the distributor, and as these goods are distributed throughout the nation, the people of every section unconsciously pay their tribute to these sinister agencies.

In this statistical age it would be interesting to learn the amount of the plunder derived by local rulers from the people of the city from whom they extort their profits. Suggestive light upon the subject was revealed in the investigation in New York City where it appeared that the bank accounts of about a dozen public officers or political leaders showed they had acquired, in a relatively short period of time, about sixteen millions of dollars, the source of which they were utterly unable to explain, but which the surrounding circumstances clearly demonstrated to be tainted. Of course, the amounts disclosed in bank accounts are but a small portion of the money which the city rulers extort from those whose interests they are pledged to conserve and protect; many are too shrewd to leave so clear a trail of their activities.

The story is too long even for adequate summarization. Yet these matters to which I have referred are not isolated instances; on the contrary, they represent methods of procedure frequently employed. They evidence what in truth and in fact, our municipal government has too often been. What is the use of gathering our ideas of municipal government from the study of the statutes which in express terms prohibit each and all of these things? The statute book does not show the real government of the city. The real government of the city consists of the manner in which its municipal functions are in fact performed. Only by appreciating the hideous system as it too often exists can we hope to be able to rid ourselves of it.

PUBLIC APATHY RESULTS FROM CIVIC EVILS

The view is oftentimes expressed that the evils which have arisen in our great cities are due to the apathy of the people. This view is only partially true. Fairness requires us to realize that to a large extent this apathy is the result of constitutional and statutory conditions designed to benefit local political machines at the expense of the public by denying them free opportunities for the expression of their will. Where these opportunities are denied, public apathy exists, but it is, in a great measure, the result, rather than the cause, of the evils. The American city has grown more rapidly than suitable

232

plans for its growth could be made, and before even an adequate social consciousness of its needs could be formed. Moreover, the city has not been free to develop. It has been obliged to make progress within the narrow limits of power granted to it by the state. It has been bound by state laws prescribing the methods by which nominations for office are to be made, by which its elections are to be conducted and its votes counted. These conditions have given rise to the political machine and the local boss, and in fact have created a class which enjoys special privileges in making nominations, conducting elections, and counting the votes. In its financial operations the city has been similarly bound and restricted, the state going so far as to prescribe by mandatory legislation the number of employees and the salaries that are to be paid to them. The cities have not yet attained home-rule powers, and, even where the grants of powers have been most liberal, they do not impair the authority of the ever-present overlordship of the state, controlled as it is by forces outside the city and not directly responsible to it. Until the way is found by which the people of the city may legally control their own government, the responsibility for the evils of the city cannot be attributed solely to popular apathy. Inaction induced by a recognition of impotence under a rigged election machinery and state control may evidence despair, but it is not apathy. In cities such as the city of Cincinnati, where the citizens are accorded the power to act, they have increasingly availed themselves of their opportunities and have manifested an alert and intelligent interest in the affairs of their city.

A recitation of the provisions of the statute book indicates the sort of government which we are supposed to receive. It is manifest from a recital of these functions how important it is that they be properly administered, and how tragic the consequences to the citizens of the city where they are not properly performed and the efficiency of their administration is perverted by the use of political influence. It is difficult to visualize a worse calamity that could overtake a city than

233

that these delicate and vital functions, affecting as they do the life, safety, and comfort of the people, should be prostituted for the purpose of strengthening a political organization and enriching its venal leaders. It would be a mistake, however, to believe that the evils end there.

CITY PROBLEMS BECOME NATIONAL IN SCOPE

The problems of city life affect not only the large numbers who live within the city, but also millions who dwell elsewhere. From the great cities radiate economic, political, and social influences, far-reaching and powerful in their effect.

We must keep in mind the fact that the powers which control such cities as New York, Philadelphia, Boston, and Chicago are powerful in the national conventions which select candidates for president and vice-president of the United States. To these national conventions the two major parties send from the cities great blocks of delegates, who often vote as a unit for the candidates whose sympathies they believe they can enlist, or from whom they expect consideration in the form of Federal patronage. Oftentimes in our national conventions, the votes of delegates from these great cities have been the deciding factor in determining the person nominated. Yet these delegates are often selected by the worst elements of the city. Not only in national conventions, but in the election of United States senators and members of the House of Representatives, or in the selection of a speaker, the power of local political machines exercises a controlling influence upon our national and foreign politics. During the last administration of President Wilson, the members of Congress from the City of New York, who were absolutely controlled by the Boss of Tammany Hall, held the balance of power. They used this power as a means of extorting Federal patronage and in influencing the determination of matters of grave national and international concern. Even more potent is the influence of these city machines, and the evils for which they are responsible, upon officials of the state of which the city is a part.

234

The influence of the city is as potent in its economic effect upon state and nation as it is in its political consequences. The food supplies which come into the market places of the cities are distributed throughout the nation to meet the needs of millions of people. For example, twenty per cent of the population of the United States receives its fresh fish through the port of New York City. Here, powerful racketeers, in league with political agencies, played a dominant part in the conduct of this industry. Every fisherman bringing a haul into New York was required to pay tribute to dock his boat, while the wholesaler paid tribute to get his fish from the dock to the counter in the market. The toll in these cases was extorted by making it impossible for those who did not pay to hire labor; in cases where payment was refused, a further payment was imposed by spraying the stock with kerosene oil. The transmission from the wholesaler to the retailer was subject to a like levy. To avoid these ministrations the dealers paid. The toll thus levied was added to the cost of the product and was collected from all those, far and wide, who bought it.

It is in the cities, also, that the forces of the underworld have their organized groups and exert their sinister powers. The underworld of New York acts in affiliation with the underworld of other great centers of population. An illicit traffic, as, for instance, the sale of narcotics, the execution of criminal designs of gangsters and gunmen, can exist only as the result of the political protection which is accorded by the governing officials of our great cities. In partial return for such political protection, these underworld forces hold themselves subject to the direction of political leaders in order to facilitate them in securing the majorities which they need on Election Day. It is from within these groups that the political leaders recruit the floaters and repeaters and guerilla warriors upon whose services they so generously draw on Election Day.

I do not wish to labor the point, but I do wish to make clear that the economic, political, and social effects of vicious municipal government are not confined to the municipal

235

limits, but operate upon the people of the nation as a whole.

EXPERIENCE SUGGESTS CERTAIN MODIFICATIONS

In the face of the challenge which the conditions prevailing under our municipal governments present, let us attempt to outline the changes which must be made to establish responsible and representative government within the American city. In order to achieve such a government, our cities must be divorced from state and national politics, and their people freed from the rule of the local boss and political machine. The principles upon which we can rely to accomplish this are few and simple.

The legislative power should be vested in a comparatively small council; the executive or administrative powers should be vested either in a mayor or city manager, and the judicial power should be vested in the inferior municipal courts, subject to the control of the higher courts. The administrative departments of the city should be relatively few and directly responsible to the mayor or the city manager, as the case may be.

In order to be representative in character, it is essential that the method of election of the council shall accord recognition to every substantial group in proportion to its numbers. The present method of voting in most cities does not do this. Insistence upon nominations for office being made in party primaries insures partisan government and otherwise increases, at the expense of the public, the power of the political machine or party boss. The system already described, known as proportional representation, or the single transferrable vote, is admirably adapted to remedying this evil and enables, in effect, the real functions of nomination and election to be performed as the result of a single act on Election Day. In relation to the executive and administrative powers, two theories are to be considered—one, that of a strong mayor elected by the people, and the other, that of a city manager

236

selected by a small municipal council. Either may be made to serve a useful purpose. In either case, mayor or city manager, the powers vested in him should be broad and he should be held immediately responsible for the manner in which those powers are exercised. There is also much to be said in favor of having the chief financial officer of the city elected by the people and held directly responsible to them for the manner in which he performs his duties. When the mayor and chief financial officer are elected by the people, it is of prime importance that they should be nominated outside of the party primary and voted for under a preferential system of voting which ensures the election of the person who is the choice of the majority of the electors. Neither in the case of members of the council nor in the case of the mayor and comptroller—or any other municipal officer who is to be elected— is there any justification for a ballot with party emblems or other party designations upon it. Municipal government is really the rendering of social services through its administrative agencies. It is not, or rather should not be, at all a matter of party control. Stringent civil service rules should be adopted, and, even more important, agencies should be established which can adequately enforce the rules which govern the civil service of the city. Civil service commissions should not be appointed and be subject to removal by partisan agencies. The selection of such commissioners should be made from groups suggested by nonpartisan cultural agencies within the community. There are no more conspicuous failures in our municipal governments than the bipartisan boards and commissions that have been appointed. They make only a nominal pretense to fairness and in practice result in a bipartisan combination of the two major political parties. Government by a partisan machine is bad, but government by two party machines is infinitely worse.

Persons in the administrative service of the city should be required to refrain from any political activities whatsoever, except that of voting, while they continue in the city employ.

The same incentive to padding the pay rolls would not exist were a place upon that pay roll to result in disqualifying the occupant from engaging in political activities.

REFORMS NEEDED IN CITY COURTS

The judicial powers which must be exercised within the city must be performed to a large extent by local inferior courts. The greatest abuses in the administration of justice have arisen from the fact that these local inferior court judges are either chosen by popular elections, having been nominated by party leaders, or else are appointed by the mayor upon the recommendation of and in deference to party leaders. This system is the fundamental vice that underlies the administration of justice in the local courts of our cities. It is the direct cause to which is attributable the practices which in some cities have made the very name of the courts of justice a designation of reproach and shame. The remedy for this evil —and it is one of the greatest evils in the government of the modern American city—is that these local judges of inferior courts should not be chosen by popular election upon the nomination of party leaders, or appointed by the mayor or any other political agency within the city. These local judges often perform the functions of magistrates. Many of them perform duties which correspond to the duties now performed in the Federal system by United States commissioners. From the inception of our government, these United States commissioners have been appointed by the judges of the higher courts. The system has worked admirably and has been practically free from political interference with the processes of justice. In many cases, the higher courts already are vested with a visitorial and supervisory power over the action of these inferior court judges and also have the power to remove them where they have been guilty of improper conduct. Our cities should go a step further and provide that the court empowered to supervise and remove inferior court judges for cause should have the power to appoint them in the first instance. Under the system which prevails in some of our cities today the higher courts have the power to remove a judge for improper action or, as was done in New York City, for being improperly influenced in his judicial conduct by a political leader. The successor of the judge who has been removed, however, is appointed, nominally by the mayor, but sometimes in fact by the same political leader. This is worse than an absurdity: it is sheer stupidity.

The conditions which prevail and the evils to which they have given rise in American cities are, of course, not uniform, but those which I have described are, to a greater or less degree, not uncommon in the administration of our city governments. All of the instances to which I have alluded were established by sworn proof introduced in the investigations made into the government of the City of New York. The principles of city government which point the way out of the existing situation are not new or untried. Generally speaking, and with modifications to meet local conditions here and there, they represent the considered judgment of many who have made a study of the problems of municipal government.

Government founded upon such principles should lift the cities out of the mire of partisan politics in which most of them are now submerged and open a new era of progress within the sphere of Western civilization. Government of this character in our centers of population would ensure rich endowments in comfort and happiness to the millions who live within them and would likewise exert an elevating and inspiring influence upon our state and national politics.

AMERICAN CITIES HAVE A RECORD OF ACHIEVEMENT

Appreciation of the abuses to which partisan political control has subjected our cities must not lead us to close our eyes to the really great achievements of the American city. Engineering skill and the art of the architect have produced public improvements and buildings which will rank among the outstanding achievements of the age in which we live. Nor is it only in these respects that the American city has glorified itself. The educational facilities which the American city has made available to its citizens are, perhaps, its foremost accomplishment, from which springs the hope that in the future defects which exist in the political government of our cities may be overcome. Another of the creditable distinctions of the American city is that it has been first among the cities to establish playgrounds for children.

Its record in providing the means for public education, the erection and maintenance of public libraries, museums of art and natural history, and its efforts to afford its citizens opportunity to hear and enjoy good music constitute some of the finest pages of its recent history. Public efforts in these directions have sometimes been supplemented by private benefactions and unofficial individual initiative, but the joint result of private and public endeavor has brought within the gates of our cities rich treasures to inspire and develop the cultural tastes of their citizens. Improvements, such as these, which have been made, even in politically controlled cities, demonstrate that there is no cause for a pessimistic attitude toward the American city. The experiment now being made in New York City is itself evidence of the improvements that can be made. The prevailing political conditions can and will be changed. Indeed, the American city offers the brightest hope for the future, but before it can realize this hope it must win its own political freedom. American citizenship can answer no more useful and patriotic call than to rid our city governments of the evils now inherent in them and, by simplifying their form and introducing representative processes within them, take a long stride toward the establishment of a democracy, national as well as local, which will be worthy of the purposes and ideals of the American people.

Chapter XV

CRIME: A SOCIAL CANCER

Lewis E. Lawes

★ ★ ★ ★

WHEN a newsboy shouts: "Policeman Shot in Daring Robbery!" or, "Man Found Murdered!" most people can hardly wait to read about the crime. If the criminal is finally apprehended, lurid accounts of his escapades fill the newspapers. Feature writers pen sensational stories about his capture, his plans to "beat the rap," his many female admirers, his contempt for law and order. Those are the details which the average citizen acquires from the press. He knows a great deal about the very last phases of the criminal's career; very little about why that career reached a murderous climax. He is deluded into believing that the perpetrator of the crime awoke one morning and decided that he no longer wanted to be a law-abiding citizen. Accordingly resentment against the offender reaches a high pitch. Months later, when the news is flashed to the world that the desperado paid his debt to society by forfeiting his life in the electric chair, citizens sit back complacently and remark that justice has triumphed.

I often wonder why the press does not also print some details about the criminal's early life, and mention the various factors, social and economic, leading to his downfall. If that were done, perhaps more people would realize that executing or imprisoning the offenders does not solve the crime problem. True, those men will not be able to engage in further depredations. But the same conditions which brought about their misfortune will create a new crop of criminals to take their place.

As long as crime has existed, there has been an emphasis on the punishment of the criminal after the offense has been committed, rather than an emphasis on prevention.

Prisons are the recipients of every known type of social failure. With the exception of those who are psychopathic or in other respects mentally unbalanced, there is hardly a man now behind bars who could not have been a useful, upright citizen had the community been aware of its obligations.

ENVIRONMENT AND CRIME

No man is born a criminal, nor does he become one in most instances unless he has lived in an unfavorable environment or associated with unsavory acquaintances. Case records at Sing Sing show that the great majority of the men were launched into criminal careers during early childhood. Furthermore, it is revealed that at no time was any concerted effort made to redirect them. To ascertain what type of preventive measures could have saved those men we should ask: "What are the characteristics of offenders now in prison?" The answer may be found when we study the life histories of some inmates.

Take the case of Richard Blake—a well-set-up youngster of ten, with nothing in his external aspect likely to arouse in the casual observer a suspicion that baffling problems lay beneath the surface. But underneath his laughter there was deep, uncomprehending pain. Richard loved his parents. The father, who was a carpenter and small contractor, used to take the boy along to his various job locations. Richard enjoyed the smell of fresh-cut wood, and was happy when he was allowed to play with some tools.

Suddenly, Richard's little world collapsed about him. There had been quarrels. Then the parents didn't live together anymore, and Richard remained with his mother. The separation, which he could not altogether understand, made him very unhappy. While he loved his mother, he also wanted to be with his father.

Outwardly there was no change in Richard. However, he began to play truant from school. Richard was interested in the kind of work his father did, and would go to watch men building houses. Furthermore, his mother was rarely at home, and he stayed away on many occasions till late at night.

He was ready enough to enter into the plans of comrades, and this quality soon involved him in most of the projects devised by the boys of his neighborhood. Unfortunately, the gang which haunted the candy store on the corner where Richard lived had developed a taste for the kind of adventures that could hardly win the approval of parents and elders. He finally joined a crowd of boys who robbed a grocery store. All were caught, and Richard was placed on probation.

Although his mother was greatly worried about him, no attempt seems to have been made at the critical moment to diagnose his difficulty. In the years that elapsed since then, he has been constantly in and out of trouble. Now, barely eighteen years old, the gates of Sing Sing have closed behind him because he was convicted of a robbery during which a storekeeper was shot.

This is by no means an isolated case. Juvenile delinquency is an all too common by-product of divorce and desertion—and in our times there is one divorce for every six marriages. I grant that other factors besides the broken home may have brought about Richard's criminal activities, but there is no doubt that had Richard's parents been able to exert a healthier influence upon him, his misfortune might have been avoided.

Other abnormal conditions in the home may sometimes bring misfortune to youngsters. After all, the home does not exist in a vacuum. It is part and parcel of the community that surrounds it.

It is no accident then, that from the chill, depressing slum areas of our big cities comes the raw material that fills the ranks of crime. In some instances, it is true, parents give way

243

to the general hopelessness of these poverty-stricken neighborhoods and become problem cases themselves. Certainly, in the homes over which they rule, their own bad example and the general vicious tone of the environment are not conducive to the flowering of high ideals.

But all too often the child's misbehavior is due, not to example, but to poverty itself—the inability of the parents to procure what they themselves recognize as the child's needs.

To single out for particular attention the case of any one of these children of the poor would be a misleading and futile gesture on my part. For there is nothing individual, nothing dramatic, about their stories. In fact, it is only through the cumulative effect of the whole that the dull monotony and the deadly sameness of their lives becomes so overwhelmingly horrible to the observer.

Let us look through the window of a typical cold-water flat. On the rickety table in the middle of the cheerless room are the few pitiful scraps that the family calls supper. Parents whose nerves are frayed by unceasing and fruitless attempts to gnaw an existence out of life find relief for their pent-up emotions through constant bickerings over the most petty and trivial matters.

The father's bitter resentment against the hopelessness that engulfs him sometimes takes expression in blows aimed at the wan face of his son, who has already found that his home life is unbearable. One day the boy packs his meager belongings and is gone.

Let us lay our scene in three homes where such discord has arisen between parents and children—Chicago, a Pennsylvania mining town, and Boston. Three cities—three boys. And the great melting pot of the road throws together those hapless creatures with a grudge against the world. There are no memories to fall back upon, nothing to brighten their future.

Somewhere, somehow, they find a gun. They will make their own "breaks."

"Reach for the sky," one of the boys tells a cashier. But a nervous finger presses the trigger.

Three youths are electrocuted; society is avenged. The names—does it matter? The ages, eighteen, nineteen, and twenty.

Fiction? These three boys died in the electric chair at Sing Sing.

Many of these underprivileged children are practically driven into crime. Deprived of their right to a normal home life, the street soon becomes the most vital part of their lives. Where there are no socially desirable influences to counteract the distorted notions that their homes have given them, there is every likelihood that delinquency will follow.

The simplest desires are often beyond the means of these youngsters. They quickly learn that they must "take" whatever they want. Many criminal careers are launched when the gang breaks into the corner candy store in order to get the sweets they cannot afford. Of course, I do not mean to say that all slum children become criminals. The important thing to bear in mind is that survey after survey has shown that most of our youthful offenders are products of large families and the overcrowded conditions of our slums.

THE FAILURE OF THE SCHOOL

In the midst of this wilderness the school should be an oasis; it should help to adjust these children to the world in which they must live. However, in looking over my records at Sing Sing, I find that the average convict does not progress beyond the fifth grade.

Sometimes the parent is forced to remove the child through sheer necessity. The school, however, fails to hold the interest of many of its pupils because no attempt is made to individualize the instruction through diagnosis of the differences in temperament, capabilities, and home environments of individual children.

Like "Fingers"—as his friends in Sing Sing call him. Fingers had once gone to school. He didn't mind learning how to read and write. "A feller is gotta know that stuff," he once told me. But when, in about the fifth grade, the teacher

245

says that Johannesburg is one of the principal cities of South Africa, Fingers asks, "So what?" And when the teacher talks about Ponce de Leon and the fountain of youth, Fingers decides that he and the school do not get along together.

To get down to the bottom of things in a hurry, as Fingers would say, he came up to Sing Sing one day. It seems that he had taken a course in pickpocketing instead of continuing his studies.

A year after he entered Sing Sing, Fingers was induced to go to the Prison School. He learned a trade, auto mechanics, and became really enthusiastic about it. Then one day he said to me. "Gee, Warden, if I'd a had a chance to study mechanics when I wuz a kid, I wouldn't be here now."

Maybe I should not have taken his remarks seriously. Perhaps he was just trying to win my sympathy. But I can't help thinking that he and many others like him could have been kept within the school system if some attempt were made to place him in a class catering to his abilities. As far as Fingers is concerned, I am certain that, had he received some vocational training during his school days, his delinquency might have been avoided. In many instances, the child who is backward in his academic studies is ashamed of the showing he makes before his brighter classmates. However, the opportunity to demonstrate his manual abilities would compensate for this.

It is painful for me to relate how many men now in prison show marked ability to engage in various trades. It is a shame that their talents come to light for the first time in a prison. It is a tragedy that we must develop their capacities behind bars, when that role should have been assumed by the schools in the first place.

There is no doubt that if more men could be induced to complete even a rudimentary education, delinquency would be minimized. It is true with regard to the usual grammar school education, but it is even more conspicuously true of the need for vocational training. It becomes clearly evident

246

when we observe that many youngsters who leave school find that their lack of training for specific work makes it impossible for them to secure employment. As a result they are bound to steal in order to eke out an existence. Some may find work, but, obviously they receive small salaries. Frequently, they are unable to satisfy their wants because of their limited earning capacities. At this point, temptation often gets the better of them, and many ultimately find themselves in prison.

Leisure-time activities cannot be overlooked when we consider those factors which influence a youngster's conduct and attitude toward life. After all, a child may receive an adequate education and live under the most wholesome home conditions, and yet be misguided by undesirable associates. The boys with whom he plays, the places where such play occurs, and the leaders with whom he comes in contact from day to day are but a few of the influences that affect the growing boy.

THE GANG SPIRIT

Most youngsters possess the tendency to group together during recreation periods. Those who comprise such groups will undoubtedly acquire the character traits of their leaders. If the head of the group already possesses habits which are socially objectionable, it is inevitable that he and his followers will find antisocial gang play their most cherished outlet. The young leader, already a delinquent, will teach his followers how to steal and will inculcate in them beliefs which will serve no other purpose than to arouse a feeling of disrespect for law and order. He will set the example for others and, because of his warped conceptions of life, will lead those who unfortunately come under his influence into channels which will cause all concerned to become menaces to the welfare of society. The great danger of gang play is that it may be carried over from childhood into adult life.

It is undeniably true that in most instances gangs exist because of inadequate or unattractive leisure-time activities.

247

The best way to break up these groups is to provide facilities for desirable play activities under competent leadership.

Recreation centers, particularly in the slum areas, are sorely lacking. Too frequently the children are forced to play in the streets. The policeman chases them because there is a likelihood that windows will be smashed during the ball game. Perhaps neighbors may have been complaining. Then again, the officer may prevent play because he feels that it is dangerous in view of the fact that automobiles whirl by. In any case, he becomes the boys' enemy and every attempt is made to outwit him. Thus, even at an early age, children learn to disrespect the men who represent authority.

Where can those youngsters go? Recreation centers and parks are not often available. They must, therefore, loiter in hallways or on street corners, perhaps frequent pool rooms and other undesirable places.

While it is true that such private institutions as the Boy Scouts, boys' clubs, and settlement houses do splendid work to obviate such conditions, the extent of their efforts is limited.

The community itself must solve the play problem. For every childrens' court there should be hundreds of playgrounds; for every reform school there should be a thousand supervised play streets. Our reformatories might then be less crowded.

Whether play activities are to be supervised by the school or other social agencies, trained recreation leaders are necessary. Very often it has been shown that when members of boy gangs come under the influence of such leaders, seldom, if ever, do they manifest any desire to rejoin their old associates. The reasons are obvious. When boys obtain healthy and attractive outlets for their energies, they are contented and will never seek other types of recreation.

Everything which the child learns tends to affect him in later years. As an individual becomes older, the habits which he has already acquired and which may be deeply ingrained in his make-up prevent him from acquiring new ones which might aid his normal growth into manhood. It is therefore essential that we do everything in our power to redirect socially maladjusted boys before it is too late. The delinquent boy is the potential adult criminal. He can only be guided from the sphere of antisocial influence, before he becomes habitually maladjusted, by removing him from an unfavorable environment and replanting him in healthier and more desirable surroundings.

During the eighteen years that I have been warden of Sing Sing Prison, approximately twenty-five thousand men have been sentenced to that institution. Those men were received singly and in groups. It is tragic to watch them as they enter the portals of the prison. Very often they are immature boys of sixteen or seventeen. Most of them come from areas that have poorly supervised play facilities. As they walk up the prison steps shackled to one another, it is apparent that the majority of them never enjoyed the happiness of youth. At an age when life should appear brightest to them, they can look forward to nothing more than an existence behind bars.

At the present time, prisons are more crowded than ever before in our history. In the state of New York, a prison costing nine million dollars, is being erected. But every time such an institution has to be built, at such tremendous cost, society should take stock of itself.

OUR SOCIAL INSTITUTIONS ARE RESPONSIBLE

Why are so many men confined behind bars? In view of the records of offenders, it is obvious that it is due to the fact that the community lacks the foresight to realize that the cost of crime prevention would be far less than any sum expended to apprehend and incarcerate the offender.

We must bear in mind that the faults of all our social institutions become the problems of penology. Prisons attempt to readopt the offender into social life after the home, the school, and the church have failed. Logic demands that the community devote more attention to strengthening the social institutions that are failing so often to make useful citizens out of those who have been on the border line between crime and a normal adjustment to society. Prisons are crowded today because society ignores these fundamental factors.

But there are other essential matters that cannot be overlooked in connection with the many problems engendered by crime.

We are constantly inculcating in the minds of young men the necessity of leading a clean life; that crime does not pay. Very frequently, however, the ethical standards of some so-called respectable people are far from praiseworthy. The distinction between crime and sharp business is often so fine that it is impossible to analyze it.

In the past ten years, we have witnessed one investigation after another which has revealed the techniques of men who possess instincts far worse than many of our criminals, but who masquerade under peculiar guises of legitimacy.

We make fine use of the radio in Sing Sing as a means of education, but the same radio brings to the ears of the embittered convict the stories of depredations upon defenseless people—even including the traditional widow and orphan— by individuals who go unpunished. Youngsters still in school cannot escape learning that a person who acquires millions through sharp business tricks can nevertheless remain a respected member of the community, especially if he contributes part of his illicit gain to some charitable enterprise. Obviously, such knowledge tends to give many people a distorted sense of morality and imbue them with false philosophies of life.

Some men on the outside wreak greater havoc than the ordinary criminal could possibly dream of. But, the one is respected and called a shrewd businessman, the other, a lawbreaker and a convict. What should be my response to the criminal who was sentenced to prison for forging a check and then asked me, "Am I better or worse than the man who forged names to a thousand telegrams?" He was referring to a case during the Congressional hearings on the Wheeler-

Rayburn Bill, when a thousand forged telegrams were sent to Senators and Congressmen asking them to vote against enactment. Perpetrators of that serious offense were known. Nothing happened.

During the past five years, we have seen hundreds of people defrauded of their last cent by dishonest bankers, mortgage brokers, officials, and others. Only in rare instances have the perpetrators of such frauds been sent to prison. Greed in high places finds an echo in petty thievery in lower scales of society. Legal larceny suggests illegal robbery.

But let us assume that society is capable of uplifting the moral standards of the nation. Another problem, greater perhaps, than any other, still confronts us. Since the depression it is apparent that more men with previous untarnished records are committing crimes than ever before. In most instances, those men are willing to work but, because of economic conditions, are unable to do so. Many more, now being trained for particular types of vocations will soon find that they will be denied the right to earn a livelihood through no fault of their own.

In the City of New York, four hundred thousand young men and women between the ages of sixteen and twenty-four are idle. That group does not include those who are still in school, those who are living at home and are not seeking employment, and those who are unemployable.

It is tragic that the depression, aside from any other consideration, has played such havoc among youth. Youngsters must spend the present in idleness; their future is dimmed with despair.

The government, it is true, has attempted to help in some respects. Some are sent to CCC camps. Others are assisted by the National Youth Administration so that they can continue their studies. But the time will come when even those youngsters must join the great army of unemployed seeking a place in the business and professional world.

Something must be done for those people. Idleness, in my estimation, is a breeder of crime. When individuals have too

251

much undisturbed leisure, they are bound to become dissatisfied with their predicament. Unless society can provide work for youth, there is no doubt that the delinquency rate will rise in the years to come.

More money is spent for advertising purposes in this country than anywhere else in the world. We attempt to create human wants. We make our advertisements as attractive as possible so that people will buy more than at present. In times past, the criminal often stole to purchase commodities which his meager earnings prevented him from obtaining. Today, some people who are thoroughly honest find that they are apt to weaken under the constant pressure of economic insecurity and their inability to obtain the ordinary necessities of life. Advertisements constantly remind them of what they might enjoy. They become embittered against society which deprives them of the right to a normal existence. Teaching them the virtues of honesty will not blind them to the fact that they are unable to obtain work. People have been known to overstep the limitations of law when they are in economic distress. We must, therefore, not frown upon expenditures which will create work for every young man and woman.

Crime is a social cancer! The causes of crime are deeply imbedded in our social structure. We must eliminate every disorder in that structure to minimize delinquency. It is said that cancer—a disease which claims thousands of lives annually—can be prevented if it is diagnosed early, that most forms of cancer have a "high cure rate" if brought under care in their incipient stages. What is said about that disease may be applicable also to crime. Redirect the child when he manifests the slightest tendency to deviate into dangerous channels; give him the care and attention necessary to develop him into a law-abiding citizen. Then give him the opportunity to engage in legitimate work. Increased budgets for all social agencies dealing with such youngsters will eventually mean decreased budgets for reformatories and prisons.

Chapter XVI

TAXATION TODAY AND TOMORROW

ALFRED G. BUEHLER

★ ★ ★ ★

A MERICANS are now paying in taxes approximately 12.5 billions ɘ year. Estimates for 1937 indicate that this huge total was then distributed roughly as follows:

	(In Billions of Dollars)
Property taxes	4.5
Commodity taxes	4.0
Income and profit taxes	2.6
Inheritance and gift taxes	0.5
Pay roll taxes	0.4
Miscellaneous taxes	0.5
Total taxes	12.5

This tremendous sum fell considerably short of Federal, state, and local government expenditures which in 1937 were approximately seventeen billions. The difference between taxes and expenditures was made up from earnings of government enterprises, receipts from borrowing, and other miscellaneous sources. If the 12½ billions in taxes had been divided equally among men, women, and children, each would have paid nearly $100. The amount collected in taxes was equivalent to nearly a fifth of the national income. The Federal government obtained approximately 5½ billions in taxes, the local governments 4½ billions, and the states 2½ billions.

How are these taxes distributed among the population? Recent studies in Illinois and New York by the Twentieth

Century Fund indicated that among the classes subject to income and inheritance taxation, or among the upper income groups, the ratio of Federal, state, and local tax payments to incomes increased as income increased. Among the lower income classes, the ratio of total tax payments to incomes increased as the incomes decreased. For the population as a whole, there appeared to be a tendency for tax payments to increase in relation to incomes as incomes increased.

There are undoubtedly many serious inequalities in American taxation, which has been shaped primarily by the forces of expediency. Our taxes are a patchwork that has been put together over the years. With some 175,000 local, state, and Federal governments in existence in a nation where local independence has been encouraged, overlapping, conflicting, unequal, and inconvenient taxation is inevitable. Instead of a rational, consistently planned system of taxation operating uniformly on a national scale, we have numerous taxes, many of which were carelessly adopted and which are at cross-purposes with each other.

THE GENERAL PROPERTY TAX

The general property tax is the most important of American taxes and is the bulwark of local taxation. It is, however, becoming less important as a state revenue. Because of the great difficulties in discovering and accurately valuing for taxation such intangible property as stocks, bonds, and other securities, and other movable personal property, the general property tax has practically disintegrated into a tax on land and its improvements. Real estate is accepted in this country as one indication of the owner's ability to pay taxes, but it is far from satisfactory as a measure of such ability since non-taxable wealth is disregarded, the personal economic status of taxpayers is ignored, and real estate valuations are not uniformly accurate.

It is well known that the valuation of property for taxation is grossly inequitable. Assessment is usually under the direction

254

of local officials who are elected by the voters without much regard for their qualifications in valuing property. Real estate, on which property taxation largely falls, may be assessed at its full market value or above or below that figure. There is a tendency for the less valuable properties to be assessed at a higher ratio of their true value than the more valuable properties. Rural property has often been assessed nearer to its true value than urban property. Real estate valuations for taxation do not, in practice, change with market values, but may be adjusted only at infrequent intervals, and then not be close to the market values. With the declining values in the real estate markets during the depression, market values have frequently fallen below assessed values of property.

Property taxation, in spite of its long-condemned weaknesses, is too important a revenue to be abandoned, but it should be reformed. It is highly difficult, if not impossible, to value personal property accurately for taxation, largely because it cannot be discovered. It would be well, therefore, to give up the attempt to reach personal property directly, and to be content with a tax upon its income. The assessment of real property for taxation should be under the direction of experts who are selected by the state tax commission on a merit basis and who can be removed for dishonesty or inefficiency. They should be full-time employees with adequate salaries to draw persons with satisfactory ability for the difficult and technical work of valuation. Assessment should be under the general supervision of the state tax commission, with assessing districts large enough to permit continuous assessment procedure. Counties or other large areas should be used as assessment districts.

The property should be assessed at its full market value. Taxpayers should be invited to determine values, and their complaints concerning valuations should be studied. The original assessments should be reviewed by a staff under the direction of the state tax commission. Property valuation is often a highly difficult task, and the best expert opinion should

255

be obtained, in conjunction with adequate mechanical aids and equipment. As long as property taxation is retained, every effort should be made to secure uniformly accurate valuations of taxable property. The general property tax, as it is now administered, is a travesty upon justice.

The recent extensive delinquency in property tax payments, the concerted efforts to secure limitations upon property tax rates, and the common denunciation of the tax by property owners indicate that its burdens have become serious. In many localities it is questionable whether property tax rates can safely be advanced without undesirable economic effects upon the community. The tendency of the states to rely less upon property taxation and the requests of state and local governments to the Federal government for aid in financing functions that were once considered largely of local concern are also symptoms of the inadequacy of the general property tax as the sole source of local revenue. If the Federal government should take over highway construction and maintenance, or other functions, this would, of course, relieve pressure upon property for taxes, but it would increase pressure in other directions. Under such conditions, with serious difficulties encountered in extensive property taxation, it is not wise further to undermine property taxation by homestead and similar exemptions. Such exemptions place additional property tax burdens upon other property owners or compel the resort to other taxes. They are commonly unfair because they give special privileges to a particular group that other groups may not share.

INCOME AND OTHER TAXES

Income, inheritance, and commodity taxes are not well adapted to local administration but call for large administrative areas. License and privilege taxes are frequently collected by state and local governments in a confusing array and without much regard for the equitable distribution of their burdens. It may be feasible in some cases for local governments to collect specific charges for special services, such as furnishing extra policemen on a particular occasion for the convenience of a certain group, in order to cover the cost and avoid tax increases. A more extensive use of special assessments on the owners of property that draw special benefits from improvements would place a larger part of the costs on such persons to the advantage of taxpayers in general. At best, however, many local governments find their revenue resources inadequate and are compelled to seek state grants or a sharing of the receipts of state imposed taxes.

The states have recently obtained great revenues from motor fuel taxes. They have secured less revenue from general taxes on commodity sales, alcoholic beverage taxes, and cigarette taxes. With the repeal of the prohibition amendment, alcoholic beverage taxes have recently provided more revenue than the highly productive tobacco taxes. The Federal government also collects a gasoline tax, which it would well relinquish to the states. The rates on the motor fuel, tobacco, and alcoholic beverage taxes are relatively high as compared with their prices, but these taxes are accepted by the public without serious opposition. Taxes on alcoholic beverages, by raising the prices, may reduce consumption somewhat to the advantage of society.

The states have diverted a growing percentage of motor fuel tax receipts away from use on the highways, but there is no compelling reason why gasoline taxes should not be employed for general governmental functions, especially if the receipts should exceed highway costs. Tobacco taxes are richly productive for the Federal government but of little importance to the states because of the difficulties arising in the taxation of a commodity that may readily be imported from other states and the problem of collecting these taxes from numerous dealers. The states could give up their tobacco and other unimportant commodity taxes to the Federal government, especially if the latter would turn the gasoline tax back to the states.

257

General taxes upon commodities and services are now imposed by over half the states and some cities, but not by the Federal government, although many national governments have adopted general sales taxes. The favorite American variety of general sales taxation is an impost upon sales at retail. The states have advantages over local governments in collecting general sales taxes, but the greatest administrative advantages would seem to lie with the Federal government. The more localized a commodity tax is, the more it restricts commerce and industry within the taxing jurisdiction. If our states are commonly to employ general sales taxation, it would be desirable to have the Federal government levy a uniform national manufacturers' sales tax and give the proceeds in full or in part to the states. Similar taxes would necessarily be laid, of course, upon imports.

It is preferable, however, for our governments to obtain needed revenues from the more equitable personal income, inheritance, and selected commodity taxes rather than from general sales taxation. Both selected and general commodity taxes tend to be passed along to consumers in higher prices and to burden the poorer consumers of the taxed commodities relatively more than the richer, but taxes on selected commodities are less objectionable because they are less universal in their application, may not apply to absolute necessities, and are more likely to reach luxuries which can bear such taxation without ill effects.

It is doubted by some observers, to be sure, whether the Federal government can eventually avoid the imposition of a manufacturers' sales tax, in view of the present level of spending which shows no signs of abating. If the Federal debt, now over thirty-seven billions, is to be reduced, tax payments must be employed for that reduction. The Federal government has embarked upon heavy expenditures for agricultural relief, public works, aid to the unemployed and destitute, and other social purposes. Military expenditures are rising because of the intense nationalism that prevails everywhere. The war

258

veterans and other groups are ever crying for more liberal spending for their benefit. In view of past experience in this and other countries, it is likely that the high level of governmental spending will continue and may increase. The normal Federal budget of seven billions annually that President Roosevelt has forecast made no allowance for debt reduction. It is also apparent that relief expenditures and military appropriations may be considerably larger than the President estimated.

Wasteful and socially undesirable expenditures should, of course, be prevented. Perhaps if all waste could be eliminated from public administration as much as ten per cent could be cut from costs. In view of present political, economic, and social conditions, it seems probable that the general spending level will not decline, although particular items may be slashed. If the Federal debt is to be lowered, more taxes must come into the treasury.

WHAT NEXT IN TAXATION?

Where can the Federal government obtain larger taxes? If the national income increases, tax payments will automatically expand. The administration has set up a goal of a national income of 100 billions, but the nation is still a long way from that objective. The national income in 1937, for example, was only sixty-seven billions. Artificial increases in the national income by rapid currency inflation would increase tax revenues, but such inflation would not increase the real income of the nation and would probably be followed by a crisis and financial collapse. It seems unlikely that increased prosperity alone, in the immediate future, will supply the tax revenues necessary to maintain balanced budgets and pare down governmental debts. The country, unfortunately, has fallen into the habit of easy spending predicated upon borrowing. Many persons consider heavier taxes and debt payments objectionable because of their burdens. But these objectors frequently overlook the advantage of public expenditures.

259

Taxes merely transfer funds from the taxpayers to governments, which pay them out to their employees and creditors, without any direct reduction of national income as long as the funds remain within the country. The national income will not be reduced by this process unless the expenditures supported by taxation are wasteful or are less effective than the private expenditure of the funds would be. If taxation is socially undesirable, it is because the expenditures maintained by taxation are socially undesirable. If governments perform their functions satisfactorily, taxes for those functions are desirable, assuming that the proper imposts are selected; and if governments cannot or will not perform their function in such a way as to improve the social welfare by spending funds more effectively than private agencies would, they should not spend upon those functions.

It seems probable that the Federal government will be compelled before long to develop new fields of tax revenue, in view of its huge spending program. It is quite possible that the next source of additional tax revenues will be the middle incomes. The Federal tax rates on the highest incomes, now ranging up to seventy-nine per cent, are so high that they tend to dry up the highest income brackets. Little, if any, additional revenue could now be obtained by further increasing these high tax rates because the higher taxes would check incentive and stimulate efforts at tax avoidance through the purchase of tax-exempt securities and other loopholes.

American governments should abandon the practice of issuing securities the income of which is exempt from income taxation. It is now held that the Federal government cannot constitutionally tax the income from state and local government securities or the salaries of employees of those governments, while the state and local governments cannot tax the income of Federal securities or the salaries of Federal employees. Such immunity from taxation is contrary to the principles of income taxation because it is unjust, giving advantages to special groups that other groups may not

260

enjoy, and it removes certain incomes which would well pay a tax from the application of income taxation. Tax-exempt investments are advantageous only to the wealthy, among personal investors, as a method of avoiding high-rate income taxation. If the high tax rates are desirable, they should be enforced by closing this loophole, and if they are not, they should be repealed. American governments can obtain adequate credit without the tax-exemption credit. They would have to pay a little more on loans, but they would gain, according to some estimates, between 100 millions and 200 millions in additional taxes.

The Federal government could give up the tax-exempt privilege on its own securities without constitutional amendment. The state and local governments are not greatly interested in giving up the long-favored tax exemption because it supposedly strengthens their credit, and, with the present low state income tax rates, they would not gain much additional revenue if the loophole were closed. The co-operation of the states in securing this abandonment of tax exemption might be obtained if the Federal government were to offer some concession to win their support, such as its withdrawal from gasoline taxation.

Considerable new revenue could be obtained by the Federal government, if, following English and European practice, it dropped the income tax exemptions down near the level of subsistence income. An exemption of $500 for single persons and $1,000 for married couples, with credit of $200 or $300 for dependents, would roughly exempt the income necessary for the simple necessities. A low tax rate of perhaps two per cent would not have drastic effects on the smallest taxable incomes. The tax rates on the middle incomes up to $100,000 or more could also be increased considerably to supply large revenues. Personal income taxes are consciously paid, and the rates may progress according to some standard of ability to pay as the incomes increase. Lowering the income tax exemption would permit collecting the tax from several million

261

families instead of two or three million and should make it possible to dispense with less equitable imposts. Moreover, a larger portion of the population would become conscious of government spending. But the chief argument for a progressive personal income tax is its fairness as a revenue measure.

The Federal estate tax, which is now levied on estates in excess of $40,000, could be made to supply greater revenues without injustice by applying the tax to smaller estates. Exemption might start at $20,000. Estate and inheritance taxes, or the so-called *death duties*, supply relatively little revenue in this country compared with England, where approximately nine per cent of national and local taxes come from the death duties as against our four per cent of total taxes. The Federal gift tax rates would require adjustment along with reforms in the estate tax. Now each gift of $5,000 to any person in a given year is exempt, inviting avoidance of at least part of the estate tax. The gift tax exemption could be reduced to $1,000 without injury of a serious nature. The Federal estate tax rises to very high rates on the largest estates, and the top rates are apparently high enough for the present.

Income taxation should be personalized so far as possible so that the tax rates could be adjusted to the particular economic status of each taxpayer. In this country corporation profits taxes have provided about as much revenue as personal income taxes, but the profits taxes lay the same rates on all stockholders regardless of the amount of their incomes and other variable conditions. The income tax could be made entirely personal by taxing stockholders' shares of the undistributed earnings of corporations as income received, in the same way that dividends are now taxed. This principle is now followed in taxing the profits of partnerships and proprietorships. Such a reform would apparently demand a constitutional amendment and would require a large administrative staff, but it might prove practicable, as well as most equitable.

262

If this plan were followed, no distinction would be made between the distributed and undistributed earnings of corporations, and no incentive would be given to pay out or withhold earnings, except insofar as corporations might have to increase their dividends so stockholders would have cash to pay their taxes. Of course any progressive personal income tax discriminates against saving because it taxes the larger incomes at higher rates than the lower incomes, since the portion of incomes saved normally increases as incomes become larger. If the income tax were personalized in this manner, the excess profits, capital stock, and undistributed profits taxes could be repealed. The normal profits tax could also be given up, unless it should be felt that a light profits tax should be retained as a benefit charge on business. Preferably, however, the normal profits tax would also be relinquished so that the stockholders could be taxed according to personal income and economic differences.

Much is to be said for an excess profits tax as a matter of principle. It permits the reaching of certain monopoly gains and other pure profits where the rate of return on investments is unusually high. But the problems of accurately valuing corporate investments, so that the rate of return may be known, are colossal and are now avoided by accepting the corporations' valuations of their investments. This tax and the capital stock taxes should be given up until an adequate administration can be established.

If the normal profits tax on corporations is retained, as it probably will be, it should be levied at a flat rate. Corporations have no ability to pay taxes apart from the abilities of their stockholders. Rate graduation cannot, therefore, be justified on grounds of ability to pay. It was stated in 1935, when rate graduation was introduced, that it would assure greater stability of tax receipts, but this advantage has not been obtained in the normal profits tax. The undistributed profits tax may be justified in principle, as a charge for the privilege of retaining earnings from dividend distribution,

263

but, if it is to be retained at all, it should, apparently, be a very moderate tax in order to avoid its drastic effects upon dividend policies and business initiative. The undistributed profits tax adopted in 1936 was a blunder which was almost unanimously opposed by businessmen from the time it was proposed and has also been roundly criticized by many economists.

In planning the income tax as a permanent feature in American taxation, the advisability of concentrating administration in the hands of the Federal government should seriously be considered. Federal administration would offer greater uniformity, simplicity, and convenience of taxation and would have the merit of considering total income in adjusting the tax rates to individual incomes. Much income is interstate in character, and the Federal government has distinct advantages in reaching income from various areas. This proposal involves the political disadvantages that may lurk in a greater centralization of governmental power. On the other hand, Federal administration of all income, commodity, business, and death taxes would have many advantages, as an administrative proposition. It was the approved method in Germany, for instance, long before the emergence of the totalitarian state. It is an open question, of course, whether such centralization might not undermine local democracy, but perhaps a scheme could be worked out that would permit the Federal government to act as the agent of the states in tax collection without a sacrifice of the independence of the states. Whether income taxes are Federally administered or not, there is a great need for co-operation of the Federal and state governments in collecting taxes from incomes.

If present taxes, including an extension of the income tax to the lower incomes, prove inadequate to support government expenditures, there remains a national manufacturers' sales tax as another source of revenue. If expenditures could be kept within bounds, such a tax would be unnecessary. It would strike at the lowest incomes indirectly and insidiously, hitting them the hardest. The only excuse that can be given for such a tax is that other taxes are unavailable and that desirable social expenditures are financed that possess merits outweighing the defects of a general sales tax. In the United States the personal income tax may still be extended to the lower incomes, so that a national general sales tax may be averted for the present at least. The states should also exhaust the possibilities of income, inheritance, and selected commodity taxation before turning to general sales taxation.

The Federal government might lay import duties on additional commodities that would provide further revenues. Coffee, tea, and cocoa, for example, are admitted without duty, but could be taxed moderately without serious social consequences. If articles like sugar, which is produced at home, are taxed, similar taxes should be levied upon domestic products so that they would not be given advantages over foreign products. Our high protective tariffs should be moderated and the protective principle should eventually be abandoned.

TAXATION AS SOCIAL CONTROL

Taxes are ordinarily thought of as revenue measures, but they may also be employed for social purposes such as reform and the regulation of production or consumption. All taxes have social effects, and it is desirable that those effects should be in harmony with the general welfare. In recent years taxes have been increasingly proposed as means of accomplishing social reforms. Where taxation is the best method of achieving a desirable social objective it is proper to employ it for social purposes. If, however, the objective in view is advantageous to only a small sector of society and is detrimental to the general welfare, or if the tax is less effective in furthering social ends, taxation as an agency of regulation or reform is not justifiable.

Taxation is often utilized for so-called *social* purposes in such a manner that the general welfare is injured rather than benefited. The protective tariff, for example, has long been known to force consumers to pay higher prices for commodities in order that home producers may not have to compete with foreign producers who are more efficient. Protective tariffs restrain international trade by penalizing exports as well as imports, engender ill will among nations, intensify nationalism, and compel consumers to pay more for their purchases and to suffer a lower level of living for the benefit of the protected domestic producers. Nations everywhere have erected tariff barriers to keep out unwanted imports, but at the same time they have been feverishly active in attempting to increase their exports. Nations cannot sell if they refuse to buy, because trade, both foreign and domestic, is two-sided. If we refuse to buy from foreign producers, they must ultimately refuse to buy from us.

The recent wave of discriminatory chain store taxation and other legislation to curb the large distributors in their competition with the less efficient small merchants and the wholesalers and manufacturers who sell through them is of an analogous nature. Instead of trying to improve their marketing methods, many small merchants cry for legislative protection and insist on their vested right to consumer patronage regardless of the way they conduct their business. The consumers, who are the most numerous groups and whose welfare should be given most weight in the controversy, are merely a pawn in the battle over their patronage. The blind tactics of those interests that seek to arrest progress and the march of efficiency so they may themselves survive invite consumer co-operation or a socialized state for the purpose of safeguarding the well-being of consumers.

Grave dangers also arise in a farm subsidy program that taxes consumers so that inefficient farmers may secure higher prices. Farm production should stop at the point where the costs of production are equal to the prices received. When farmers persist in producing more than the markets can absorb at prices covering costs, as under our present economic system, it becomes dangerous to invite habitual overproduction

266

by subsidizing a depressed industry. The more depressed agriculture becomes, the larger the subsidy it will need, but as subsidies increase, the farm situation is aggravated, and the vicious cycle goes on. The agricultural problem is a matter of vast social importance, but one may doubt the wisdom of trying to solve a problem by inviting its continuance.

Taxation too often strikes at effects rather than causes. It is too frequently proposed to cure social ills by those who little understand its effects. The undistributed profits tax was blindly rushed through Congress as a measure that would protect the small corporation against the big corporation, but it has apparently reacted to the advantage of the larger corporations. The undistributed profits tax has also been disappointing as a revenue. Instead of increasing income tax receipts by the estimated 620 millions in 1937, it supplied only 380 millions, according to treasury reports. Both its reform and its revenue possibilities were greatly misunderstood.

Many persons urge high income and inheritance taxes as a means of securing a more equitable distribution of wealth and income. Within limits, this proposition is defensible and supplies additional arguments for progressive taxation. Experience shows that equalities in wealth and income distribution may be mitigated by taxation. On the other hand, if the tax rates become too high, initiative and enterprise may be stifled and industry may be depressed. Revenues may also decline as the tax rates rise, so there is a practical limit to the possibilities of progression as an equalizer of incomes. As indicated previously, we are now apparently at the point where the middle incomes will need to be taxed more heavily, and this will level off the middle as well as the upper incomes. The ultimate issue here is the desirability of equalizing wealth and income, and the place where the equalization process should be discontinued.

The use of taxation for social reforms and for the regulation of production and consumption is a proposal all too frequently fraught with dangers. Social taxation is a field that should be entered only with extreme caution and moderation. Taxation is usually a very crude instrument of reform. The numerous abuses of taxation for the gain of particular groups, the misunderstanding concerning the effects of taxation, and its usual ineffectiveness as a medium of reform militate against its widespread employment as an agency of general reform, although it may operate satisfactorily in particular instances.

Chapter XVII

WHAT PRICE SOCIAL SECURITY?

ABRAHAM EPSTEIN

★ ★ ★ ★

FOR nearly half a century, while one European nation after another was establishing social insurance programs to alleviate the economic insecurity of its workers, America looked on contemptuously and, despite its growing industrialism, refused to face its own similar problems. Strange as it may now seem, opposition to governmental action on social security characterized not only American industrialists and businessmen, but pervaded the organized American labor movement as well.

American labor unions opposed at first even the enactment of workmen's compensation laws, although for the past twenty-five years the American Federation of Labor and its state affiliates have devoted their attention almost exclusively to the development of this branch of social insurance. Despite the fact that the A. F. of L. convention of 1918 endorsed the principle of old age pensions, its highest ranking officers persisted in obstructing the passage of these laws in the early twenties. During the pioneering struggle for health insurance twenty years ago, American labor leaders closely collaborated with the opponents of labor against this legislation. The A. F. of L. continued opposing all unemployment insurance legislation until 1932 when the Cincinnati convention belatedly reversed its previous opposition. Not until its convention in 1935 did the A. F. of L. finally give a mild blessing to health insurance.

SOCIAL INSURANCE: A NEW CONCEPT IN THE UNITED STATES

Although social insurance has dominated European politics for nearly a century, it was never an issue in any of our elections until it suddenly loomed on the political horizon in the 1936 campaign. Not even in 1932, when the New Deal was ushered in, did either of the leading political parties elevate the question of social security to a campaign issue. So far removed was social insurance from the consciousness of America that prior to 1934 it was not even deemed worthy of academic discussion, and few, if any, American universities gave a full course on the subject. Although there was considerable, though thoroughly confused, discussion of unemployment insurance before the introduction of the social security bill in Congress in 1935, it is significant that up to that time not a half dozen articles had been published on the important problem of old age insurance.

Americans scorned social insurance as detrimental to our ideals and traditions, as destructive of individual character, initiative, and the virility of the race, as ruinous to thrift and morals, and as subversive of the basic principles of our government. The bogey which social insurance symbolized in the United States was illustrated in a statement by the U. S. Secretary of Agriculture a short time before the Federal government began lending billions of dollars to private banks and insurance companies. The secretary opposed the extension of food relief to drought-stricken farmers on the ground that if public loans were given for the feeding of men it would "approach perilously near the dole system and would be a move in the wrong direction." He made an exception in favor of seed, fertilizer, and feed for work animals.

Only in the light of the abysmal ignorance and blind prejudice which existed up to the time of the presentation of the Social Security Act can we understand the misconceptions embodied in it, its speedy and practically unanimous adoption by Congress, and the developments since its passage. It would

270

never have been adopted without the stirring events which preceded it—the closing of the banks, the establishment and collapse of the National Recovery Administration, the Agricultural Adjustment Act, and the Civil Works Administration. The passage of the Social Security Act resulted not from any new understanding of the necessity and advantages of social insurance but from the search for another panacea, made politically necessary by the years of depression, starvation, and despair. Senator Huey Long, Dr. Townsend, Father Coughlin, and a host of lesser prophets had not only aroused the American people to the economic ills besetting them but had extravagantly raised their hopes of the millennium. The widespread ignorance of the limitations and possibilities of social insurance easily transformed the slogan "social security" in the minds of the people into a magic formula fulfilling all the heralded promises. Thus, no sooner had the President promised on June 8, 1934, to undertake "the great task of furthering the security of the citizen and his family through social insurance" than the message was hailed from one end of the country to the other as "the beginning of a new era," "humanity's greatest boon," "the advent of a new social order," "the translation of the cross of Christ."

The Gargantuan bill not only was inspired by, but was swept through Congress mainly on the strength of, the tremendous surge of interest for the aged, brought to a fever pitch by the Townsend agitation for $200 monthly pensions to all who have reached the age of sixty. The movement for old age protection dates back over a generation, and for nearly a decade Congress had discussed the Dill-Connery bill to subsidize state pension systems, but no desire for Congressional action had been evidenced until 1933, when the Townsend pressure was approaching its peak. With this demand at its height in 1934, the administration seized the opportunity, not only to build a more comprehensive program of social security, but to make tremendous political capital at the same time. Instead of submitting to a com-

271

mission of experts a program for social security which it has taken European nations decades to elaborate, the President entrusted its formulation to five of the then busiest and most harassed members of his Cabinet. This committee in turn transferred the actual elaboration of the program to a miscellany of advisory councils and committees in which, strangely, the leading American students and experts of social insurance were conspicuous by their absence. The unwarranted pressure for haste prevented the Cabinet committee from sending a delegation abroad to study the European experience. Its work, moreover, was handicapped from the very start by the absence of any specific instructions from the President as to what economic risks should be covered by the contemplated legislation. That the President himself had no clear idea of the scope of the program was evidenced by the fact that two months before the bill was introduced in Congress he doubted "whether this was the time for federal action on old age security." Only two weeks before its introduction, even the chairman of the Cabinet committee did not know what particular unemployment insurance plan the President would favor.

As a result, the people were kept in the dark for months and no public discussion whatsoever preceded the presentation of the measure to Congress. Provisions against sickness, which lend themselves best to social insurance and have generally been the first to be adopted abroad, were urged as a basic need by the Cabinet committee. These provisions, however, were opposed by the well-organized medical profession and were therefore eliminated. The committee's report on this problem, promised for a few months later, has not yet seen the light of day.

In Congress the bill met the destiny of all New Deal proposals of that period. Never before had Congress faced a bill so novel to its philosophy, so comprehensive in scope, so complex in administration, and one involving so large a tax. Added to these difficulties was the hasty and slipshod drafting of the

272

original bill, which forced the House Ways and Means Committee to order its own draftsmen to rewrite it. The congressional finance committees in charge of the bill found the entire proposal not only unfamiliar but irritating. Beset by numerous legislative programs and unable to give genuine study to the subject, their chief consideration was that the bill was an Administration measure on the "must" list. The House Committee of Ways and Means did not even disguise its impatience with witnesses outside the Administration fold. It not only attempted to limit all other testimony to five minutes but on one occasion forcibly ejected a spokesman who overstepped the allotted time.

These events made inevitable the desultory debates in Congress. The vociferous Townsend agitation frightened congressmen into a desire to do something for the needy aged, and they were thus interested in the bill's provisions for noncontributory pensions. They utilized the occasion to deliver florid orations on the glories of old age and to assure their constituents of their profound affection for America's old fathers and mothers. Few members of Congress were interested in, or had any notion of, the insurance plans of the act. Of the 247 pages of actual House debate not half a dozen were devoted to a genuine discussion of the entire bill. Five full days of Senate debate was reported in the *Congressional Record*, but, with the exception of the explanatory remarks, not even half a column of the *Record* was given over to discussion of the unprecedented scheme of unemployment insurance. The portentous contributory old age insurance plan rated less than a page in the hundreds of columns of senatorial argument. The adjournment of Congress in the fall of 1935 without voting any appropriation for inaugurating the act was but a fitting climax to a tragic spectacle of ignorance and ineptitude.

That a vast social security program, little discussed and less known, hurriedly framed and perfunctorily adopted, should leave much to be desired was to be expected. As enacted, the law embodies a miscellany of ten different welfare and insurance programs based on a variety of philosophies of Federal-state operation. It is administered by five different Federal agencies. While constructive discussion of the problems involved would normally have followed the passage of the act, its complex and all-inclusive nature has obstructed such consideration. The variety of good, bad, and indifferent provisions prevent any general characterization, and those interested in defending it merely emphasize its good provisions. Thus, for example, the Social Security Board is able to ignore all the fundamental issues raised by the act and yet convey the impression that all is well: Witness the board's statement in the Second Annual Report that "it would be impossible to make a count of the individuals whose well-being and peace of mind have been protected by the Social Security Act." The "well-being" results only from the sound, but less significant, assistance provisions contained in the act. But readers of the report are unaware of this and assume that the act as a whole is to be commended. On the other hand, the enemies of the legislation stress only the worst features, such as the fantastic 47 billion dollars' reserve contemplated under the old age insurance system. The act is rarely analyzed in its entirety since the multiplicity and variety of the problems involved cannot be discussed fully in one article or one speech. Added to these difficulties is the pervading feeling that to criticize New Deal legislation is to be classed as an *economic royalist*, while approval of some of the provisions stamps one as a devout New Dealer.

SOCIAL SECURITY ACT OF 1935 ANALYZED

Although we cannot hope in these pages to discuss all the problems raised by the Social Security Act, the main issues are clearly revealed by a brief analysis of the general objectives of social insurance, their distortions in the act, and the developments since its passage.

Of the ten programs embodied in the Social Security Act the most far-reaching and socially significant are the provisions for old age and for unemployment insurance. The problems raised by these programs stem entirely from the fact that, although dubbed *social insurance* measures, they flagrantly violate all the elementary principles of social insurance evolved successfully in Europe over a period of nearly fifty years.

The basic aims of social insurance are threefold:

1. To provide as *adequate protection* as the nation can afford against the loss of wages when, through no fault of their own, either because of old age or unemployment, workers are unable to earn their usual livelihood. It goes without saying that, until a nation can extend such protection to those who, by one sacrifice or another, can take care of themselves, the first objective is to provide for those who are in greatest need.

2. To eliminate to the greatest extent possible the long-standing degradation and humiliation of poor relief through dignified and self-respecting social insurance grants accorded as a matter of right. This is essential because poor relief is based on the conception that poverty results from individual maladjustment and shiftlessness, whereas modern unemployment and the scrapping of older workers are due largely to social and economic forces beyond the worker's control.

3. To employ social insurance as a means not only of enhancing the security of the individual worker but, at the same time, of safeguarding the stability of society by a better balance in the national economy. Such a conception is based on the axiom that the workers can be made more secure only as the security of society as a whole is advanced, and that this is attainable only by an increase in the purchasing power of the masses.

In short, the primary aim of a social insurance program for old age is to extend as much protection as possible in such a manner that all stigma of charity will be eliminated. Similarly, the aim of unemployment insurance is to provide self-respecting security to those who lose their jobs and are in need. In both instances, the aim must be to increase consumption by these groups in order that production and employment will be increased thereby and the welfare of the nation as a whole promoted.

Although these objectives are universally accepted as fundamental to sound social insurance, they are completely repudiated by our insurance programs. The first aim—adequate protection—cannot be achieved under our old age insurance system for a generation to come because, instead of protecting those workers who need it most, the benefits are apportioned in exact ratio to previous earning, regardless of the needs of the individual. Thus, the highest annuities will be given to those with the most years of remunerative employment at the highest wages. On the other hand, the most unfortunate— those workers who have had the least employment and earned the lowest wages—will receive the lowest pensions. Although it is the needy older and middle-aged workers who constitute the pressing problem of old age indigency, our system will provide fairly adequate protection only to the youth of today when they reach old age, and then only if inflation does not depress the value of the dollar. The maximum of $85 a month written into the law may be completely dismissed from consideration since it can be secured only by the very few who earn at least $3,000 every single year for forty-three years. The great mass of our workers, earning an average of about $100 a month, must work for at least twenty, and more likely thirty, years before they can obtain as much as about $30 a month. Indeed, when the payment of annuities begins in 1942 only the luckier aged workers will receive a pension of about $15 a month. Since the act makes no provision whatsoever for an insured man's wife unless she, too, is a wage earner, the great majority of aged couples will be expected to "live happily ever after" on their $15 monthly. Regardless of their needs, those who have earned the least will receive as little as $10 a month, the minimum provided by the law—a sum they, too, will have to share with their wives. In terms of protection against old age dependency, therefore, the American old age insurance system provides no security for the mass of aged and middle-aged today.

Our systems of unemployment insurance suffer from a similar lack of realism in their approach to the problem of unemployment. Although here, too, the chief aim should be to protect those workers who suffer most from unemployment and low wages, our laws, on the contrary, extend the greatest security to those workers who suffer least from unemployment and who earn the highest wages. None of our fifty-one statutes gives the slightest consideration to those who have been continuously unemployed either before or since the enactment of the law. These unfortunates are left entirely to the vagaries of emergency relief and WPA. To be entitled to any insurance benefits, a worker must not only have worked recently and earned a minimum sum in wages, but even after qualifying, the amount and duration of the benefits are set in exact proportion to his previous earnings. The workers with the steadiest employment and highest wages may receive as much as $15 a week for fifteen or sixteen weeks. But those who are destitute because of little employment and low wages receive total benefits as low as $15 or $21 for an entire year, no matter what their financial plight or the number of their dependents. Thus the neediest unemployed, the chief concern of unemployment insurance, receive the least protection.

The present programs of old age and unemployment insurance violate just as flagrantly the second objective of social insurance—elimination of the stigma of charity now attached to state noncontributory pensions and to relief.

Since annuities of less than an average of $30 a month per person do not offer any security and since the mass of our workers cannot obtain even this amount during the next twenty or thirty years, all the needy aged beneficiaries during this long period will be forced to apply for supplementary help to the relief agencies or to the presumably humiliating noncontributory pension systems. Thus the objective of old age insurance—to render to worn-out workers aid that is not an affront to dignity and self-respect—is completely nullified for practically all the needy older and middle-aged workers for whom this legislation is primarily instituted.

The same is true of the unemployment insurance systems. With benefits as low as $15 or $20 a month, with a long wait ranging from three to five weeks in the different states before any benefits are received, the bulk of the needy unemployed will not be able to escape the stigma of relief even for a single week. Many of them will not be able to sustain themselves through their long waiting period without resorting to emergency relief. Again, since checks of $5 or $7 a week will not anywhere in the country suffice to cover the needs of most unemployed workers, especially those with families, most of them will be obliged to secure supplementary relief even during the few weeks when they receive insurance benefits. And all those in need will be forced to resort to full relief again immediately on the expiration of their short benefit period. They will thus have to be given full relief before the meager insurance checks come to them, partial relief during the short period of insurance benefits, and full relief again immediately thereafter. The objective of aid decently proffered to the unemployed is thus completely nullified for the very persons who should be the chief concern of unemployment insurance legislation.

In addition, as constituted today, both insurance systems require a variety of separate and distinct agencies to cater simultaneously to the needs of the same person. This will not only tremendously increase the cost of administration, but will prove exasperating to the recipients because of the perpetual shunting from one system to another with all the attendant annoyances, special regulations, and long-drawn-out delays.

The third objective of social insurance—greater social stability through a better balance in our economy—is likewise frustrated by both our old age and unemployment insurance programs. This aim can be achieved only when the government contributes to social insurance out of progressive

278

income and inheritance taxes, thereby making possible a general increase in purchasing power. Only to the extent that income not now used for consumption can be transformed into benefits for the needy aged and unemployed, can mass purchasing power be underpinned. A program of social insurance which places the cost upon workers' incomes and employers' pay rolls cannot accomplish this since it involves, at best, merely a distribution of poverty among the poor. For no one disputes the fact that taxes on workers' wages reduce their purchasing power. Furthermore, quibbling economists to the contrary notwithstanding, it is generally conceded that inasmuch as a tax on pay rolls is an item in the cost of production, it is generally passed on to the consumer. Since the wage and salary earning groups constitute the bulk of consumers, it is obvious that the workers' purchasing power is further reduced by this increase in prices.

The principle that every stratum of society should share in the cost of old age dependency has been incorporated in all old age insurance systems in the world; it was accepted even by Bismarck half a century ago. Our government, however, scrupulously avoids the use of progressive taxation for the purpose of sustaining and increasing the purchasing power of the masses and thereby creating a more balanced national economy. Indeed, our government goes out of its way to relieve the wealthier groups from their share of the future burdens of old age dependency and unemployment which, through the poor laws, they have helped to carry for over three hundred years. Because of this, our programs are not only confined to distributing charity among the poor but may actually result in a decrease in the purchasing power of the masses.

It is the lack of governmental contributions which chiefly accounts for the 47 billion dollars' reserve contemplated under the old age insurance plan. This has become a grave issue. Reserves by their very nature can be built up only by hoarding the taxes as they are collected. The idea underlying our old age insurance system is to accumulate fantastic reserves by setting the contributions higher than is necessary for the present generation, and by keeping the payments at a low level. However, since this hoarded money is derived exclusively from direct levies on wages and pay rolls which reduce purchasing power, the unnecessarily heavy taxes coupled with low benefits doubly reduce the consuming power of the masses. Since no funds at all come from the higher income brackets to offset this tremendous withdrawal and since the reserve funds now being spent by the government do not result in a proportionate increase in purchasing power, the greatly reduced income of the workers must inevitably lead to decreased consumption, curtailed production, diminished profits, and intensified unemployment. Our social security measures are definitely tending in the direction of greater general insecurity.

Moreover, although somewhat higher ratios of annuities to earnings are to be awarded to the present aged and middle-aged, the cost of these extra allowances are borne entirely by the younger wage and salary earners through considerably higher taxes on their part. This means that purchasing power is taken away from the group which needs it most—the workers with families to support and children to raise. In addition, it must also be remembered that the larger the pay-roll tax, the greater is the inducement for the substitution of man-power by laborsaving machinery. The fact that practically the only business index on the upgrade throughout 1937 was that of laborsaving machinery is a warning which must not be ignored.

SOCIAL INSURANCE COMPARED WITH PRIVATE INSURANCE

The above tragic and unparalleled distortions of the fundamental conceptions and aims of social insurance are due to the confusion between social insurance and private insurance prevailing in the United States. For, while we remain abysmally ignorant of all that social insurance implies, Ameri-

280

cans, more than any other people, have been "educated" to the meaning of private insurance. The framers of the Social Security Act sought to establish a gigantic scheme of private insurance because they could envisage governmental social insurance only in terms of private insurance. Indeed, to this day American writers on social insurance continue to draw fine though meaningless distinctions between social insurance and relief; they waste reams of paper on vapid discussion of the insurability of unemployment; above all, they suffer from the delusion that the actuary must determine all policies in social as well as in private insurance.

There are obvious and basic differences both in aims and methods between private and social insurance. The aim of the private insurance company is simple. Its objective is to provide protection in accordance with the means of the policyholder. Because its premiums are paid voluntarily, it must adhere strictly to the principles of actuarial science, since no one will freely pay higher premiums without receiving commensurate returns. In view of the fact that its only sources of income are premium payments and the interest derived from them, it must lay aside contingency reserves in order to enable it to pay its obligations during periods when revenues fall. Having no responsibility other than the payment of the face value of the policy, regardless of the actual needs of the policyholder or the purchasing power of money, its obligations are fully met by setting aside of such reserves.

Altogether different are the aim and purpose of governmental social insurance, the very development of which has arisen from the fact that the limitations of private insurance make it ineffective as a medium of protection against the major hazards haunting the workers. Private insurance offers benefits only in accordance with premiums paid, and workers can pay only small, if any, premiums; therefore a governmental social insurance plan cannot follow actuarial principles. Its aim is rather to extend relatively greater protection to those workers who are in greatest need of governmental support. Since contributions in social insurance are compulsory rather than voluntary, the program is concerned chiefly with social need rather than strict equity among the insured. Social insurance seeks chiefly to establish a minimum of economic sustenance for all workers regardless of the premiums they are able to pay. In order to accomplish this the premium rates in social insurance are dictated by intelligent social policy, that is, a statesman-like fusion of financial expediency and social wisdom, rather than by cold and abstract actuarial computations. In social insurance the actuary determines only the costs, not the direction of the program. A private insurance company has no further responsibility beyond the payment of the face value of the policy, regardless of the then prevailing purchasing power of the dollar, but a government cannot dismiss its obligations to its needy citizens by the payment of a specified amount utterly unrelated to a minimum of subsistence. So long as this sum is inadequate for the support of an aged or unemployed person, either now or in the future, the government must supplement it out of other funds, actuarial formulas notwithstanding.

Since a nation must in one way or another provide benefits adequate to meet need as long as that need exists, a governmental social insurance plan does not require large reserves. A government does not need reserves to pay the benefits because, unlike a private insurance company, it does not rely solely on premiums, but rather on its unlimited power of taxation. Social insurance funds are derived not from voluntary contributions but from enforced taxes. A participant in a governmental plan cannot discontinue his payments as a private policyholder can. Unlike a private insurance company, also, a nation cannot invest its funds in private industry and share in the profits. It invests funds only in its own securities and pays interest to itself. The building up of huge governmental social insurance reserves is, therefore, not only an empty gesture in terms of the future, because of the rapid changes in the value of money, but reserves of such astronomical sums as 47 billion dollars are fraught with the gravest economic and social dangers since they freeze sorely needed purchasing power.

POLITICS ENTERS INTO THE PROGRAM

The extraordinary circumstances surrounding the inauguration of the Social Security Act have not confined the dangerous social and economic trends to the insurance programs. They have seeped even into the act's sound and constructive subsidy provisions for the aged, the blind, and for dependent children. With a national election approaching, Federal grants were rushed to the states with breakneck speed. Although Federal appropriations were not available until February, 1936, a mad scramble to pay as many pensions as possible was precipitated in the last few months before the election. Oklahoma, one of the worst offenders in making a political racket of the old age pension system, received its Federal subsidy for the aged a few weeks before election. Indeed, so eager were the states and the Social Security Board to pension the aged before the elections that two states were allotted Federal funds without as much as troubling their legislatures to enact specific pension laws. The Louisiana pension law was not signed by the governor until June 26, 1936, but Social Security Board grants were made available as of June 19. Many other states were allotted Federal money even though their laws did not conform with the basic requirements of the Federal act. These questionable procedures were all lamely excused later by the Social Security Board on the ground that "the immediate necessity for aiding the needy outweighed considerations of administrative nicety."

As a result, the old age assistance systems, which before the enactment of the Federal law had rarely been dominated by political influences, have since become cesspools of political corruption in many states. They have been brought in line with our traditional spendthrift way of using pension systems for the political good they do. A recent investigation in Okla-

283

homa, for example, disclosed that thirteen counties had more pensioners than the entire aged population recorded by the 1930 census, that a state investigator was received by a pensioner's butler, and that hundreds of grants were made in the names of dead persons and to people who have never filed applications for aid.

The price exacted by the Social Security Act is thus tremendous. Only the promises of the millennium, assimilated into the act and nurtured by the administration, have lulled the American people into the belief that they have finally arrived in the promised land of security. As a matter of fact, in following the principles and methods of private insurance, our programs completely reverse the aims of genuine social insurance and make impossible the protection of the workers either in old age or unemployment. It will do no harm to repeat that the present heavy and menacing taxes not only merely distribute poverty among the poor and relieve the wealthy from sharing in the cost of indigence, but they definitely prevent the extension of social security to other indispensable programs, such as sickness and invalidity. At the same time, the high reserves contemplated tend definitely in the direction of greater general insecurity rather than security.

As this brief analysis indicates, many changes are necessary in the present Social Security Act if it is to be converted into a constructive measure for social good. First and foremost, the present trends toward general insecurity resulting from the contemplated huge reserves and lack of a government contribution must be reversed by paying adequate grants through as large a governmental subsidy as possible from progressive taxation. For none of the objectives sought through social insurance can be attained without such a contribution. The old age insurance program must be so changed that it will meet the needs of the aged and the middle-aged. Protection for the unemployed must be granted by flat benefits in accordance with their need and for as long as the need exists. Our present systems of work relief, emergency relief, and insurance must be co-ordinated. The costly and top-heavy administrative system with its duplications must be eliminated and replaced with a co-ordinated, simple, and relatively inexpensive plan making use of flat benefits and government contributions. Only after these improvements are incorporated should the program be extended to the large groups now excluded. It goes without saying, of course, that political manipulation of social security must be completely eradicated. In a word, the act must be immediately converted into a genuine instrument for social security before it shatters the longstanding dream of the American people that the social structure can be improved in an orderly fashion by government underwriting of certain social risks.

Chapter XVIII

WHICH WAY AMERICAN LABOR?

HERMAN FELDMAN

★ ★ ★ ★

IN CURRENT discussion of labor developments, three questions
are certainly among those uppermost in people's minds.
The harassed employer and the distressed citizen alike ask:
Will the labor factions now engaged in an embittered struggle
finally annihilate one another, or will some basis be found for a
united front? The sympathizer with labor asks: Will labor
unionism recede in membership and power or will the end of
the decade find it larger in membership and more securely
entrenched than ever? The economist and the sociologist ask:
Would a strong labor movement mean economic retardation
to the country and internal strife between classes, or would it
mean constructive co-operation toward a common goal of
national well being? These three major issues, considered in the
light of recent events, will form the subject matter of the present chapter.

THE HOUSE OF LABOR: DIVIDED OR ONE?

Struggles within the ranks of labor may be classified into
four types: jurisdictional disputes, intraunion factional outbreaks, clashes of dual unions, and civil wars of dual federations. The present situation involves a convergence of all these
varieties of disputes and in particularly malignant combina-
tions. A word about these forms of labor union distemper may
indicate the complications of the malady.

A jurisdictional dispute, recurrent as a source of trouble
within the A. F. of L., is a border incident between unions

286

having chartered or acknowledged spheres of operation but conflicting with regard to jurisdiction over an overlapping kind of work. The classic example is the question whether carpenters or sheet metalworkers are entitled to make wood doors incased in tin. If the unions involved in such disputes are members of the same federation, there is likely to be a national labor authority, no matter how imperfect, that will endeavor to adjust the cause of the difficulty. When this is not the case it is warfare to the hilt.

An intraunion fractional dispute may be defined as one in which some new or upstart group within a labor union challenges the existing leadership, either because of a clash of ideas or because of a mere collision of personalities. Such a factional rebellion is usually of temporary and local importance when it is isolated and unsupported from the outside. But the ever-present possibility of a dual federation encourages intraunion factional disputes of a more deep-seated nature, so that a new union challenging the old may emerge and thus precipitate the clash of dual unionism. This does not mean, however, that a dual federation will inevitably result. Until 1937, factional outbreaks and dual unions made trouble in only a few of the 110 national unions constituting the A. F. of L., and a conflict of this sort was not regarded as the outpost of a rival federation. Today, because of artificial stimulation from the outside, every petty squabble becomes magnified, local adjustment becomes extremely difficult, and the elimination of a weaker force is made less easy. Thus when there are dual federations, labor is in the grip of a civil war.

GENESIS OF THE PRESENT TROUBLE

This most dangerous form of rivalry is a type of conflict from which the labor movement has been free for half a century. The A. F. of L., organized in 1886 under its present name, was a revolt from the Knights of Labor, then at its zenith, but the latter was so poorly adapted to the practical needs of the labor movement that it at once began to decline

287

and within a few years had become unimportant. In the decade 1910–1920, the International Workers of the World made trouble sporadically in certain branches, such as textiles, longshore labor, logging, and mining, but as a whole, until 1937, the A. F. of L. had unquestioned supremacy as a federation of unions.

The Committee for Industrial Organization, popularly called the CIO, started informally on November 10, 1935, not as a seceding group or dual federation, but merely as a committee of eight A. F. of L. unions which wanted to further the industrial form of unionization within the steel, automobile, and other mass industries. The Executive Council of the A. F. of L. might well have made concessions strategically to confine the scope of CIO activity to a limited area. Instead, the council suspended this group and engaged in a series of acts which hopelessly widened the rift. The CIO leaders, exasperated by this treatment and denouncing vigorously the actions of their opponents, retaliated by setting up a dual labor federation in April, 1937.

The new group included some of the most powerful and best seasoned unions in the country, such as the United Mine Workers, the International Ladies' Garment Workers, and the Amalgamated Clothing Workers. As it grew, it added to its roster new and vigorous unions started in various fields, so that by the fall of 1937 it could claim some thirty-four separate national unions and some three million or more members. This meant that it was not easily to be disposed of and that a battle of the giants was in prospect.

Was this break in the ranks of organized labor a mere surface occurrence, or was it the result of forces long held in abeyance? There is a popular impression that the emergence of CIO was due to its advocacy of a form of labor organization, *viz.*, vertical unionism, in contrast with the dominant craft structure of the unions in the A. F. of L. This is to exaggerate a question of method, and therefore it is necessary to clarify the point.

288

The A. F. of L. has consisted of about 110 independent national unions, each with separate charters and jurisdiction over the whole country. Of this group, two, the United Mine Workers and the Brewery Workers, were practically the only ones organized as unions of the purely industrial type. What this means is that the United Mine Workers accepts as members everyone working in or around a mine, whether a carpenter, electrician, machinist, or coal digger. The Brewery Workers includes teamsters, firemen, engineers, and other employees incidental to brewing operations. A few other unions, such as the International Ladies' Garment Workers, are of a quasi-industrial type. They include all those employees directly concerned in making clothing or whatever the product of the industry may be, but not other groups incidentally connected with the industry, such as electricians or machinists.

The rest of the 110 unions of the A. F. of L. are predominantly of the craft type, *i.e.*, their jurisdiction extends only to a particular occupation within a given shop. For example, in a printing plant, the compositor who sets the type belongs to a wholly different union from the pressman who prints the sheets or the bookbinder who binds them, and these groups are further subdivided as far as unions are concerned. Thus, in the pressroom alone there are three separate national craft unions, *viz.*, the Pressmen's Union, the Press Assistants' Union, and the Paper Handlers' Union.

The craft form of organizing labor does not, of itself, make impossible the organization of the unskilled; it merely makes organization more difficult in certain industries. In the building trades there are unions for unskilled building laborers, so that these unskilled are organized, though in their own separate organizations. It is likewise theoretically possible for an automobile plant to have several craft unions of workers and at least one huge union for the unskilled. If the A. F. of L. had pursued the policy of organizing the unskilled workers, even on such a divided basis, there would have been no grounds for the charge that its structural base was inherently unsuitable to the organization of workers in industries in which mass production prevails.

THE BASIC COMPLAINTS OF THE CIO

The CIO is not opposed to craft unions wherever these have been able to achieve the primary purpose of organizing the workers. For example, the CIO had no intention of attempting to invade such well-organized fields as those of the building trades, the railroads, and other industries in which, in spite of the craft structure, the extent of organization is very broad.

The basic fault which the leaders of the CIO found with the A. F. of L. was the fact that, with an achievable labor union membership of perhaps ten million, or more, and a potential wage-earning membership of perhaps twenty million, the A. F. of L. had, by 1935, in fact, organized merely some three and a half millions—this in spite of the opportunities afforded by the NRA. The organized groups represented predominantly the skilled workers of the country, so that the great mass of the unskilled workers were outside the doors. Thus the CIO group felt it had strong reasons for exasperation with the A. F. of L. on these grounds:

1. That the A. F. of L. leadership was one primarily interested in maintaining the working conditions and relative superiority of the skilled as compared with organizing the great mass of the unskilled.

2. That the denial of this would mean that A. F. of L. leaders had not the zeal, courage, ability, or what it takes to go out and organize these workers in steel, automobile, rubber, chemical, and other mass-production industries, as shown by the fact that they had not for over three decades of the past centuries made any headway in those industries.

3. That, even if these two assertions were questioned, a fundamental reason for the failure of the A. F. of L. in certain important areas in which it was weak was its craft structure, for this emphasized separateness of interest of various groups

290

within an industry, gave the employer a chance to play off one against another, and served in defeating major advances on the organizing front.

The CIO differs from the A. F. of L. chiefly, therefore, in these three particulars: (1) in being primarily interested in organizing the unorganized, constituting chiefly the semiskilled and the unskilled; (2) in supplying a fresh, vigorous, and capable leadership that within the first year captured sectors which had defied the whole A. F. of L. for decades; (3) in being free of the structural rigidity of the charted policies of the A. F. of L., so that the industrial form of organization can be used wherever it is appropriate.

ELEMENTS OF THE CONFLICT

The existence of two rival federations fighting each other at every conceivable point of friction is a terrifying prospect for the future of a country which has long been wallowing in economic depression and which will require several years of prosperity to regain a feeling of security. It is an unendurable situation, for, in addition to strikes against employers and union strikes against each other, there are developing such paralyzing and impoverishing expedients as the use of boycotts to nullify legitimate victories. The reuniting of the two federations into one organization is the imperative need of the moment. What are the obstacles to such an outcome?

One fortunate fact is that the clash represents no fundamental social antagonism. There is no desire for warfare among the mass of wage earners themselves. Twenty of the chief labor leaders of the country, intent on obtaining a reconciliation could, with a little inner strategy, effect some sort of compromise in a short time. This view does not underestimate the complexity of making an integration of the old into the new, but merely to point out where the log jam is centered.

Let us look for a moment at the A. F. of L. Some of the leaders of its organization have been in control of their particular segments for decades. Although a few years ago not a few unions were threatened with extinction, the same leaders are still at the top of the pile, in berths that are much more secure than they had been for a long while. But they know that many of its members lean toward the CIO structure and leadership. If they admitted the CIO, with its asserted three million membership (or whatever it may now be as a result of the "recession"), the control of the A. F. of L. might pass to the leaders of the CIO. Democratic control of a labor organization requires acquiescence in such political overturns, but the desire of the leaders to hold on to their status makes them willing to go to any lengths to maintain their grip of that part of the labor movement which is subject to their control.

Let us now look at the CIO. The convictions of the CIO leaders, their astonishing rank and file support, and their tremendous early success made them overconfident of their strength, but the recession has had a chastening effect. CIO leaders know too well that the A. F. of L. is imbedded institutionally, that it is an uncomfortable antagonist, and that a permanent break is neither to labor's interest nor to that of CIO. But these leaders are certain that merging with the A. F. of L. without a very definite change of spirit and principle on the part of the latter would be to lose the value of all CIO efforts to achieve structural adaptations in certain of the mass industries. This would impair the continued organizing of the unorganized.

BASES OF RECONCILIATION

Evidence on the part of the A. F. of L. of a sincere desire for adjustment to the new spirit and structure and of willingness to make a real place for the CIO following and programs would put a tremendous pressure on Lewis and others whom the A. F. of L. denounce for recalcitrance.

On March 10, 1937, in a radio address, Homer Martin, president of the United Automobile Workers, a CIO affiliate, outlined a basic plan for negotiating an end to the labor feud. He urged:

> A definite and clearly stated recognition by the A. F. of L. of the principle and policy of industrial unionism for the mass production industries, to remove the doubt existing in the minds of some as to the extent to which the A. F. of L. had agreed to accept this policy and principle in the recent peace negotiations.
>
> Immediate steps to solve the jurisdictional problems affecting such CIO unions as are functioning in fields where older A. F. of L. unions are in existence.
>
> Submission of jurisdictional adjustments to subcommittees with a time limit for achieving results. In the event subcommittees are unable to reach an agreement their controversy would be submitted to a super-committee representing the A. F. of L. and CIO. Should this fail, the jurisdictional problems would be put before an arbitrator or arbitration committee.
>
> It should be understood and agreed that none of the CIO unions are to be admitted piece-meal or by groups into the A. F. of L. upon the attainment of a peace basis, but that the admission of the CIO unions is to be achieved as a body upon the clearing up of the entire situation.

A solution can only lie in some such constructive program and in a peace without defeat. On the part of the existing hierarchy of the A. F. of L., certain craft unions must be willing to waive jurisdiction over members of their trade employed in certain mass industries and thus accept a permanent restriction upon their unjustified notion of unlimited charter rights. The field left to craft unions would be big enough. The existing hierarchy of the A. F. of L. itself must integrate the new forces by giving them independent status in their fields as chartered members of the federation. In its turn, the CIO must be reasonable and conciliatory so that the medicine the craft unions will have to take will not be too hard to swallow in one gulp. For either the A. F. of L. or the CIO to refuse to negotiate on terms such as these would constitute a costly betrayal of labor and a flagrant disregard of the economic interests of the country.

Within both camps there have been elements working quietly for reconciliation, but their efforts have had little result. The temporary successes of one or the other side occasionally blind them to real perils of the schism. The wound is too wide to be healed by nature and requires a surgical suture.

If labor continues recalcitrant, what force in the community can bludgeon the two sides into a compromise? Perhaps only the President himself. He must do more than call for a plague on both their houses, for the plague is likely to carry off many not themselves involved. The mass of wage earners, as well as employers and the general public, would support him in a move demanding that such a compromise, on general terms clearly outlined in advance, be affected through the aid and decisions of jointly selected arbitrators.

WILL UNION MEMBERSHIP INCREASE OR DECREASE?

Previous to the New Deal, the most rapid growth in union membership occurred during the War period. From its peak of over 4,078,000 members, in 1920, the trend had been persistently downward to a low point of almost half this figure in 1933. A sudden advance began at that time, largely because of a governmental policy favoring unionism, together with legislation designed to protect workers in the process of establishing collective bargaining. This was embodied in clause 7a of the NIRA. In this early period the expansion of unionism occurred chiefly in unions already in the field and partially organized. The bituminous coal division of the United Mine Workers not only "came back" but reached an all-time peak; the women's garment union doubled its membership and extended its control to new geographical and industrial areas; the brewery industry took on new life after the repeal of prohibition; the longshore and marine industries, the boot and shoe industry, and others made rapid strides.

Employers, by various devices of opposition, effected a slowing down of this movement, so that organization was said to be almost at a standstill at the time of the invalidation of the NIRA in May, 1935. However, the National Labor Relations

294

Act was substituted almost immediately, and in November, 1936, with the re-election of Roosevelt, a new and unparalled period of organization began.

ANNO MIRABILIS: 1937

The year 1937 then made its mark as the most notable in labor history. It is the year in which the Supreme Court astonished the country in upholding the validity of the National Labor Relations Act, thus crippling employer opposition to unions and giving labor powerful legal support to its organizing efforts. It is the year in which the CIO became a rival federation of labor and achieved its dramatic successes. Its invasion of the mass production industries resulted in the capitulation of the United States Steel Company, Jones & Laughlin, and some 400 smaller steel companies. In the automobile industry, free of any union until 1933, its union achieved 380 agreements, with some 400,000 workers; in the rubber industry a new union claimed 75,000 members, and in the electrical and radio workers the CIO claimed 125,000, aside from the expansion in the same field by the Electrical Workers of the A. F. of L. The Textile Union, which was one of the original groups of the CIO, grew from less than 100,000 members to about 275,000. The CIO also enrolled some 65,000 members in the petroleum industry and about 50,000 subway, bus, and taxicab employees in the City of New York.

The A. F. of L. at the same time was expanding existing unions, the most significant achievement being a culmination of organization activities begun a year or two earlier in the railroads, and the expansion of the machinists and of the electrical workers in certain of the mass-production industries.

What it all amounted to, in membership figures, is that the A. F. of L. unions reported as of October 1, 1937, a total dues-paying membership of 3,377,000, and the CIO, almost as many. The CIO figures are probably more nebulous but they are impressive. In January, 1938, one high official of the CIO claimed that his organization had almost 4,000,000 members.

295

That there was probably a membership of 7,000,000 or more in the two federations in 1937 is reasonable. Add to this, the four railroad brotherhoods, not in either federation, along with certain other independents, and there may have been a moment in 1937 when it would not have been serious exaggeration to assert an 8,000,000 membership in all unions in existence in the country.

The grave decline in employment characterizing the early part of 1938 should have meant a rapid dwindling of membership, but the extent of these losses was balanced by other factors. In spite of the recession, the impetus with which certain new industries have been invaded has yielded new agreements steadily since October, 1937. Agreements have been won by maritime workers, metal workers, and such new groups as clerks and agents of insurance companies, employees of telegraph and telephone companies, employees of retail stores, office workers, and white-collar workers generally.

EFFECTS OF THE CONFLICT ON LABOR ORGANIZATION

This unusual trend, occurring in spite of interunion strife and hard times, may be understood in the light of certain peculiar conditions growing out of the recent schism. In trying to determine what will be the future course of the labor movement and whether we are again likely to see any such decline as occurred in 1920, there are several factors which must be evaluated.

We need deal only cursorily with the ultimate effects of a prolonged economic depression. For a variety of obvious reasons, labor union membership suffers severely during a serious depression, and if this is in prospect, it is certain to leave unions in a weakened state. Let us rather evaluate the less obvious factors.

For several reasons the conflict of dual federations has thus far helped rather than hurt the cause of unionism. In the first place, the competition of the two sides has made for more vigorous campaigning in many areas in which the A. F. of L. had been inactive. The break of the CIO released from control many militant leaders who were under the thumb of A. F. of L. discipline, and the new vigor of the competition has by contagion been imparted to the A. F. of L. as well.

In the second place, in order to try to meet this aggressive competitor on its own ground, the A. F. of L. has begun to minimize the structural difficulties which formerly impeded it. Certain craft unions have adopted an industrial basis, at least for the time. The carpenters' union, the machinists' union, and other dyed-in-the-wool craft unions have set out to take all the membership they can. As an example, Local No. 3 of the Brotherhood of Electrical Workers, operating in the New York area, has taken in the semiskilled and the unskilled workers in electrical equipment plants in Westchester, New Jersey, and Long Island, so that at the end of 1937, it had almost doubled its membership in the metropolitan area.

A third factor, of particular significance so far as the A. F. of L. is concerned, is that the militancy, temporary irresponsibility, and communist flavor of certain CIO units, scared employers into regarding the A. F. of L. as much the less of two evils. The leaders of the CIO seemed too much intent on establishing a virile labor movement, while certain of the A. F. of L. unions seemed more interested in merely extending their membership. The A. F. of L. seemed, therefore, to offer less threat to the *status quo*. As a result, many employers have been trying to checkmate the CIO by tying up with the A. F. of L., in some cases even urging company unions to take out charters with the A. F. of L. In turn, A. F. of L. unions have rushed in to sign contracts with employers in fields where they have had no majority following. The National Labor Relations Board in a number of cases has had to intervene to upset such labor highjacking, by insisting on an election to determine whom the workers wished to have as their representatives. This, however, has evoked from the A. F. of L. loud condemnation of the NLRB as interfering with democracy!

INFLUENCE AND STATUS OF THE WAGNER ACT

Will the two federations continue to gain as much in results as in rivalry? The effect in the future is more likely to be otherwise. Admittedly, much of the increase in labor strength has been due to the favorable political conditions in nation and state. The very special protection granted by the National Labor Relations Act is an essential basis of labor advance. If a reaction in public opinion against unions were to wipe the act off the books, an antiunion drive by employers could demolish much of the structure labor unionism has built up in these few years. To maintain popular favor, the National Labor Relations Act must prove that it offers a peaceful way of solving the labor struggle, on the thesis that, once the right to collective bargaining is granted, the cause of most labor disputes is removed.

But instead, the notion is gaining ground that the act is no real aid. For example, certain of the lumber mills of the Pacific Coast are willing to deal either with the CIO or with the A. F. of L., whichever happens to get a majority. An election held in the plant should, theoretically, have been the means of relieving the situation; but actually boycotts were evoked by unions handling the goods in transit, and so the struggle continued. This kind of situation is certain to exasperate not merely the general public but also the members of unions themselves. If, therefore, conditions of this sort continue and hard times are a background, there will be a popular reaction against unions and against the National Labor Relations Act. This, along with other causes, will halt the growth of federations, and cause their membership to decline to a much lower total figure than could be jointly attained under a unified organization.

The possibility of the repeal of the National Labor Relations Act by such an eventual ebb tide of public opinion is the greater because it is constantly being exposed to attacks by the A. F. of L. for exceeding its powers and for being dictatorial, fascist, and an instrument of tyranny. This situation may be explained as follows: When an election is held in a plant, the question involved is what groups of employees should be included in that election. For example, in a tobacco plant of 1,500 workers, should the twenty machinists or ten electrical workers vote separately with regard to their right to be represented by separate unions, or should their vote be part of that of the employees as a whole? If, because of the intervention of some craft union, the former decision is made, the NLRB may in effect be forcing the breakup into crafts of workers organized by the CIO as a unit. It would mean also that the CIO unit in doing the spade work in opening up new territory would be contributing time and money partly to help a craft union become entrenched in a new area.

The NLRB has said that the "appropriate unit" in certain industries might involve a separation of certain crafts from the general election to be held for the rest, but, because in other cases it has not so held, it is assailed. The exact basis of these attacks and their refinements will not be appreciated by the general public, which is gradually getting the notion that, since the employers do not like the act, and since the federations themselves seem dissatisfied with it, and since labor troubles seem not to have diminished, perhaps the best thing to do is to throw the whole thing out. In all fairness to the CIO it should be said that the general tenor of its criticism of the act has been more friendly and cautious than that of the A. F. of L.

In the meantime, employers are countering by offering the alternative of so-called *independent unions*, started by workmen under the subtly protecting aegis of employers and industrial relations executives. The technique of employers in launching and maintaining such independent nonfederation groups is constantly improving, and the movement is getting beyond the pale of NLRB intervention. The appeal in these associations is particularly strong just now as a reaction to the destructive conflict going on within the house of labor.

A popular change of heart toward labor and the repeal of the act by the process of amendment will permit employers to use more direct and vigorous methods to beat unionism down. If this occurs, the unions will have themselves largely to blame for not reconciling their differences of a purely internal nature, thus combining to advance the labor movement as a whole. When wisdom comes—assuming that it will—the labor union movement will have been dealt severe blows, and, because of its strategic failures, an uphill effort to repair the damage will again be required.

LABOR IN POWER: PROGRESS OR RETARDATION?

But let us consider the possibility, indeed, the probability that organized labor will ultimately become stronger, and ask: What will its influence be on the economic and political life of the nation?

Popular discussion of this aspect of labor unionism centers around the *responsibility* of unions, a term which tends to obscure vital problems by emphasis on transitional ones. The term needs to be clarified by reference to current criticism of unions.

What many people have in mind when they think of trade union responsibility is the observance of decorum and good faith in collective bargaining. They cite, as examples, disturbances of the peace, illegal acts to obtain recognition, and unauthorized strikes occurring in spite of contracts outlawing such practices. Such violations, incidentally, are held to be a peculiar trait of the CIO, an assertion which would seem to simplify the matter, but which shows an absence of true perspective on the part of those making it.

This first phase of trade unionism responsibility is of minor concern because it may be regarded largely as a transitional phenomenon occurring during a period when unionism is new to the rank and file. At such a time, certain leaders whose temperaments are unstable or obstructive are likely to be sifted out and "liquidated." For the steam rollers of the strong men soon give more stable leaders the control. Such stability is manifested by many of the officers of the A. F. of L. unions, as well as by those of the older divisions of the CIO, such as the United Mine Workers. The control exercised by the older unions in the CIO over its officers is at least on a par with that exercised by the A. F. of L.

Another class of criticisms of trade union irresponsibility, held by a large number of critics of unions, starts at this point. They see trade union bosses entrenched at various points who handle large funds without accounting for them properly, who levy secret tribute on employers, or who are, in certain cases, merely racketeers. Such charges are too frequent to be waved off, although the cure most frequently advanced, *viz.*, the incorporation of unions, is a misguided one. The demand for honesty in office, indispensable in trade union administration, is, however, an achievable goal; but it is not the crux of the trade union problem.

SIGNIFICANT ASPECT OF LABOR UNION "RESPONSIBILITY"

It is a third aspect of trade union responsibility which represents the essence of future difficulty. The question is: Responsibility to whom? Shall trade unions and their leaders be considered, at best, narrow and grasping groups, vigorously, although honestly, trying to benefit merely themselves, without regard for the economic and social outcome? Or shall they be expected to shoulder the obligation of a semipublic agency having a responsibility for the economic and social well-being of the country as a whole?

This is no mere rhetorical question, for, realistically viewed, unions consist of groups of workers who wish to obtain some benefits for themselves. Those in a union are often the same type of persons as those who belong to the American Legion, the Townsend movement, or to the Ku Klux Klan. To endow any group of people with a special nobility because of the fact that they call themselves a union is naive.

Labor organization may be a different kind of influence at different stages of its development. When conditions in an industry are notoriously bad, everything a union does to

301

improve the conditions of the group may be to the social good. As a union progresses in power, a stage is reached when it may present a totally different aspect from the one in which it began. A craft which first raises its level from $4 to $6 a day may appeal to our sympathy, but not when it becomes a monopoly and asks more than twice that sum. The workers who, terrorized by corrupt foremen and harsh supervisors, courageously achieve humane working rules may cease to evoke admiration when they use their power to make wasteful regulations which lower efficiency and output. Attempts to get national legislation to curb oriental immigration are more praiseworthy than the exertion of influence at the national capital to obstruct tariff revisions on products worked on by craft unions. As unions increase in power to the point of actually dominating economic policies, a greater obligation is imposed upon them to engage in economic thinking commensurate with their new responsibilities. There is a notion, for example, on the part of many unions that wages must never be lowered, and that the union must at all times press for increases in pay. This seemingly desirable social aspiration may, in fact, be irreconcilable with economic realities and may impose unjust burdens on other workers and on the public. A phase of this problem was recently pointed out by Prof. Sumner H. Slichter when he stated:

> When collective bargaining is first instituted, there is usually a certain amount of slack that can be taken up without serious harm to employment. After this initial period is over, however, the rate at which collective bargaining can raise wages in industry as a whole cannot be much more than the rate of increase in the productivity of labor. This increase during the last several generations seems to have averaged less than 2 per cent a year.[1]

There is greater danger than mere unfairness in misguided or narrow policies regarding wages, technique, or discipline. This danger is that such policies will ultimately exasperate large numbers of people who, first of all, want work and peace. One acute observer, Dorothy Thompson, points ominously to the danger of this as it may now be developing in France. In her column in the New York *Herald Tribune* of February 2, 1938, she states:

> The French workers, who support the rearmament program and are second to no class in France in their ardor to protect France from Fascist aggression, are balking at the use of electric riveters in the nationalized munitions factories, and the result is that the rearmament program is running far behind schedule and costing far more than it should.
>
> In France one hears precisely what one heard in Germany in the early 1930's: "Cela ne peut pas durer"—it can't go on like this. A Frenchman who is in close touch with the situation at home told me this week, "We should have Fascism in France already if Germany and Italy had not done it first." There is the same demand on the part of the middle classes for "social and national disciplines" which is the precursor of all Fascist revolts. Fascism seems to be staved off in France only by the Frenchness of the French.

SOCIAL OBJECTIVES PARAMOUNT

In essence, therefore, the efforts being made to instill a measure of democracy in industry are only the beginnings of an evolution of relations which may lead to one of two objectives. The fact that the intent of the movement is democratic does not of itself safeguard us from a collapse of democracy. The success of the industrial marriages of employees and unions will depend on the determination of the individual and the union, in spite of increasing power, to exercise moderation and square dealing. This implies the increasing capacity to subordinate selfish and personal aims *reasonably* to the ideal of the social good.

NOTE

[1] "The Contents of Collective Agreements," in *The Society for the Advancement of Management Journal*, January, 1938, p. 19.

Chapter XIX

THE FARMER'S PROBLEM
IS YOUR PROBLEM

ARTHUR P. CHEW

★ ★ ★ ★

ANALYSIS of the farmer's problem is a study in human interests. This makes it somewhat different from the analysis of the agricultural problem in general. It deals with the needs of individuals and families, rather than with the technical and economic requirements of an impersonal industry. Need it be said that the welfare of the farmers is not always identical with the progress and prosperity of the farming business? Wealth may accumulate and men decay, as Goldsmith said. There have been poor farmers in thriving agricultural systems from time immemorial. Farm wealth is not accumulating very rapidly just now; but even if it were, we might still have a farmers' problem. Farmers in the United States have more things to think about than merely the total volume of the agricultural earnings, as will presently appear.

FARMERS—REAL AND OTHERWISE

But first, who are the farmers? This is not a simple matter. We cannot divide the population sharply into the farmers and the nonfarmers, for between farm and nonfarm occupations there is a continual interchange of personnel, brought about by the ebb and flow of population between country and town. Before 1930 the movement toward the city was much greater than the movement toward the farm. During the depression, however, the net migration was toward the farms. In 1932,

304

about 266,000 more persons moved from the urban centers to the farms than moved from farms to urban centers. This interchange of population between the country and the town shows that large numbers have no fixed roots either in agricultural or in nonagricultural occupations. Always the so-called *farm population* includes great numbers who are not farmers.

In 1936, the flow of population began once more to ebb away from the farms. In that year the net migration toward the cities was 446,000 persons. It drew from agriculture many persons who had gone reluctantly to farms or who had over-stayed their welcome on the old farmstead. Normally, the interchange of population between town and country is partly seasonal; it involves a two-way movement of migratory laborers. Normally, some of the interchange reflects the decision or the compulsion of individuals to make a permanent change in their way of life. All in all, it is a very large movement. In 1936, for example, about 1,165,000 persons moved from the farms to the villages, towns, and cities, while 719,000 persons moved in the opposite direction. Extreme mobility is a remarkable feature of the American scene. It has no counterpart in any other country and adds much to the difficulty of saying who are the farmers.

There is another confusing element. Millions of people, mostly unemployed, returned to the land during the depression. Millions of them were still there in 1935. Another surplus farm group, mostly young people, were on the farms because the cities and towns could not absorb them. As a result, the farm population was six or seven millions greater than it would have been normally. Small poor farms increased tremendously between 1930 and 1935; the census reported an additional 500,000 of these properties, most of them in areas of hilly, eroding land or near the large industrial cities. These were the so-called *subsistence farms*—which means that they did not yield a subsistence. The occupants were farmers only by courtesy title. There should be another name for them and also for the urban refugees and the farm-reared youngsters

305

who would be in the cities if they could get work there. These groups are not commercially necessary in agriculture. Often, moreover, they depend for a living on part-time nonfarm work, on the bounty of relatives, or on relief.

Besides the crop of subsistence farmers produced by the depression, there is a group that is historically older. It comprises our rural primitives—the hill folk, the Florida crackers, the small graziers of semiarid regions, and a varied assortment of part-time farmers. These part-time farmers are generally in a desperate situation. Rural industries which formerly gave them both a market and some part-time work have moved away, their land has eroded, and they have few sources of cash income. On the 500,000 "self-sufficing" farms recorded by census enumerators only about $140 worth of produce per farm is sold annually. Two-thirds of what they produce is food and fuel for consumption on the farm. Such so-called *subsistence* and *part-time* farms abound in the southern Appalachians, in the cut-over region of the lake states, in the Ozarks, and in the northeastern states. Actually, they do not provide a subsistence. In a sensible allocation of our land among suitable uses, most of these farms would be in forestry, or in wildlife conservation, or in recreation areas. They are a symptom of chronic economic depression, rather than an integral part of the agricultural system. We may regard them as a poor form of relief, which a better economy would eliminate.

Moreover, many of the people who are in agriculture to stay and who belong there still ought not to be called farmers. In the busy months, our farms employ about 2,700,000 persons as farm laborers; many of them work on the farms for only a few weeks. Economic planning should provide for their welfare, but it should not call them *farmers*. Then there are the share croppers, who operate more than 700,000 farms and constitute more than a third of all the farm tenants in the Southern states. They contribute to the farm business only their own labor and that of their families. The landlord provides the land, the work stock, the tools, and the seed, and usually furnishes food and other necessaries. Thousands of so-called *tenant farmers* are in a similar position. They do not manage their farms but work under close supervision. Moreover, they have no real claim upon the products. Ought we to call them farmers? It is a nice question. One does not call the factory hand a manufacturer, and it seems unreasonable to call the farmhand a farmer. He belongs to a farm-labor group that has its own problems, frequently dissimilar to the problems of the true farmer.

FARM FINANCES

These eliminations, however, still leave an immense farm population and nearly 6 million farms. Fully half the farm families are financially insecure. That was the finding of the President's Committee on Farm Tenancy in 1937. Indeed, the committee found one farm family out of four in a precarious position. About fifteen per cent of the farm families earned gross incomes in 1929 of less than $400; and 1929 was a good year. About twenty-eight per cent of farm families had gross incomes of less than $600; about forty-nine per cent had gross incomes of less than $1,000. The typical farm of northern Europe produces more than that. In fact, the less productive half of our farms produced in 1929 only about eleven per cent of all farm products sold or traded. It would be possible, in a favorable market situation, to increase production that much on the better farms. Then, commercially speaking, the poorer half of the farms would be unnecessary. It does not follow, of course, that because half the country's farms contribute little to the feeding and clothing of nonfarm people they should be eliminated forthwith. They feed their occupants, and that is something in these days. But the living they provide is far from the theoretical American standard.

There is an immense difference between the small poor farms, the great ranches of the Western plains, and the so-called *industrial farms* of the Pacific slope. The difference is one of kind as well as of degree. Many of the poorer farmers are virtually outside the money economy, whereas the great rancher or fruit grower is an important capitalist. In 1929, some 8,000 large farms, most of them fruit, truck, specialty-crop, dairy, or cattle farms had an averate wage bill of $13,385, as compared with an average of only $135 on about 6 million family-size farms. The problems of the small farmer are very different from those of the large operator. Indeed, the small and the large farmers often have divergent interests, comparable to the divergent interests of labor and capital.

Up the ladder a rung or two from the small poor farms are the farmers of the South, who have only about half as much income per capita as the farmers in other sections. This generalization takes in the plantation owners and the independent farmers, as well as the tenants and the share croppers. Many Southern farm families, even among the whites, do not possess even a mule and a few farm tools; tenant earnings in the South are usually below a decent subsistence level. Two-thirds of the country's less productive farms are in the South, though there are many also in the Middle West and in the North Central and northeastern states.

THE FAMILY-SIZED FARM AND ITS PROBLEMS

Generally speaking, the farms of the United States are still family-size farms. They require only the labor of the farm family, with a little hired labor besides in the busy seasons. Farms specializing in grain as a money crop usually run over 260 acres; but half our general farms and dairy farms are less than 100 acres in size, and half the so-called *self-sufficing* farms are less than 50 acres. Mechanization has increased somewhat the average size of farms for the country as a whole, and some conspicuous developments have taken place in corporation and chain farming. Nevertheless the great majority of the farms are relatively small and represent a cross between the old agricultural self-sufficiency and the modern commercial system of farming. Similarity of size, however, does not imply similarity of requirements.

When we talk about the farmer's problem, it is the family-size farm that we should have in mind. Obviously, the conditions of life on such farms have lately changed to correspond with social changes elsewhere. Modern communications have ended rural isolation; agriculture is highly mechanized; farm people use goods and services identical with those used in cities; education in the country resembles education in the town. American agriculture still has its roots in the family, which is both the social and the economic unit. Neither the collective farm on the Russian model nor the great corporation farm offers an attractive rival pattern. Acceptance of the typical farm family as a unit is fundamental in the shaping of our agricultural policy.

Needless to say, however, farm families differ greatly in their relationship to the land, and in this fact lies another fundamental consideration in agricultural policy making. Agriculture has an internal as well as an external maladjustment. According to statistics, owner-operated farms outnumber the tenant farms, and the owner-operated acreage exceeds the tenant-operated acreage. Many so-called *owner-farmers*, however, have only a nominal ownership; the real owner is an absent mortgagee or creditor. For example, in 1930, the equities of farm owners in Illinois, Iowa, and South Dakota averaged less than 30 per cent of the value of their farms. Taking the country as a whole, the equity of the farm operators amounts only to about 42 per cent of the value of the farm real estate. This equity, moreover, is a diminishing quantity. In 1920 it was 50 per cent; in 1900, 54 per cent; and in 1890, 59 per cent. Farm land and buildings in this country were valued in 1930 at $47,379,000,000; but $27,978,000,000 was the property of others than the immediate farm operator. Thousands of so-called *owner-farmers* have only a labor interest and not an investment interest in their farms.

Tenancy is increasing very rapidly. The proportion of the farms operated by tenants in 1935 was 42 per cent, as compared with only 38 per cent in 1920. Farm land operated under lease in 1935 was 45 per cent of the total, as against only 31 per cent in 1900. In some states tenants operated nearly three-quarters of the farm land. Tenant operation covers 73 per cent of the cotton farms. There was a little less tenancy in the South in 1935 than in 1930, but the change was not an improvement. It meant that numerous former tenants and croppers had become wage hands while others had gone on the relief rolls. Among white farmers in the Southern states, 46 per cent are tenants. Elsewhere the proportion is 30 per cent. This growth of tenancy implies an increased separation of agricultural labor from agricultural capital, and shows that agricultural policy should consider the landless as well as the landed farm folk.

In the farm tenure situation, we find at one extreme the absentee owner, who may not even visit the farm, much less do any of the farm work; and at the other extreme, the propertyless tenant or cropper. In between are hybrid types— the owner-operator who rents some additional land; the tenant with considerable working capital; the tenant with little or no working capital; share-rent tenants; and cash-rent tenants. Some farm tenants are capable managers; others need constant and minute supervision. In most states of the North and West, the tenant farmers generally lease farms of a higher average value than those of full owner-operators. The better farms more frequently permit of tenant operation.

Owners of profitable farms move off and let others do the work, and the arrangement may be mutually advantageous. Tenancy is not necessarily bad in itself; it may be a step toward farm ownership. In recent years, however, it has been increased by those who have descended rather than ascended the tenure ladder, and it has developed serious evils. Occupants of the different tenure positions have different problems, as well as problems shared in common with all farm operators; they have problems of status, of contract, and of custom which may be as difficult as any with which agriculture has to deal.

The tenure situation produces conflict between ownership and operation. It is not enough to increase the earnings; they must be divided fairly. Contention arises between landlords and tenants, and between mortgagees and mortgagors, in other words, between the claimants to an investment return on the land and capital and the claimants to a reward for labor and management. From time to time, the claims become irreconcilable, particularly in the depressions that follow booms. In every boom would-be land buyers bid up the price of land: they force valuations far above value, which depends on earning power. The ensuing reaction, with its foreclosures and bankruptcies, widens the breach between ownership and operation, and this calls for drastic action. Witness the Frazier-Lemke Moratorium Act, which delays foreclosure and virtually compels creditors to reach an accommodation with mortgagors.

In our period of the open frontier, when land was plentiful and population scarce, this problem arose only occasionally. The path to farm ownership was easy then. There was good land to be had free, or at a very low price. No one had to work long for another, either as laborer or tenant, if he cared to set up in farming for himself. Hence the dominant feature of the land tenure situation was owner-operation. As the country filled up, and the good free or cheap land disappeared, the situation changed. Newcomers had to become tenants or buy land on terms that gave the former owners an excessive proportion of the earnings for a long time. In short, the land became burdened with debt; moreover, capital charges increased with earnings. There seemed to be no remedy, and ownership and operation began to fight. Ownership enforced its claims through fixed charges; operation had to be content with what was left. Relatively a new one in the United States, *this problem is old in other countries.* It does not solve itself, but calls increasingly for the intervention of public agencies. In this country, *it is the neglected half* of the agricultural prob-

311

lem, though the Federal government and many of the state governments have begun to study and to deal with it.

RELIEF BY LEGISLATION

We may observe it, for example, in the Netherlands. After the World War, disparities developed there between farm rents and agricultural prices. Rents reflected high land values established during the war; agricultural prices reflected the impoverishment of consumers. Thousands of farm tenants faced bankruptcy, but special legislation relieved them. The Crisis Farm Tenancy Act of 1932 permitted any farm tenant who could not pay his rent to seek a voluntary adjustment under the auspices of his district court. Failure to get relief in that way opened up to him another course: he could appear with his landlord before a special chamber which had authority to revise the rental payments. This legislation proved very successful. Moreover, the government lent money to laborers and part-time farmers for the purchase of farms. In 1930 nearly sixty per cent of the farmers were landowners; they occupied fifty-one per cent of the land.

The population of the Netherlands, however, is very dense, and the demand for farms continued to exceed the supply. For this reason, the government, besides making leases subject to review and requiring landlords to compensate tenants for farm improvements, retained the ownership of certain land reclaimed from the Zuider Zee, and arranged to lease it in inalienable holdings. This land policy of the Dutch government made for the greater security of both landlords and tenants. Its basic principle was the intervention of the public authority for the readjustment of tenure conditions in times of depression. In the United States the pressure of population on the land supply is much less; but it exists, and gives rise to identical problems. Necessarily the solution for us, too, depends on legislation. Potentially, the problem of tenure is as important a farm problem as that of raising and maintaining the aggregate farm income.

FARM INCOME

It is obvious, however, that farm income should be raised; as between the various claimants, it is essential *to have something to divide.* And this brings us to the most general problem of the agricultural industry. Farm income was about sixteen or seventeen per cent of the national income before the war; it dropped after the war to about eleven per cent, and in the depression of 1929–1932 to about six per cent. By 1937 it had climbed back to ten per cent. That is modest for twenty-five per cent of the population. It would be at least thirteen per cent if the prewar relationship prevailed between the farm population and the farm share of the national income. Many students of the problem would regard even that percentage as extremely low. There is more dispute over the division of an *inadequate* total farm income among the various claimants than there would be over the division of a sufficient amount. As we might say, the distribution of a shortage is more vexing than the distribution of an abundance. Little progress toward an amicable adjustment of the disputes that arise between landlords and tenants, between mortgagors and mortgagees, and between farm operators and farm laborers, can be made until the farm income rises. First there must be a correct distribution of the national income between farmers and nonfarmers.

Most people know that the depression of 1929–1932 increased an already serious disparity between farm and nonfarm prices. In that period farm commodity prices dropped from about fifty per cent above the prewar level to about fifty per cent below it; other prices declined far less. Simultaneously, the annual gross farm income dropped from nearly 12 billion dollars to about 5 billion dollars, with the result that in 1932 the farmers received per capita only about a quarter as much income as the gainfully occupied in the nonfarm population. (They received half as much per capita as the nonfarmers before the war.) In 1937, with the government payments

313

included, the gross farm income was back to a point not far below the 1929 level, though the farm share of the national income, if we take the prewar relationship as a criterion, was still about 1½ billion dollars low.

The recovery, however, was precarious. It resulted in large part from legislation, which the United States Supreme Court subsequently invalidated in the Hoosac Mills case decision. (*United States v. Butler*, 297 U.S. 1.) Other factors, such as dollar revaluation and farm credit relief, played a part in the improvement. Big crops in 1937 caused prices to decline again, and obliged Congress and the nation to reopen the whole agricultural question. Once more it has become evident, as clearly as it was evident in 1933, that the situation requires special legislation.

It will help us to see why if we glance over the record. Our agricultural industry grew up in a reciprocal relationship with European manufacturing. This factor was basic in our agricultural expansion during the nineteenth century; it established a division of labor between the new world and the old. The United States was the breadbasket, Europe was the workshop, and our farmers could usually sell all that they produced at satisfactory prices. Not counting forest products, our agricultural exports rose from about 300 million dollars in value in 1870 to nearly 900 million dollars before the close of the century. Then began a decline which continued until the World War.

THE CRISIS IN AGRICULTURE

Temporarily, the war drew us back into heavy production for export. More American beef, pork, and cereals went to Europe in 1918 than at the height of our agricultural export trade in the nineties. The agricultural exports, including cotton, jumped to a point forty-five per cent above the prewar level. Suddenly, however, and with an accelerating speed, export trade began to shrink again, and after 1929 farm exports dropped more than sixty per cent. In the fiscal year

314

1937 they were the smallest that they had been in sixty years. This slump in exports synchronized with the trade depression and reduced consumption at home. It constituted a major agricultural disaster.

Therefore, the farmers had to seek the help of the government. They could not suddenly stop their production for export and get themselves on a domestic basis overnight. They were involved too deeply. They had been exporting about 13.2 per cent of their production, and the trade constituted about a third of our total exports. It was necessary to retreat strategically. When an industry has an export surplus from year to year, the prices obtainable for the export proportion determine the prices obtainable for the whole output. In a competitive, wholly unregulated market, low prices for export goods mean low prices also for similar goods offered to domestic consumers. With the export surplus hanging back, the home market becomes a bargain counter. It was necessary to break with the conventional system, and to invoke promptly a double remedy, one aspect of it designed gradually to eliminate the surpluses, and the other to inhibit, meantime, their normal effect on prices at home. The government's answer to this problem was the AAA, which organized the farmers for concerted crop reduction and simultaneously lifted domestic prices.

It does not appear that this operation inflicted any hardship on the consumer. In 1936, after a certain measure of crop limitation, and two great droughts besides, food prices in this country were still fifteen to twenty per cent below the pre-depression level. How low they would have fallen had the consumer been free to take advantage of the glut in the export trade and to get farm products at a fraction of their value, no one can tell. They would probably have been low enough to bankrupt millions of farmers. That would have meant, eventually, an approach to scarcity of farm products, coupled with a partial paralysis of farmer buying power—especially from the cities. As things turned out, the consumer paid a

315

little more for his food and clothing than he would have had to pay otherwise and had the satisfaction of co-operating effectively in a general economic recovery. As a result, the incomes of wage earners and of other city dwellers increased with the incomes of the farmers.

Probably the AAA promoted a *quicker* readjustment in the farm situation than would have been possible otherwise. It may not have promoted any *greater* readjustment, and certainly not any greater *limitation of the output*, than would have come about eventually in any case. It should be recalled that in 1932 farm commodity prices were fifty per cent below the prewar level. Except the droughts of 1934 and 1936 nothing that has happened since then would have raised them spontaneously, and the continuance of such prices would have driven thousands of farmers out of production and into the bankruptcy courts. With the foreign market drastically curtailed, the natural response of the American farmer would have been a drastic curtailment of his output. This natural response would have been harshly competitive and therefore generally ruinous. It would have had the same effect on prices in the end as the method which replaced it and which kept the farmers on their farms.

But the farm problem has not yet been solved, and we see now that it has a threefold aspect. It requires an increase in the total farm income, a more equitable distribution of that income among the different categories of producers, and a general movement for the conservation of agricultural resources. This final aspect of the matter, with which there is no space here to deal, arises from the fact that more than 200 million acres of our crop land have already been impoverished by erosion, and that an additional larger area is eroding and needs protection. Permanent farm prosperity requires not merely the adjustment of production for the maintenance of reasonable prices, but the conservation of resources. If the farmers allow their soil to deteriorate, so that the costs of production rise, nonfarmers will have a just complaint;

they will distinguish sharply between aiding the farmers in times of unavoidable calamity and paying for their inefficiency.

AGRICULTURE AS A NATIONAL PROBLEM

Regarded in this manner, we see that the farmer's problem is merely part of our national economic problem. It is necessary to restore urban as well as rural industry; otherwise, the land will be overmanned, the soil will erode and will deteriorate from various malpractices, farm prices will be low, and agriculture will be unable to buy much from the cities. There is need for more consumption both at home and abroad. This means there is need for more production; for production is income, and income is purchasing power. Moreover, urban and rural production must be correctly balanced; in other words, present increase in production must lie with industry rather than with agriculture; otherwise, temporary agricultural gluts will occur, and prices will fluctuate disastrously. In short, the farm problem, at bottom, is one with the economic problem as a whole. It must be formulated correctly, however, if we expect to find a solution.

THE FARM PROBLEM AND FOREIGN TRADE

We have already noted the fact that our agricultural problem has a vital connection with the international balance of trade. This country first developed a favorable balance of trade about ten years after the Civil War. Farm commodities constituted the bulk of it until the end of the nineteenth century; then factory goods began to figure in the excess of exports over imports. The favorable trade balance jumped to the billions during the World War; it touched the peak at $4,015,-000,000 in 1919. Thereafter, however, the national export surplus declined. In 1936, it amounted only to 43 million dollars on merchandise account; in 1937, it recovered to 262 million dollars. These figures help us to see what is wrong with our economy. With a production capacity far beyond the buying power of the home population, we have no place to put the surplus.

As a result of its long dependence on foreign trade, American agriculture identifies farm relief with the export opportunity. Crop adjustment it regards as a mere stopgap. Full recovery, it still believes, awaits a relatively free movement of cotton, grain, cereals, and meats into foreign markets. It proposes to export crops and to take factory goods in exchange. But the surplus problem is not exclusively agricultural; it is industrial as well, and the manufacturer, like the farmer, produces more than he can sell. There is no general gain in exchanging a farm surplus for an industrial surplus, and only a temporary gain for agriculture.

It is an old story that agriculture and industry have their ups and downs together. Neither can prosper independently. Farmers could not permanently benefit from a policy that disregarded industrial requirements. More imports without more consumption domestically would mean domestic unemployment. Farm exports paid for with imported nonfarm goods would then be worthless. The resulting congestion in the industrial markets, with the associated price declines and unemployment, would curtail the home demand for agricultural products. Loss of trade at home would offset the sales abroad.

Merely outbound trade involves indefinite foreign lending without provision for taking payment on the due dates. To think of money in this connection is, of course, misleading. Foreign lending really means an exportation of goods on credit. It leads to imperialism because the difficulty of bringing back the goods or their equivalent tempts the lending country to try to surround them where they are with a military cordon. That may lead to war.

Yet taking imports for exports is only part of the remedy. It merely changes the form of the commodity surplus, without lessening the volume of it at all. *It does not balance consumption with production capacity.* There are only two ways to do that. One is to increase the number of consumers sufficiently through an increase in one-way foreign trade; in short, to boost exports more than imports. That is the way of economic and eventually political expansion. The other is to increase sufficiently our domestic consumption.

But taking imports for exports will accomplish that, you may say. True it will change the distribution of the national income by causing the prices of both imported and domestic factory goods to decline. That would be the same as an increase in the real incomes of the poor. It would be so if nothing else happened. But wages would tend to decline. With prices falling, profits vanishing, and jobs diminishing in number, it would be impossible to keep wages up. We see once more that the end result of a big influx of imports might be reduced consumption. Without buying power to absorb them, such imports would cause industrial depression eventually.

Suppose, however, it were possible to receive imports freely, and yet not reduce consumption of domestic products at all. It would take a miracle to do it, but the result would be a drastic redistribution of the national income, and a true solution of the surplus problem. We should have a free-trader's paradise, where surpluses would be transformed at once into things desired. The credit for the miracle, however, would belong not to the freer interchange of domestic for foreign products, which would be merely incidental, but to the underlying redistribution of the nation's buying power which would be the indispensable prerequisite of the increased mass consumption.

In the end, the only dependable way to increase consumption is to increase it per capita domestically. No one yet knows precisely how this may be done. Every method suggested bristles with difficulties. Increased consumption through public expenditure means higher taxes. Increased consumption through higher wages means lower profits. Nevertheless, a way must be sought. Practically every government in the world has found itself obliged to tackle the problem of redistributing income in one way or another.

THE CRITICAL POINT

Here we come to the crucial point. Why bother unduly about foreign trade, if the ultimate market is really domestic; if what goes out, or its equivalent, must eventually come back to be consumed? Redistribute buying power and the foreign trade situation will take care of itself; it will become a spontaneous affair of reciprocal imports. With buying power well diffused, Americans will be able to consume most of the farm surpluses. Some cotton may be left over, and a little wheat and tobacco; but in the absence of a sufficient foreign market, the growers can produce something else—something wanted at home. There is a large potential demand for dairy products, meats, fruits, and vegetables, and for agricultural products in industrial uses. To be able to satisfy this demand would be infinitely better than making a fetish out of imports and exports. It gets us nowhere to concentrate on foreign trade and ignore the related problem of consumption, which remains the same whether traffic with foreign countries be large or small. The real task is to make consumption match production domestically.

There will always be need, of course, for foreign trade. It will always be useful to exchange unlike things; to trade cotton for rubber or wheat for coffee. Indeed, the nations may often usefully exchange similar things if the qualities vary; there are comparative national advantages even in the same lines of production. Hence, removal of unnecessary impediments to international trade is desirable. As the free traders demonstrated long ago, the wealth of nations increases when they observe the law of comparative advantage and specialize in the things they can produce best. The point to bear in mind is that greater international trade is not in itself the remedy for the problem of the surplus.

This country can face the issue more easily than most countries. Growth of population here is slowing down, and by 1960 our numbers may be stationary. We shall never have a land

320

shortage. We have far more agricultural-production capacity than we can use and a great reservoir of potential farm land besides. Our farmers could feed three times the country's present population. Nothing drives us to seize land and other natural resources abroad. Other countries have a biological as well as an economic drive toward imperialism; they have tremendous pressure of population on resources, as well as specialized forms of production that depend on foreign trade. This country has only the economic drive; only the desire for a favorable balance of trade to offset underconsumption domestically. It has the alternative of consuming domestically its surpluses, or their equivalent in suitable imports.

Concretely, the task is to continue the greater development of industry than of agriculture within the United States, and to consume the increased factory production through lower prices or higher wage levels or expanded public works. The logic involved is simple. Industrial consumption can be expanded almost indefinitely, whereas agricultural consumption turns on the capacity of the human stomach. In the aggregate, however, the human stomach has never been satisfied. Increased industrial production, therefore, will increase the domestic demand for farm goods, because it will increase the income of the urban poor. It will give us domestic prosperity and keep us out of foreign adventures. True, it involves some redistribution of the national income; but that is preferable to sending much of the income abroad and never getting it back.

Chapter XX

THE RELATION OF GOVERNMENT
TO BUSINESS

WALTER E. SPAHR

★ ★ ★ ★

THE relation of government to business involves two fundamental considerations: (1) the question of *the proper relationship* of government to business, and (2) the *nature of the relationship* which prevails between government and business in the United States.

The first question implies a comprehensive survey of the world's experiences with governmental relations to business, and a knowledge of the general principles derived from these experiences. The second involves a descriptive account of our governmental system, and a presentation of the principles of our constitutional law. Both issues are so large, and extend so far beyond the space at our disposal, that it is impossible to attempt more than a very brief survey of broad principles.

How are we to answer the question: *What is the proper relationship of government to business?* Are there any basic principles of proper relationship to which we may look for guidance?

If we can suggest, however briefly, the fundamental principles which indicate the nature and appropriate functions of government itself, we may then be able to apply these principles to the more specific question of the proper relation of government to business.

Since there is a wide variety of governments and of peoples governed, it is necessary to search for those broad basic principles that seem to explain why peoples of all kinds have government, and for the basic functions which it is expected that governments should perform. These principles must be broad enough to apply to a government structure, such as we have in the United States, in which we have layer piled upon layer, ranging from local, through state, to Federal government.

DANGER IN EXTREMES

Students of government have bequeathed to us a body of organized information and of scholarly thought in which we may find those principles which appeal to intelligent people because they seem to represent the essence of the valuable lessons learned by mankind throughout the ages.

Such accumulated wisdom teaches us that there are dangers in any extreme form of government, whether it be of the laissez-faire school, or socialism, or any other exaggerated form of paternalism, and that the best government is found in some area lying between these extremes.

From those few instances in which there has been no government or very little government, we may conclude that government, and a considerable amount of government, is a necessity. Individually, man has been able to accomplish little. In fact, he is poorly equipped to dominate many of the lower animals. His accomplishments have been in consequence of his joining forces with his fellows. This has meant society, and society requires government. Societies with little government have experienced bitter lessons. The strong have oppressed the weak; the net results have been poverty, ignorance, disease, misery.

Similarly, history is replete with the evidence of human suffering caused by governments with autocratic or absolute powers. Indeed, it seems probable that more human suffering has resulted from too much government than from too little. Human history records the tragedies of mankind resulting from the oppression of governments; it tells of the continuous struggle of individuals to free themselves from such oppression and to devise a system of government which will provide an

323

orderly society and at the same time give to the individual the widest possible freedom for his utmost self-development. Neither socialism nor extreme *laissez faire* will accomplish these aims. Both theories of government have been demonstrated to be inimical to human welfare; both bring a degree of suffering and distress which people have learned that they may escape under a more moderate system.

Still speaking generally, it may be said that a fundamental principle of a good government is that its end or basic purpose is to accomplish the objects of organized society. One prime objective is the greatest self-development of those individuals who compose society. Because society comprises an infinite variety of individuals seeking self-expression, social progress lies in the direction of finding ways to enable this great variety of individuals to function and develop freely without any individual trespassing upon the same rights of others. In other words, society must make the best possible use of all resources, including human good will and ingenuity, for the purpose of better satisfying human wants and of minimizing human suffering and distress.

AIMS OF GOOD GOVERNMENT

In accomplishing its fundamental purposes, a beneficent government will follow certain aims and methods generally acknowledged to be sound:

1. A good government endeavors to raise the average level of living of society. It is held in economics that those things are good which raise the average standard of living without increasing the inequalities in the ownership of wealth. And in this we are to think not only of the present but of the future, since ways are found to increase the standard of living in the present at the expense of the future.

2. A good government endeavors to enlarge the scope of individual liberty. The material standard of well-being does not constitute the sole criterion of what is good for humanity; alongside this material standard is the important matter of

individual liberty. For centuries, people have fought perhaps as strenuously for liberty as for material goods. One may find food, shelter, clothes, safety, and security within the walls of a prison, but at the price of liberty. Many men have sacrificed all their worldly goods, and even their lives, to obtain freedom. Individual liberty has been considered a priceless heritage. It has been man's perpetual aspiration. He has struggled for ages to enlarge the scope of individual liberty, including the freedom necessary to develop his personality to the limits of his physical and mental capacities and to safeguard the same freedom for his fellows. The justice and desirability of such freedom are recognized by all truly enlightened and free people. When we curb this freedom, we take a step backward. When we find new ways to enlarge this freedom, we progress.

Such freedom recognizes, above all things, the sacredness of one's personality. Probably every important religion in the world has recognized and clung to this great fact. It ran like a theme through the teachings of Christ. It lies at the bottom of that fine courtesy with which the refined person deals with his fellow men. It is probably one of the most vitally fundamental elements in human existence.

3. A good government fosters equality of competition and protects the weak against the strong. Human beings apparently have never devised a better means of encouraging individual development and social progress than by fostering equality of competition, impelled by the profit motive, and by providing at the same time the means of protecting the weak against the strong. There is probably no better means of determining the social value and proper prices of commodities and services than free and fair competition. But free competition of itself is not enough; it also must be fair. And fairness of competition implies either equality in strength or conformity to what appear to be fair rules of competition when the competitors are of unequal strength. The test of the fairness of these rules is found in whether or not they tend to foster

the conditions that would prevail if the competitors had equal strength in competition. It seems quite clear that all deviations from this principle by governments have been injurious to social well-being.

The application of this principle requires that monopolies be regulated, to the end that the conditions of free competition may prevail; that the weak be protected against the strong, to the end that competition may be fair; that prices, with certain exceptions, be neither fixed nor controlled but the results of this free and fair competition, to the end that they may reflect accurately society's appraisal of the value to it of these goods and services.

The appropriate exceptions to the rule against price fixing are found in the necessity for the government to fix (*a*) the weight of, and consequently the price for, the metallic unit used as a standard in its monetary system, and (*b*) the rates charged by public and private monopolies which are permitted to operate in lieu of competitive enterprises.

4. A good government will recognize the fact that a society of free people is a co-operative enterprise. Even though the government of a modern society may recognize the virtues of competition, and do much to foster it, an enlightened government, earnestly striving to increase the well-being of society, will also recognize and conform to the fact that society is at the same time a co-operative enterprise.

All agents engaged in the production, exchange, and consumption of goods and services, and in the distribution of the national income both compete and co-operate with one another. In production, employers, employees, and owners of natural resources and capital equipment must co-operate. All are necessary, and it is as futile to argue that one of these agents of production is more important than the others as it would be to contend that any one leg of a four-leg table is more important than the other three.

The better the co-operation among the agents of production and consumption, the better is the well-being of society

326

promoted. A fostering of free and fair competition does not militate against such co-operation. Indeed, quite the converse is true. The smoother the competition, the more effective is the co-operation. Co-operation, under conditions of free and fair competition, becomes practically automatic and almost completely devoid of conscious effort. When competition operates less freely and less fairly, co-operation becomes more difficult and requires a greater amount of conscious effort.

5. A good government will provide those agencies which ensure peace. Co-operation among the agents of production, exchange, and consumption and in sharing the national income requires peace. When conflicts of interest appear, they must be eliminated quickly by means of devices that will provide justice and mercy, and restore peace. In general, this means that courts must be provided to which people with conflicting interests may repair, since adjudication offers more promise of ensuring justice than does resort to force, except as used by the state to enforce those of its laws which are based upon the principles of justice, mercy, and peace.

In recognition of these facts, a good government will never cease cultivating and improving upon the devices and rules which aid co-operation and a better understanding of its necessity and virtues. It will always occupy a neutral position with respect to the importance or interests of any one of the classes of the agents of production in recognition of the fact that all are necessary, that all must co-operate, that all are equally entitled to justice, and that this justice probably can be obtained in no better way than through the smooth operation of free and fair competition and the consequent automatic and largely unconscious co-operation.

6. A good government will exercise only those powers granted to it by the people being governed. The state is the organic agent of society created by that society to promote its best interests. Thus a government which is granted powers, usually in the form of a constitution, for the purpose of aiding society in attaining its aims, cannot step beyond the scope of

the authority granted it by the society from which its powers are derived without ceasing to be a good government. Briefly stated, a good government will be a constitutional government. It will neither exercise powers nor engage in interferences with social practices when such governmental acts exceed the provisions of the organic law according to which society has decided that it expects its government to be guided.

7. A good government will undertake no activities that can be performed as well or better by private individuals or associations. A fundamental purpose of government is to provide society with the regulations and the enforcement of these regulations, which this society desires, as a means of protecting individuals in their efforts to live and to make a living. People do not wish to be deprived of opportunities to gain a livelihood, and they do not, in principle, willingly organize an agency which will deprive them of these opportunities.

Those who regard this principle as questionable, or who suggest that the state should be free at its option to compete with, or to enter into "partnership" with, the people who provide it with its authority, open the door to socialism—a form of government which cannot meet the objective tests as to what constitutes good government. Unless this principle is recognized and adhered to, we have no criterion by which we can define the extent to which a government may appropriately enter into competition with citizens or deprive them of their opportunities to make a living without being employees of the state.

Moreover, when a state enters into competition with its citizens, or creates a government monopoly in a business in which private enterprise could be as efficient or more efficient than the state, it has substituted government monopoly or ownership for regulation. This is an admission that, as a regulative agent, it has been unsuccessful. Yet the government's function is to regulate, not to own, business; and, ownership and operation of a business by a government are more difficult and create more problems for all concerned than does government regulation. Furthermore, governments rarely count with any high degree of accuracy their costs of doing business; their losses are levied upon the taxpayers; the forces which usually exact penalties for inefficiency in management and in service practically cease to operate; and society suffers as a consequence.

8. A good government will recognize the natural limits to appropriate state action. Quite apart from the matter of constitutional authority granted to the state, there are natural limits to appropriate action by government.

The state provides the agency which enables people to co-operate to attain ends which are to their mutual advantage. But there are limits beyond which co-operative activities through the agency of the state bring more disadvantages than advantages; and it is at this point that the state should cease its efforts to act for the people as their co-operative agent.

A very large proportion of human activities can, with great advantage to all, be left to private arrangements in which people are free to enter into contract; to exercise their ingenuity in production, invention, and discovery; to pursue their pleasure in music, art, literature, entertainment, and recreation; to choose their friends and associates through the organization of clubs, fraternities, partnerships, and similar organizations; to organize for religious purposes their churches, synagogues, cathedrals, and tabernacles; to pursue knowledge through the establishment of educational institutions; to save by creating savings and insurance institutions; to engage in humanitarian activities by establishing hospitals, the Red Cross, foundations, and eleemosynary institutions.

Then it is to be remembered that government is not an end; it is a means. It is no bigger and no more important than the society which creates it and which it is designed to serve. Whenever government takes steps which reveal that it is assuming that society should serve it, rather than it serve society, it has stepped beyond the natural limits of its appropriate functions and action.

9. A good government will seek competent advice on intricate matters. Every government is confronted with a wide variety of questions. They may involve matters falling into the provinces of chemistry, physics, geology, mechanical engineering, hydroelectric engineering, civil engineering, naval and military affairs, economics, constitutional law, insurance, and so on. No government is wise, nor is it pursuing the proper course, when it submits questions of chemistry to those who are not competent chemists, or engineering questions to others than competent engineers, or economic questions to other than competent economists.

In the fields of the exact sciences, this principle is ordinarily recognized, but often, if not usually, matters of economics, such as questions involving money and banking, tariffs, public finance, labor, agriculture, public utilities, and transportation, are not submitted to economists and others having long and practical experience in these matters, but to the general public. Some economic questions are as intricate in nature as those in the fields of the so-called exact sciences, and the period of training required of the economist before he is competent to render valuable opinions regarding the best solutions may be even longer than that required of the chemist. Nevertheless, these are facts often overlooked by government officials. Because the economist uses common language, rather than such specialized symbols as those characterizing chemistry, the layman generally supposes that he is automatically admitted to an understanding of most or all economic principles. Consequently governments, unless they are very wise, often arrive at their answers to, and policies regarding, economic questions of major importance, not by consulting the most competent and objective economists, but by arranging for the general public to vote upon the issues. The same is true of important and really intricate matters in constitutional law, sociology, political science, and international law.

It is the duty of an intelligent government to submit all such questions to the best trained people at its disposal and then to take appropriate steps to inform the general public regarding those matters of which a very large proportion of the people have no clear understanding. A government becomes particularly untrustworthy, and even extremely dangerous, as an agent of the people, when it not only submits involved questions to the incompetent general public for a vote on what the answers should be but goes even further and appeals to the emotions of the untutored people in an effort to obtain a vote that will maintain the party in power, even though this be at the expense of the national welfare.

In early times, when a pestilence appeared, some savage tribes would beat their tom-toms to drive away the evil spirits. In modern times, we have learned to call in medical authorities when a pestilence strikes us; we do not use tom-toms; neither do we vote on the issue. But in matters of economics, sociology, and political science, we are hardly safely beyond the tom-tom stage in the devices used to arrive at the supposed solutions to the problems involved. We contrive to vote on many of these issues, and pretend that we have voted intelligently on them. Before we cast our votes the political tom-toms beat, the public is stirred, if possible, into an emotional frenzy, flags wave, slogans are used to hypnotize, torches burn, the voters march and sing and shout, the demagogues and patent medicine men orate and praise and condemn, the scientists hang their heads in shame. Then the votes are cast, and the shout goes up that the correct answer has been given. This voting is widely supposed to solve all problems no matter how intricate or technical they may be. Those in power speak of a mandate, and this mandate is not only assumed to be specific and wise, but it is stretched to satisfy the caprice of those in power or to cover any issue that may confront them.

331

Resort to these devices reflects badly upon the government which employs them, and the dangers to society that are involved in their use are incalculable. When a government indulges in such practices, the intellectual resources of a country are not properly utilized, the methods employed are almost certain to lead to the wrong answers and policies, the government ceases to be a reliable agent of the people, and the prospects of ensuring the effective functioning of a popular government are dangerously impaired.

To submit intricate questions to the untutored rather than to the tutored is social folly; and to legislate for the benefit of pressure groups and in accordance with the strength of their pressure is equally indefensible. Both methods of developing government policies and solutions constitute a social cancer which slowly undermines good government, impairs social health, and retards human progress. Indeed, it may set in motion forces sufficient to lead the nation into a period of social retrogression and disintegration.

In this brief review of the nature and functions of government, some of the fundamental principles have emerged which should determine the proper relationship of government to business.

But, in addition, the nature of the relationship which a particular government actually maintains with business falling within its jurisdiction is conditioned in a marked degree by the structure of the government. For instance, in the United States, the central government is only one of our various layers of government, and its powers in general, as well as those controlling its relationship to business, must be regarded in the light of the Federal Constitution and the powers reserved by the people for the respective states and for themselves as individuals.

THE RELATIONSHIP BETWEEN GOVERNMENT AND BUSINESS IN THE UNITED STATES

Although the powers of the Federal government are defined in broad terms in the Constitution of the United States, the general nature of these powers, specifically stated or fairly implied, are better understood when regarded in the light of the circumstances which gave rise to the Constitution and to the division of powers between the Federal and state governments.

It was because of the weaknesses of the Articles of Confederation that the framers of the Constitution provided for a central government with powers considered sufficient to ensure its strength and sufficiency. But the Federal government was given only such powers as it seemed to the framers that experience had shown were necessary. *Consequently, the Federal government was made a government of delegated powers.* The powers granted to this central government were those which it was assumed could not be discharged properly by the individual states.

All other powers were reserved to the states, which thus became bodies with general powers, except as the people reserved certain powers for themselves. More specifically, the ninth amendment of the Constitution reads: "The enumeration in the Constitution, of certain rights, shall not be construed to deny or disparage others retained by the people." The tenth amendment reads: "The powers not delegated to the United States by the Constitution, are reserved to the States respectively, or to the people."

Thus, in principle, the Federal government cannot legally exercise any powers of government except those expressly granted to it by the Constitution or fairly implied from that instrument.

The final determination of the scope of the Federal government's powers rests with the United States Supreme Court, which, by clear implication, as lucidly expounded by Chief Justice John Marshall in the case of *Marbury v. Madison* in 1803, was charged with the unavoidable responsibility of giving the official and final interpretation to the meaning of the Constitution. Article VI of the Constitution provides, among other things, that "This Constitution, and the laws of the United States which shall be made in pursuance

thereof . . . shall be the supreme law of the land. . . . "
Laws of Congress not made "in pursuance thereof," are not
part of the supreme law of the land, and, as Marshall pointed
out, "It is emphatically the duty of the judiciary to say what
the law is. If a law be in opposition to the Constitution, it is
the very essence of judicial duty to say which shall govern."[1]

The passage of time has seen many things that were of local
or state interest become of national concern as a consequence
of the developments in transportation facilities, the growth of
huge corporations, and the inability or unwillingness of the
states to cope with many of the agricultural, industrial, and
social problems which clearly reach beyond the boundary
lines of any one state. The determination of the scope of the
authority of the Federal government with respect to these new
problems has rested, as it should, upon the interpretation of
the meaning of the Constitution by the United States Supreme
Court and, when this defined authority has proved unsatisfactory, upon the willingness of the people to amend the
Constitution. The assumption of powers by the Federal government by other means is unconstitutional and revolutionary.

It is not possible here to do more than to indicate, in a general way, the principal powers possessed by our governments
and to distinguish between those possessed by the Federal
government and by the states and local units. The principles,
which must apply in the control of business by government,
should nevertheless be apparent.

THE FEDERAL GOVERNMENT AND BUSINESS

The Federal government has the power to regulate or to
affect favorably or unfavorably business activity by exercising
the following powers:

Congress may lay and collect taxes, duties, imposts, and
exercises. All these must be uniform throughout the United
States. The sixteenth amendment to the Constitution gave
Congress power to collect taxes on incomes without apportion-
ment among the states and without regard to our census or

enumeration. Congress may not tax state functions, nor the salary of state officers, nor the property or borrowing power of a state or municipal corporation. It may levy tariffs on imports but may not lay any tax or duty on articles exported from any state.

Congress may borrow money to pay its debts.

It may regulate commerce with foreign nations, and among the several states, and with the Indian tribes. One of our great problems today is to determine where interstate commerce begins and ends. In general, the powers to regulate commerce fall into three classes: (*a*) that class in which the jurisdiction of Congress is exclusive and in which the states cannot interfere at all; (*b*) that class in which the jurisdiction is concurrent, in which the states may act in the absence of action by Congress; and (*c*) that class in which purely intrastate commerce prevails, regarding which the power of the state is exclusive.

Congress may establish uniform laws on the subject of bankruptcies throughout the United States.

Congress may coin money, regulate the value thereof, and of foreign coin, and fix the standard of weights and measures.[2]

Congress may establish post offices and post roads, and regulate the use of the mails. It may exclude from the mails matter that is fraudulent or otherwise injurious to the public, and it may refuse to deliver mail to persons who are using the postal service for improper purposes. The powers of the Federal government under this heading are extensive and not clearly defined.

Congress has power to grant patents and copyrights.

It may declare war, raise and support armies, and provide and maintain a navy.

It may make laws which shall be necessary and proper for carrying into execution the foregoing powers and all other powers vested by the Constitution in the government of the United States, or in any department or officer thereof.

Then the Constitution specifies certain things which the Federal government may not do that have a direct bearing upon its power to regulate business. For instance, the Constitution provides that the right of the people to be secure in their persons, houses, papers, and effects against unreasonable searches and seizures, shall not be violated, and no warrants shall issue, but upon probable cause, supported by oath or affirmation, and particularly describing the place to be searched, and the person or things to be seized.

No person shall be deprived of life, liberty, or property, without *due process of law*. This "due process of law," by which Congress is limited in the fifth amendment, and the states by the fourteenth amendment, is equivalent to the "law of the land," and is intended to protect the citizen against arbitrary action, and to secure to all persons equal and impartial justice under the law. Due process of law also means law in its regular course of administration through courts of justice.

Although the Federal government may exercise the power of *eminent domain*, it may not take private property for public use without just compensation. This prohibition as to the exercise of the power of eminent domain is placed upon the Federal government by the fifth amendment to the Constitution, and upon the states by the fourteenth amendment.

Contrary to a common notion, there is no specific provision in the Constitution of the United States which prohibits the Federal government from *impairing the obligation of contracts*. This prohibition of Article I, Section 10, applies to the state legislatures and constitutions. But the absence of such provision does not mean that the United States government may abrogate at pleasure such contracts as are subject to its jurisdiction. Contracts are property, and the fifth amendment forbids the United States to take property without due process of law.

The Federal government may also do many things, affecting business, when it takes steps to promote public health, safety, morals, order, or the general welfare. Since legislation for these purposes is known as an exercise of the *police power* when utilized by the states, it has sometimes been contended that

336

THE RELATION OF GOVERNMENT TO BUSINESS

the Federal government is likewise employing its police power when its legislation is for these same general purposes. Fundamentally, there is no such thing as a Federal police power, and, when the Federal government legislates in behalf of the general welfare, it must find authority for such legislation under other powers specifically granted to it or reasonably implied from these specifically enumerated powers.

The power of the Federal government to regulate monopolies and to pass such statutes as the Sherman Anti-Trust Law is derived from its authority to regulate interstate and foreign commerce. The same is true of its power to regulate the meat packers and the stockyards and the stock and grain exchanges.

The efforts of the Federal government to regulate hours, wages, and working conditions of laborers, and to control or prohibit child labor, have been rendered difficult because of the absence of a Federal police power, and because of the difficulty of finding other specific authority in the Constitution for legislation of this type.

The same general difficulties have been experienced with respect to the legislation of recent years relating to agriculture. For example, it would seem difficult, indeed, to find constitutional authority for the Agricultural Adjustment Act of 1938, without stretching the Constitution beyond any reasonable interpretation.

STATE GOVERNMENT AND BUSINESS

The states of the union are bodies of general powers, and they may exercise any powers not delegated to the United States government by the Constitution of the United States, or not reserved by the people to themselves. The general rule is that the states have the authority not specifically denied to them by their state constitutions, except in those instances in which the Constitution of the United States is supreme, whereas the Federal government has only that

337

authority specifically or impliedly granted to it in its Constitution. A state legislative act cannot be declared void unless conflict with the Constitution of the United States or with the state's constitution can be demonstrated.

The Constitution of the United States prohibits any state from passing an ex post facto law, or a law impairing the obligation of contract. The prohibition as to ex post facto laws relates only to certain classes of retroactive criminal statutes. This prohibition does not operate against the Federal government.

No state, according to the fourteenth amendment to the Constitution, shall make or enforce any law which shall abridge the privileges or immunities of citizens of the United States; nor shall any state deprive any person of life, liberty, or property, without due process of law; nor deny to any person within its jurisdiction the equal protection of the laws. The due process clause places important restrictions on the states in their use of the police power. This prohibition not only means that people may not be deprived arbitrarily and without some reasonable ground of their personal liberty, but it also protects their freedom to make contracts, to engage in occupations, or to acquire and use property. Deprivation of property, however, may take place in a variety of ways besides outright confiscation. A state may place such restrictions upon the possession, use, or transfer of property as to constitute a deprivation of some or all of its essential incidents.

Since the states may exercise a police power, there is a great variety of ways in which they may regulate business. Under this power the states may take steps to protect the public health, including that of persons and animals; they may legislate in the interest of public morals, safety, order, and comfort; they may license people for certain occupations and activities and impose restraints and prescribe such requirements as seem proper; they may legislate with respect to dependent, delinquent, and defective persons, and regarding marriage, divorce, and other aspects of domestic relations.

338

In general, the courts have allowed the legislatures less latitude in regulations affecting economic and business interests than in those dealing with social problems. This has been particularly marked with respect to legislation calculated to restrict or impair competition. Legislation to curb unfair methods of competition ordinarily is upheld, but the tendency has been to eliminate those laws that would restrict the free struggle for life. Under their police power, we find states legislating in the economic fields against fraud and oppressive practices by economically superior persons. Businesses affected with a public interest may be regulated as to rates, and charters and franchises may be required. The ownership of property is regulated, and liabilities of owners of business may be specified.

The guarantee by the fourteenth amendment of equal protection of the laws to all persons within the jurisdiction of a state does not mean that all persons, property, or occupations must be treated alike by a state. In the interests of public welfare, persons, property, and occupations may be classified, and laws made applicable, but uniformly applicable, to all persons falling within the same group. All classifications for purposes of regulation must be based upon some difference which bears a reasonable and just relation to the act in respect to which the classification is proposed. For example, it is reasonable to tax Ford cars at one rate and Cadillacs at another, but it would be unreasonable to tax blonde drivers of Fords at one rate and brunettes at another. Such a classification would be arbitrary and without any reasonable basis.

The constitutional prohibitions of the fourteenth amendment apply to corporations as well as to natural persons, since the United States Supreme Court has held that corporations are persons within the law. But a corporation is a person within the meaning of the fifth and fourteenth amendments only as to property, not as to life and liberty.

The states may affect or regulate business through the use of their power to tax, the power of eminent domain, or even

339

by the exercise of the power to destroy property without compensation as, for example, when diseased cattle are killed, or buildings destroyed to prevent the spread of a conflagration, or property upon the scene of active hostilities is seized and used by military officers.

No state may impair the obligation of contract. Although this statement may appear simple, the proposition involves so many intricacies and so much interpretation that we cannot clarify its implications here.

LOCAL GOVERNMENT AND BUSINESS

Local government in the United States, with a few exceptions, comprises counties which, in turn, are divided into townships, towns, and perhaps other districts of various kinds, such as school and improvement districts. (In Louisiana the state is divided into parishes instead of counties. In some of our states, particularly in New England and Long Island, the "towns" comprise or overshadow the county.)

Although these local governmental units enjoy large powers of self-government through elective officers and may be subject to only slight supervision and control by state officers, the extent of the powers of the local governmental units is determined by the state constitutions and statutes. In general, every county and subdivision is a political unit having certain financial, legislative, judicial, and police powers, but all these are under the absolute control of the state legislature which may create or abolish these local offices, distribute functions, and regulate in minute detail if it so desires, provided the state constitution does not restrict the legislature in any of these respects. The degree of "home rule" granted through constitutional provisions to these local units varies considerably among the states.

All these variations in the nature and extent of the authority and functions of local governmental units make it exceedingly difficult to present any generalizations of value regarding the relationship between these governments and business.

340

These local governments, in general, may levy and collect taxes and borrow money to take care of local needs; they may spend money for the construction or improvement of highways or streets, for local governmental buildings, for the performance of governmental functions, for relief of the poor, for construction of parks, schools, and playgrounds; they may license people for certain purposes; they may regulate the use of land for building and the height and type of buildings; they may register deeds and record titles to land and mortgages, loans, and other instruments which affect such titles; they build and manage schools; they may issue marriage licenses and record marriages, births, deaths; they may establish or supervise sewage systems, waterworks, and lighting plants; they may establish and finance courts and police officers; they have general authority over fire prevention and protection.

A large number of local activities have become matters of state interest, with the consequence that there has been a tendency to transfer an increasing amount of authority from local to state governments, just as the states have been seeing much of their authority transferred to Washington. The growth of transportation facilities, the increasing ease of travel and communication, the growth of big business, the division of labor, and a multitude of similar and related factors are responsible for this tendency toward greater centralization of government. The various relations of government to business have been shifting correspondingly.

WE HAVE BECOME A NATION OF LAW WORSHIPERS

The reliance of the American people upon laws to solve their various problems—whether of business or otherwise—has become a remarkable phenomenon. When difficulties arise, the first reaction of people, in general, is that a law should be passed. And there is an increasing tendency in this country to pass more and more laws with respect to more and more things. This has become strikingly true of the Federal government. At some sessions of Congress a thousand or more laws are passed. The accumulation of statutes, particularly during recent years, is one of the most amazing commentaries on modern times. Our present faith in the efficacy of lawmaking, especially in the value of thousands of laws that are neither read nor understood by a large proportion of our people, presents a problem for the social psychologist. We are being swamped with laws; we have so many on our statute books that we do not know what they are; the general public makes no pretense of reading them; we do not know when we are violating or obeying them, and yet there is a persistent clamor for more.

We are living in a period of frenzied legislation, the vague notion or superstition being that if only we can pass a law—its economic soundness often being not a paramount consideration—our problem or problems will be solved and we shall be saved from our troubles. The passage, in February, 1938, of the Agricultural Adjustment Act provided a striking illustration of our naïve faith in lawmaking as a means of curing our economic ills. Congressmen and the Administration demanded that this law be enacted, although it was conceded that few Congressmen understood it, and it was known that the farmers in general had not read it and did not know the nature and implications of its provisions.

One may advance several plausible reasons for this childish faith in the virtues of statutes that are neither read nor understood generally. Among these reasons may be an undermined confidence in the virtues of competition and self-reliance, and a lack of understanding and perspective regarding the importance of the World War and of the unwise acts of governments in contributing to postwar and current economic and social maladjustments. Whatever the reason may be, we have become a nation of law worshipers.

At the same time, these laws are slowly breaking our backs. They have brought upon us greater costs; heavier taxation; an unprecedented and mounting public debt; more governmental supervision; a growth in bureaucracy; a pronounced trend toward personal government; a development of class consciousness, class strife, and class hatred; a startling spread of demagoguery in politics; a serious decline in objective statesmanship; an insidious attack upon the virtues of hard work, thrift, and self-reliance; a conspicuous disregard for economic principles; a growing and disturbing complexity in life and business; a loss of freedom; a spreading pessimism and fear regarding the future; and the consequent development of a great weight which is bearing down more heavily upon us each year, with real prospects that in the end it may crush all that is worth while and healthy in our economic, social, and political life. Indeed, the increasing burden of these laws, combined with the danger of impairing our public credit and with numerous other forces now undermining our national well-being, may prove to be the principal factor which will destroy our democratic form of government and bring this nation under the control, or heel, of "a man on horseback."

REACTIONISM AND COERCION VS. LIBERALISM

There appears to be a vague notion among our people that all these laws and related developments are symptomatic of progress. Often they are pointed to as a mark of growing liberalism in this country.

The fact seems to be that they are indicative, rather, of an insidious social disease which is slowly undermining our general social health and well-being, and pointing toward some form of social retrogression. They clearly indicate an increasing amount of coercion, much of which is undoubtedly of an undesirable sort.

Time and experience have made it amply clear that those things which do not raise the average plane of living, and which impair, rather than enlarge, the freedom of the individual, are reactionary in nature. Most unfortunately, this

343

spreading spirit of coercion and reactionism is today frequently called *liberalism,* and the advocates of this coercion and authoritarianism often call themselves *liberals.* But this reversion to coercion is the antithesis of liberalism; it is reactionism and retrogression. The philosophy of these self-styled, but false, liberals is that the individual must be regimented for his own sake—a philosophy that has characterized tyrants, dictators, coercionists, and reactionaries throughout human history. True liberalism has been associated with that long, painful struggle of humanity to free itself from regimentation, coercion, and authoritarianism.

People today—in the United States as well as in Europe—have fallen under the spell of words. Label a thing *liberal,* and the unthinking people will follow, advocate, or pursue it as though hypnotized. Label a thing *conservative,* and they will mark it down as bad at once. The gullibility revealed is amazing; the faith in labels is tragic.

At present these modern Pied Pipers of Hamelin are rapidly leading our people back along the path of coercion and retrogression. What, if anything, will awaken enough people from their soporific lethargy to arrest this backward march is not at all apparent.

The battle today is between the genuine liberals and the forces of coercion and retrogression; and the liberals are battling for some of the most vital things in life—for an improvement in our economic well-being, for constitutional and good government, and for a greater individual freedom and a wider recognition of the sacredness of the individual personality.

NOTES

1 Although the authority of the United States Supreme Court, to declare unconstitutional those laws, Federal or state, which in the opinion of that court are contrary to the Constitution, has been questioned from time to time by those who wish Congress to have freedom to pass such laws as it may desire, it cannot be said that Marshall's ringing statement that "all laws repugnant to the Constitution are void and courts are bound to say so" has been challenged with any success.

The validity of Marshall's statement has been made conclusive by a variety of evidence and by such statements as that of Alexander Hamilton, who, in expounding the new constitution in *The Federalist*, wrote: "No legislative act contrary to the Constitution is valid. To deny this would be to affirm that the servant is above his master, that men acting by virtue of powers conferred upon them may do what is forbidden them to do." Hamilton continued: "The interpretation of the laws is the proper and peculiar province of the the Courts. A Constitution is, in fact, and must be regarded by the Judges, as a fundamental law." (*The Federalist*, No. LXXVIII).

Among other leading persons in the Constitutional Convention who are on record as supporting the position later taken by Marshall were James Madison, Gouverneur Morris, James Wilson, Elbridge Gerry, and even Luther Martin of Maryland who strongly opposed a proposal to create an executive-judicial body with revisionary or veto powers with respect to laws of Congress. The rejection of the latter proposal by the Convention is not to be confused with the question of whether the Convention ever rejected or refused to grant to the United States Supreme Court the power to declare unconstitutional those acts of Congress considered repugnant to the Constitution. This confusion has sometimes appeared in the arguments of those who wish to strip the Supreme Court of this power. The question of whether the Supreme Court should have this authority never came before the members of the Convention for formal consideration; it was taken for granted—unfortunately. Ira Jewell Williams, Jr., in "A Republic— If You Can Keep It," *The Saturday Evening Post*, January 15, 1938, page 36, says that the evidence "is that forty-five of the fifty-five delegates, including twenty-four of the twenty-five leaders, acknowledged the existence of the power and knew that it was being conferred." For a recent and effective treatment of this issue, see the *Adverse Report of the Senate Committee on the Reorganization of the Federal Judiciary*, Report 711 to accompany S1392, 75th Cong., 1st Sess., June 14, 1937.

[2] The expression "regulate the value thereof," does not refer to regulation of the price level, as frequently asserted by those persons who wish Congress to attempt to regulate the price level or its reciprocal, the value of money. The value of money clause, as used in the Constitution, refers specifically to the power of Congress to fix the size of the standard monetary unit, the fineness of coin, and the denominations of our currency. The meaning of this clause was thoroughly examined and expounded by the United States Supreme Court in the famous cases of *Juilliard v. Greenman*, 110 U.S. 421; 28 L. ed. 204 (1884); and *Knox v. Lee*, 12 Wall. 532; 20 L. Ed. 306 (1870). There is no basis whatever for the assumptions or assertions of those advocates of price level stabilization who insist that "regulate the value thereof" means that Congress was charged with responsibility of stabilizing the price level, and that so long as the price level fluctuates Congress is failing in its duty to stabilize the value of money.

345

Chapter XXI

THE CONSTITUTION AND THE SUPREME COURT

Rinehart J. Swenson

★ ★ ★ ★

THERE is an all too common belief, shared by laymen and the legal profession alike, that the Constitution of the United States is in the nature of a contract defining legal rights and duties of parties, *in terms which are unchangeable and unmistakably clear and definite,* and which it is the duty of courts to enforce as part of the judicial function to administer justice. In truth, the Constitution which George Washington swore to preserve, protect, and defend is not the same instrument which Franklin Delano Roosevelt swore, in identical words, to support. The Constitution of today has been "adapted to the various crises of human affairs," as John Marshall said it must be, until it no more resembles the original document than the United States of today resembles the union of the original thirteen states. The United States has not been shaped to the Constitution; the Constitution, in spite of resistance at certain points, has expanded with the nation.

The Constitution reflects two sound principles of constitution making: it contains only fundamental matter, which changes slowly, and it is written in general terms, which give it elasticity. In consequence, it has not been necessary to make many verbal changes in the original document. However, the framers of the Constitution foresaw the possible need for such changes and, accordingly, incorporated an amending clause, which prescribes the procedure for making formal modifications whenever deficiencies should appear which the generality of the document could not cure. Twenty-one amendments have been added to the Constitution, but actually the amending procedure has been used only twelve times, as the first ten amendments, generally referred to as the Bill of Rights, were ratified together in 1791. The twenty-first amendment repeals the eighteenth, and the thirteenth, fourteenth, and fifteenth were made possible only by the Civil War and could not have been adopted voluntarily. There remain nineteen effective amendments; sixteen were adopted in accordance with the spirit of the Constitution; the first twelve of these were ratified by 1804, making them virtually a part of the original document; thus leaving a net of four properly adopted amendments since 1804.

FLEXIBILITY OF THE CONSTITUTION

Fortunately, the adaptation or expansion of the Constitution has not been confined to formal amendments. Such rigidity would have been fatal to the Constitution and to the Union. The Constitution owes its greatest flexibility, not to the amending clause, but to the theory of constitutional interpretation adopted by the national government—in the last analysis by the Supreme Court. This is not to say that judicial interpretation has always given flexibility to constitutional provisions; on the contrary, the controlling majority of the Supreme Court has, with fair consistency, resisted democratic innovations, or even major social revolutions such as happened in the administrations of Jefferson, Jackson, Lincoln, and Franklin Roosevelt. But political pressure and periodic infusions of new blood have kept the Court from lagging too far behind the procession.

From 1789 to 1801 the Federalists were in control of all three branches of the national government, and until 1835 the Supreme Court was dominated by Mr. Chief Justice

Marshall, the supreme nationalist. The central idea of the Federalist constitutional theory, as developed by Hamilton, Webster, and Marshall, was that the Constitution was the work of the people as a whole, not of the states, and that its primary purpose was to establish a strong national government to which the state governments would be subordinate, a purpose implicit in the supremacy clause. To effect this end the provisions of the Constitution were to be given an adaptive interpretation. That is, the Constitution was a plastic instrument to be adapted to a growing American nationalism. The adaptation, it may be observed, did not embrace the prevailing republican doctrine, except when the latter made concessions to nationalism.

John Marshall died in 1835, and within two years the Supreme Court was practically remade, with Roger Taney as chief justice, and five new associate justices. Four additional changes in the membership of the court had been made by 1845. Under the leadership of Taney the court changed from a constitutional theory of *nationalism* to one of *states' rights*. According to the latter theory, the Constitution was regarded as essentially a *static compact* between one-time independent states, which divided the powers of government between "two authorities of equal dignity, the states and the national government," and into two clearly separable spheres: the powers delegated to the United States related to the *general* welfare, while the powers reserved to the states were those of *local* or internal government. The constitutional compact was to be strictly construed in the interest of the parties to it, that is, the states. Adaptation, if necessary, should be effected through the process of amendment and not by construction. Thus the earlier states' rights doctrine was adapted to changed conditions—an adaptation which rejected nullification and secession, for Roger Taney was no less a Unionist than John Marshall, but which aimed to preserve the Federal equilibrium by conserving the residual powers of the states and confining the delegated powers of the national government within the original constitutional intent.

John Marshall was primarily interested in "expounding" the Constitution, in designing basic constitutional patterns for a larger national life, a more perfect union. To him the bench was a forum, and opinions were lectures on nationalism. Roger Taney was more interested in the "application" of the Constitution as a design for living. He was more concerned with social and economic problems than with theories of constitutional interpretation, but inasmuch as he regarded these problems as falling properly within the province of state power, the Constitution was to be construed accordingly.

Thus the Supreme Court has fashioned two opposed theories of constitutional construction, equally authoritative, which have controlled and directed the evolution of the Constitution. Under the guise of interpretation, the Constitution has been expanded or shrunk to fit the views on public policy held by the prevailing majority of the Court.

Woodrow Wilson fittingly described the Supreme Court as "a constitutional convention in continuous session," and, without disparagement or even criticism, he pointed out that at the hands of that Court "the Constitution has received an adaptation and an elaboration which would fill its framers of the simple days of 1787 with nothing less than amazement." Having supplied itself with two equally respectable views of the Constitution, one for elasticity and one for rigidity, the Court has shaped legislative policy by requiring it to conform to that view of the Constitution which the Court *elected to adopt with respect to any given legislative act.* In short, as *Governor* Hughes once observed, "the Constitution is what the judges say it is." This is inevitable since the judges have an uncontrolled discretion in selecting the rule or principle which is to guide them in defining and giving effect to constitutional words, phrases, or clauses. When those who wear the ermine also carry the scepter the result is not always fortunate, as the following exhibits indicate.

SOME IRRECONCILABLE INCONSISTENCIES

The Sixteenth Amendment authorizes Congress "to lay and collect taxes on incomes, *from whatever source derived.*" But in spite of the plain language of this amendment, the Supreme Court has held that Congress may not tax, as income, stock dividends distributed from the profits of a corporation; nor may the salaries of judges of constitutional courts be taxed, as such a tax would destroy the independence of the judiciary and so violate Article III of the Constitution. Four justices dissented in the former case, and the latter drew the fire of Mr. Justice Holmes who objected to a construction of the Constitution which made the judges "a privileged class, free from bearing their share of the cost of the institutions upon which their well-being if not their life depends." In thus protecting the salaries of Federal judges, including their own, from bearing any share of the tax burden, the Court violated an elementary principle of constitutional and statutory construction, namely, that when there is repugnancy between two provisions of a constitution or law, the later provision supersedes the earlier. And as they had a pecuniary interest in the case, the judges should have had more regard for the plain meaning of simple words.

The Fifth and Fourteenth Amendments provide that Congress and the states, respectively, may not deprive "any person" of "life, liberty, or property, without due process of law." For a long time the Supreme Court and leading commentators on the Constitution held that the words "due process of law" as used in these amendments were intended to convey the same meaning as the words "the law of the land" in Magna Carta. But through judicial translation, due process in the United States has come to differ from due process, or the law of the land, in England in two most important respects: (1) in England it operates as a check upon the Crown but not upon Parliament, while in the United States it limits both the executive and the legislative branches; and (2) in England it

350

relates to *procedure* only, while in the United States it includes *substantive*, or essential, rights as well. Thus *due process* has become a device by which the Supreme Court censors legislation affecting our social and economic life. This judicial censorship has brought forth many protests from dissenting justices, such as this now famous statement by Mr. Justice Holmes: "As the decisions now stand, I see hardly any limit but the sky to the invalidating of those rights if they happen to strike a majority of this Court as for any reason undesirable. I cannot believe that the amendment was intended to give us carte blanche to embody our economic or moral beliefs in its prohibitions." Furthermore, in 1882 a Federal court held, for the first time, that a private business corporation is a "person" within the meaning of the due process clause, of the Fourteenth Amendment, and this was affirmed by the Supreme Court in 1886. This ruling is based upon statements by Roscoe Conkling and John A. Bingham, insinuating that they, as members of the congressional committee which framed the amendment, deliberately substituted the term *persons* for *citizens* in the original draft, in order to include artificial persons. Recent examinations of the journal of the committee indicate that Conkling deliberately misconstrued the action of the committee in order to impress an altogether too receptive court. In thus extending to corporations the benefits of a constitutional provision which was meant, so far as the Congress and the ratifying states were concerned, for natural persons, the court found it necessary to give the clause a double meaning, which emphasizes the dubiousness of the ruling: when applied to natural persons, it protects "life, liberty, or property," but when applied to corporations it can have reference *only* to "property," as the life and liberty of the corporators are not the life and liberty of the corporation.

The so-called *contract clause* of the Constitution, Article I, Section 10, which declares that "no State shall . . . pass any . . . law impairing the obligation of contracts" was unquestionably directed at the cheap money acts of the states which impaired the obligations of *private* contracts. But through judicial interpretation the clause was extended in the case of *Fletcher v. Peck*, in 1810, to include legislative grants, as of public lands, even when fraudulent, and, in the Dartmouth College Case, in 1819, to ordinary corporate franchises or charters. The latter decision was followed by an unparalleled orgy of corruption making it imperative for the states to take steps, in self-protection, to checkmate it, through the adoption of constitutional or general statutory provisions declaring all business charters of the future subject to amendment or repeal. A reconstructed Court came to the aid of the states by holding that the ruling in the Dartmouth College case did not affect a state's police power or its power of eminent domain, obviously corrective measures.

The commerce clause delegates to Congress the power "to regulate commerce with foreign nations, and among the several stages, and with the Indian tribes." In the hands of the Supreme Court this clause has taken on the characteristics of an accordion—it has been extended and contracted to express the changing moods of the judges as they improvise on the *commerce* theme. In a multitude of cases, there are infinite variables, harmonies, and discords. A manufacturer, miner, and farmer are not in commerce and, therefore, not subject to Federal regulation, even though most of the products which they produce are intended for interstate or foreign trade; but warehouses and stockyards are in commerce since the cotton or grain or live stock in which they deal are intended for interstate commerce. A contract for the manufacture and shipment in interstate commerce of an automobile is commerce; but the manufacturing of the automobile covered in the contract is not a part of commerce. The Sherman Anti-Trust Act did not apply to a combination of sugar refiners, since "manufacture succeeds to commerce and is not a part of it"; but this law did apply to a combination of meat packers, even though the acts held illegal were *in them-*

352

selves local, because they were a part of a general scheme which *as a whole* affected interstate commerce. The labor relations of a mine operator, however extensive their effect upon commerce, were held to be "local" and not in interstate commerce with the result that the Federal Bituminous Coal Conservation Act of 1935 was invalidated; but in 1925 a strike of miners was held to affect directly interstate commerce in coal and, therefore, to come within the prohibitions of the Sherman Anti-Trust Act. In 1937 the National Labor Relations Act of 1935 was upheld on the ground that the labor relations of large-scale industry had a direct effect upon interstate commerce. Even though the word *commerce* appears but once in a simple sentence it has at least two different meanings: the congressional power over *foreign* commerce is *plenary* and includes the power to prohibit such commerce; but the power over *interstate* commerce is *limited* (1) by the requirement that it must be exercised to promote, not to prohibit, commerce between the states and (2) by the police power of the states in certain judicially approved cases. Yet, Congress may prohibit the transportation in interstate commerce of lottery tickets, impure food, stolen automobiles, prize fight films, prostitutes, and prison-made goods; but Congress may not close the channels of interstate commerce to goods produced by the labor of children, unless, perhaps, it would be in aid of a state law forbidding the importation of such goods. In the child labor case, the court pointed out that Congress might prohibit the use of the instrumentalities of interstate commerce for the transportation of goods which *in themselves* are harmful or dangerous to the public welfare, such as adulterated foods, or goods which would have a harmful effect *after* transportation, such as lottery tickets, but that Congress may not ban otherwise legitimate articles of commerce because of alleged evils connected with their manufacture *before* transportation, because conditions affecting production are subject to regulation by the state alone under its police power.[1] Thus a distinction without a difference is made the basis for the anticonstitutional doctrine that the delegated power of Congress to regulate interstate commerce is limited by the reserved police power of a state. Furthermore, this distinction does not explain the prohibition on stolen automobiles or prison-made goods.

On the other hand, a state, in the exercise of its police or commerce powers, may affect interstate commerce only indirectly. Accordingly a state may not forbid, in the absence of a confirming act of Congress, the importation of legitimate articles of commerce while in the original package; but states may exclude prison-made goods, and, by analogy, it has been suggested that they may exclude goods made by children, although an elementary regard for consistency would seem to exclude both types of legislation. State quarantine laws and a law forbidding the running of freight trains on the Sabbath have been held not to affect interstate commerce directly, even though they fixed positive prohibitions upon traffic. The state of Florida was held competent to protect its citrus industry by forbidding the marketing beyond the state of poor and immature fruit; but North Dakota could not protect its wheat industry through regulations forbidding the exportation out of the state of wheat, until the price should rise above the cost of production. A statute of New Jersey which forbade the taking or sending out of the state of game birds killed within the state was upheld; but an act of Louisiana which prohibited the exportation of unshelled shrimp was held to be an unconstitutional burden upon interstate commerce. And in the decision holding the Agricultural Adjustment Act of 1933 unconstitutional, the power of a state to regulate intrastate commerce was held to limit the delegated powers of Congress to tax and to spend for the general welfare, a doctrine which, if generally applied, would destroy the supremacy clause of the Constitution and undermine the Union.

Thus the commerce clause, as applied by the courts, defies rationalization and understanding. Lost in a maze of legal

354

technicality, judges have drifted into all manner of irreconcilable inconsistencies, from which they will not or cannot, with the aid of the legal profession, be extricated.

THE SUPREME COURT AS ARBITER

As the final interpreter of the Constitution, the Supreme Court has become, with the general approval of the American people, a third chamber of every legislative body in the United States. Any national or state legislative act may be brought before that court for review, and it will then be tested by certain *judicially defined* standards or devices. For instance, a tax must not be "confiscatory," regulations affecting the service or rates of a public utility must be "reasonable," that is, they must allow the utility to earn a "fair return" on the "fair value" of the property used by the public. A state regulation of common carriers can "affect" *interstate* commerce only "indirectly," and a national regulation of carriers must not "affect" *intrastate* commerce "directly." The taxing power, the power of eminent domain, and the police power can be exercised only for some "public purpose." A tax, upon an object not otherwise subject to regulation by the taxing authority, is valid only if the "primary purpose" of the law is to secure revenue and its regulatory or penalizing effect is "incidental," and legislative power may not be delegated to an executive or administrative agency unless the legislature prescribes an adequate "legislative standard."

But the application of all these tests involves the exercise of discretion or judgment. If the legislative and judicial judgments do not agree, the latter will prevail, and the judicial will is substituted for the legislative will in the formulation of public policy. Hence, the American system of government is properly described as one of judicial supremacy, while parliamentary systems are based upon the supremacy of the legislature. Inasmuch as the Supreme Court consists of nine judges who hold office during good behavior, they are not subject to any direct popular or political control, as are legislators

355

who must stand for reelection at stated times. And as this court is the sole judge of its own constitutional powers, it is not subject to any legal restraint save its "own sense of self-restraint." Thus ultimate governmental power is vested in from five (a majority) to nine politically and legally irresponsible judges; or it may be that this power is exercised by the odd judge, that is, the judge who breaks the tie vote in five to four decisions. This is by definition an oligarchy, whatever may be said in defense or praise of the manner in which the judges have exercised their dictatorial powers. The often repeated statement that judicial supremacy ensures the protection of the individual against arbitrary action by the legislative and executive departments hardly rises to the dignity of an argument, as there can be no place in a democracy for judicial or any other guardianship. A free people must rely upon an effective use of the suffrage and not upon the benevolence of their wise men. There is no escape from the responsibilities of democracy save through the surrender of democracy itself. "In short," says Professor Edward S. Corwin, "having gone in for political democracy, it might have been as well if we had courageously faced the logical consequences of our choice from the outset, instead of trying 'to cover our bet' by resigning the ultimate voice as to matters of vital social import to the consciences of nine estimable elderly gentlemen."

THE COURT'S POWERS: WHENCE DERIVED?

Whence came this power of constitutional adaptation by judicial interpretation? The Constitution nowhere, in terms, defines the judicial power of the United States as including the power to pass upon the constitutionality of acts of Congress. Whether the framers of the Constitution intended to confer this important power by implication is a moot question. After much searching analysis and considerable wishful interpretation, researchers arrive at opposed conclusions in respect to the intent of the fathers. Psychoanalysis aside, the record of the Constitutional Convention discloses that that body considered three separate propositions affecting the judicial function: (1) provision for a national judiciary, (2) provision for negativing state legislation, and (3) provision for negativing national legislation. The first proposition became Article III of the Constitution. This article does not contain any direct reference to judicial review, and no reference was made to the subject during the debate on the article. The second proposition was incorporated in the supremacy clause, the keystone of the Federal system, which declares the supremacy of national over state law and binds state judges thereby. Thus provision was made for judicial review of *state* legislation. The third proposition, the revisionary clause, would have associated the judges of the Supreme Court with the President in the exercise of the veto power. This proposal was rejected at least three times by the Convention which deliberately voted to repose the veto power in the executive alone. This action was based upon an outspoken opposition to "the interference of the judges in the Legislative business." In the course of the debate on this proposition, some of the delegates seemed to assume that judicial review of acts of Congress was to be implied from the judiciary article, Article III, because this power was inherent in the judicial function; but it is significant that this group, for the most part, *strenuously opposed giving the judges any part in the legislative function.* Judges should be "the Expositors of the Laws," not "Legislators." It is clear that, if judicial review of national legislation was contemplated by the members of the Convention, that power had only a remote relation to the distinctly political judicial veto power as exercised today. It appears that to the fathers the judicial function had reference to the *interpretation* and not to the *application* of the Constitution, and that interpretation did not involve supervision of legislative policy.

But it is idle to pursue the elusive question further. Whether the Constitution was intended to embody the principle of judicial review of both national and state legislation or of state legislation only is a matter of fruitless speculation. Judicial review in the former sense is constitutional today because the American people have acquiesced in John Marshall's strained construction in the case of *Marbury v. Madison*, the first decision declaring a section of an act of Congress unconstitutional. But what the fathers put into the Constitution by construction the sons can take out by construction. The current argument to the effect that judicial supremacy cannot be disturbed except through formal amendment to the Constitution is a lawyer's trick to preserve the *status quo*, to "freeze" accepted doctrine into the Constitution. Beneficiaries of judicial conservatism have successfully resisted desirable constitutional change by appealing to the doctrine of the divine origin of the Constitution and then taking refuge behind the amending clause. Accordingly support of *their* Constitution has become at once a profession of the true American faith, an act of piety, and a fetish. The sons are by way of forgetting the admonition of one of the fathers, John Marshall, to "never forget that it is a constitution we are expounding."

NOTE

[1] The Fair Labor Standards Act of 1938 contains child labor provisions which are practically identical with the Federal Child Labor Act of 1916, held unconstitutional in the first Child Labor Case in 1917. A reorganized Supreme Court is now expected to sustain the new law.

Chapter XXII

THE DECLINE OF THE STATES

Roy V. Peel

★ ★ ★ ★

OVER thirty years ago, Elihu Root predicted that the states of the American union would lose power. The prediction has come true, and the time to face the facts is now. No longer need citizens lend a willing ear to the plaintive protests of a Coolidge or a Ritchie striving vainly to resurrect a defunct instrument of government. Even President Roosevelt, when he says: "The preservation of home rule by the States is not a cry of jealous commonwealths seeking their own aggrandizement. . . . It is a fundamental necessity if we are to remain a truly united nation," is not to be taken too seriously. The greatest inroads on state sovereignty have been made by his direction; to make these changes acceptable it has been deemed necessary to invoke the ancient deities. But political slogans cannot forever restrain the march of progress.

All life changes. Forms that once served the needs of man yield under pressure, sometimes gradually, sometimes suddenly and violently. The one inescapable fact of modern society is change. Adaptation to changes becomes, then, the first obligation of government, which is men acting together to promote their joint interests; but almost on a level with this principle is the reciprocal principle of stability, which resists, retards, and embarrasses progress but does not stop it. The stabilizing impulses of people are reflected in their institutions, in their written constitutions and unwritten customs, in their courts, which are manned by the aged and firm defenders of

359

the *status quo*, in their legislatures with defined powers and limitations, and in their administrators with prescribed duties and obligations. In the American system, security against too rapid change is found in the checks and balances, composed, on the one hand, of a separation of power between legislators, executives, and judges and, on the other hand, of the distribution of powers between the nation and the states.

One of the acts of the present government which has excited the greatest alarm and precipitated the most violent debate on current policies, is the Reorganization bill which was designed to strengthen the executive and to give him power commensurate with his responsibility and adequate to the nation's needs. This bill was based on the historic principle of the strong executive, accepted—in principle—by every serious student of administration. The opposition to it came from legislators, who keenly felt the loss of privileges which their predecessors were supposed to have enjoyed, privileges which, however, when exercised, were not free from the most scathing contemporary condemnation nor from the most solemn adverse judgment of posterity.

It is not within the purview of this chapter to prolong the discussion, but one must note that the very same complexities and perplexities which gave rise to demands for national *centralization* also precipitated governmental *integration*. In England, the delegation of political power by Parliament to administrative departments incited Lord Hewart to raise the cry of despotism. In America, similar tendencies on all levels of government evoke an equally pathetic and futile opposition. To no avail. The accommodation of institutions to new demands thrives on attack. Every year has witnessed in city, state, and nation new gains for executive independence and administrative reorganization. The effort to reorganize, begun in 1894, has in part succeeded in 1938 despite the defeat of the Reorganization bill.

In addition to the Reorganization bill, the Roosevelt Administration has roused the foes of progress by a whole series of measures calculated to weaken the integrity of the states. Most notable is the work of the National Resources Committee, which has not only surveyed present trends but also indicated a course of future development wherein the states will gradually yield authority. Although the issue is now being drawn in dramatic fashion, the origins of this movement may be traced back to the earliest days of the nation. In essence, consolidation is Hamiltonian in theory. Lincoln, Blaine, Theodore Roosevelt, and Herbert Hoover—Republicans all—have been its stoutest defenders; and yet, by the irony of circumstance, it was Jefferson, Madison, and Franklin Roosevelt who have actually done more to promote centralization than their historic rivals.

Before proceeding with our exposition, it is essential that we consider the relation of these matters to fundamental principles. The objective of government is to protect and serve its citizens. "It is co-operative enterprise," writes Morgenthau, "which provides highways, schools, police protection, libraries, health protection, relief to the unfortunate and other such services." The critera of its efficacy are moral, legal, political, and economic. In a totalitarian state, the emphasis is on the state itself, not on the individual. Democracies are grounded in faith and trust in the individual. If any one technique of governance distinguishes the democracy from the dictatorship, it lies in the application of the belief that persuasion is preferable to force. In principle, a democracy is a limited government. The consolidation of power, whether in the form of integration or centralization, is no denial of this principle because power takes various forms. Each case has to be decided on its merits. Where there are sufficient safeguards to liberty and equality, there is democracy. The essential test of government is not, therefore, its form, but its results in terms of the welfare of the masses.

The American colonies were established as separate units, but within a very short time were consolidated and subjected to uniform regulation by Parliament. During the confederation period there was some tendency to multiplication of authorities, which was reversed by the Constitution in 1789. Three million people lived in the United States at that time; today the nation supports 130 million and governs them by means of one national, 48 state, and nearly 200,000 separate local agencies. In New York State alone, there are over 14,000 distinct, semi-independent governments. There is widespread acceptance of Senator Byrd's opinion that "There are too many governments and there is too little efficiency."

Many people, including Senator Byrd, Governor Lowden, and Secretary Morgenthau, believe that this problem can be met by abolishing or consolidating the smaller, nonsovereign units, such as counties and special districts. Others agree with Professor Edward S. Corwin of Princeton University that "the concept of dual federalism was always highly artificial, owing not a little to the accidental circumstance that the members of the union were called 'states'"; and they urge that the states themselves be liquidated.

FACTORS OF STATE PARTICULARISM

Nothing is more paradoxical than the persistence of states' rights sentiment in the face of growing national supremacy. It is no answer to this puzzle to say that historical forces have given American statehood a peculiar virility, because such forces have worked elsewhere to different ends. Nevertheless, one powerful factor in the formation of the attitudes and institutions which comprise the American "state system" is historical. The first colonies were independent settlements, some of them organized under the English Parliament and kings, others founded by the Swedes and the Dutch under letters patent. A few of them were actually laid out on the map in advance of settlement. But the boundaries were irregularly ordained and, in some instances, overlapping. Gradually, by conquest and then by legislation or royal proclamation, conflicts of jurisdiction were resolved, and the colonies burgeoned as living organisms.

362

The colonists considered themselves members of their own "states." Not until repressive legislation and oppressive administrative action began to fall upon them without regard to position or type of charter did they give any evidence of that fellow feeling which betokens the emergence of national consciousness. Even so, Franklin's "severed snake" cartoon and other propaganda devices were not effective until a war had been fought (in which the people were divided three ways—loyalist, patriot, and indifferent), until independence had been gained, and until eleven years of economic rivalry had prepared them for the new union.

Differences in racial composition, religious persuasion, culture, economic organization and practices accentuated the separatistic tendencies of the states. Loyalties were rooted in the states, where distances, social connections, and commercial intercourse all contrived to produce reality, whereas the nation was still a symbol of uncertain cohesive quality. Long after the first Americanization campaigns had been initiated, states were resisting the authority of the national government. Every state in the union, at some time or other, nullified a national law. By the time the state system had spread to the West, every possible element in state separatistic identity had been explored and every artificial device for autonomy had been employed. The identification of great names with the state, state flags, state songs, state regiments, state societies, state delegations, state histories, state resources, and state institutions—these were the instruments and implements of state pride and state identity. In the years since the Civil War, state separatism has lost much of its vigor, but the longer reorganization is deferred, the more potent is the factor of historical traditions.

The second factor in state separatism is geographic. Slight differences in climate, soil structure, land use, resources, and topography distinguish adjoining states. In some cases, rivers, watersheds, bays, and other natural features physically separate states. Thus geographic forces contributed to sepa-

363

ratism. By legal tokens, historically derived, the Western Reserve in Ohio was a part of Connecticut, the territory west of the mountains belonged to Virginia and North Carolina, and Delaware consisted of the three lower counties of Pennsylvania. Geography detached them from the claimant state.

The third factor in separatism is population. The Swedes conferred a distinction on Delaware, the Dutch on New York, the English Puritans on Massachusetts, the English cavaliers on Virginia, the Quakers on Pennsylvania, and the English working classes on Georgia. Each state came to have a peculiar composition of population elements, which by its institutions and occupations was accoutered with dress, dialect, and deportment fitting its special role. The Virginians cultivated a sense of divine importance and the Pennsylvanians looked with disdain on the uncouth New Yorkers. Said Maclay: "These Yorkers are the vilest of people. Their vices have not the palliation of being manly." Reciprocal aversions were picturesquely phrased.

Naturally, politicians and plutocrats aspiring to leadership nourished these sentiments as accompaniments to their own aspirations. Luther Martin and William Paterson drew upon the small states, undernourished and inferior in prestige, to sustain their plans of decentralization. Decades later, another Marylander, Albert Ritchie, loomed as one of the stoutest defenders of states' rights; and Frank Hague, in New Jersey, attempted to enforce some peculiar interpretations of the Constitution. Throughout the union, the chief advocates of states' rights were always the persons whose concern for particularistic doctrines of sovereignty was subordinate to their ambition.

Hand in hand with these factors moved the force of economic organization. Early transportation facilities within states and the conditioning of the market tended to confine commercial organization within state lines. Ships sailed with letters of marque and reprisal from the colonial governments. When these were withdrawn, harbors, warehouses, and auxiliary enterprises kept the shipping firms tied down to particular states. Antagonistic legislation, such as tariffs, affected the whole economic structure of the state, and economics and politics joined hands in defense of state interests. Later legislation reinforced the state system. State banks were established, some, as in New York, protected by state safety funds, implementing collective responsibility. In New York, too, the Erie Canal bound together the fragments of empire. Turnpikes and the railroad joined eastern Pennsylvania to the trans-Allegheny sections. In every state, differential legislation with respect to land tenure and use, subsidies to business and regulations thereof, banking systems and commercial practices, fixed the state system—apparently irrevocably.

The last and greatest bulwark of state particularism is the law. The Constitution definitely committed certain powers to the states and granted others by implication. All persons who inherited or acquired exceptional privileges under this arrangement fought for its retention and extension. Later, when the growth of national power began to threaten entrenched privilege, the holders called on the states for protection. The courts strove to be impartial, with curious results. Thus, Marshall: " . . . the United States form, for many and for most important purposes, a single nation. . . . In war we are one people. In making peace we are one and the same people. In many other respects the American people are one, and the government which is alone capable of controlling and managing their interests in all these respects, is the government of the Union."

GROWTH OF NATIONAL POWER

Federalism in the United States has had a checkered career. Up to 1860, it was still particularistic, the idea of independent states slowly yielding to the idea of nationality. Even Taney, famed for his sectionalism, expounded a national doctrine. Since Lincoln, the nation has been dominant. The Civil War signalized the triumph of the union; but doubts remained. In

1876, Blaine temporarily revived the sentiment of sectionalism, with unfortunate repercussions in state electoral legislation and in Southern treatment of the Negro question. Blaine himself, despite his cultivation of local pride in the "State of Maine," was not particularist. He even outgrew his sectionalism, and became one of the outstanding advocates of national supremacy. Conkling, his rival, perverted the Fourteenth Amendment, originally intended as a measure in defense of Negroes, and made it into a measure in defense of corporations, weakening thereby the alliance of states and business which had been fostered by the Dartmouth College case. By the turn of the century, the idea of state independence was dormant. The vast industrial and transportation enterprises, which now span the continent, had broken down the barriers which state lines had erected. Newspaper chains, art, music, literature (especially textbooks like McGuffey's *Readers*), and later the movies and then the radio obliterated state lines.

The only obstacles to national supremacy for many years were constitutional amendments, which, requiring the assent of three-fourths of the states, gave the latter an additional significance every time they came up. The Eighteenth Amendment was passed in the approved fashion, but until its repeal its opponents never stopped attacking it as an unwarranted invasion of powers reserved to the states. Similarly, the Nineteenth Amendment was delayed, and the Child Labor amendment—not yet ratified by a sufficient number of states— was obstructed, by the transparent friends of states' rights.

The soothsayers continue to invoke the ancient doctrines in defense of child labor, unregulated marketing of milk, and the unregulated exchange of stocks and bonds.

Even the National Resources Committee, which shall presently be cited as the recorder of a vast change in our Federal system, concluded that

. . . it is neither possible nor desirable to alter state boundaries. The territorial arrangements involved in the States have been "frozen" both legally and psychologically for so long a period that the disadvantages in changing them would outweigh the advantages. Moreover, the very fact that the States are heterogeneous units seems to be of considerable value politically. The attendant disunity of interests and clash of objectives provide a perpetual guaranty of those checks, balances and compromises which are the backbone of the American political system. (December, 1935, report, *Regional Factors in National Planning*, page 20.)

Through the agency of historical, geographic, demographic, political, economic, and legal forces, the nation has preserved the illusion of being an "indissoluble union of indestructible states." Yet, as we have seen, national centralization has become stronger with the passing of time. At present, the decline of the states is reflected in four tendencies.

1. THE TWILIGHT ZONE

In the first place, the national government has taken over powers formerly lodged with the states, or at least exercised by them in default of national action. Corwin remarks that, with regard to the reserved powers of the states, "there are two lines of precedents between which the Court may choose at will, one of which asserts in effect that when an exercise of national power is *otherwise* constitutional, there is no reserved power to nullify it; while the other treats the 'reserved power' of the States as constituting an independent limitation on national power." Here is a twilight zone, where the express delegations of power are not precise enough in practice. Under the leadership of nationally minded men, the national government has extended its sphere, most notably in the control of certain types of intrastate commerce, banking, housing, health, education, relief, and the suppression of crime.

These extensions of national power shade off into fields wherein the states have not functioned at all, or to no appreciable degree. They have been slow to control activities accompanying the new forms of social and economic intercourse, or resulting from crises and calamities which have afflicted us severely in recent time. Duncan Aikman, in *The New York Times*, described the new nationalism as follows:

The whole financial structure of the country, for instance, with its thousands of bankers and regiments of legal and technical advisers, is bound to Washington through the control exercised by the Federal Reserve system. Every corporate business in the United States, moreover, except the few with a definitely intra-state character, has a stake in the regulations of the Securities Exchange Commission. So many of the government's economic and social policies touch labor directly that the capital swarms with labor leaders, resident and transient. A government which once gave farmers free seeds and circulars now ties 30,000,000 agriculturalists to its activities with vast programs of economic aid and regulation, with scores of enterprises in technical service . . . [spending] tens of millions through . . . the pension and insurance provisions of the social-security program. . . .

Business men and industrialists [journey to Washington to consult] about price and distribution problems under the Robinson-Patman Act; about wage and labor problems under the Walsh-Healey Act; about corporate and personal taxes under the many-pronged New Deal revenue laws; about trade practices and the whole field of competitive endeavor under the expanding authority of the Federal Trade Commission. The Bureau of Standards, the Commissions which watch his transportation, communication, power and tariff interests, or the scores of bureaus and divisions in the Departments of Commerce, Labor and Agriculture. . . .

Since 1911, the national government has extended its powers indirectly as well as directly through the grants-in-aid. Although legally considered a contractual process, the practice of conditional grants and loans actually promotes nationalism, for the national government retains complete control. The latest example of this type of relationship is the Social Security Act of 1935.

There are then, three ways in which the Federal government clips the authority of the states: by exercising powers formerly considered state powers, by exercising new powers, and by giving funds to states on the condition that states match Federal contributions and submit to Federal supervision.

2. COMPACTS AMONG THE STATES

The states have contributed, wisely, of course, to the diminution of their sovereign powers by concluding compacts among themselves. The basis for this practice is found in the Constitution. Article one, Section ten reads: "No State shall, without the consent of Congress . . . enter into any agreement or compact with another State . . . " The Court has declared such agreements to be legally binding and enforceable. By means of the "supremacy" clause, a national agency, the Supreme Court, enforces such compacts.

To date, Congress has given its assent to forty-four compacts, dealing with eight kinds of situations. By this device (1) boundary disputes are settled and territory ceded; (2) interstate debts are adjusted; (3) interstate rendition of fugitives from justice is facilitated; (4) public utilities of an interstate character (*e.g.*, tunnels, canals) are submitted to uniform controls; (5) uniform legislation on a score of subjects is provided; (6) interstate accounting and taxation reciprocity is arranged; (7) river and harbors are developed; and (8) extraordinary measures in the conservation of national resources are taken.

In theory, sovereign bodies do not abandon any rights when they yield them under treaty or agreement. Practically, they do; and, if all signs do not fail, control over sanitation, crime, water power, harbors, and many other problems arising in boundary areas, particularly in metropolitan districts, will quickly pass to bistate and tristate boards, set up under the auspices of Congress. Disputes relating to these and all other matters concerning states directly are reviewable only in the national Supreme Court. Interstate compacts, are, therefore, unmistakable signs of the decline of the states.

3. INTERSTATE CO-OPERATION

It is alleged that interstate co-operation of a less formal character, such as is found in the Council of State Governments, constitutes a real defense of states' rights. Some authorities on government believe that co-operation permits states to manage engineering enterprises in an effective and dignified manner. H. W. Toll, Executive Director of the Council of State Governments, has been a pioneer in the effort to bring the states closer together. Others, who have studied the situation from different points of view, are skeptical of the future of interstate planning compacts.

A close examination of the work of co-operative agencies, such as the American Legislators Association and the numerous other interstate organizations which have their headquarters in Chicago, confirms the view that this movement has as its result the uniformity and simplification of state administrative practices. This is clear gain. But as Hubert R. Gallagher, writing in the *National Municipal Review*, points out, the real test will come when

. . . the cooperative commissions take the offensive in economic fields which in the past have been so clogged with the petty jealousies of individual states, with selfish business and industrial interests tugging their legislatures first one way and then another, that attempts to bring about constructive legislation and progressive administration have often been blocked.

4. THE NATION AND THE CITIES

To this problem we shall revert in a moment. Meanwhile, the national government has begun to draw the cities within its own orbit. Cities are nowhere mentioned in the Constitution. They received no notice in any national law until a few short years ago. Since 1932, however, the Federal government has dealt with cities on such a large scale as practically to exclude the states.

The average citizen probably does not realize that fifty per cent of the American people live in metropolitan communities of 100,000 and over. Since 1790, urban population has multiplied 300 times; the rural population, only 15 times. Seventy-four per cent of industrial wage earners live in the 155 largest city-counties, and eighty per cent of all salaried employees live there. The value of goods produced in these centers amounts to seventy-three per cent of the country's total. If the United States is a democracy and if the satisfaction of the masses is our chief aim, then the cities are three times as important as all the rest of the country.

Prior to Hoover's administration, the cities were shamefully neglected, even betrayed by their own agents. Relief was sought in home rule. Only seventeen states, however, permit their chief cities any substantial powers by this instrument. Governors and state legislators resist it desperately; courts construe the doctrine narrowly. Clarence G. Dykstra, on whose authority the figures here cited are given, holds that state supervision over municipal activities (finance, personnel, and highways—the author would add elections) is "partial in scope and confusing in administration." The worst evils of personnel administration are due to state interference. In recent years, states have compensated for pressure put upon them by the national government and by the need for regional co-operation by laying extra burdens on the cities and tenaciously imposing their intervention in matters associating cities and the nation.

Every municipal authority worth his salt joins Dykstra in condemning state control of cities. Charles E. Merriam of the University of Chicago says:

> Most states do not now correspond to economic and social unities, and their validity as units of organization and representation may be and has been seriously challenged . . . Certainly as guides and guardians of cities, the states have been singularly ill-equipped and ill-qualified. Conceivably, states might be very useful to cities as administrative superiors, supervising such affairs as finances and police, but practically they have no such function as a rule, and it does not seem probable they will have in the near future, so far as metropolitan regions are concerned.

Let it be emphatically observed, however, that none of these experts wants cities to be freed from higher controls. Some agency should control them—*but not the state*. Manhandled and neglected by the states, the cities have turned to the Federal government. P. V. Betters found that scores of services were being rendered cities by nearly every department in the Federal government. In the case of San Diego, selecting one city at random, he reported that the total operating costs in the city were $4,511,277.74 for the fiscal year 1936–1937, and

371

Federal WPA expenditures for the same period were $3,796,-163—hardly a million dollars less.

Frances L. Reinhold, writing in the *National Municipal Review* in August of 1936, listed the important national-city relations as follows:

Glass-Steagall Act	banking
CCC Act	relief and works
TVA Act	general
NIR Act	recovery, relief
PWA (CWA, FERA, LWP, WPA, etc.)	recovery, relief
NHA Act	housing
AAA	lightening of local relief burdens
Summers-Wilcox Act	municipal bankruptcies (declared unconstitutional)
21 crime acts	crime control
Social Security Act	security relief
Utilities Act of 1935	regulation and loans
Revenue acts	deposit insurance

This by no means exhausts the list. By various acts, over 11 billion dollars has been appropriated, and, one can say, there would simply have been no relief for the cities if the national government had not stepped in. Not only has Washington saved human lives, but also millions of Federal funds have gone toward the conserving and improving of property values, plant, and equipment in cities.

Who can honestly reject Merriam's dictum that "the state is a fifth wheel so far as city government is concerned"? The only defenses of state dominance over cities are based on the irrelevant ground that somewhere, in between, there must be a regional agency.

Serious students are inclined to agree with President Dodds of Princeton, who suggested that "In the course of the years, the present circumstances of area and frontier of the states may be modified, but I do not foresee an abandonment of the principle of national federalism although its internal structure may be changed as time progresses." Such modifications are no new thing.

THE FUTURE OF THE STATES

The ancestors of the states, the colonies, were hardly established before they sectionalized and then coalesced into a national union. Various forces, as we have seen, kept alive the idea of state sovereignty, but the same forces were stimulating sectionalism, and other forces were working to achieve national supremacy. The balance of forces clearly indicates a contemporary retrogression of the states. All signs point to further decline. What, then, will be the future structure of American government?

The possible answers range from (1) restoration of the states to the condition they were in one hundred years ago; (2) the conferring of new powers on the states, commensurate with the tasks imposed on governments under present conditions; (3) the breaking up of certain states to create city-states; and (4) the displacement of states by political regions.

The advocates of the first alternative are inspired by a nostalgia for bygone days, and may be dismissed with a sympathetic shrug. The proponents of the second alternative stand on firmer ground. It is their contention that the Federal government is going too heavily in debt, but how they expect the states to perform additional functions—which in the pre-New Deal period were causing costs to rise one hundred per cent—any more cheaply than the national government performs them at present, is not made clear. The chief objection seems to be to the Works Progress Administration which, it is alleged, fosters indolence and inefficiency. These critics fail to consider that the national policy, supported by the states, is to emphasize the relief aspect of the WPA.

The Chicago school of experts and some Eastern authorities believe that it is desirable to conserve the states because of their antiquity and apparent usefulness in warding off sectional conflicts. Nearly all authorities agree that any sudden and organic attempt to divest the states of their so-called *independence* would release prejudices and political interests of

373

tremendous drive. But all authorities insist that states must improve their own organizations and administrative efficiency, cut their costs, professionalize their legislatures, and, not inconsistently, democratize their entire political structures.

To the writer, these proposals seem to be impossible of application. Of the alternative methods of reorganization, Merriam's plea for city-states merits earnest consideration. Our large metropolitan centers, such as New York, Chicago, St. Louis, Los Angeles, Detroit, Seattle—to name but a few— cover, in fact, wider areas than are indicated by their boundaries. Some sprawl over several states, and the existing incompatability of social and economic organization, on the one hand, and political control, on the other, is deplorable. From the City of New York, a half million souls pass out every night to the suburbs, leaving cares and responsibilities behind them. Significantly, some of the stoutest champions of good government in the city—men like Buttenheim, Seabury, Moses—are domiciled beyond its borders. The legalized xenophobians of the city regard them as outsiders. This is merely one type of difficulty found in our present metropolitan cities. Others have been exhaustively presented in various planning studies—notably in New York, Philadelphia, Chicago, St. Louis, and Boston. The mass of evidence is overwhelming. Metropolitan cities must be constituted on the basis of their actual—not historical—boundaries and be given authority adequate to their needs and appropriate to their position in the national scheme.

The final solution is the substitution of regions for states. This proposal has the merit of retaining federalism, and it can be developed in such a flexible manner as to permit local self-government to survive. Schemes of adaptation are based on three factors; area, functions, and powers.

It has already been suggested that the solution to this problem found by the framers of our Constitution was unique. Federalism had been projected by the ancient Greeks, but its actual practice began here in the United States in 1787. The

374

only flaw in it was its rigid assumption of *indestructible* states. Did Jefferson have such an inflexible system in mind when he wrote:

> But it is not by the consolidation of powers, but by their distribution, that good government is effected. Were not this great country already divided into states, that division must be made, that each might do for itself what concerns itself directly, and what it can so much better do than a distant authority. . . . It is by . . . partition of cares, descending in gradation from general to particular, that the mass of human affairs may be best managed for the good and prosperity of all.

Jefferson's behavior in office and his other writings lead one to believe that he would be "open to reason" today. It is not only in America that growth has been curtailed by illogical and obstructive boundaries. Let us see what experience other powers have had in the "partition of cares."

The dawn of history found men in Europe grouped according to area. Nomadic tribes were confined by natural frontiers; when they did succeed in passing them they settled somewhere. Thus the Slavs eventually occupied West Central Europe and Hither Asia, the Vikings spread out over the world and then fell back upon the homeland in the North. New nations were formed out of mixtures of peoples and developed unique characteristics. Under Rome the whole Mediterranean and the southern portion of the continent of Europe were organized as an imperium, which was in fact a kind of federation. The imperium broke up, to be followed by an "organization of chaos"—feudalism, which was in turn to yield to nationalism and capitalism. For centuries, the central problem of nationalism, *viz.,* finding frontiers which would demark one sovereign national state from another, kept Europe in turmoil; and even today, with Germany occupying Austria, there is striking evidence of the persistence of the conflict and confusion of ideas.

The case of Germany is especially interesting because here are people who retained separate governmental entities until 1870, and even after that date persisted in acknowledging sub-divisional entities, the nomenclature of which had scant reference to historical origins or racial characters. A new principle of unity was introduced by Adolf Hitler, who cut across territorial divisions of the people to ordain pure and impure racial groups, and projected the state to encompass minorities lodged in alien lands. By the doctrine of totalitarianism, area differences were submerged—for how long, it is too early to say.

France, nationalized under Philip Augustus in 1209, nevertheless retains regions, cultural and governmental. For administrative purposes, areas were fixed (called *departments*) and the form of the state government was unified. But, today, the sentiment of regionalism is stronger than ever. Sweden, once divided into three parts, Svealand, Gotland, and Norrland, broke up into provinces, which still exist, but alongside of them are administrative counties formed in the time of Gustavus Adolphus. England applied the same solution to the problem of administration, but the problem of federalism in the British Isles received a complex answer, resulting in nearly complete independence for southern Ireland, semi-autonomous statutes for Scotland, co-ordination for Northern Ireland, and incorporation for Wales and Cornwall. As in France, regionalism reappeared, taking the form of demands for *devolution*, a unique solution which space forbids us to dilate upon. "Local government in Britain," said the English authority, Robson, "is still suffering from area difficulties, due to the failure to write the Benthamite scheme of creating areas appropriate to function into the Municipal Act." Throughout the world, the story has been the same—powerful regional ferments at work, sometimes rising above the threshold of internationalism, on other occasions caught and controlled by internal reorganizations.

When the Russian state was formed, it rested upon a theory of class which ignored racial and nationality differences. Hence the fear and hatred with which the new "nation" was regarded. On the other hand, the political theory of the

Russian state was essentially *regionalistic*. Bakunine advocated a state which "had no other basis than the natural interest, needs and attractions, of man, nor other principle than the free federation of individuals into communes, communes into provinces, provinces into nations, and finally the latter into the United States of Europe, and later of the entire world." This doctrine, profoundly impressed by American example, was written into the Constitution, and there was added to it the provision calling for the right of free secession.

THE FACT OF REGIONALISM

Regionalism differs from states' rights in that it rejects the validity of state boundaries as appropriate to their uses. It is not necessarily antagonistic to federalism, since federalism defines only the relation between the larger unit and the smaller one, whatever that may be. Legally, the American union may be a federation of states; politically, it is a compact among sections. The first region was New England, which formed, as early as 1643, a New England Federation. New York was almost a region by itself, as was Pennsylvania, but these two states later combined with New Jersey and Delaware to form the Middle Atlantic states. For enumeration purposes, Maryland fell also in this category, but from Virginia south the land was known as the South. Historical accident and geographic factors, as well as demographic influences, set off North from South Carolina, and West Virginia from the Old Dominion. In the Constitutional Convention, clear blocks of delegates from the North and the South, as well as from the East and the West, were apparent.

The Northwest Territory was the historical and legal ancestor of the Middle West. In time, the border states acquired a definite character, emphasized by their neutral position during the Civil War. The "deep" South or the old South was set off from them. As the march of empire proceeded westward, the West itself became a section, united in

1812 by the expansionists, and later bound by common interest in internal improvements, land policies, and tariff interests.

The Louisiana Purchase split up into the Middle West and the Mountain states. Texas, Arizona, and New Mexico, fruits of the Mexican War, coalesced into the Southwest. Beyond the Rockies, the Pacific Coast gave form to the three westernmost states. Within each group minor subdivisions appeared, each with well-defined characteristics. In speech, physique, attitudes, and traditional loyalties and aversions, the residents of sections came to have vastly more significance than residents of states. To these factors others have been added.

Frank S. Turner was the first to turn academic attention to the fact of regionalism. Since he first published his "Section and Nation," in the *Yale Review* in October, 1922, historians have hastened to document his generalizations. An amazing number of other scholars have contributed to the study of the subject, and not a few have submitted elaborate proposals for the reorganization of the United States government on a regional basis. To save space, reference is here made to W. B. Graves's article, "The Future of the American States," in the *American Political Science Review* for February, 1936, and to Howard W. Odum's various works on regionalism, wherein all the important proposals for regional reorganization are extensively discussed. The curious reader can find ample citations from authority there.

Eleven years ago the present writer called for the reconstruction of the United States on the principle of regionalism; since that time, the trend toward this type of reorganization has intensified a hundredfold. Naturally, there is no disposition to retreat now.

We have seen how nationalism overcame states' rights and other local manifestations with the victory of the Union armies in the Civil War. By 1900, ignoring interludes, nationalism had taken firm hold, and its external expression, imperialism, appeared. The political aspect of American imperialism

378

languished; economic imperialism and financial penetration displaced it. Then, after the World War, a new federalistic concept of international organization was given reality by Woodrow Wilson. It rose and fell, and as it fell, a recrudescence of regionalism was brought about by the depression.

Various social and literary agencies took note of this new regionalism. The geographers increased their activity and published works depicting the physiographic features of America. Natural catastrophies and economic maladjustments, bringing private and public remedies in their train, emphasized once again the regional areas of America in terms of watersheds; river systems, such as the Mississippi and the Ohio; power areas, such as Boulder Dam; soil areas, crop areas, forest areas; petroleum districts; coal, iron, copper, silver, and gold sections. Whenever public measures were asked for, it was clearly seen that differences of opinion with reference to them coincided with territorial boundaries.

To a degree, the man-made regimentations of transportation and industry, often accelerated by governmental action, cut across these natural sections. Wealth and industry were concentrated in the Omaha-Boston belt, the plains crop and grazing areas were tied to Fort Worth and Kansas City, and then to Chicago. Southern California, haven of retired Iowa farmers, became the moving picture capital. Economic necessity drove textile mills from New England to the South, and factories to the Middle West; the long overlordship which Northern financiers had exercised, first over the South, later over the West, manifested itself more openly as steel mills were established in Birmingham and realignments in elections reflected changed attitudes.

Governmental action sought to re-establish sectional identities of interest and sectional equality. The Federal Reserve System, as modified in the Owens-Glass bill from the early Aldrich-Vreeland proposals, decentralized credit. But not satisfactorily. So great was the pull of the speculative market in New York City of the 1920's that a banker of

379

Colorado rushed into New York and illegally restored to his depositors their life savings. Meanwhile, the necessities of commercial intercourse, only slightly hampered by interstate restrictions, produced market areas which disregarded state lines. In art, speech, literature, and all cultural aspects of American life, sectional patterns were prevalent.

Buttressing all these forces were demographic factors. Immigrant groups tended to settle in sections. New generations of Scandinavians, distinct from the early colonists, peopled the prairies and the cities of the Middle West. Germans concentrated in Missouri, Illinois, and Wisconsin; the Irish, Jews, and Italians in the East; Orientals in the West, and Negroes in the South. Well-marked areas of nationality centralization appeared, giving cultural character to each region, and mightily influencing commercial, political, and governmental regimentation.

Studies of political distributions showed that alignments in Congress were more dependent upon section than party. In Nebraska, third party voting has been accelerated by drought. Geography, occupations, nationality traditions, all combined to leave a sectional impress on forms of political association. The Democrats solidified the South, the Farmer-Laborites and the Progressives spread like a fan around the headwaters of the Mississippi, bipartisanship flourished in the Mountain states, and northern New England remained rock-ribbed Republican, until Irish and French-Canadian immigration altered responses to political appeals. On particular issues fought out within states, it appears that divisions were along sectional lines, although on this point there is a difference of opinion.

The necessities of administration are transforming the legal state federalism of the nation into regionalism. The Federal Reserve system, based on studies of regional interests, has been mentioned. The composition of its governing board and the delimitation of its districts served political purposes. The Army Corps areas, however, are related more directly to

380

resources, topography, and tactics of defense. Agricultural, industrial, and financial regions established by the government at Washington were modeled after various standards, in which the political element was likewise dormant. But private and state associations, such as the one supporting the St. Lawrence Waterway projects, were partly political. All together these manifold alignments of interests prove that regionalism has reasserted itself and requires a modification in the structure of the state which would be more radical than mere administrative readjustment.

In the encyclopedic National Resources Committee reports (especially *Regional Factors in National Planning* and *Our Cities*), all the agencies promoting regionalism were enumerated. Amazing is the number of Federal administrative agencies which, more or less, disregard state lines. Over one hundred different national agencies maintain from three to seven hundred and fifty different regional or zone districts. Although the urbanism committee (and W. F. Ogburn in a special study) found a high degree of similarity in cities in the United States, so numerous were the "different" types of areas, that the committee was embarrassed by its riches. Various methods of determining composite areas were invented. The one favored—organization for planning purposes—stressed physiographic factors.

None of the scholars engaged on these gigantic research projects felt inclined to urge the abolition of the states. The writer of this article is, however, in the company of cautious and conservative men when he invites serious attention to the gravity of the problem and urges that the obsolete ideal of sovereign states be relinquished for a new federalism of regions. Is it not true that powers, obligations, responsibilities, and potentialities in the present Federal system are hopelessly confused? And is it not a fact that the word "local" has no longer any clear meaning? Sentiments of pride and illusions of integrity and virility must not interfere with the efficient and appropriate organization of our national life, for we are confronted with a crisis fully as great as that which confronted us in 1787.

To these visions of the future of the United States, one would be impelled to add a postscript. Regions established might be limited to nine or twelve, and their political representation in Congress made proportionate to their internal divisions. Administrative areas could be consolidated, and yet made flexible enough to be readily adjusted to future emergencies. The sweep of national centralization will undoubtedly force many problems out of range of regional conflict, but such as remain—obviously fewer in number—will, one imagines, yield readily to simplified and uniform procedures now being developed by interstate co-operation.

In this volume, others discuss the implications of new doctrines of welfare and social responsibility. But no proposal— or prediction—of a real reorganization can afford to ignore the theory of class conflict. What effect would regional recognition have on antagonisms between worker, farmer, and businessman? It would diminish them, since it would clarify and simplify the nature of these antagonisms. In every prediction regarding the reorganized structure of society, the assumption is inherent that reallocation of functions, reformation of institutions, and revision of attitudes are essential. Eventually, Vaccaro's dream of natural states, which he develops in *Les Bases sociologiques du droit et de l'état,* will become a reality here, as well as in the turbulent continents of Europe and Asia.

Part Four

OUR RELATIONS ABROAD

Chapter XXIII

THE INTERNATIONAL SCENE

HENRY C. WOLFE

★ ★ ★ ★

O N NOVEMBER 11, 1918, the guns stopped firing on the
Western front. For the preceding four years and three
months millions of men along the tortuous line of
trenches from Switzerland to the North Sea had been devoting
all their time and their energies to killing their opponents.
The most gigantic slaughter of history had taken the flower of
youth in the warring countries. Men had lived like animals in
filthy, vermin-infested trenches. They had turned the peaceful
countryside of Belgium and eastern France into an abattoir.
They had fought like maniacs, slaying men whom they had
never seen before, disemboweling others who, like themselves,
had been driven into the shambles. They had choked from poison
gas; they had been nauseated by the stench of rotting flesh
whenever the wind blew across no man's land and brought
them the odors of the human scarecrows hanging on the
barbed wire. The soldier in the trenches became a grim fatal-
ist; he came to doubt that he would ever live a normal life
again. He thought little of the future; he lived only for the
moment.

When the "Cease fire!" order came on that November 11,
he crawled out of his muddy trenches and looked across that
desolate expanse of ground that had been no man's land. The
soldiers of the Allied forces watched "poor old Fritz" come up
out of his burrow. Both sides were sick of killing, maiming,
destroying. When the guns stopped barking every man drew a
sigh of relief. If this "war to end war" accomplished its pur-

385

pose, perhaps the sacrifice was not altogether in vain. The front line soldier devoutly hoped so. He had suffered in the trenches; he was ready now to make political and economic sacrifices in order to build a stable and enduring peace.

Paris, London, New York, and other cities in the Allied countries went hysterical with joy that November 11. The war was over! The London *Times* expressed the general feeling of mankind: "The 'cease fire' of yesterday must be final and universal." Fathers, husbands, brothers, sons were coming home. Prussian militarism had been destroyed. Parents and children could go to sleep now without fear of being killed by the droning monsters in the skies. Democracy had triumphed, and the world was going to be a better place in which to live. Hadn't the citizens in the victorious Allied countries been assured of the high purposes of their governments? Had not the peoples of the defeated Central Powers heard of the famous Fourteen Points, the slogans, the promises, the ideals that were to be the basis of peace on earth and good will toward all men?

THEN CAME VERSAILLES!

It was a far cry from the simple trust of the man in the trenches and of the humble civilian back home to the greed and chicanery of many of the politicians who assembled at Paris early in 1919 to begin that long wrangle called the peace conference. The young conscript who had gone valiantly to his death had never heard of secret treaties. The legless veteran who lived had not been—and was not then—animated by a desire to destroy his late enemy. The muddy men who had come home held no hatred against their recent opponents. Is it fantastic to believe that delegations of front line soldiers— not professional officers—from the Allies and the Central Powers could have reached an honest, lasting understanding? Certainly they could hardly have made a sorrier job of it than the politicians and generals who congregated on the banks of the Seine.

386

Allied victory accomplished the announced objectives of the respective governments. The Kaiser had run off ingloriously to Holland; General Ludendorff, wearing smoked glasses and a false beard, had escaped to Sweden; the military autocracy symbolized by Potsdam had crashed. The scar-faced Prussian lieutenant no longer dared elbow civilians off the sidewalk. The once mighty German military machine was in ruins. Belgium was freed of the Teutonic invader, and French troops occupied Alsace-Lorraine. Allied military power was established along the vineyard-covered slopes of the Rhine.

And what about the internal affairs of Germany? A democratic government had succeeded the Hohenzollern autocracy. Two socialists, Friedrich Ebert and Philip Scheidemann, had become, respectively, president and chancellor of the German republic. The militarists, the pan-Germans, the reactionaries had been discredited. The German people had come into power. Men and women who had been ostracized by the Junker class, who had been imprisoned, who had suffered martyrdom in the cause of democracy, were the new rulers of the Reich. This is attested by the fact that in the parliamentary elections of January, 1919, the Majority Socialists polled 11,112,450 votes against only 2,729,186 for the Conservatives. The recently dominant Prussian military clique was defeated under an avalanche of republican and pacifist votes.

Here was Europe's opportunity. Here was the ideal foundation for building a new continent. The men who governed the Weimar Republic were ready to meet the representatives of other nations in an effort to clean up the wreckage of the great war, to clear the path for economic recovery, to remove the causes of future conflicts. With these German republicans in power, war ceased to be "the national industry of Prussia." If Europe could at long last create a political, social, and economic structure of peace and equal opportunity among the various nations, the enormous sacrifices of fifty-one months of war would not all have been in vain.

It was the cardinal mistake, the criminal folly, of the victorious nations that they did not grasp the opportunity inherent in the existence of the republican German government. But, as a Frenchman remarked, "the war will be continued by other means." Not even the food blockade was removed so that starving children and old people in defeated Germany could survive. Herbert Hoover, the United States Food Administrator, protested " . . . we do not kick a man in the stomach after we have licked him." But the victors, especially the French, would make only negligible concessions to the vanquished. Marshal Foch succinctly expressed the French government's attitude toward the post-Armistice food blockade of the Reich when he said that it was a means of "compelling Germany to bow to our wishes."

The reader will do well to keep in mind the fact that many of the starving German children had not even been born when the war began. No one could accuse them of complicity in bringing on that tragedy. And the children and old people who were suffering most lived in the poor districts of the cities. In Berlin, Hamburg, Dresden, and other population centers, children with gray, expressionless faces looked like little spectres from some strange phantom land. Some of these mites had never known the experience of a full meal. It is they who were the real victims of the hunger blockade.

In a vigorous speech at Weimar on February 6, 1919, President Ebert warned the Allies not to push the German people beyond the limits of endurance. He asked for union of Austria and Germany, and the Reich's admission to the League of Nations. But his pleas fell on deaf ears. Clemenceau, cynical and vengeful, expressed his attitude toward the German people when he said that there were "twenty million too many" of them. More than anyone else at the so-called Peace Conference, the "Tiger" typified the spirit that wrote the Carthaginian treaty which ended the hopes for a permanent settlement of Europe's war-fostering problems. The dragon's teeth sowed at Versailles were to sprout into crushing armament burdens a few years later. Senator William E. Borah has called this pact the "mother of modern armaments" and the breeder of dictators.

There were at Versailles, it is true, prophetic voices which protested against the stupid, destructive treaties written there. Among the British, General Jan C. Smuts perceived the folly of such a dictated settlement, and John Maynard Keynes pointed out the economic disaster that was certain to follow. But men like Smuts, Keynes, and some of the American delegates were voices crying in the wilderness. Clemenceau, Lloyd George, Orlando, and others who represented a narrow, nationalistic viewpoint carried the day. The Treaty of Versailles was the monument to their labors. And what has followed has been the crowning example of the truth that no problem is ever solved by injustice.

When Germany's diplomatic mission was called to the Peace Conference on May 7, the chief delegate told that body that, as the result of the Allied blockade, 100,000 Germans had died since the Armistice. Nevertheless, the blockade was never completely relinquished until the German delegates signed the treaty on June 28, in the Galerie des Glaces at Versailles.

And when the Germans, Austrians, Hungarians, Bulgarians, and Turks signed their respective treaties, did war in Europe come to an end? These pacts did not bring peace. Indeed, Europe was torn by strife on a dozen fronts. A Balkanized Continent was drenched with blood, and its economic resources were further wasted by conflicts over boundaries, over ideologies, over the spoils of the "war to end war." From the Bay of Biscay to Vladivostok, millions of men were still under arms.

Finns, Poles, Estonians, Letts, Lithuanians, and Rumanians fought with Russians. Yudenitch, Kolchak, Petlura, Denikine, and other White Russian leaders battled with the newly created Red army under Trotzsky. Japanese, Americans, British, French, Poles, Czechs, and White Russians campaigned over the dreary wastes of Siberia. When Estonians and Letts

389

were not fighting the Soviet, they fought each other. Poles and Lithuanians clashed. Czechs and Poles fought over Teschen. Letts and Poles came to blows over Dunaburg. German free-booting armies roamed the Baltic countries and fought together with Finns against Russians, or alone against Poles, Letts, Lithuanians and Estonians. One Greek army went to Odessa and joined the anti-Soviet forces there. Another Greek army plunged into Asia Minor in an attempt to establish a great empire in the hinterland of Smyrna. Millions of refugees were shunted back and forth across wide areas. Disease and famine stalked in the paths of the armies.

A short-lived communist government was set up in Hungary, and the Hungarians fought the Czechs and Rumanians. The flamboyant Italian poet-warrior Gabriele D'Annunzio and his legionaries marched into the city of Fiume, a port claimed by both Italy and Yugoslavia, and in defiance of the Peace Conference established a puppet state that some observers believe was the forerunner of Mussolini's fascist regime. Meanwhile, a hard-pressed German republic was struggling to feed its people, withstand pressure from the Allies, and defend itself against communist outbreaks in Silesia, Saxony, Bavaria, Hamburg, and other districts. And while President Ebert and his collaborators were striving to prevent the Reich from sinking into anarchy, they had also to struggle to quell French-fostered separatist movements in the Rhineland and south Germany.

In Part V of the Treaty of Versailles it was stipulated that Germany was to disarm "in order to render possible the initiation of a general limitation of armaments of all nations." It was a constructive provision. Had this moral obligation of the victors been honored, the world today might be a normal, civilized community of nations, instead of a madly arming group of nations preparing for another major conflict. But the Allies did not, unfortunately, honor this implied promise to cut down their armaments. *And this Allied disregard of their own treaty was, perhaps, the major factor that created in Germany the*

390

resentment which destroyed the Weimar Republic. For German reactionaries could make capital of the fact that the disarmed Second Reich was surrounded by heavily armed enemies. Not even the brief era of Locarno could turn the tide.

The one issue on which all Germans could agree was their hostility to the "diktat" of Versailles. The German liberals hoped that they could revise the hated treaty by negotiation. The German reactionaries thundered their denunciation of the treaty and of the democratic government. The Junkers could point to heavily armed France, Poland, and Czechoslovakia; they could point to the Reich's "open frontiers," to the French occupation of the Ruhr, to the Lithuanian seizure of the German-populated city of Memel. "Those Socialists can never protect the Fatherland!" roared the German militarists, the monarchists, the reactionaries of all colors.

Inflation! That word may mean much or little to the reader. But to the Germany of 1922 and 1923 it meant chaos, suffering, and tragedy. A visitor could drop a million-mark note into the hat of a Berlin beggar, only to have the note thrown away. The beggar threw the million-mark note away because he could buy nothing with so small a sum. A single potato might cost a billion marks. The German lower middle class, the backbone of the Weimar Republic, was hardest hit of all economic groups in the Reich. These people who lost their financial independence, their life savings, their insurance, went down under a deluge of paper marks. More unemployment and suffering came in the wake of the tidal wave of inflation.

The world-wide depression exaggerated the cleavage between the so-called "have" and "have not" nations. It was inevitable that people in countries like Germany and Italy should attribute much of their suffering to their lack of rich colonial possessions. Politicians could point to the "satiated" colonial powers, Britain, France, and the Netherlands, and tell their followers that acquisition of territory from these colonial empires would solve the local problems of unemployment and depression. "Why should small states like Portugal and the Netherlands have vast over-seas possessions, while the great German Reich has no colonies?" German agitators demanded. It was an appeal that stirred Germans of all political parties.

In France and Britain, the German demand for return of the Reich's prewar colonies was answered by the statement that colonies are a liability, not an asset. The colonial powers produced statistics to show that Germany sent few emigrants to her colonies before the war, that these colonies provided only a small part of the Reich's raw materials imports. "And," said the spokesmen of the colonial powers, "anyone can buy raw materials in the world market. Every producer is glad to sell his products." Much of this is true, no doubt, and in a normal world lack of colonies should not affect a nation adversely. But since 1914 this has not been a normal world. And the "have nots" have been confronted with serious problems inherent in currency wars, mounting tariff walls, and other trade restrictions. Economic relations have been turned into political weapons, and war has been transferred from the trenches to the marts of commerce. The international struggle to gain raw materials has been waged with increasing violence.

Meanwhile, down in the Bavarian capital of Munich, a bizarre individual who wore a Charlie Chaplin mustache was ranting in an uncouth Austrian accent at small meetings of malcontents. He was leading a so-called .workers' party on patterned lines of national socialism, as distinguished from international socialism. His name was Adolf Hitler. During the early part of 1923, few people paid any attention either to the leader or his following. There were many cranks abroad in Europe. But in early November, 1923, this agitator and a motley following that included General Ludendorff, the aviator hero, Goering, an Austrian princeling, and an assortment of adventurers, ex-soldiers, and unemployed staged a revolution. From the place of its inception it was called the *beer-hall Putsch.*

German troops and police promptly quelled the uprising, killing several of the revolutionists. The mustached, ranting leader was arrested and sentenced to prison. Europe laughed. How droll it was for the one-time house painter to dream that he could overthrow the German government. Just imagine such a clown in the role of dictator! It was a thought that amused those whom he was attacking. Few took his ambitions seriously. Yet powerful forces were at work to serve the program of the crank who was imprisoned in the fortress of Landsberg am Lech writing a book called *Mein Kampf*.

By this time, Benito Mussolini, the erstwhile radical agitator, and his black-shirted Fascisti had taken over control of Italy. Doughty Mustapha Kemal Pasha and his Turks had driven the Greek army into the sea at Smyrna and had torn the Treaty of Sèvres to bits. The French were waging war against Abdel Krim and his Riffs. And the belligerent Italian Duce had sent his battle fleet to bombard the Greek city of Corfu. Soon French artillery would bombard the ancient city of Damascus. A world economic boom was under way. Small states scattered from the Aegean to the Arctic quarreled, erected trade barriers, threatened and belabored one another.

The League of Nations, perhaps the one hopeful result of the Peace Conference, was dominated by France and her allies. When the defeated nations were finally admitted to the society of Geneva, they found themselves outvoted. Disillusioned, they became convinced that the victors of the World War were using this great international organization as a means to perpetuate the peace treaties and guarantee the territorial *status quo*. Gradually, the conviction spread among the defeated peoples that peaceable revision was impossible, that revision could be achieved only by force. Clemenceau was dead, but Poincaré lived. A Briand and a Stresemann could settle Franco-German problems and disputes to their mutual satisfaction; they could advocate good will and the spirit of live and let live. But they could not win the support of

393

chauvinists in France or reactionaries in Germany. The day would soon come when Stresemann's grave in Berlin would be desecrated by rowdies; Briand's sincere and arduous work for peace would be sneered at in Paris.

THE "HAVE NOTS" STRIKE

Economic disaster speeds the progress of political and social decay. Spiritually, the world of 1929 was in no way prepared for the approaching ordeal. Politicians in many countries had deluded their followers with false promises; they had enacted legislation that defied the laws of economics, of common sense, of common morality. They had sowed the wind; now they were to reap the whirlwind. Democracy, in whose cause a great war had allegedly been fought, was suddenly assailed from many quarters. As the army of unemployed increased in country after country after the economic collapse, the appeals of demagogues found eager, pathetic recruits. Desperate men were willing to listen to any charlatan who promised to lead them out of the wilderness of despair toward work and bread.

The year 1931 found the German democracy fighting with its back to the wall against increasingly difficult problems. Millions of men without work clamored for the means to live. The leader of the tragicomic beer-hall revolution had become a powerful political figure. Resentment against the Treaty of Versailles and the sufferings of the unemployed had helped him to mount to a position where he was a serious challenge to the government. But his triumph was then by no means certain. Chancellor Bruening was waging a brave struggle to save the republic. He still held an ace. The time had come to play it. He attempted to establish an Austro-German customs union, an arrangement that would have stimulated the exchange of goods between the two countries and would have bolstered the waning prestige of the Weimar Republic. But the French, with the passive consent of the British, stepped

394

in and stopped this measure. The World Court, by a close vote, upheld the French stand. Bruening had played his ace and lost. Most important of all, the "have not" nations now became convinced that it was vain to hope for revision of the peace treaties by peaceful methods. Hitler could boast: "I told you that force is the only factor that counts in international relations!"

Partly as the result of the failure to create an Austro-German customs union, the great Austrian bank, the Kredit-Anstalt, collapsed. A train of disaster followed this event. All Central Europe felt the adverse effects of this catastrophe. They spread across Germany and into England. In a few months the American economic system was assailed by the destructive forces let loose on the Danube. The foundations of public law and morality throughout the world were undermined still further. The triumph of Hitler and his Nazis now became all but inevitable.

In September, 1931, the Japanese began their campaign in Manchuria. International aggression on a large scale was beginning. Europe was not, however, more than casually interested. China was a long way off, and there were few European financial stakes in Manchuria. Let the Chinese worry. President Hoover and Secretary of State Stimson foresaw that what was happening in Manchuria in 1931 would probably happen later in other places. But Washington's efforts to enlist the support of Britain, France, and the League of Nations failed dismally. There was, indeed, no little support for the Japanese on the part of Europeans who were to howl loudly against these same Nipponese six years later when the Mikado's armies launched their invasion of the Yangtze valley. For our efforts to stop Tokio's rape of Manchuria we met only with cynical indifference in Europe, hostility in Japan. It was difficult to escape the conclusion that, despite all the oratory and propaganda about collective security and the rights of small or weak nations, the great powers would move to stop aggression only when their own interests were threatened.

The beginning of 1932 found Dr. Bruening still holding the chancellorship in Germany. But his failure to obtain satisfactory concessions from the Allies destroyed his prestige within Germany. Had the *status quo* powers been willing to aid the Second Reich, Bruening could have said to the German people: "You see, I can obtain justice for you. There is nothing that Hitler and his Nazis can do for you that I can't do." If that had happened, the history of Europe in the intervening six years would undoubtedly have been vastly different. And today, that unhappy and jittery Continent might well be on the road to economic recovery and international political pacification. But Allied politicians lacked vision.

On May 30, Chancellor Bruening went out. Colonel von Papen became the new Reichschancellor. In July, the Lausanne Conference secured for Germany virtual cancellation of reparations. But this move came too late. It might have saved Bruening if it had come a year or more earlier, but the political wheels were spinning too swiftly now to be slowed down by belated Allied concessions. The brown shirts who were bidding for power cared nothing for Germany's reparations obligations. In early December, General von Schleicher succeeded von Papen and began the fateful fifty-seven-day regime that was to lead up to that climax on the evening of January 30, 1933, when Adolf Hitler, as chancellor, was acclaimed by his triumphant Nazi legions. That evening an epoch came to an end. Europe passed from the postwar era of Versailles to the prewar era of Adolf Hitler and his Third Reich.

HITLER DOMINATES THE WORLD SCENE

Since Hitler became Reichschancellor, Europe has lived in a state of tension, in an atmosphere of alarm. Crisis has followed crisis with bewildering, breath-taking rapidity.

The Continent has been poised on the brink of war not once but a dozen times. Yet the incredible feature of this period has been Allied unwillingness to grapple with the realities inherent in Hitler's challenge. When the Nazis came to power, Poland, not to say France, could have smashed the military machine of the Third Reich. The well-trained, but inadequately equipped, Reichswehr could not have stood against the French, Czechs, Belgians, and Poles for even a few weeks. Yet every general staff in Europe knew that Hitler was beginning the creation of a great military establishment, which, unless destroyed by its enemies, would challenge the political and territorial *status quo* of the Old World.

The following year, the Nazis indulged in the luxury of the "blood purge" which liquidated the notorious Captain Roehm and scores of Storm Troop leaders. Twenty-five days later the Austrian Nazis started a Putsch in Vienna that went amiss. Engelbert Dollfuss, the Austrian chancellor, was murdered, but the revolution failed, and Hitler suffered a humiliating diplomatic defeat at the hands of Mussolini. For the Duce rushed his crack motorized divisions to the Brenner Pass and threatened to enter Austria if Hitler sent his troops into that endangered state. Fortunately for the Fuehrer, he did not tempt fate on this occasion; an outbreak of hostilities in Austria would have pitted his new army against heavy odds, probably complicated by French intervention.

TREATY EVASIONS BEGET UNDECLARED WARS

The following March 16, however, Hitler had recovered sufficient reassurance to announce conscription in Germany. He was boldly breaking one of the fetters of Versailles. Europe rocked with excitement, but nothing was done to stop the military growth of the Third Reich. Four months later, the Continent was rumbling with the approaching Ethiopian crisis. London and Rome were beginning to growl ominously at each other, and Geneva started to mobilize world public opinion against aggression. For this time aggression was taking place dangerously near Great Britain's lifeline. France, fearful that league action against the Duce would turn him toward Hitler, held back. The league, led by Britain, challenged the Duce. And the Duce took up the challenge.

The Ethiopian War, in reality a sideshow so far as military operations were concerned, was a prologue for great dramas then in the making. Italy defied the sanctions of fifty-three nations and made war on another league member. Hitler sat back and enjoyed the show and learned from it. Then came the Hoare-Laval plan, an attempt, on the part of Britain's Sir Samuel Hoare and France's Pierre Laval, to settle the Italo-Ethiopian conflict by Ethiopian concessions to Italy. British public opinion would have none of it. The protest which went up drove Sir Samuel out of the foreign secretaryship and destroyed the plan of settlement. A few months later, however, Sir Samuel had the satisfaction of seeing his critics forced to stand by while Mussolini gobbled up the whole of Ethiopia. Thus another precedent of successful aggression followed the Japanese seizure of Manchuria.

Hardly was the fighting over in Ethiopia before the bloody Spanish civil war broke out. The ingredients of the Iberian conflict had been brewing for years; scarcely had the first day passed when foreign interference added pepper to the broth. Flushed by his victory in Ethiopia, Mussolini turned his attention to Spain. Before long he received help from Hitler. The fascist dictators were supporting the Insurgents led by General Franco. The Spanish Loyalists soon received aid from the Soviet Union and unofficial help from France. From a civil conflict the fighting in Spain quickly developed into the "little world war" which pitted ideology against ideology, Italian against Russian, Catalonian against Moor, the Spaniard from Burgos against his fellow countryman from Valencia, German against the foreign shock trooper of the Loyalist International Brigade. Men from the far corners of the earth came to suffer and die in the trenches before

Madrid or in the mountains of Aragon. Nonintervention agreements were turned into cruel farces.

The Spanish conflict gave the interventionists an excellent opportunity to experiment with their newest war weapons. While German and Italian tanks went over the top, German and Italian bombers harried the cities of Loyalist Spain. German antiaircraft artillery, guarded so carefully that not even Insurgent officers could approach the guns, was tested under war conditions. On the Loyalist side of the lines French, Czech, and Russian war material was put to similar tests. By means of the brutal raids on Barcelona by their bombers in March, 1938—raids that left hundreds of dead in their wake—Berlin and Rome were staging a frightful warning for the people of London and Paris. "What we are doing to Barcelona today," the actions of these raiders plainly said, "we can do to British, French, or Czech cities tomorrow!" Tragic Spain provided the stage on which the rival European coalitions enacted their bloody dress rehearsal for the next major war.

While world attention had been concentrated upon Europe's quarrels, two South American nations, Paraguay and Bolivia, were fighting a long, costly war over disputed territory along their common jungle frontier in the Gran Chaco. Outside mediation had little effect on these land-locked fighters. Only bloodletting and exhaustion finally brought to a close one of the most bitterly fought conflicts of recent years.

Undoubtedly emboldened by her success in Manchuria, the Italian conquest of Ethiopia, Hitler's growing challenge to Europe, and the course of the conflict in Spain, Japan launched a new war in China early in July, 1937. Like other conflicts of today, it followed the technique of stream-lined aggression. Japan made no declaration of war against China. And Tokio optimistically predicted that within a few weeks her armies would have gained their objectives and the "punitive expedition" would be over. But Nippon's war

399

lords were due for a rude surprise. China's armies fought stubbornly, if not expertly. Japan soon found the conflict a costly affair, not only in terms of money but also in man power. And there has been the constant danger that Japan's actions in China would involve her in serious trouble with other powers.

HITLER STRIKES ANEW

At a moment when Europe's attention was turned toward the Far East and Spain, Hitler suddenly launched a campaign of aggression. The prelude was a split in the ranks of the army hierarchy, the exit of von Blomberg as minister of defense, and the seizure of supreme control of the Reich's armed forces by the Fuehrer. A week later the world was startled by news that Chancellor Schuschnigg of Austria had crossed the German frontier to confer with Hitler in the latter's retreat at Berchtesgaden. Conflicting reports of the meeting were spread, but informed students of the Austro-German situation knew that Dr. Schuschnigg's meeting with his bellicose and imperialist neighbor was the beginning of the end of Austrian independence.

On March 11, while France was in the throes of a political crisis that left the Third Republic without a cabinet, while Russia was staging a demoralizing public trial, while Britain was trying to come to terms with Italy on questions involving Britain's safety and prestige in the Mediterranean, Hitler struck. The Fuehrer gave his order for Reich troops to march into Austria. A few hours later Hitler's field-gray battalions arrived at the Brenner Pass. They paraded triumphantly through Vienna, they approached the uneasy frontiers of Czechoslovakia, Hungary, and Yugoslavia. *Anschluss*, so long an explosive European political issue, had been immediately achieved. The union of Germany and Austria that the Allies had forbidden the democratic Second Reich to consummate was hammered out defiantly by the Third Reich's mailed fist. Has history any dénouement of more biting irony?

Not only has Hitler added more than six millions to the population of greater Germany, he has gained control of Austria's gold reserve, timber, ore, and cattle. But even more important to his long-range plans of pan-German imperialism, he has gained political and strategical advantages of tremendous importance. The *Drang nach Osten* has taken a long stride toward distant objectives. The Nazi propaganda and economic offensives down the Danube are being pursued with increasing energy. And Czechoslovakia, that "island of democracy in a sea of dictatorships," has been partitioned and reduced to the status of a harmless neutral state.

The Czechoslovakia that emerged from the Peace Conference was a hodge-podge state consisting of various races and peoples. It lacked homogeneity. But what it lacked in ethnic unity it made up in economic balance. Of all the countries in Central Europe the nation of Masaryk and Benes probably had the best economic system. While many other European states veered either to the extreme left or to the extreme right, Czechoslovakia pursued a sane middle course. Her social legislation set a precedent in postwar Central Europe. There is, of course, no gainsaying the fact that the Czechs made certain mistakes in their treatment of their minorities. It cannot be denied that there was some injustice. Nevertheless, the minorities in Czechoslovakia have been treated better than those in any other country in Danubia.

But Czechoslovakia occupied the unenviable position of being located athwart Hitler's path toward the East. The Fuehrer could not safely push down the Danube toward the Rumanian oil fields and the black earth of the Ukraine as long as a strong, independent Czechoslovakia remained on his left flank. He would have to reduce that Bohemia which Bismarck called "a fortress erected by God in the heart of Europe." The Nazi campaign against Czechoslovakia began shortly after Hitler came to power in the Reich. Germany's nonaggression pact with Poland, her remilitarization of the Rhineland, her support of the German-Italian-Japanese anti-

Communist pact, her subjugation of Austria—these were all part of Hitler's strategy to isolate and destroy Czechoslovakia.

In August, 1936, President Benes of Czechoslovakia told the writer that he could obtain a German guarantee of the Czechoslovakian frontiers from Hitler, provided the Czechs would drop their pacts with France and the Soviet Union. Hitler was ready to recognize the territorial integrity of Czechoslovakia if Dr. Benes would break off his alliances. This the Czechs refused to do. They steadfastly stood by their international agreements. When Hitler realized that he could not drive the Czechs into breaking their pacts, he set out to dismember the Republic.

After the fall of Austria the Nazi drive against Czechoslovakia began in earnest. In May, 1938, German military measures caused the Czechs to mobilize suddenly in order to meet the threat across their frontier. For a time this Czech action was heralded as a German defeat. Newspaper editorials in the Western democracies pointed out that the Czechs had demonstrated that all a nation had to do was take a strong line against Hitler. By the end of July, however, it became evident that Hitler was preparing to march against Czechoslovakia. In an effort to postpone, if not prevent, war, Britain sent Lord Runciman to Czechoslovakia as a mediator between the Czechoslovak Government and the Sudeten German minority. During August and the early days of September these negotiations dragged on while the crisis became steadily more menacing. France, as an ally of Czechoslovakia, continued to promise aid to the Czechs in case Hitler attacked them. The British, while not actually committed to go to war to save the Czechs, gave the impression that Prague could count upon the Empire's support against Hitler. On September 12, Hitler made a martial address to the Nuremberg Congress. His threatening speech left Europe gasping. At last the Continent was on the brink of a general war.

Then came Prime Minister Chamberlain's dramatic flight to Berchtesgaden to talk personally with Hitler. And out of that conference emerged the plan to dismember Czecho-slovakia. French consent to the plan came quickly. Astonished by the defection of their French ally, the Czechs stubbornly clamored for support against the Nazi enemy. The Czech army was willing to fight. Then came Godesberg, where Hitler and Chamberlain again conferred. The Fuehrer had raised his demands since the meeting at Berchtesgaden. Chamberlain objected, returned to London, and took his case to Parliament. All Europe expected immediate war. Then, through the intervention of Mussolini, Hitler invited the Duce, Chamberlain, and Premier Daladier of France to Munich. That fateful conference handed Sudetenland over to Hitler. The Czechs were not even permitted the opportunity to make a suggestion. It was a conference ruled by panic. The following day Czech generals returned their French and British decorations to Paris and London. On October 1 Hitler's troops crossed the border into the Sudeten districts of Czechoslovakia.

The lesson to be drawn from the Munich conference was not lost on the other small countries of Central Europe and the Balkans. They all realized that pacts, treaties, and agreements had become scraps of paper. No longer could a little nation depend upon aid from the Western democracies. They would have to make the best terms they could with the German Nazi colossus. For France, the Munich settlement spelled the end of her postwar political and military empire in Central Europe. For Germany, the Munich conference meant the consummation of another major victory in her program to gain hegemony over Europe.

Let us not forget that the well-organized Nazi propaganda among the millions of Teutons scattered in colonies, from the Gulf of Finland in the north to Serbia in the south, has often fallen on fertile soil. For in certain localities the majority population has treated the Germanic minority with less than justice. Consequently, those Teutons who have grievances have eagerly joined the most intolerant imperialist program of this era—the Nazi drive to the East. In country after country, in the path of the *Drang nach Osten*, it is the Teutonic minorities that compose Hitler's "Fifth Columns."

THE OUTLOOK IN INTERNATIONAL AFFAIRS

The Europe of 1938 is a community of nations poised on the brink of war. "Today Europe is neither at war nor at peace but stands at armed attention," said Stanley Baldwin. And the Duce expresses the brutal philosophy of fascism when he proclaims to his cheering black-shirt followers: "We Fascists reject the myth of perpetual peace, which never existed and never can exist." There is no peace in Europe, yet the general conflagration that all countries fear is not at this writing a certainty. Armaments pile upon armaments; taxes become a crushing burden; children go to school hungry in order that impoverished governments may pay for instruments of death. Yet bankrupt world statesmanship seems to have nothing better to offer than the accumulation of greater and still greater armies, navies, and bombing fleets. Where are the statesmen who could be solving these crushing problems? When asked that question, former Premier Caillaux of France replied: "They were all killed in the war."

Certain it is that the statesmanship which ruled at the Congress of Vienna was conspicuously absent at Versailles. Even a vain aristocrat like Metternich did not attempt to load down defeated France with humiliating restrictions that would soon endanger peace. Partly because of the comparative mildness of the Vienna pacts, Europe was not plagued for a century with another general war. Had there been similar foresight among the men who dictated the Versailles Treaty, the Germany of Ebert, Scheidemann, Rathenau, Erzberger, and Bruening might well be a powerful factor for European peace and economic stabilization today. But in place of those German pacifists and republicans a great nation of seventy-seven million people is ruled by the demoniac intolerance and brutality of Hitler, Goering, Goebbels, Himmler, and Streicher. Nazi militarism has replaced the Weimar Republic's pacifism; the mailed fist of Hitler and Goering has replaced the olive branch of Stresemann and Bruening.

And what do we face in the conduct of international relations today? There is the bald truth expressed by Prime Minister Neville Chamberlain that "in war there are no winners." Many people realize that another great international conflict will destroy what is left of our civilization. And yet, in common honesty we must admit that the statesmanship to cope with our international problems, to lead us out of the morass of fear, suspicion, and greed is not in sight today. Can the world hold off the universal catastrophe of war until a new generation with new vision and new leadership shall come into power in the principal nations in the world? On the answer to that question may rest the fate of our society for the next century.

Chapter XXIV

THE FALLACY OF ECONOMIC NATIONALISM

PETER MOLYNEAUX

★ ★ ★ ★

W E ARE living in a time of disturbance and unsettlement. As I write this the nations are in the midst of one of those periodical crises which have become all too familiar. In my morning newspaper, Walter Lippmann tells me that "no one now living has known a more solemn hour than that through which we are now passing," and news from the principal capitals of the world tends to support this rather arresting statement. But there have been numerous other "solemn hours" during the past two decades, and I feel sure there will be still others during the years ahead.

Contemplating all this, I find myself recalling an anecdote which the late Newton D. Baker, former secretary of war, never tired of telling. It concerns a conversation Secretary Baker had with General Tasker Bliss, late one night in 1918, in his office in the War Department. They talked about the war, and Secretary Baker asked the General how long he thought it would last. After a moment of contemplation, General Bliss replied, "About thirty years, I should say." "Oh!" exclaimed Secretary Baker, "surely this can't go on for thirty years!" "No, oh, no," said the General, "not this particular incident. This will die down. And then out of the muck and moil, the turmoil, the indecisions, the injustices of the arrangements that are made at the end of this incident, a fresh incident will break out, and it will take about the life of a generation to end this war."

THE AFTERMATH OF THE WORLD WAR

Today, after two-thirds of General Bliss's estimated thirty years have passed, the World War is still very much with us. In a very true sense it has continued during the past twenty years and is still continuing. I mean that genuine peace among the nations has not been established. "It is not too much to say," writes Dr. James T. Shotwell, who was with the American delegation at Paris in 1919, "that the Peace Conference never met. The Conference of Paris was a meeting of the enemies of the Central Powers, which dictated treaties for each of the ex-enemy states and hardly listened at all to their protests against the conditions imposed upon them."

Dr. Shotwell observes that "the leaders of liberal Germany" at the time "had dared to hope that a peace based upon the Wilsonian program would offer the new German Republic an opportunity to cooperate to the full in building the structure of a world community." This hope turned out to be futile, of course. No such peace was established and no such opportunity was offered. On the contrary, the enemy status of the two groups of nations was in fact maintained, in spite of all formal arrangements which pretended it was otherwise, and in a very true sense the war was continued. The prolonged maintenance of this condition set the stage for Hitler. And since the coming of Hitler there has been an ever-present danger that even the fighting will be resumed.

I am aware that this view of the matter could be carried too far. But whether or not the fighting is resumed, in the near future or later, it will remain true, I think, that most of the calamities which have come upon us and which have agonized mankind during the past two decades and most of the major problems which perplex us today have been the result of the failure to establish peace on a firm foundation in 1919. Whether "a peace based on the Wilsonian program" was possible in 1919, is something I would not argue. I would not undertake even to prove that such a peace is politically possible today. It may be that mankind is headed inexorably toward catastrophe because of the incapacity of men to manage competently the business of living together on the earth and of getting an increasingly better living out of it. I do not believe anything of this kind, of course, but it could turn out to be true. What I do think is that if we are ever to have an orderly world again, a world in which the people of the principal countries, including our own, can live and labor in peaceful security and resume the ways of progress, it will be brought about through the more or less general application of a program which in its broad outlines will approximate the principles enunciated by Woodrow Wilson.

ECONOMIC NATIONALISM EMERGES

One element of the Wilson program I regard as fundamentally essential to such a world. It is that which was set forth in the third of the now almost forgotten Fourteen Points, which proposed "the removal, so far as possible, of all economic barriers and the establishment of equality of trade conditions among all the nations consenting to the peace and associating themselves for its maintenance." In no single respect has the course of the world during the past twenty years run so decidedly counter to the Wilson program as in this one. Not only have the nations, our own included, failed to remove economic barriers, but they have vied with one another in increasing the height and effectiveness of such barriers, and in devising new ways of making economic intercourse across international boundaries more difficult. The policy which this tendency embodies has come to be known as *economic nationalism*, and it is my belief that a more prosperous, a more secure, a more stable, and a more peaceful world can be ensured in the future only through a reversal of this policy.

Moreover, aside from the circumstance that it is only in such a world that the people of any country can hope to live in enduring security, it is my conviction that the highest interests and welfare of the American people require that the government of the United States shall veer steadily away from the policy of economic nationalism and shall adopt an increasingly liberal policy with respect to the commercial relations of this country with the rest of the world, *regardless of the policies of other countries.*

At the outset, it is desirable to make clear that I use the term *economic nationalism* in no narrow sense. There are certain aspects of American commercial policy and certain popular prejudices widely prevalent among the American people which I think may be properly described by that term. But I am not concerned to insist on any precise definition of the term itself. And I want especially to avoid setting up a sharp antithesis, dividing all possible aspects of policy into two exclusive groups, one comprehending the policy of economic nationalism and the other constituting the opposite policy, which might be called *economic internationalism.* As the Hutchins Commission pointed out, every policy is "national" in the sense that it is intended to promote the interest of the nation that adopts it.

THE IMPORTANCE OF FOREIGN TRADE

The economic nationalism of the United States, so far as it has any formal theoretical basis at all, springs from the assumption that *export* trade is not a significant nor more than a negligible factor in our domestic economy. This assumption is usually supported by the generalization that we have never exported more than ten per cent of our total annual production of movable goods and that consequently a decrease or an increase of our exports cannot have much effect on our prosperity, one way or the other. On the other hand, American economic nationalism assumes that *import* trade has a very decided effect upon our domestic economy. Indeed, its basic idea may be said to be the assumption that it is better in all circumstances, practically regardless of cost, to produce almost anything within the borders of our own country than to import it from another country. It assumes that the importation of goods from abroad, except such goods as cannot be produced in this country, provides employment for foreign labor which otherwise would go to American labor, and that in most instances it actually displaces American labor and causes unemployment.

These two major assumptions of economic nationalism, as we know it in the United States, are largely fallacious. Its assumption that export trade is not a significant, or more than negligible, factor in our domestic economy is entirely fallacious since precisely the opposite is true. We have had abundant experience during the past twenty-five years which proves that a vigorous and expanding export trade is absolutely essential to our domestic prosperity. The generalization that we have never exported more than ten per cent of our total production of movable goods is misleading and does not justify in any degree the inference which is drawn from it. For whole industries in the United States, of which the production of cotton is the most notable but is by no means unique, depend upon export markets to such an extent that their prosperity is determined entirely by the volume of exports and by world prices for their products. And the producers of such products constitute so large a percentage of domestic consumers of all other American goods that the domestic market for almost everything is affected, one way or the other, by the volume and the value of such exports.

THE FALLACY OF SELF-SUFFICIENCY

The assumption that it is better in all circumstances, practically regardless of cost, to produce almost anything within the borders of our own country than to import it from another country is also fallacious. It is not better, *in all*

410

circumstances, for example, for a country like Germany to produce wheat at a cost greatly in excess of the price at which it could obtain that wheat abroad in exchange for the proceeds of the products of highly efficient and low-cost German industries sold abroad. Nor is it better, *in all circumstances*, for a country like Hungary to produce motor vehicles at a cost more than twice the price at which it could obtain these motor vehicles abroad in exchange for the products of highly efficient and low-cost Hungarian industries sold abroad. And if this policy is not better, in all circumstances, for other countries, it is not better, in all circumstances, for the United States. There may be circumstances in which such a policy would be justified, but no such circumstances exist for the United States at present, or are likely to exist during an indefinite future.

Finally, the idea that the importation of goods invariably deprives American labor of employment is based entirely on the erroneous assumption that the volume of trade and of consumption is narrowly limited and that the domestic producer must lose whatever trade the foreign producer obtains. Goods which come into our domestic market from abroad very largely represent foreign demand for American goods. The importation and domestic consumption of foreign goods create foreign purchasing power for American goods within our own borders, and the exercise of such foreign purchasing power in turn creates domestic purchasing power among the domestic producers of commodities for export, and thus the total volume of business is increased.

In spite of their fallacious character, however, these basic assumptions of economic nationalism have hitherto determined the commercial policy of the United States. They have found expression in a commercial policy which has never been concerned with increasing exports or expanding markets for American products abroad, but, on the contrary, has always been directed primarily and almost solely toward limit-

411

ing the importation from other countries of goods of any character that might be produced in any considerable quantity within our own borders.

This policy has always had an adverse effect upon the material interests and the living standard of substantial portions of the population of the United States, particularly of the farm population. For it has tended to create and to maintain a domestic price level, insulated from the average price level of the rest of the world and usually much higher. And this has tended to reduce the income and the purchasing power of American producers of export commodities, the prices of which are determined in a world market. It has been said that this policy has compelled American producers of exports "to sell cheap and to buy dear."

So long as the United States was a debtor country, the policy worked after a fashion. It did have the effect of reducing certain regions of the country to a position of economic inferiority and of submerging certain segments of the population below the average living standard, but it did not contract or limit the export market for American products. The reason our export market was not seriously affected by the limitations placed on imports was that American payments abroad of interest due on debts and other obligations to foreigners and of such items as the expenditures of tourists and the remittance of immigrants to relatives in foreign countries provided a fund of American dollars in foreign hands for the purchase of a large percentage of our exports. But ever since the United States was transformed into a creditor country, during the World War, a radically different situation has existed. The policy of limiting imports has come to have the effect of limiting the volume of exports as well, and the consequent reduction of exports has destroyed a margin of domestic purchasing power which has upset the internal economy of the United States. Today, therefore, economic nationalism is entirely untenable as a desirable policy for the United States.

412

UNITED STATES BECOMES A CREDITOR NATION

In a message to Congress on December 2, 1919, President Wilson called attention to the circumstance that the status of the United States had been changed from that of a debtor country to that of a creditor country, and he pointed out that this would require a change of its traditional commercial policy. He said:

> The productivity of the country, greatly stimulated by the war, must find an outlet by exports to foreign countries, and any measures taken to prevent imports will inevitably curtail exports, force curtailment of production, load the banking machinery of the country with credits to carry unsold products, and produce industrial stagnation and unemployment. . . . Whatever, therefore, may have been our views during the period of growth of American business concerning tariff legislation, we must now adjust our own economic life to a changed condition growing out of the fact that American business is full grown and that America is the greatest capitalist in the world.

More than eighteen years have passed since that message was sent to Congress, and meantime the recommendation to "adjust our economic life to a changed condition" has been completely ignored. In spite of the creditor status of the United States and the increased dependence of its domestic economy on export outlets, the traditional commercial policy has been not only continued, but has even been intensified. This has been the source of most of the economic unsettlement in the United States during recent years, and it has been a strong contributing factor toward a condition of disturbance and unsettlement in other parts of the world.

As soon as President Wilson passed from the scene, the United States promptly adopted new "measures to prevent imports." Congress enacted the so-called Emergency Tariff Act in 1921 and followed this immediately with a general upward revision of rates in the Fordney-McCumber Act of 1922. The unwise character of this course was not at once apparent because a combination of circumstances served to

413

postpone its inevitable consequences. The postwar deflation of 1921 and 1922 was accompanied by a steep reduction of the value of our exports, and between 1921 and 1924, with debt payments from abroad generally suspended, the United States proceeded to drain the prostrate world of gold, importing more than the world's production of the precious metal during this period. Then, with an abnormal supply of gold and with a cheap-money banking policy in effect in this country, Americans began buying foreign bonds and other securities at the rate of more than a billion dollars a year. The dollar exchange thus made available was sufficient to enable the world to meet its debt payments to the United States each year and to pay also for the excess of an expanding volume of American exports. And so the "new era" between 1924 and 1929 was launched.

Of course, this beautiful arrangement was foredoomed to collapse, as was pointed out at the time by more than one competent economist. Dr. Benjamin M. Anderson, Jr., of the Chase National Bank, for example, sounded a warning as early as the summer of 1925. In the August issue of the *Chase Economic Bulletin* that year, he pointed out that it was not to be expected that this arrangement could long continue and that there would be an "appalling credit congestion when the day of reckoning finally comes." He continued:

> For this combination of high-protective-tariff policy and cheap-money policy in the existing world unbalance, we shall ultimately pay with a congested investment market accompanied by a sharp falling off of our export trade. With an early modification of our tariff policy and a modification of our Federal Reserve bank policy, it is still possible to avoid congestion in our commodity markets and our general business situation.

That was in 1925. But the American people went merrily on their way, and even when the inevitable "day of reckoning" finally arrived, late in 1929, when their purchase of foreign securities fell off and exports dropped in value by more than one-fourth, almost over night, it found them still unwilling to change their traditional commercial policy. On the contrary, the American tariff wall was promptly raised higher than ever, for before the end of June, 1930, Congress had enacted the Hawley-Smoot Tariff Act, and, over the protest of more than a thousand competent economists, President Hoover signed it.

From that point the debacle was on in dead earnest. The first inevitable result was the collapse of international payments, and, in the summer of 1931, President Hoover was compelled to declare a moratorium on intergovernmental debts. By the end of 1932, the value of American exports had fallen to a point more than sixty-nine per cent below the level of 1929, lower than any year since 1901. And, as President Wilson had predicted, this collapse of export trade "forced curtailment of production" and "produced industrial stagnation and unemployment."

ATTEMPTS TO REGAIN TRADE

Since then, we have had only the artificial and temporary relief provided by dollar devaluation and unprecedented government spending. To be sure, since 1934, we have had the so-called *reciprocal trade policy*, the intent of which is to restore our lost export markets. But in actual practice our commercial policy has remained unchanged—our high tariffs have not been repealed, and our export markets have not been recovered. The value of American exports in 1937 was less than that of the exports of any year between 1919 and 1931. Never before in our history has American export trade experienced such a steep decline as occurred between 1929 and 1932, and never has it remained depressed for so long a period. This is the distinctive thing about the depression which began in 1929. It is different from all previous depressions in this respect. Fundamentally, it has been due to the disappearance of a considerable margin of domestic purchasing power as a result of the loss of export trade. And the delay in recovery has been due to failure to restore this lost export trade. Government spending between 1934 and 1937, while it lasted, replaced this missing margin temporarily and after a fashion, but as soon as it was reduced, production and employment went into a tailspin.

This, I believe, must always be the case. The only escape from an indefinite period of huge government spending and its ultimate consequences, and from a radical derangement and a violent readjustment of our domestic affairs, in my opinion, lies in the direction of a complete revision of our commercial policy so as to make it square with the new status of the United States as a creditor country.

The stock argument against such revision of our commercial policy is that our industries are already "adjusted" to the high tariff system and that consequently any material change in the tariff rates would cause widespread economic disturbance. The circumstance that we have had the most widespread and the greatest amount of economic disturbance in our history under the highest tariff rates on record and that this disturbed condition continues unabated in the ninth year of the depression, ought to be sufficient refutation of the validity of that argument. However, we have yet to experience the full extent of the radical derangement and violent readjustment of our domestic affairs which are in process as a result of our attempt to maintain a debtor commercial policy in spite of our creditor status.

One example will suffice to illustrate this. The decline in the export market for American cotton, in the face of record-breaking consumption of cotton, all kinds included, outside the United States, is the most striking feature of the effect of this policy, owing to the fact that cotton hitherto has been by all odds the leading American export commodity. The same influences have reduced our export trade generally and have affected our whole economic structure adversely. But the case of cotton is the most spectacular and its effects will provide us with an example illustrating the whole process.

POPULATION PRESSURE AND FOREIGN TRADE

Recently, the Public Affairs Committee, composed of such men as Raymond Leslie Buell of the Foreign Policy Association, Harold G. Moulton of the Brookings Institution, Evans Clark of the Twentieth Century Fund, William T. Foster of the Pollak Foundation, George Soule of the National Bureau of Economic Research, and other similarly competent students of American affairs, published a short digest, prepared by Clifton T. Little, of *A Study of Population Redistribution*. For a more detailed consideration of the subject, it referred the reader to a report entitled *Migration and Economic Opportunity*, published by the University of Pennsylvania Press in 1936. But two quotations from this digest will adequately serve our purpose here.

The digest is based on a study of population in the United States as a whole and the need of its redistribution, and it deals with several regions in which population pressure was found to exist. One of those regions is what the report designates as *the Old Cotton Belt*. It takes note of the declining export market for American cotton, and it explores all the possibilities of other employment in the South for the labor which is thus being displaced. It points out that formerly fully half of the average American cotton crop was absorbed by the export market, and then it says this:

Without a restoration of this foreign market, only one-half of the present agricultural population of the Cotton Belt can possibly maintain even the accustomed standard of living, much less improve it.

Then, after exploring all the possibilities of new forms of employment in the South, on the farm and in industry, the digest of the report continues as follows:

But these prospects are not nearly enough. Despite expansion in employment which can reasonably be visualized for the immediate future, the Old Cotton Belt must plan for emigration. If the world market for cotton is permanently lost, it may become necessary for six or seven million persons to leave and seek employment in other parts of the country.

This, be it understood, is not the wild proposal of some ignorant visionary. It is the considered finding and deliberate recommendation of competent economic and sociological investigators. I know of no reason to question the soundness of their conclusions.

But let us consider for a moment what this all means. In the northeastern corner of the United States there is a region which includes thirteen states and which comprises 13.8 per cent of the land area of the country. The states I have in mind are Connecticut, Massachusetts, Rhode Island, New Jersey, New York, Pennsylvania, Maryland (including the District of Columbia), Ohio, West Virginia, Michigan, Illinois, Indiana, and Missouri. The combined area of these states is 417,511 square miles, and their combined population at the time of the last census was 62,869,290. The area, as I have said, constitutes 13.8 per cent of the total area of the United States, and the population of this area is 51.2 per cent of the total population of the United States. The density is 150.5 per square mile.

Now, compare these thirteen states with the thirteen states which comprise the South. The latter are Virginia, Kentucky, Tennessee, North Carolina, South Carolina, Georgia, Florida, Alabama, Mississippi, Louisiana, Arkansas, Oklahoma, and Texas. The combined area of these states is 853,244 square miles, and their combined population is 33,771,653. The area constitutes 28.1 per cent of the total area of the United States, and the population of this area is 27.5 per cent of the total population of the United States. The density is 39.5 to the square mile.

It is this latter area, the larger area with the smaller population, in which population pressure is found to exist, and which "must plan for emigration," presumably, to some extent at least, to the smaller area with the larger population. I am not questioning, as I have said, the soundness of this view. In fact, I believe it is substantially correct. But what shall be said of the economy of a country in which such a situation

418

arises? Is it a sound economy for a country like the United States, which extends from one ocean to the other and from the frozen north to the tropics? Is it a sound economy which creates such a situation? Is it an economy that ought to be maintained and perpetuated, from the standpoint of the interests of the country as a whole, and at the cost of the violent readjustment which must inexorably result?

This is a single illustration, though the most striking one, of the effect which the traditional commercial policy of the United States, the policy of economic nationalism, must have henceforth on the life of the American people. Are there compensating benefits to the American people as a whole to be derived from the perpetuation of this policy which may be said to justify such violent readjustment and such a waste of the resources of America? I think not. And accordingly, I believe that this policy is entirely untenable as a desirable one for the United States in the years ahead.

Woodrow Wilson said, in that message to Congress on December 2, 1919, now nearly twenty years ago:

> The prejudices and passions engendered by decades of controversy between two schools of political and economic thought, the one believers in protection of American industries, the other believers in tariff for revenue only, must be subordinated to the single consideration of the public interest in the light of utterly changed conditions. . . . Whatever, therefore, may have been our views during the period of growth of American business concerning tariff legislation, we must now adjust our own economic life to a changed condition growing out of the fact that American business is full grown and that America is the greatest capitalist in the world.

419

Chapter XXV

IS NEUTRALITY POSSIBLE FOR AMERICA?

GERALD P. NYE

★ ★ ★ ★

W HEN the World War came to an end, with its appalling waste of human life and of material resources as well, with its aftermath of depression from which we are still suffering, we were all resolved never to let it happen again. Today, every newspaper reader knows how close the world may be to another holocaust—completely fatal, perhaps, to civilization as we cherish it. Woodrow Wilson's charge to his countrymen to be "neutral in thought and deed" fell upon many unwilling ears. We were the witnesses of the violation of Belgium, involving the disregard of a solemn international undertaking; we believed that we were called upon to act in defense of a civilization and a political theory more precious than life itself. Today, we in America are not so certain that we have a mission to perform in settling the quarrels of the Old World. We are not even sure that we are competent to decide in all cases as to the justice of the dispute: we are, however, profoundly convinced that the method of war is no way to bring about the establishment of justice, political freedom, or peace itself. The best place for us to exert our influence to establish these blessings is in our own country. Those of us who see in the strict application of the principle of neutrality a way by which America may save herself from being drawn into an impend-

420

ing conflict are used to meeting the bitter insinuation that we belong in the "peace-at-any-price" ranks, that we are "spineless pacifists," or "fatuous isolationists." But I should like to ask what possible shame can attach to America for taking advantage of both her geographical and historical position to keep out of the present chaos in Europe? What shame is there in trying to limit the area of conflict rather than extend it? What ethical obtuseness in attempting to keep one clear pool of sanity in the world?

There is little doubt in any one's mind today that the European situation means trouble for us in America. That it is a challenge is beyond debate. How we are to meet the challenge is a matter upon which there are divergent opinions. As between a so-called "collective security," the terms of which have never yet been clearly defined, and a policy of neutrality which will involve some sacrifice of profits and even of something superficially accepted as prestige, I prefer the policy of neutrality—the planned intention of keeping out of other people's wars.

One way to approach the subject of neutrality is to inquire closely what neutrality is not.

AMERICA IS AS AMERICA DOES

The United States has a way of saying to the nations of the world, "Oh, if only you were all as peace-loving as we are, we could get out from under the terrific burdens involved in preparing for war! If only other nations would follow our example!" Suppose we scrutinize for a moment our example. When Congress voted to spend billions of dollars in a gigantic national recovery program, what was the first use we made of this money? The very first allocation, for 231 million dollars was turned over by executive order to the United States Navy for the building of more ships. More ships, to get ready for another war, to be followed by another depression, and another spending program, including more ships! If only other nations would follow our example!

No one is more jealously interested in my country's maintaining adequate national defense than I am. But I am sick of the things that are being done in the name of the national defense. For ten years I have sat upon the Senate Appropriations Committee. For ten years, without a miss in any one year, I have listened to talk about the perils of war with Japan, and I am reporting the exact truth when I say that the annual war scare always comes just before the introduction of the annual appropriation bills for the army and navy. When those bills are enacted into law, there is an immediate improvement in the relations between Japan and the United States.

When President Roosevelt was assistant secretary of the navy, he wrote an article for *Asia* in which he remarked that there wasn't any likelihood of war between these two countries so long as five cents' worth of common sense remained in either of them. In the kind of war which Japan and America would have to fight, if they fought at all, he believed there would be no possibility of a decisive victory for either nation; that such a war could end only when one or the other country bled to death through the pocketbook; that "war" between Japan and the United States was nothing more than the result of an apprehensive habit of mind. But suppose relations between these two countries are really strained—as the proponents of a big shipbuilding program would lead us to infer—is it common sense for us to send our warships near Japanese waters—thousands of miles away from our shores, and right under the noses of the Japanese—for signal practice and maneuvering? A recent visit to Japan convinced me that the worst phase of this rivalry in shipbuilding, this exhibitionism, and the general policy of preparation for a war that is not national defense is the mutual distrust which it engenders. While so many of our citizens are made to fear Japan's intentions, the people of Japan are being agitated by their own military leaders, and by our own aggressiveness, into fear that the United States is preparing to attack Japan. Thus the way is cleared for increased appropriations for the "defense" of the Japanese. It is a game that has no end. Here, at least, is one nation that has followed our example.

Now, I am convinced that if Japan had a navy twenty times its present size she couldn't get within several hundred miles of our shore under conditions of modern warfare that depend upon the use of airplanes, submarines, and coast defenses. Nor could we get within striking distance of her coasts. The truth is that our military plans are not built up and financed on a reasonable basis of true national defense. If they were, we should have a different allocation of funds— more for coast defenses, for instance, and less for battleships. Even before the introduction of the President's national defense program for 1938, we were spending in the neighborhood of a billion dollars a year for our army and navy, of which fabulous sum the navy has been receiving about 600 million dollars. During this period the rise in appropriations for the army was 150 million dollars. To what astounding figures we shall aspire no man knows, but the present additional appropriation for the navy under the Vinson Act amounts to 200 million dollars.

What a pity it is that other nations are not as peace-minded as ourselves! And as little inclined to go in for armament races! And, make no mistake, these huge appropriations as at present allocated can by no stretch of the imagination be considered essential to the national defense, even if we include in that the defense of Alaska, the Panama Canal, Hawaii, and Puerto Rico. Our appropriations are built around blueprints that call for the transportation of three million men across thousands of ocean miles to fight, I presume, in the name of national defense, on somebody else's land, or in someone else's waters. It is largely for these outlays that the people of America are shouldering a load of taxation that is growing heavier every year. It is a burden that will cripple America as surely as it has already crippled nations of the Old World. It is a burden the only escape from which is to make the war machine pay for itself by wars of aggression carried on by ruthless dictatorships.

SOCIAL BENEFITS SACRIFICED TO WAR

But there is still another side to this outlay for war preparedness and the conduct of war. What alternative use could we have made, for instance, of the money that four years of war cost this world? Dr. Nicholas Murray Butler has made an inventory of what we could do for mankind if we had that money today. We could buy five-acre plots of land at $100 an acre, build homes upon the land costing $2,500, furnish them for $1,000, and give such a home scot-free to every family resident (in 1935) in Russia, Italy, France, Belgium, Germany, Scotland, Ireland, Wales, England, Australia, Canada, and the United States. Every city of approximately 20,000 people in those countries could have a two million dollar hospital, a three million dollar library, and a ten million dollar university. With part of the balance invested at five per cent, we could pay salaries of a thousand dollars apiece to 125,000 teachers and 125,000 nurses, and then we would have enough money left to buy up every penny's worth of property in Belgium and in Germany. Think of the social benefits the world has sacrificed to pursue a war which brought us all only a depression and more war!

Or suppose we think only of what is actually happening in our own country every year. When the appropriation for the Office of Education comes before Congress, the legislators begin at once to quibble. They take out their knives and whet them, and then they proceed to cut those appropriations to the bone. The same thing happens with the appropriation for the state department. This department is maintained at the cost of something like a paltry thirteen million dollars a year. But suppose someone should have the temerity to propose an additional million in order that the secretary of state might enlarge the scope of his activities in the name of world peace. Such a proposal would be laughed out of court. Men would

424

say, "What! Increase our budgets in times like these? The man is mad!"

But when the appropriations for the maintenance of the army and navy come before Congress, our economists in the House and the Senate are as silent as the grave. There isn't any fear then about increasing budgets. So well does the cry of "preparedness" do its work, that I once proposed to a body of teachers that they should learn to call education *National Defense*, and I presume a similar shibboleth could be invented for the advancement of the state department.

Now, what possible explanation can be found for this inconsistency and madness?

PROFITEERS IN WAR MATERIALS

Let me remind you of a few outstanding facts with regard to the methods of doing business in the materials of war. These facts were revealed in the course of the investigations by the Senate Munitions Committee.

I have already mentioned that the first money allocated under the national recovery program went by executive order for the building of warships. Before any member of Congress knew that shipbuilding was to be permitted under the public works program, the shipbuilders knew it. Less than two weeks after that program had been enacted into law, on March 14, 1933, to be exact, one of the lobbyists wrote to the shipbuilders that he thought it would be very wise if his employers would "come down to Washington and talk things over with the gang." When the Munitions Committee asked him to be a little more explicit as to his reference to "the gang," this lobbyist refused for more than an hour to answer our question. We reminded him that although counsel who advise a witness not to answer questions never go to jail, witnesses themselves, acting upon the advice of counsel, do go to jail. The witness thereupon named certain admirals and commanders in the United States Navy and certain officials in the navy department. There was a good deal of testimony bearing on the rather close relations that were maintained between the officials of our navy and the shipbuilders. The president of one of the great shipbuilding companies wrote as follows to his board of directors:

> I know from my talks with some of the representatives of the navy that they are desirous of finding substantial reason for awarding this work to the largest possible extent to our private yards rather than to the government's own ship-building yards. There was also expressed to us the desire that the builders themselves get together and agree, as far as we could, upon what each would bid, and then bid on nothing else.

So here is the spectacle of our own navy helping these shipbuilders to plunder Uncle Sam! The letter goes on to state that, according to the writer's understanding, "This would mean for Bethlehem twenty-eight million dollars, Newport News thirty million dollars, and for the New York Ship Building Company twenty-eight million dollars." When the bids were opened ten days later, it was revealed that this official had not missed his guess by a single ship. The pie had indeed been divided into precisely these nearly equal parts. Those who have learned to play this national defense racket know what they are doing at every turn of the road. And mark the fact that there are always two parties to a racket. Let me quote from a letter written by a member of Congress who had been of great assistance to the shipbuilders at the time of this public works episode:

> As you perhaps know [he is addressing the shipbuilders], a Congressman must derive some of his income from other sources than being a member of the House of Representatives.

He then goes on to explain what kind of business he is in and just how the shipbuilders can put dollars in his pocket by buying from his company. Of course that is not bribery; it is just good business, and besides it is in the name of national defense. I have used illustrations that happen to concern the shipbuilders, but I might equally as well have chosen testimony involving the ammunition makers and the makers of ordinance. These racketeers maintain a very expensive lobby in Washington. The record now on file contains overwhelming evidence of their activities, and the evidence is derived in great measure from their own letters. Some of the letters concern their attempt to prevent the passage of the Nye resolution calling for the munitions investigation. There is also evidence of their deliberate and methodical purpose to wreck disarmament conferences. It was the president of the Bethlehem Ship-building Company who testified to what a horror he had of war. He said he was sure that all businessmen in America would strenuously oppose these mad naval races if they could have their way. But that did not prevent his company from paying one-third of the cost of sending a representative to the Geneva Disarmament Conference in 1926. You may remember some of his testimony. He stated that it was the navy, the officials of the Navy Department, who gave him secret documents and instructed him go to go Geneva to accomplish the wrecking of any disarmament program there. The navy told him to go and the shipbuilders paid the bill. And then we wonder why these conferences prove, one after another, to be such tragic failures. They will continue to be failures so long as we and the other nations send to them men trained in naval and military schools, or men who are acting primarily in the interests of the stockholders of munitions companies. This racket is an international racket, the business of which is to build up hate and fear and suspicion in all the countries of the world. Peru, for example, got advice from a commission of our naval experts, and on the strength of that advice she ordered a fleet of submarines and destroyers. When Colombia heard about that, she too wanted advice from a commission of our naval experts, and she too ordered submarines, as a defense, of course, against Peru's submarines. These orders were placed with American firms and were a cause for great self-congratulation on the part of American business. But suppose we send our boys down to those troubled waters some day to straighten out a difficulty which we as neighbor and adviser have been chiefly responsible for promoting? Statistics of the Bureau of Commerce show that day by day and week by week huge cargoes of munitions leave our shores for nearly every nation on the globe—including the Japanese nation, about whom the war propagandists have so much to say. Our boys couldn't go to war anywhere without having our own munitions fired back at them. And yet decent American businessmen will say that to have a war is the only way in which business will "pick up." They will tell you that, if we are to have adequate production capacity at home to meet the possible emergencies of war, we must increase the foreign market for American-made ships and American-made munitions. In other words, we must sell now to countries who may some day be our foes, in order that we may have productive capacity if and when the rest of the world decides to use what we sold them against us. A good policy! Don't alter it. Don't rock the boat.

THE ARGUMENT FOR MANDATORY LEGISLATION

Enough has been said to make it plain to the reader what neutrality is not. These matters caused the country grave concern when they were revealed by the Munitions Inquiry; familiarity with them must not lead us to view them with indifference. The serious danger to our peace, to say nothing about our standards of common honor and decency, is so obvious that a way out of the bog in which we find ourselves must be found. A policy of strict neutrality, to become mandatory as soon as the war infection manifests itself, appears to be such a way of escape. The advantages of such mandatory legislation are easily apparent. Valuable time is saved at a critical moment in world affairs when a situation involving the question of our neutrality is settled automatically and in advance of the crisis. It is then the choice of no single individual and is not directed against the interests of any particular nation or group of nations. It is simply the law of the land, a law familiar to every foreign power. Nations intent upon war are given notice and may weigh for themselves the effect of such a policy upon their ability to buy arms and other war supplies in our markets. These are very definite advantages which cannot be lightly dismissed. To such a mandatory embargo against the shipment of munitions was added, specifically for our own protection against involvement in war, the so-called *cash and carry* provision.

PRACTICAL AND THEORETICAL PROBLEMS OF NEUTRALITY

Experience has taught us much since the passage of the compromise measure signed by the President in August, 1935. It has become clear that the cash and carry principle may work out in practice to the advantage of one combatant and the disadvantage of another. This is not neutrality. The embargo on shipments to Spain, as instigated by the Administration in January, 1937, was not neutrality; it was an effort at collective security, done in co-operation with England and France and their famous Non-Intervention Committee. It has become plain that certain commodities such as cotton and oil, which are legitimate and profitable exports upon which we rely for revenue in time of peace, become highly controversial and more than ever profitable in time of war. We cannot assume that public opinion today would support a mandatory embargo upon such exports, even though an embargo might be the means of checking war. We cannot assume that any executive would use his discretionary powers to list such exports as contraband in the face of strong popular dissent. We can, however, remind our people in season and out of the pitfalls that we fell into twenty years ago; and we can use every effort to educate them to resist the selfish influences which sometimes warp and destroy their better judgment. Because of these selfish influences, neutrality in the strict sense of the word has never been tried.

Neutrality legislation as we have had it in America has been a makeshift imposed by conditions of haste and emergency and by a none too intelligent compromise between conflicting views—so much so that I moved recently for the repeal of the Neutrality Act. At the moment when its repeal seemed assured, it became the center of a whirlwind of activity from certain pressure groups among whom our Church groups were conspicuous because of their official sympathy with the Insurgent forces now fighting in Spain. It should also be plain to Americans that the passage of repeal would have acted as a checkmate upon the present policies of Great Britain.

NEUTRALITY AND FUTURE POLICY

The whole question of neutrality, both in principle and as it may be enacted into law, is one of such difficulty that much thought and research are needed before we can hope to arrive at an acceptable formula. We have made some gains. The creation of a Munitions Control Board, which is a provision for some degree of supervision over the manufacture, exportation, and importation of munitions is a move in the right direction. It must, in my opinion, lead ultimately to the government's becoming the manufacturer of its own national defense machinery and the court of last resort as to all questions involving the sale and export of munitions.

The discussion of the subject, which has been stimulated by the passage of the act and the important considerations which have developed as to its functioning, has exerted a wholesome influence upon American thought. Problems which had been confined to the consideration of diplomats and students of international law have been opened up for discussion among our citizens, and the bearing of such problems upon the all important question of the maintenance of peace is now becoming plain to everyone. When an American gunboat and Standard Oil tankers, huddled together in the waters of a nation at war, are torpedoed by military planes, the people are sobered, but they do not let the incident impel them to get into the war themselves. Their comments have a healthy skepticism: "What business had the gunboat to be there anyhow? I'll

430

bet the gas that ran the motors in those bombing planes was delivered to Japan in the same tankers that were hit! And no doubt the shrapnel was made from some of the scrap iron we've been selling to Japan." There is no longer resentment against the doctrine that some degree of restriction must be laid upon the freedom of the individual to involve his country in any risks he may choose to take for his own profit or convenience in areas that are infected by war. Although the prohibition against loans to foreign countries engaged in war—which was one of the provisions of the original resolution—was never enacted into law, an informed public opinion has put bankers and governments on notice that such loans will not be tolerated, even if and when the present restriction against loans to debtor nations is canceled. These are signs of greater maturity and self control in our attitude toward the problems of war. They indicate that the American people will soon make an unmistakable demand to be consulted by means of a war referendum before war is declared.

The legislative problem of taking the profits out of war and out of war preparedness has hardly as yet been approached. There is a bill now under discussion before Congress which has unfortunately become known as a bill to take the profits out of war. Our people will do well to scrutinize severely all legislation that is presented with that ostensible purpose. The bill to which I refer has been fathered by the American Legion, and is known as the Shepherd-May bill; it is a peculiarly wrong-headed and vicious example of "bargain" legislation, in which everybody gets something—except possibly the men who are to be killed on foreign battlefields in the next war. Perhaps the proponents of the measure do not expect to hear very much from them. At any rate, the bill undertakes to draft between two and three million men for "national defense"—an obvious smoke-screen for conscription for service overseas. There are other dangerous provisions against which we should be on our guard, as for example, the complete subjugation of our civil life to an undisguised dictatorship to be set up by the executive.

431

The drafting of labor under such a dictatorship would become a reality in everything but name, and organized labor would run the risk of dissolution.

As to the matter of war profits, there is a provision authorizing the President to freeze prices as of the date on which war is declared. This is supposed to be a threat to capital, giving it notice that there is no use trying to raise prices to make bigger profits. The experience of the country during the World War should be enough to show the futility of such an edict. At that time the steel companies refused to produce at certain prices, on the ground that some high-cost producers were making no profit. The increases they demanded were given them. But years later when the matter was investigated by the Senate, it was found that these very same high-cost producers had been making a profit of ninety per cent! History will repeat itself. The bill has a further provision for taking from the producer ninety-five per cent of profits above an average of the three years next preceding the year in which the United States becomes engaged in war. The immediate effect of that provision would be to put a premium on all sales of war material in peace time. Thus the bill would positively encourage war booms. Moreover, such firms as Carnegie Steel, the Du Pont interests, or the Sperry Gyroscope concern who are now under contract and are making big profits, would scarcely be disheartened by the prospect of "only" five per cent additional profit during war time.

Those persons who put human life above property are also offered something in this proposed legislation, but it is only a few fine phrases. The treatment to be accorded citizens generally, and labor in particular, would depend upon the emotional reactions of the President, but the treatment to be accorded capital is specifically provided for in the terms of the bill. Be assured, moreover, that the next war, as it is envisaged by the miliary and naval experts who force our appropriations, is a war to be fought on foreign soil and in distant waters. It is for this reason that bills calling for unconditional power over the lives of men are being offered. In the event of invasion or attack by a foreign power, no conscription would be needed—men would flock to the defense of America *unless*, indeed, our war preparations burden us so heavily that education, health, housing, and social insurance of all kinds fall to so low a level that this country is no longer a country which men and women will spontaneously desire to save.

The truth is that unless a halt is called upon war preparations that are not for defense and upon the enactment of laws for the complete mobilization of our civil organization in wartime, America will succumb to war psychology and will be drawn inevitably into actual conflict. Neutrality, aided by the natural advantages of our physical so-called *isolation*, or neutrality, happily in co-operation with other nations, if that can be safely accomplished, appears to be the solution. It is a problem that challenges the best minds.

NEUTRALITY OR "COLLECTIVE SECURITY"?

There is no machinery left for collective action among the nations of the world today, unless we except the League of Nations, which has been called by its own adherents "futile and hopeless." There are certain military alliances. Is it proposed that we shall tack on to one or more of these to ensure our American security? There is something very puzzling about those alliances. It cannot have escaped your notice that England and France are demonstrating the amazing fact that there is something more precious to them than the saving of their own national existence, their own form of government—not to mention the independence of Austria, Spain, and Czechoslovakia. The thing that might actually ensure collective security in Europe is a firm military alliance with Russia, the most consistently peaceful of any of those three great powers. Such an alliance, however, would seem to be more abhorent to France and Great Britain than is the loss of their own power, more abhorent than the loss of peace itself.

When we are asked to underwrite a campaign for collective security, it is plain that we are not being invited to assist in the defense of powers, or to co-operate with powers that can properly be called *democratic*. The defense of the British and French empires, were we to lend ourselves to a policy of collective security with those countries, would involve the continued subjugation of hundreds of millions of black and brown peoples among whom the spirit of revolt is already manifest. With Britain as our associate in a pledge of collective security, we should derive some protection from the activities of the British navy in Pacific waters where American interests ought not to lie. But do we want to pledge ourselves to help Britain hang on to the spoils of the last war? Hongkong was Britain's toll from the unholy opium war. Do we want to help her to hold it? Collective effort is the way to win a hand in so doing.

It has been said that the leadership of the future lies with us; that it is henceforth for us to tell Great Britain and France what the terms of collective action are to be. Let me remind you, not cynically, but only in the interests of historic realism rather than of wishful thinking, that such leadership precisely was President Wilson's dream.

For better or worse, we are part of a world order, and it is always possible that challenges may come which we cannot ignore and which will take us as a co-operator into another world war. But let us refrain from writing the ticket of procedure even before we know who our allies are to be, what the cause is to be, what the jeopardy is going to be, what the cost is going to be, and, above all, what the chances of winning the cause for which we may be willing to fight. If America lends herself to participation in another foreign cause, she would do well to ask to see all the cards face up on the table before she consents to being collected into another collective security program. In other words, our interest in world affairs does not extend to giving a blank check to all of Europe's confused and secretive diplomacy. As to the inroads of fascism in South America, they can only be met by showing democracy to be

434

preferable to anything that totalitarian dictators may have to offer. Scrupulous fairness in our trade and in our governmental relations with South America is the best form of insurance against the spread of fascist doctrine there.

Not long ago President Roosevelt said, "We shun political commitments which might entangle us in foreign wars." And again, "We are not isolationists, except in so far as we seek to isolate ourselves completely from wars." May we continue to hew to that line here in America, strengthening our written neutrality policy which is intended to deny us the taste of profit from the blood of other nations' wars, and so checking our growing appetite for more and more of that profit. If we will cease letting American corporations, assisted by our military establishment, arm all the world with instruments of warfare; if we will stop financing other people's wars; if we will make profit from any other war in which we may engage impossible, and destroy as far as possible the motive of profit in our mad armament races; if we will learn to be content with a national defense that guarantees protection against attack; if we will give to the people a voice in determining whether this country shall engage in foreign war; if we will do these things, we shall not write off all danger of war, but we shall very definitely assure a fuller measure of security to the finest democracy to be found upon this earth.

Chapter XXVI

THE ROAD TO PEACE

CLARK M. EICHELBERGER

★ ★ ★ ★

THE road to peace for the United States and for the rest of the nations is to be found through increasing co-operation in a highly developed society of nations. Some future generation may live in a world in which national sovereignty counts for much less than it does today. In it there will be new forms of group loyalty and patriotism. But our generation, at least, lives in a period of intense nationalism, and our problem is that of building a system composed of sovereign nations, yet capable of providing expanding machinery to meet the ever-increasing complexities of life, capable of providing economic justice, and strong enough to prevent aggression.

It is necessary in order to see the magnitude of this task to examine the world of today. It might be said that mankind stands between two periods of history. As far back as we can look, there was room for nations to move about. There was always a horizon challenging a few brave adventurers to find new land and resources beyond.

Some one has said that modern history began with the discovery of precious metals in the New World and ended with the development of oil gushers in Texas. In that brief period of time, the best land of the world was taken. The resources of the world became known. Geographers, scientists, and industrialists now know where practically all the deposits of raw materials are to be found. Every square inch of land is claimed by some highly conscious nation. The pioneer and the colonial periods of history have practically passed. As far into the future as we can see, we must adjust the problems of some sixty nations to an earth the limits of which we have reached and understand.

At the moment when the land of the world was fully explored and its resources discovered the population of the world reached its highest point. Within the past one hundred years the world population has more than doubled.

Moreover, the discoveries of steam and electricity which opened the eighteenth century led to a development of communications which means the literal annihilation of time and space. One may fly around the world in a few days; one may talk around the world in a few seconds. Professor Eugene Staley and his associates at the Fletcher School of Law and Diplomacy have developed a series of charts by which one may compare the time elements involved in distance. For illustration, a chart showing the amount of time required for travel from Boston to parts of the thirteen colonies at the time of the Revolutionary War as compared with the distance one may travel from Boston in the same space of time today, would show that the world is actually smaller in the time element than were the thirteen colonies in 1776.

ECONOMIC INTERDEPENDENCE

Another development that has been taking place has been the rapid industrialization of the peoples of the world, at first affecting a few nations in Western Europe and the United States and finally affecting nations almost everywhere. The simple economic organization of the pioneer families, who raised all that they needed to eat and made their own clothes and built their own log cabins, has given way to a most complex industrial system. Great cities have been built. Salesmen have gone to the far-off corners of the earth, there to sell the so-called surplus products of the factories of the more highly industrialized nations. Not only has the individual tended to be less and less self-sufficient, but the nation has as well. Wallace

McClure in *World Prosperity*, points this out in an effective manner:

> As all peoples that are well advanced in civilization require raw materials which are in fact produced only in a few restricted localities, the wiser proponents of economic independence incline to seek it through the development of international arrangements whereby all countries may be assured of access to supplies of such raw materials as they need wherever such materials may be extracted from or produced upon the earth. The only practicable economic independence, that is, the continuing unthreatened use of the material things deemed necessary for preserving national safety and maintaining a gradually rising standard of living for the masses of people, must, indeed, be sought through international cooperation and cannot be achieved by any state acting alone.

As the world has become united economically its political problems tend to become world-wide. The assassination of the Archduke of Austria in 1914 set in motion a train of circumstances which we know as the World War. Conflict anywhere threatens to become world conflict. The economic consequences of a threat of war are almost equally disturbing. All nations today are part of a world depression. President Roosevelt has estimated that a third of the people of this country live below a decent standard of living. The percentage must be so much higher for part of the world at least that we can probably say that half the people of this earth are on the verge of misery and starvation. There are many causes for this situation at a moment when science makes it possible for us to provide a decent standard of living for all people, but the fear of war, with its accompanying economic nationalism and its resultant trade barriers, is one of the greatest factors.

The world-wide fear of war has produced a most fantastic arms race. When the Premier of France recently asked for the largest peace-time budget in French history, he frankly told the Chamber of Deputies they had no alternative but to make such expenditures if the other nations did likewise, but that he realized that their continuance over a long period of time would bankrupt the country. The prime minister of another great government is reported to have warned the workers of his country that they need expect no legislation for social improvement within this generation because of arms expenditures. The German dictator has told his people not to complain if they do not have enough butter because he will guarantee that they shall have enough cannon. The United States has a part in this arms race. Enormous sums are being spent and the energies of the world utilized in military preparations at a tremendous cost in fear of war, economic depression, and a greatly reduced standard of living. It is becoming increasingly clear that no amount of recovery measures which the United States or any other country may take can produce lasting prosperity unless accompanied by efforts that will succeed in removing the fear of war and in establishing world-wide confidence and security.

At the close of the World War the nations realized that the answer to this world dilemma was a well-organized community of sovereign nations. It does not detract from the idealism of these conceptions to say that they were hammered on the anvil of necessity. When a group of men on a frontier found that lawlessness would destroy them, they sought first to establish law and order as best they could, and from that rough beginning of community life they proceeded to organize their more constructive activities.

FOUR BASIC OBLIGATIONS

Necessity has forced the nations in the last eighteen years to undertake certain basic obligations of human society. Even in the face of the present world-wide reaction, we are amazed at what has been accomplished. In the various treaties signed since the Armistice, the world has made tremendous strides in the development of an organized community of nations, despite the present world reaction against them and the inclination of nations to return to prewar anarchy.

The nations have accepted four basic obligations of human society and have created the machinery to give them effect.

439

As for the first two obligations, the nations have renounced war as an instrument of national policy and have agreed not to settle their disputes by other than peaceful means. Thus, the century-old legal sanctions of international law concerning war have been swept aside and war itself has been renounced. These two obligations are specifically stated in the Kellogg Pact and are inherent in the League of Nations Covenant.

In the third place, under Article 11 of the Covenant of the League of Nations, in other documents, and in the repeated declarations of statesmen, the nations have accepted the principles of collective responsibility for individual respect of the renunciation of war. Under Article 11 of the Covenant of the League of Nations, the nations agreed that war or its threat was the concern of all. This collective responsibility has been supplemented by definite obligations for collective security.

And in the fourth place, recognizing that in an expanding society peace would be impossible unless there were adequate provisions for justice, the nations declared, in Part 13 of the Treaty of Versailles, that world peace is dependent upon international social and economic justice. The principles of this declaration find expression in the International Labor Organization.

In his address at Nashville, Tenn., June 3, 1938, Secretary of State Cordell Hull said:

> On a number of recent occasions, I have set forth some of the principles which, in my opinion, are indispensable to a satisfactory international order. The most important of these are as follows:
>
> Maintenance of peace should be constantly advocated and practiced. . . .
>
> All nations should, through voluntary self-restraint, abstain from use of force in pursuit of policy and from interference in the internal affairs of other nations. . . .
>
> All nations should seek to adjust problems arising in their international relations by processes of peaceful negotiation and agreement. . . .
>
> All nations should uphold the principle of the sanctity of treaties and of faithful observance of international agreements. . . .

Modification of provisions of treaties, when need therefor arises, should be by orderly processes carried out in a spirit of mutual helpfulness and accommodation. . . .

Each nation should respect the rights of others and perform scrupulously its own established obligations. . . .

Steps should be taken toward promotion of economic security and stability the world over through lowering or removal of barriers to international trade, according effective equality of commercial opportunity, and application of the principle of equality of commercial treatment. . . .

All nations should be prepared to limit and progressively reduce their armaments. . . .

Apart from the question of alliances with others, each nation should be prepared to engage in cooperative effort, by peaceful and practicable means, in support of these principles.

Hand in hand with acceptance of these obligations has come the machinery to give them effect. The League of Nations has expanded its activities to cover practically every phase of human existence. The International Labor Organization, now with the membership of the United States, is striving to secure a greater degree of co-operation in the raising of labor and living standards. The Permanent Court of International Justice continues to give decisions in legal disputes and clear the way for a greater degree of agreement between nations.

The League of Nations, one may say without detracting from the greatness of Woodrow Wilson's vision, was not a theoretical scheme beyond the capacity of mankind. It was the result of necessity. The nations had reached that place where war was too costly; where no one could really win; where war would destroy all mankind.

The road to peace lies in strengthening the four major obligations of human society: renunciation of war; settlement of disputes only by peaceful means; acceptance of the principle of collective responsibility; and establishment of international social justice. The road to peace lies in the nations' accepting the basic rules of human conduct which Secretary of State Hull has announced. The road to peace lies in the strengthening of the machinery of the League of Nations, the

441

Permanent Court of International Justice, and the International Labor Organization to provide the means, the spirit, and the technique for translation of these basic obligations and rules of conduct into practical realization.

These together constitute the road to peace.

A PRACTICAL PROGRAM

What must the nations do immediately to stem the retreat to destruction? In the first place man must restore his faith in his capacity to create a new world. This faith has been the distinguishing mark of our postwar period. As long as that faith prevailed the community of nations grew strong; when that faith dimmed man returned to the old paths, disastrous paths, but ones with which he was familiar. It is not surprising that great declarations of moral principle could not become fixed in the minds of statesmen of the old school in eighteen years. Man's faith in his capacity to build a warless world must be renewed.

In the second place, the principle of collective security must be restored. It is generally assumed that at least ninety per cent of the people of the world wish peace. That peace is menaced because the nations that wish it remain divided as to policy. The three democracies of France, Great Britain, and the United States alone possess three-fourths of the world's gold; they control one-half of its shipping; they produce more than one-half of its steel and three-fourths of its oil.

These nations, plus the many others who wish peace, have in their hands the means by which to enforce it. By remaining disunited and refusing to fulfill their obligations under international society, they see the philosophy of dictatorship repudiating the principles of decent human conduct which have grown out of long practice and which were defined in the Kellogg Pact and the League of Nations Covenant. These dictators have started upon a program of conquest which has already claimed Ethiopia and Austria, has fed the flames of the Spanish Civil War, and even as this is being

442

written, is effecting the dismemberment of Czechoslovakia. At the same moment that this chain of events is getting under way in Europe, Japan is involving one-fourth of the world in the Far Eastern tragedy. If these forces continue, the light of human freedom will be extinguished from a great portion of the globe. Ignorance, brutality, oppression, and fanaticism will be the dominant forces in the lives of hundreds of millions of human beings. A great part of the world will enter another night of the dark ages.

Recently the Munich Conference succeeded in removing the immediate menace of a general European war. But the sense of relief was tempered by a growing realization of the price that had been paid. Neither by its technique or its results did the conference bode well for the future. Upon Czechoslovakia, last stronghold of democracy in Central Europe, was forced a process of dismemberment which rendered her relatively defenseless and which opened the way to Germany's eastward expansion. The politics of threat and force had gained another victory, and the hope of an orderly world had suffered another defeat. Perhaps at the moment nothing else could have been done, but if the peace-loving nations had had sufficient wisdom to consider ways of peaceful change, sufficient strength to stand firm for international order, that moment need never have arrived.

The moral solidarity of the nations that wish peace, if co-ordinated and united, might be sufficient to restore peace. But if the united moral forces of the world are not sufficient, united action of a stronger kind is necessary. The tremendous resources of the peace-loving nations could be controlled with a twofold purpose: to prevent the aggressor from waging war and also from any consolidation of his gains. On June 1, 1938, statistics showed that fifty-four per cent of the materials which Japan needed to wage war were coming from the United States, at the very moment when the government of this country was protesting the bombardment of civilians and insisting upon the sanctity of the Kellogg Pact.

In the third place, having re-established their moral solidarity and having decided to deny their vast resources to any aggressor, the ninety per cent who want peace should proceed to establish among themselves a liberal international economic order with equality of access to raw materials, freer access to markets, and equal opportunity in colonial areas. All nations, despite their systems of internal government, should be admitted as equals to this liberal economic order in return for a reaffirmation of pledges not to wage war and to settle disputes only by peaceful processes.

It is clear that no amount of territorial adjustment, even if it could be undertaken peaceably, would afford each nation equal resources. Some nations, such as the Scandinavian countries, whose territory is not rich and who have few colonies are the most peaceable, for they have decided that they can live through international economic co-operation. Other countries are demanding colonies to satisfy wounded prestige and are rationalizing these demands in terms of economic necessity. Certain nations, such as Great Britain, France, the Soviet Union, and the United States, have a very large share of raw materials. These nations alone have seventy-eight per cent of the world's gold supply. And yet the wealthiest nation cannot be self-sufficient, and the poorest can live if it is industrious and can find foreign markets for its industry.

A recent League of Nations committee on raw materials reported that less than two per cent of the raw materials now produced come from colonial areas; that ninety-eight per cent come from independent countries or self-sufficient dominions.

One of the most encouraging facts today is the agreement among the experts as to how these problems can be approached. There is great unanimity among the committees of experts of the Carnegie Endowment for International Peace and the International Chamber of Commerce; the report of former Premier Van Zeeland of Belgium; the reports of the economic and financial committees of the League of Nations; and finally the committee of experts appointed by the National Peace Conference to report to the Economic Conference held in Washington, March 23–26, 1938. These experts agree that the problem of raw materials is to be solved not by conquest or further colonial expansion, but by facilitating equality of access to the raw materials of the world. The experts also agree that these raw materials must be paid for in goods and services, and, therefore, trade barriers must be reduced and international trade stimulated as a means of payment. Currencies should be stabilized, and the principle of the open door and equality of opportunity guaranteed in the mandated areas should be extended to all crown colonies. The standard of living and of labor should be raised in all countries, and particularly in the so-called *backward countries*, more nearly to approach standards of more advanced countries.

All the experts are agreed that the International Labor Organization should be given the support of world-wide public opinion in its effort to accomplish this improvement in standards. It has, furthermore, been suggested (and a committee of the League of Nations has had the matter under advisement) that another autonomous body be created called the International Economic Organization, capable of facing problems of raw materials, trade barriers, and currency with the same technique that the International Labor Organization is using for industry and labor.

The machinery of the League of Nations, weakened in the last few years by the desertion of the statesmen who have lost the vision, must be strengthened. It must be given a staff and a budget adequate to deal with its complex problems. A community of nations is an impossibility without adequate machinery, as any municipality would be impossible without administrative machinery. As an indication of how little money the world spends on the administrative machinery for peace in comparison with its military budgets, one might point out that if Great Britain and the United States were to give the League of Nations the equivalent of the cost of the

445

two 45,000-ton battleships which the two nations are planning to build, and this money were properly invested, it would pay the peace budget of the League of Nations from now until the end of time.

THE RESPONSIBILITY OF THE UNITED STATES

What of the United States? After all other nations have been given their share of the blame for the present retreat from the obligations of the society of nations, the fact remains that the greatest obstacle to the building of peace in the past eighteen years has been the moral neutrality of the United States.

The American people won the war and lost the peace. After having turned the tide of victory in 1917 and suggested the establishment of the League of Nations, they tried to retreat to the frontier hoping that they might escape international obligations. The leadership which this country rejected in 1919 haunts it in 1938.

As an illustration of the results of a policy of moral neutrality, one might cite the neutrality legislation now on our statute books. The neutrality law gives the President no authority to discriminate between the aggressor and victim. It has not proved to be the road to peace. It has served as an encouragement to aggression by proclaiming in advance the moral neutrality of the United States in issues of right and wrong.

The worst feature of our neutrality policy is that it is a policy calculated to determine in advance this government's course in case war breaks out. It has nothing in it of a constructive nature providing for either consultation or co-operation on the part of the United States with other countries in withholding materials of war from the aggressor. Furthermore, by giving the President and the secretary of state little choice in the matter of invocation, it places the conduct of American foreign affairs in the hands of foreign dictators and generals rather than in the hands of the secretary of state and the President, where those powers rightly belong.

446

The United States cannot afford to be lulled to sleep by a false sense of security. Suppose the rest of the world were engulfed in war? We would be forced to reduce our standard of living, regiment our lives, and suffer a considerable reduction of our freedom. Worst of all, could the world long be half democratic and half fascist, half free and half slave, half respecting the ideals of peace and half ridiculing and threatening those ideals? If Europe enters the dark ages, the United States, to say the least, would be living in perpetual twilight.

Moreover, what assurance have we that the United States would not become involved in the actual conflict? If the threats of Hitler are to be taken literally, when he says, "Today all Germany is ours; tomorrow the whole world," the ambition of dictators will not stop at the borders of American territory, interests, or ideals.

There is nothing in the historical experience of the United States from colonial days down to 1920 that gives us any assurance we could avoid participation in another war.

A destiny which the American people did not ask for and probably do not wish, has given them a responsibility for leadership which they cannot avoid. Great Britain had the leadership of the world in the 19th and the early part of the 20th century. It is not my purpose to judge whether or not she used that leadership wisely. But Great Britain and all the other belligerents except the United States lost the World War in that they emerged weaker instead of stronger. The United States alone gained strength and influence. Whether we like it or not, the influence and leadership which were Great Britain's in the 19th century have now become the responsibility of the United States. If we refuse this leadership, the world may not be able to advance without it. But the United States has the opportunity to lead the world in the development of a peaceful international society.

Most of the people of the world do not wish war. Their brains and conscience protest against it. Have they the courage and the vision to develop further those policies of cooperation which alone point the road to peace?

BIBLIOGRAPHY[1]

CHAPTER I

THE CURRENT CRISIS: ITS CAUSES

BARNES, H. E.: *Can Man Be Civilized?* New York: Coward McCann, Inc., 1932

BRAINARD, D. S., and ZELENY, L. D.: *Problems of Our Times*, 3 vols., New York: McGraw-Hill Book Company, Inc., 1938.

CASSON, S.: *Progress and Catastrophe*, London: H. Hamilton, 1937.

COLE, G. D. H.: *The Intelligent Man's Guide through World Chaos*, London: Victor Gollancz, Ltd., 1932.

GRATTAN, C. H.: *Preface to Chaos*, New York: Dodge Publishing Company, 1936.

LANGDON-DAVIES, J.: *A Short History of the Future*, New York: Dodd, Mead & Company, Inc., 1936.

OGBURN, W. F.: *You and Machines*, Washington, D. C.: National Capital Press, Inc., 1934.

ROBINSON, J. H.: *The Human Comedy*, New York: Harper & Brothers, 1937.

RYAN, J. A.: *A Better Economic Order*, New York: Harper & Brothers, 1936.

WELLS, H. G.: *The Shape of Things to Come*, London: Hutchinson and Company, Ltd., 1933.

CHAPTER II

SOCIAL PROGRESS THROUGH EDUCATION

BEAR, R. M.: *Social Functions of Education*, New York: The Macmillan Company, 1937.

COUNTS, G. S.: *Social Foundations of Education*, New York: Charles Scribner's Sons, 1934.

DEARBORN, N. H.: "Beyond the Eastern Horizon," *Journal of Adult Education*, January, 1938, pp. 53–56.

DEWEY, J.: *The Way Out of Educational Confusion*, Cambridge: Harvard University Press, 1931.

FOERSTER, N.: *The American State University: Its Relation to Democracy*, Chapel Hill, N. C.: University of North Carolina Press, 1937.

KREY, A. C., and others: *American Historical Association: Conclusions and Recommendations of the Commission on Social Studies*, New York: Charles Scribner's Sons, 1934.

LANGFORD, H. D.: *Education and Social Conflict*, New York: The Macmillan Company, 1936.

MYERS, A., and WILLIAMS, C. O.: *Education in a Democracy*, New York: Prentice-Hall, Inc., 1937.

[1] Includes references to viewpoints which differ from those of the contributor of the chapter.

Recent Social Trends in the United States, 2 vols., New York: McGraw-Hill Book Company, Inc., 1933.
The Unique Function of Education in the American Democracy (Report), Washington, D. C.: National Education Association, 1937.

CHAPTER III

DEMOCRACY AS A WAY OF LIFE

ASCOLI, M., and LEHMAN F. (eds.): *Political and Economic Democracy*, New York: W. W. Norton and Company, Inc., 1937.
BODE, B. H.: *Democracy as a Way of Life*, New York: The Macmillan Company, 1937.
DEWEY, J.: *Liberalism and Social Action*, New York: G. P. Putnam's Sons, 1935.
HOOK, SIDNEY: "Democracy as a Way of Life," *Southern Review*, vol. 4, No. 1, pp. 45–57, Summer, 1938.
KALLEN, H. M., and others: *Freedom in the Modern World*, New York: Coward-McCann, Inc., 1928.
LASKI, H.: *Democracy in Crisis*, Chapel Hill, N. C.: University of North Carolina Press, 1935.
MANN, T.: *The Coming Victory of Democracy*, New York: Alfred A. Knopf, 1938.
MILL, J. S.: *On Liberty*, edited by Matthew Copithorne, Boston: Little, Brown & Company, 1921.
RUGG, H. O.: *America's March toward Democracy*, Boston: Ginn and Company, 1937.
SWABEY, M. T.: *Theory of the Democratic State*, Cambridge: Harvard University Press, 1937.
SWIFT, L. B.: *How We Got Our Liberties*, Indianapolis: Bobbs-Merrill Company, 1928.

CHAPTER IV

TODAY'S PROPAGANDA AND TOMORROW'S REALITY

DOOB, L.: *Propaganda: Its Psychology and Technique*, New York: Henry Holt & Company, Inc., 1935.
HOWE, Q.: *England Expects Every American to Do His Duty*, New York: Simon & Schuster, Inc., 1937.
IRWIN, W.: *Propaganda and the News*, New York: McGraw-Hill Book Company, Inc., 1936.
JASTROW, J.: *The Betrayal of Intelligence*, New York: Greenberg, Publisher, Inc., 1938.
LUMLEY, F. E.: *The Propaganda Menace*, New York: D. Appleton-Century Company, Inc., 1933.
RIEGAL, O. W.: *Mobilizing for Chaos: The Story of the New Propaganda*, New Haven: Yale University Press, 1934.
ROBINSON, J. H.: *Mind in the Making*, New York: Harper & Brothers, 1930.
SUMNER, W. G.: *Folkways*, Boston: Ginn and Company, 1906.
WHITE, A. D.: *A History of the Warfare between Science and Theology*, New York: D. Appleton-Century Company, Inc., 1910.

BIBLIOGRAPHY

YOUNG, E. J.: *Looking Behind the Censorships*, Philadelphia: J. B. Lippincott Company, 1938.

CHAPTER V

ACADEMIC FREEDOM

A Gage on Teaching, New York: American Civil Liberties Union, 1936.
BEALE, H. K.: *Are American Teachers Free?* New York: Charles Scribner's Sons, 1936.
DEWEY, J., and OTHERS: *The Social Frontier*, Vol. II, No. 6, March, 1936.
ICKES, H. L.: "Academic Freedom," *School and Society*, June 8, 1935, pp. 753–759.
KILPATRICK, W. H.: *Source Book in the Philosophy of Education*, rev. ed. (See index), New York: The Macmillan Company, 1934.
LOWELL, A. L.: *Annual Report*, 1916–1917, Cambridge: Harvard University Press, 1917.
NOCK, A. J.: *Free Speech and Plain Language*, New York: W. Morrow & Co., Inc., 1937.
RAUP, B.: *Education and Organized Interests in America*, New York: G. P. Putnam's Sons, 1936.
STUDEBAKER, J. W.: *Plain Talk*, Washington, D. C.: National Home Library Association, 1936.
The Teacher and Society, first year-book of the John Dewey Society, New York: D. Appleton-Century Company, Inc., 1937.

CHAPTER VI

GOALS IN A CHANGING WORLD

ADLER, M. J.: *What Man Has Made of Man*, New York: Longmans, Green & Company, 1937.
BEEVERS, J.: *World without Faith*, New York: Harper & Brothers, 1936.
COUDENHOVE, I. F.: *The Burden of Belief*, New York: Sheed and Ward, 1935.
FARIS, E.: *The Nature of Human Nature*, New York: McGraw-Hill Book Company, Inc., 1937.
HILTON, E.: *Problems and Values of Today*, Boston: Little, Brown & Company, 1938.
HUXLEY, A.: *Ends and Means*, New York: Harper & Brothers, 1937.
MORRISON, B., and RUEVE, S.: *Think and Live*, New York: Bruce Publishing Company, 1937.
OGBURN, W. F.: *The Family*, Boston: Houghton Mifflin Company, 1934.
SOCKMAN, R. W.: *Morals of Tomorrow*, New York: Harper & Brothers, 1931.
VANN, G.: *Morals Makyth Man*, New York: The Macmillan Company, 1938.

CHAPTER VII

CAPITALISM WILL SURVIVE!

ALLEN, L. W.: *Limited Capitalism, The Road to Unlimited Prosperity*, New York: Strand Publishers, 1934.

451

ARNOLD, T. W.: *Folklore of Capitalism*, New Haven: Yale University Press, 1937.

COREY, L.: *Decline of American Capitalism*, New York: Covici Friede, Inc., 1934.

CROMWELL, J. H.: *In Defense of Capitalism*, New York: Charles Scribner's Sons, 1937.

DOHLBERG, A. O.: *When Competition Goes on Strike*, New York: Harper & Brothers, 1938.

FANFANI, A.: *Protestantism, Capitalism and Catholicism*, New York: Sheed and Ward, 1935.

GASKILL, W. B.: *Profit and Social Security*, New York: Harper & Brothers, 1935.

MOULTON, H. G.: *Formation of Capital*, Washington, D. C.: The Brookings Institution, 1935.

PITKIN, W. B.: *Capitalism Carries On*, New York: McGraw-Hill Book Company, Inc., 1935.

SOKOLSKY, G. E.: *Labor's Fight for Power*, New York: Doubleday, Doran & Company, Inc., 1934.

CHAPTER VIII

IS FASCISM A WAY OUT?

ASHTON, E. B.: *The Fascist, His State and His Mind*, New York: W. Morrow & Co., Inc., 1937.

BRADY, R. G.: *The Spirit and Structure of German Fascism*, New York: Viking Press, Inc., 1937.

DENNIS, L.: *The Coming American Fascism*, New York: Harper & Brothers, 1936.

EINZIG, P.: *The Economic Functions of Fascism*, New York: The Macmillan Company, 1933.

FLORINSKY, M. T.: *Fascism and National Socialism*, New York: The Macmillan Company, 1936.

HAIDER, C.: *Do We Want Fascism?* New York: Reynold & Hitchcock, Inc., 1934.

HITLER, A.: *My Battle*, abridged and translated by E. T. S. Dugdale, Boston: Houghton Mifflin Company, 1933.

LICHTENBERGER, H.: *The Third Reich*, New York: Greystone Press, 1937.

NORLIN, G.: *Fascism and Citizenship*, Chapel Hill, N. C.: University of North Carolina Press, 1934.

SILONE, I.: *Bread and Wine*, New York: Harper & Brothers, 1937.

CHAPTER IX

WHAT DOES SOCIALISM OFFER?

BELLOC, H.: *The Restoration of Property*, New York: Sheed and Ward, 1936.

CHESTERTON, G. K.: *Outline of Sanity*, New York: Dodd, Mead & Company, Inc., 1927.

GURIAN, W.: *The Rise and Decline of Marxism*, London: Burns, Oates and Washbourne, 1938.

HALL, R. L.: *Economic System in a Socialist State*, New York: The Macmillan Company, 1937.

LAIDLER, H. W.: *Program for Modern America*, New York: The Thomas Y. Crowell Company, 1936.

MISES, L. VON: *Socialism*, New York: The Macmillan Company, 1937.

STRACHEY, E. J.: *The Nature of Capitalist Crisis*, New York: Covici Friede, Inc., 1935.

———: *Why You Should Be a Socialist*, London: Victor Gollancz, Ltd., 1938.

THOMAS, N.: *Choice before Us; Mankind at the Crossroads*, New York: The Macmillan Company, 1934.

THOMAS, N.: *Human Exploitation in the United States*, New York: Frederick A. Stokes Co., 1934.

CHAPTER X

DOES COMMUNISM POINT THE WAY?

BERDYAYEV, N. A.: *Origin of Russian Communism*, London: G. Blas, 1937.

BRAMELD, T.: *A Philosophic Approach to Communism*, Chicago: University of Chicago Press, 1933.

BROWDER, E. R.: *Religion and Communism*, New York: Workers Library Publishers, Inc., 1935.

———: *What Is Communism?* New York: Vanguard Press, Inc., 1936.

CHAMBERLAIN, W. H.: *Collectivism: A False Utopia*, New York: The Macmillan Company, 1937.

HECKER, J. F.: *The Communist Answer to the World's Needs*, New York: John Wiley & Sons, Inc., 1934.

LYONS, E.: *Assignment in Utopia*, New York: Harcourt, Brace & Company, Inc., 1937.

ROTHSCHILD, R.: *Jefferson, Lenin, Socrates! Three Gods Give an Evening to Politics*, New York: Random House, Inc., 1936.

SPINKA, M.: *Christianity Confronts Communism*, New York: Harper & Brothers, 1936.

WEBB, S., and WEBB, B.: *Soviet Communism: A New Civilization*, two vols., New York: Charles Scribner's Sons, 1936.

CHAPTER XI

TECHNOLOGY DEMANDS A PLANNING ECONOMY

CHASE, S.: *The Economy of Abundance*, New York: The Macmillan Company, 1934.

FAIRCHILD, H. P.: *Profits or Prosperity*, New York: Harper & Brothers, 1932.

HENDERSON, F.: *The Economic Consequences of Power Production*, London: Geo. Allen and Unwin, Ltd., 1931.

LEVEN, M., MOULTON, H. G., and WARBURTON, C.: *America's Capacity to Consume*, Washington, D. C.: The Brookings Institution, 1934.

LOEB, H., and OTHERS: *The Chart of Plenty*, New York: Viking Press, Inc., 1935.

MACKENZIE, FINDLAY, and others: *Planned Society—Yesterday, Today, Tomorrow*, New York: Prentice-Hall, Inc., 1937.

MARTIN, P. M.: *Prohibiting Poverty*, New York: Farrar & Rinehart, Inc., 1933.

NOURSE, E. G., and OTHERS: *America's Capacity to Produce*, Washington, D. C.: The Brookings Institution, 1934.
RUGG, H.: *The Great Technology*, New York: Reynal & Hitchcock, Inc., 1933.
SOULE, G.: *A Planned Society*, New York: The Macmillan Company, 1932.
VEBLEN, T.: *The Engineers and the Price System*, New York: B. W. Huebsch, Inc., 1921.

CHAPTER XII

THE COOPERATIVE WAY

BAKER, J.: *Cooperative Enterprise*, New York: Vanguard Press, Inc., 1937.
CHILDS, M. W.: *Sweden: The Middle Way*, New Haven: Yale University Press, 1936.
DANIELS, J.: *Cooperation: An American Way*, New York: Covici Friede, Inc., 1938.
DURELL, F.: *Cooperation, Its Essence and Background*, New York: Bruce Humphries, Inc., 1936.
FOWLER, B. B.: *Consumer Cooperation in America*, New York: Vanguard Press, Inc., 1936.
FOWLER, B. B.: *The Lord Helps Those . . .* , New York: Vanguard Press, Inc., 1938.
KAGAWA, T.: *Brotherhood Economics*, New York: Harper & Brothers, 1936.
NEIFELD, M. R.: *Cooperative Consumer Credit*, New York: Harper & Brothers, 1936.
President's Commission of Inquiry on Cooperative Enterprise in Europe, Washington, D. C.: U. S. Printing Office, Superintendent of Documents, 1937.
WARBASSE, J. P.: *Cooperative Democracy through Voluntary Association of People as Consumers*, 3d rev. ed., New York: Harper & Brothers, 1936.

CHAPTER XIII

A GOVERNMENT OF MEN

Better Government Personnel, Report of the Commission of Inquiry on Public Service Personnel, New York: McGraw-Hill Book Company, Inc., 1935.
BROOKS, R. C.: *Political Parties and Electoral Problems*, 3d. ed., New York: Harper & Brothers, 1936.
BRUCE, H. R.: *American Parties and Politics*, 3d ed., New York: Henry Holt & Company, Inc., 1936.
GAUS, J. J., WHITE, L. D., and DINOCK, M. E.: *Frontiers of Public Administration*, Chicago: University of Chicago Press, 1936.
MACKENZIE, C. W.: *Party Government in the United States*, New York: Ronald Press Company, 1938.
MERRIAM, C. E.: *The Role of Politics in Social Change*, New York: New York University Press, 1937.
MERRIAM, L.: *Public Service and Special Training*, Chicago: University of Chicago Press, 1936.
PFIFFNER, J. McD.: *Public Administration*, New York: Ronald Press Company, 1935.

454

University Training for the National Service, Report of Proceedings of a Conference Held at the University of Minnesota July 14–17, 1931. Minneapolis: University of Minnesota Press, 1932.

WHITE, L. D.: *Government Career Service*, Chicago: University of Chicago Press, 1936.

CHAPTER XIV

REFORM BEGINS AT HOME: THE AMERICAN CITY

BEARD, C. A.: *American Government and Politics*, New York: The Macmillan Company, 1936.

FAIRLIE, J. A.: *Municipal Administration*, New York: The Macmillan Company, 1922.

LYND, R. S., and LYND, H.: *Middletown in Transition*, New York: Harcourt, Brace & Company, Inc., 1937.

MCKENZIE, R. D.: *The Metropolitan Community*, New York: McGraw-Hill Book Company, 1933.

NATIONAL RESOURCES COMMITTEE: *Our Cities* (Report), Washington, D. C.: United States Government Printing Office, September, 1937.

NORTHROP, W. B., and NORTHROP J. B.: *The Insolence of Office*, New York: G. P. Putnam's Sons, 1932.

PEEL, R. V.: *Political Clubs in New York City*, New York: G. P. Putnam's Sons, 1935.

Reports to the Legislature of Samuel Seabury, Counsel to the "Joint Legislative Committee to Investigate the Administration of the Various Departments of the Government of the City of New York," made between January 25, 1932, and December 27, 1932.

Reports to the Appellate Division of the Supreme Court, First Department, of Samuel Seabury, Referee, in "The Investigation of The Magistrates' Courts in the First Judicial Department and the Magistrates thereof, and of Attorneys-at-law Practicing in said Courts," made between January 2, 1931, and March 28, 1932.

Report to Governor Franklin D. Roosevelt of Samuel Seabury, Commissioner, "In the Matter of The Investigation, under Commission issued by the Governor of the State of New York, of Charges Made Against Hon. Thomas C. T. Crain, District Attorney of New York County," dated August 31, 1931.

SEABURY, S.: "New Methods in City Government," *The Consensus*, April, 1933, pp. 14–20.

STEFFENS, L.: *The Shame of Cities*, rev. ed., New York: McClure, Phillips and Company, 1937.

WEBER, A. F.: *Growth of Cities in Nineteenth Century: A Study in Statistics*, New York: The Macmillan Company, 1899.

CHAPTER XV

CRIME: A SOCIAL CANCER

BATES, S.: *Prisons and Beyond*, New York: The Macmillan Company, 1936.

BEELEY, A. L.: *Social Planning for Crime Control*. Salt Lake City: University of Utah, 1935.

BIERSTADT, E. H.: *What Do You Know about Crime?* New York: Frederick A. Stokes Company, 1935.

BROWN, J.: *Under the Surface of Crime,* New York: Industrial and Educational Publication Company, 1934.

GILLIN, J. L.: *Criminology and Penology,* rev. ed., New York: D. Appleton-Century Company, Inc., 1935.

GLUECK, S., and GLUECK, E. (eds.): *Preventing Crime,* New York: McGraw-Hill Book Company, Inc., 1936.

LAWES, L. E.: *Life and Death in Sing Sing,* Garden City, N. Y.: Doubleday, Doran & Company, Inc., 1937.

TANNENBAUM, F.: *Crime and the Community,* Boston: Ginn and Company, 1938.

TEETERS, N. K.: *They Were in Prison,* Philadelphia: John C. Winston Company, 1937.

United States National Commission on Law Observances and Enforcement. *Report on the Causes of Crime,* Washington, D. C.: United States Government Printing Office, 1931.

CHAPTER XVI

TAXATION TODAY AND TOMORROW

COCHRAN, H. P.: *Scientific Tax Reduction,* New York: Funk & Wagnalls Company, 1937.

COLM, G., and COLM, L. F.: *Economic Consequences of Recent American Tax Policy,* New York: New School for Social Research, 1937.

GREENWOOD, E.: *Spenders All,* New York: D. Appleton-Century Company, Inc., 1935.

HODES, B.: *It's Your Money,* Chicago: Reilly & Lee Company, 1935.

NEWCOMER, M.: *Index of the Taxpaying Ability of State and Local Governments,* New York: Teachers College Publications, Columbia University, 1935.

STAMP, J. C.: *Fundamental Principles of Taxation in the Light of Modern Developments,* rev. ed., New York: The Macmillan Company, 1936.

Tax Policy League: *Direct and Indirect Taxes,* New York City: The League, 1937.

"The Federal Tax System," *Fortune,* January, 1938, pp. 46–47, 102, 104, 106, 109.

"United States' Taxes," *Fortune,* December, 1937, pp. 107–109, 188, 190, 195–196, 198, 200, 202, 205.

UNTEREINER, R. E.: *The Tax Racket,* Philadelphia: J. B. Lippincott Company, 1933.

CHAPTER XVII

WHAT PRICE SOCIAL SECURITY?

BURNS, E. M.: *Toward Social Security,* New York: McGraw-Hill Book Company, Inc., 1936.

DORMAN, M. J.: *Age before Booty,* New York: G. P. Putnam's Sons, 1936.

DOUGLAS, P. H.: *Social Security in the United States,* New York: McGraw-Hill Book Company, Inc., 1936.

EPSTEIN, A.: *Insecurity: a Challenge to America*, 3d ed. rev., New York: Random House, Inc., 1936.

LUTZ, H. L.: *Insecurity of the Security Program*, Princeton, N. J.: Princeton University Press, 1936.

More Security for Old Age, New York: Twentieth Century Fund, Inc., 1937.

Social Security in the United States (Report), New York: National Association for Social Security, Inc., 1937.

RUBINOV, I. M.: *The Quest for Security*, New York: Henrv Holt & Company, Inc., 1934.

STEWART, M. S.: *Social Security*, New York: W. W. Norton and Company, Inc., 1937.

WYATT, B. E., and OTHERS: *Social Security Again in Operation*, Washington, D. C.: Graphic Arts Press, 1937.

CHAPTER XVIII

WHICH WAY AMERICAN LABOR?

ADAMIC, L.: *Dynamite*, rev. ed., New York: Viking Press, Inc., 1934.

ANDREWS, J. B.: *Administrative Labor Legislation*, New York: Harper & Brothers, 1936.

BROOKS, R. R. R.: *When Labor Organizes*, New Haven: Yale University Press, 1937.

CHAMBERS, W.: *Labor Units and the Public*, New York: Coward-McCann, Inc., 1936.

CLARK, H. F., and OTHERS: *Life Earnings in Selected Occupations in the United States*, New York: Harper & Brothers, 1937.

CLARK, M. R., and SIMON, S. F.: *Labor Movement in America*, New York: W. W. Norton and Company, Inc., 1938.

FELDMAN, H.: *Problems in Labor Relations*, New York: The Macmillan Company, 1937.

KEIR, R. M.: *Labor Problems from Both Sides*, New York: Ronald Press Company, 1938.

LEVINSON, E.: *Labor on the March*, New York: Harper & Brothers, 1938.

PATTERSON, S.: *Social Aspects of Industry*, New York: McGraw-Hill Book Company, Inc., 1935.

CHAPTER XIX

THE FARMER'S PROBLEM IS YOUR PROBLEM

CHASE, S.: *Rich Land, Poor Land*, New York: McGraw-Hill Book Company, Inc., 1936.

DAVIS, K. C.: *Modern Productive Farming*, 6th ed., Philadelphia: J. B. Lippincott Company, 1932.

GOLDSTEIN, I. M.: *Agricultural Crisis*, New York: Reynal & Hitchcock, Inc., 1935.

HUTCHESON, T. B., and OTHERS: *Production of Field Crops*, New York: McGraw-Hill Book Company, Inc., 1936.

JOHNSON, C., and OTHERS: *Collapse of Cotton Tenancy*, Chapel Hill, N. C.: University of North Carolina Press, 1935.

KAINS, M. G.: *Five Acres*, New York: Greenberg, Publisher, Inc., 1935.

KOLB, J., and BRUNNER, E.: *Study of Rural Society, Its Organization and Changes*, Boston: Houghton Mifflin Company, 1935.

MALOTT, D. W.: *Problems in Agricultural Marketing*, New York: McGraw-Hill Book Company, Inc., 1938.

SMART, C. A.: *R. F. D.*, New York: W. W. Norton and Company, Inc., 1938.

WALLACE, H. A.: *America Must Choose*, New York: Foreign Policy Association, 1934.

CHAPTER XX

THE RELATION OF GOVERNMENT TO BUSINESS

BOSSARD, J. H. S.: *Social Change and Social Problems*, rev. ed., New York: Harper & Brothers, 1938.

CHASE, S.: *Government in Business*, New York: The Macmillan Company, 1935.

HEIMANN, E.: *Communism, Fascism or Democracy?* New York: W. W. Norton and Company, Inc., 1938.

HOOVER, C. B.: *Dictators and Democracies,* New York: The Macmillan Company, 1937.

HOOVER, H.: *The Challenge to Liberty*, New York: Charles Scribner's Sons, 1935.

KING, W.: *Industry and Humanity*, New York: The Macmillan Company, 1935.

LAWRENCE, D.: *Beyond the New Deal*, New York: McGraw-Hill Book Company, Inc., 1934.

LIPPMANN, W.: *An Inquiry into the Principles of the Good Society*, Boston: Little, Brown & Company, 1937.

SWENSON, R. J.: *The National Government and Business*, New York: D. Appleton-Century Company, Inc., 1924.

WILSON, W.: *The State*, special edition revised to December, 1918, by Edward Elliott, Boston: D. C. Heath & Company, 1918.

CHAPTER XXI

THE CONSTITUTION AND THE SUPREME COURT

ALFANGE, D.: *Supreme Court and the National Will*, Garden City, N. Y.: Doubleday, Doran & Company, Inc., 1937.

BEARD, C. A.: *Economic Interpretation of the Constitution of the United States*, New York: The Macmillan Company, 1935.

BECK, J. M.: *The Constitution of the United States; Yesterday, Today, and Tomorrow*, Garden City, N. Y.: Doubleday, Doran & Company, Inc., 1924.

CORWIN, E.: *Twilight of the Supreme Court*, New Haven: Yale University Press, 1934.

CUSHMAN, R. E.: *Leading Constitutional Decisions*, New York: F. S. Crofts and Company, 1937.

ELLIOTT, W.: *The Need for Constitutional Reform*, New York: McGraw-Hill Book Company, Inc., 1935.

LAWRENCE, D.: *Nine Honest Men*, New York: D. Appleton-Century Company, Inc., 1936.

LYON, H.: *The Constitution and the Men Who Made It*, New York: Houghton Mifflin Company, 1936.

PEARSON, D., and ALLEN, R. S.: *Nine Old Men*, Garden City, N. Y.: Doubleday, Doran & Company, Inc., 1936.

WALKER, E. F., and KERSEY, V.: *Our National Constitution*, New York: Charles Scribner's Sons, 1938.

CHAPTER XXII

THE DECLINE OF THE STATES

BROMAGE, A. W.: *State Government and Administration in the United States*, New York: Harper & Brothers, 1936.

COMEY, A. C., and OTHERS: *State and National Planning*, Cambridge: Harvard University Press, 1937.

CORWIN, E. S.: *The Commerce Power versus States Rights*, Princeton, N. J.: Princeton University Press, 1936.

GRAVES, W. B.: *American State Government*, Boston: D. C. Heath & Company, 1936.

HOPKINS, M. A.: *Planning the Social Order*, New York: Doubleday, Doran & Company, Inc., 1937.

KEY, V. O.: *Administration of Federal Grants to States*, Chicago: Public Administration Service, 1937.

LASKI, H. J.: *State, in Theory and Practice*, New York: Viking Press, Inc., 1935.

National Resources Committee: *Regional Planning* (Report), Washington, D. C.: United States Government Printing Office, June, 1938.

PORTER, K. H.: *State Administration*, New York: F. S. Crofts and Company, 1938.

WATKINS, F.: *State as a Concept of Political Science*, New York: Harper & Brothers, 1934.

CHAPTER XXIII

THE INTERNATIONAL SCENE

GUNTHER, J.: *Inside Europe*, rev. ed., New York: Harper & Brothers, 1937.

HODGES, C.: *The Background of International Relations*, New York: John Wiley & Sons, Inc., 1935.

ROWAN-ROBINSON, H.: *Sanctions Begone!* London: William Clowes and Sons, Ltd., 1936.

SFORZA, C.: *Europe and Europeans*, Indianapolis: Bobbs-Merrill Company, 1936.

SHOTWELL, J. T.: *On the Rim of the Abyss*, New York: The Macmillan Company, 1936.

SLOCOMBE, G. E.: *Mirror to Geneva*, New York: Henry Holt & Company, Inc., 1938.

SHUMAN, F.: *International Politics*, New York: McGraw-Hill Book Company, Inc., 1937.

SKELTON, O. D.: *Our Generation: Its Gains and Losses,* Columbus: University of Ohio Press, 1938.
WHITAKER, J. T.: *And Fear Came,* New York: The Macmillan Company, 1936.
WOLFE, H. C.: *The German Octopus,* Garden City, N. Y.: Doubleday, Doran & Company, Inc., 1938.

CHAPTER XXIV

THE FALLACY OF ECONOMIC NATIONALISM

BEARD, C. A.: *The Open Door at Home,* New York: The Macmillan Company, 1934.
BINKLEY, R. C.: *Realism and Nationalism,* New York: Harper & Brothers, 1935.
DELAISI, F.: *Political Myths and Economic Realities,* New York: Viking Press, Inc., 1927.
FRANK, J.: *Save America First,* New York: Harper & Brothers, 1938.
GREENBERG, L. S.: *Nationalism in a Changing World,* New York: Greenberg, Publisher, Inc., 1937.
LAWLEY, F. E.: *Growth of Collective Economy,* 2 vols., London: P. S. King and Sons, 1938.
POTTER, P. B.: *Introduction to the Study of International Organization,* 4th ed., New York: D. Appleton-Century Company, Inc., 1935.
SALTER, J. A.: *World Trade and Its Future,* Pennsylvania: University of Pennsylvania Press, 1936.
SPRING, G. M.: *Nationalism on the Defensive,* Glendale, Calif.: Arthur Clark Company, 1937.
WILLCOX, O. W.: *Nations Can Live at Home,* New York: W. W. Norton and Company, Inc., 1935.

CHAPTER XXV

IS NEUTRALITY POSSIBLE FOR AMERICA?

BEARD, C. A.: *The Devil Theory of War,* New York: The Vanguard Press, Inc., 1936.
BORCHARD, E. M., LAGE, W. P.: *Neutrality for the United States,* New Haven: Yale University Press, 1937.
ISHIMARU, T.: *The Next World War,* London: Hurst and Blackett, Ltd., 1937.
KULSRUD, C. J.: *Maritime Neutrality to 1780,* Boston: Little, Brown & Company, 1936.
MARSHALL-CORNWALL, J. H.: *Geographic Disarmament,* New York: Oxford University Press, 1935.
NEUMANN, R.: *Zaharoff, the Armament King,* New York: Alfred A. Knopf, Inc., 1935.
TANSILL, C. C.: *America Goes to War,* Boston: Little, Brown & Company, 1938.
TILDEN, F.: *The World in Debt,* New York: Funk & Wagnalls Company, 1936.
RAUSCHENBUSH, S.: *War Madness,* Washington, D. C.: National Home Library Association, 1937.

BIBLIOGRAPHY

WOOLEY, M. E.: *Internationalism and Disarmament,* New York: The Macmillan Company, 1935.

CHAPTER XXVI

THE ROAD TO PEACE

BUTLER, N. M.: *The Family of Nations: Its Needs and Its Problems,* New York: Charles Scribner's Sons, 1938.

FAGLEY, R.: *Proposed Roads to Peace,* Boston: Pilgrim Press, 1935.

MADARIAGA, S. DE: *World's Design,* London: Geo. Allen and Unwin, 1938.

MCPHERSON, I. M.: *Educating Children for Peace,* New York: Abingdon Press, 1936.

RICHARDS, L. P.: *Realistic Pacifism,* New York: Willett, Clark and Company, 1935.

SIMONDS, F. H., and EMENY, B.: *Price of Peace,* New York: Harper & Brothers, 1935.

STEED, H. W.: *Vital Peace,* New York: The Macmillan Company, 1936.

STRATTON, G.: *International Delusions,* New York: Houghton Mifflin Company, 1936.

VOLLENHOVEN, C. VAN: *Law of Peace,* New York: The Macmillan Company, 1936.

WRIGHT, P. Q.: *Causes of War and the Conditions of Peace,* New York: Longmans Green & Company, 1935.

461

INDEX

467